Understanding Human Trafficking, Corruption, and the Optics of Misconduct in the Public, Private, and NGO Sectors

Understanding Human Trafficking, Corruption, and the Optics of Misconduct in the Public, Private, and NGO Sectors

Causes, Actors, and Solutions

Luz Estella Nagle
PROFESSOR OF LAW
STETSON UNIVERSITY COLLEGE OF LAW

CAROLINA ACADEMIC PRESS
Durham, North Carolina

Library of Congress Cataloging-in-Publication Data

Names: Nagle, Luz Estella, author.
Title: Understanding human trafficking, corruption, and the optics of
  misconduct in the public, private, and NGO sectors : causes, actors, and
  solutions / Luz Estella Nagle.
Description: Durham, North Carolina : Carolina Academic Press, [2017] |
  Includes bibliographical references and index.
Identifiers: LCCN 2017017148 | ISBN 9781531001964 (alk. paper)
Subjects: LCSH: Human trafficking--Law and legislation. | Human
  trafficking--Investigation. | Human trafficking--Prevention. | Human
  trafficking (International law)
Classification: LCC K5297 .N33 2017 | DDC 345/.02551--dc23
LC record available at https://lccn.loc.gov/2017017148

CAROLINA ACADEMIC PRESS, LLC
700 Kent Street
Durham, North Carolina 27701
Telephone (919) 489-7486
Fax (919) 493-5668
www.cap-press.com

Printed in the United States of America

Dedicated to my beautiful and brilliant daughters,
who are the lights of my life,
and to my husband, whose faith in me never wavers ...

for the survivors, wherever they may be ...

Contents

Foreword

by Ian McDougal

According to the US State Department's 2016 *Trafficking in Persons Report*, human trafficking is a US$150 billion industry. Only the trade in drugs is bigger. Bigger than what, you may ask? Bigger than the trade in human slavery. I should pause there to allow those words to register. Yes ... Slavery is what it is. Slavery is still taking place in the modern world.

This trade in human slavery, still prevalent in the year 2017, isn't just a sleepy backwater of crime. It is one of the largest illegal trades the world has ever known. Human trafficking is different from people smuggling. People smuggling involves a person voluntarily requesting or hiring another individual to covertly transport them. Though illegal, there may be no deception or coercion involved. After entry into the target country, the smuggled person is apparently free. Human trafficking, on the other hand, is a crime against the victim because of the coercion, imprisonment (whether physically or as a result of coercion), and exploitation.

But, you may ask, why don't I hear more about it? My answer is that it is a "trade" that hides in plain sight. Unless you know what you are looking for, you can easily mistake it for something else. While some victims are hidden from the outside world, many toil in forced labor where they actually have contact with everyday members of society. Yet the reality of their situation is unknown and legal systems are often not in place to protect them. Some victims of human slavery actually perform their work in plain sight, but unrecognized. It is a global problem that touches almost everywhere; it can be found in expected places like strip clubs, massage parlors and, an increasing favorite in our consumer-based society, nail salons. It is also found in places you might consider more unexpected; factory sweatshops, construction sites, hotels and resorts; even in farms and private homes as domestic slaves.

The reach and impact of human trafficking from an economic perspective is staggering. My opinion is that the absence of a strong foundation of the Rule of Law is often a contributory factor. But that is not always the case; the trade in human trafficked people just within and across the United States is enormous; a shadow world outside of the Rule of Law. Globally, there are tens of millions of people trapped in various forms of slavery throughout the world today. Researchers, and the UN, estimate different numbers, but it seems a consensus estimated figure is that over 20 million people are enslaved worldwide.

The UN International Labor Organisation estimates that about 78 percent of that number toil in forced labor slavery in industries where manual labor is needed—such as farming, ranching, logging, mining, fishing, and brick-making—and in service industries working as dish washers, janitors, gardeners, and maids. In almost every country around the world, people are forced into domestic slavery; working in households as domestic slaves—unable to escape.

Sex slavery, that is people trapped into forced prostitution, accounts for about 22 percent. Child slavery accounts for around 26 percent of all trafficking victims. However, in some parts of Africa and the Mekong region, children are the majority of trafficking victims (up to 100 percent in parts of West Africa).

But the bare statistics don't really convey the human stories, the impact on lives and the scale of the enterprises. Professor Luz Nagle's amazing work recounts instances such as:

> "*Criminal organizations operating in Greece traffic Roma women from Albania and Bulgaria to be placed in 'baby mills' where those who are not already pregnant are impregnated by gang members and forced to produce babies that are then sold through adoption agencies in Athens where there are no laws against privately arranged adoptions.*"

It is when you read examples such as this that the true horror, evil and scale of the criminal undertaking becomes apparent. Remember, the people held, right now as you read these words, are not statistics; they are human beings held in conditions unimaginable to most of us.

Although it doesn't seem to make the headlines in this age of reality TV stars, the international community is taking some steps to address the problem at a macro level. Professor Nagle outlines, in far greater detail than here, that in 2000, the United Nations adopted the *Convention against Transnational Organized Crime*, also called the *Palermo Convention*. This is a comprehensive international convention against transnational organized crime incorporating international laws to address trafficking in women and children, the illicit manufacturing of and trafficking in firearms and ammunition, and illegal trafficking in and transportation of migrants.

The purpose of the *Convention* is to promote cooperation to prevent and combat transnational organized crime more effectively. The *Convention* is supplemented by the *Palermo Protocols*: The *Protocol to Prevent, Suppress and Punish Trafficking in Persons, Especially Women and Children*, and the *Protocol against the Smuggling of Migrants by Land, Sea and Air*.

As of 2008, there were 143 parties to the United Nations *Convention against Transnational Organized Crime*, 119 parties to the United Nations *Protocol to Prevent, Suppress and Punish Trafficking in Persons*, and 112 parties to the United Nations *Protocol against the Smuggling of Migrants by Land, Sea and Air*. The *Trafficking Protocol* is unique from other treaties, because it was created as a law enforcement instrument, which, in theory, gives it more influence than aspirational agreements. Provisions within the *Trafficking Protocol* state that parties must take action to:

- penalize trafficking;
- protect victims of trafficking; and
- grant victims temporary or permanent residence in the countries of destination.

Therefore, if a state is a party to the *Convention* and its *Protocols*, it has an obligation to create legislation that supports these provisions at the domestic level.

At this time, the United Nations tells us, 61 countries have passed national laws with this primary focus. Almost 90 percent of these laws have been enacted in the last five years, demonstrating a clear acknowledgement of the dangers of human trafficking and an increasing commitment towards addressing this critical world-wide issue. Many nations address human trafficking in their criminal or penal codes; these are not included in the 61. So there is still a way to go.

Regional and domestic instruments that have played a key role in the prevention and elimination of human trafficking include: The United States *Victims of Trafficking and Violence Protection Act* (2000), and the Council of Europe *Convention on Action against Trafficking in Human Beings* (2008). Regions throughout the world are also starting to make cooperative efforts to end trafficking. For example, in 2005, the Coordinated Mekong Ministerial Initiative against Trafficking (COMMIT), a sub-regional group composed of China, Laos, Thailand, Cambodia, Myanmar, and Vietnam, was established. Its purpose is to create policies for anti-trafficking measures in the region, allowing each state to create legislation that is in agreement with these provisions.

This fascinating book goes into much more detail about these various (and many more) international instruments. As Professor Nagle emphasizes throughout its pages, addressing corruption and enhancing the Rule of Law still remain key in the fight to eliminating human slavery and trafficking. Corruption of officials basically facilitates the continuation of this trade. The biggest question in those regions, therefore, remains enforcement. All the laws and international instruments in the world do not matter where corrupt law enforcement officials are paid to turn a blind eye. These activities are still prevalent in many places and regions. It is a binding theme that runs through the book.

To the debate on human trafficking, and for the raising of awareness, this book is undoubtedly a major contribution. I also think it is quite unique in its punchy prose style and the power of its message and conclusions. What Professor Nagle has produced is a major academic contribution, built on solid research, yet reads in part like an investigative journalism crime exposé! It is a great, and innovative, effort which I hope goes some way to continuing to raise awareness and contributing to the debate.

The underlying message that comes out of this work is that human slavery and trafficking is one of the great global problems of our time. In fact, a massive global problem. Even though some high profile cases of potentially fraudulent victim claims come to light (and Professor Nagle also shines a harsh light on those!), that should not take away from the power of the underlying issue. It affects every town, city and country in the world. It affects millions of people and, because of its connection to such things as prostitution, provision of services and the like, it can hide in plain sight, leaving the majority of people unaware of how big a problem it is.

Our challenge is to raise awareness and support actions to reduce this modern plague. It is another reason (amongst many) why this excellent book by Professor Nagle is such a valuable tool. Information/knowledge is the enemy of human trafficking. Works such as this contribute another step in the fight against it.

Mr. Ian McDougall
Executive Vice President and General Counsel
LexisNexis
October 25, 2016

Preface

This project began as a book about human trafficking and how the presence of corruption fuels and sustains a pernicious global criminal enterprise.[1] It soon became much more than that. Beyond a straight forward legal analysis of the two criminal acts, there are layers of misconduct present in human trafficking that range from overt criminal acts (bribery, extortion, coercion, fraud) to behavior that may be unlawful but difficult to prove (false advertising, misrepresentation, poor judgment), to conduct that while not unlawful may not pass the "smell test" and has a detrimental impact on the credibility of a government entity, a private business, or a non-government organization involved in the anti-trafficking movement.

An abundance of journalists, researchers and government watchdogs has rapidly expanded the evidence of public corruption in various types of human trafficking through well-documented reporting and a growing body of cases and outcomes. Private corruption and misconduct, primarily related to labor trafficking, is in many ways far more complex and difficult to target and prosecute, in part due to challenges inherent to lifting the corporate veil that protects individuals and entities engaged in corrupt acts and misconduct related to human trafficking. The "stickiest" area of research and investigations concerns the non-government organizations and individuals in the anti-trafficking movement whose conduct spans the gamut of being overtly corrupt (graft, embezzlement, fraud), to not being corrupt per se, but giving the appearance or the "optics" of misconduct (narratives that may not pass careful scrutiny,

---

1. The connection between corruption and human rights is recent. *See* Int'l Council on Human Rights Pol'y, *Corruption and Human Rights: Making the Connection* (2009), http://www.ichrp.org/files/reports/40/131_web.pdf. *See also* Anne T. Gallagher, The International Law of Human Trafficking 442 (2010).

use of unreliable or discredited facts and statistics, using methods to elicit donations that play on people's emotions and sentiments), to behavior that harms
the anti-trafficking movement (impropriety between government officials and
NGOs, libeling competing organizations, and simply lying about an organization's work). While the majority of the individuals involved in the anti-trafficking movement are true crusaders and dedicate their entire lives and
resources to combating human trafficking, a few scam artists and charlatans
have used the fight against human trafficking for personal gain and notoriety.
Their known presence in the movement has led some critics to refer to the
anti-trafficking NGO sector as the "rescue industry."[2] We will look at some of
the controversial organizations within this sector, not to pass judgment on
their activities, but to raise awareness among potential volunteers, donors, and
supporters in order to make informed assessments and conclusions.

The discussions, findings and recommendations set forth in this book are
based on several sources—existing scholarship, government reports and studies, news sources, position statements made by experts, trafficking survivors
and advocates, and interviews with leaders in the anti-trafficking movement.
In the course of research, several anti-human trafficking non-government organizations (hereinafter HT NGOs) were approached for information about
their operations, program resources, and financial management, but there
were few replies. One NGO stated, apologetically, that "the information available tends to be generalized and this hasn't been an area of study that we have
so far developed."

What we learn from the content in the following chapters reflects the difficult task before criminal justice actors and watch-dog groups to identify and
charge corruption-related trafficking offenses, and to take proactive and deci-
sive steps to stop corruption in public, private and non-government segments
of society, as well as to monitor, vet, and safeguard the credibility of the anti-
trafficking movement. If we are going to address the full scale of human trafficking and what we deem as modern-day slavery, then we must understand
the meaning of the crimes, the cultural and historical underpinnings, and the

---

2. Term coined by Dr. Laura Agustín, a noted anthropologist who studies and writes
on undocumented immigration, human trafficking, and the sex industry. Agustín has a lot
to say about the rescue industry, which springs from the idea that being unable to see social ills creates the need for self-identified experts to inform us about them. Her term "rescue industry" was created "after years of study to describe non-self-critical helpers who
assume they Know Better than the rest of us how we all out to live." See http://www.auraa-
gustin.com/.

motivations of corrupt actors in public, private, and non-government sectors that are in some way or form connected to human trafficking crimes.

One of the challenges realized in writing this book is that the nature of the subject is constantly shifting and evolving, so that data relied upon two or three years ago may be too outdated to be of use now, or in some cases has been discredited and set aside. As this book was nearing completion, two startling investigative reports came to light that underscore the need to pay far greater attention to the links between various forms of corruption and various forms of trafficking in human beings. The first investigation, conducted by the Associated Press for more than a year, concerns the commercial fishing industry in Hawaii, in which foreign undocumented laborers originating primarily from Southeast Asian nations have been kept as de facto prisoners on fishing vessels for years at a time without ever stepping foot on United States territory and thereby remaining exempt from federal labor laws.[3]

The conditions in which "hundreds" of deck hands and fish processors are kept on these American-owned and American-registered fishing vessels would be in violation of several applicable labor regulations and laws in the United States, but for the active collusion of a now-deceased U.S. Senator from Hawaii to protect the Hawaiian fishing industry from foreign competition and a loophole in federal labor law that allows the foreign workers to labor away on U.S. vessels, but exempts them from labor protections. According to the AP, the fleet of some 140 boats specialize in catching premium ahi tuna and swordfish that end up in high-end markets like Whole Foods and in restaurants catering to affluent customers.

Over the course of six months, the Associated Press examined copious numbers of labor contracts and business records and interviewed boat owners, labor brokers, and more than 50 fishermen from San Francisco to Hawaii to Indonesia. "The investigation found men living in squalor on some boats, forced to use buckets instead of toilets, suffering running sores from bed bugs and sometimes lacking sufficient food. It also revealed instances of human trafficking." What is particularly onerous about the reports is that federal contractors paid to monitor the industry have been aware of the depredations perpetrated against the foreign undocumented workers, but seem indifferent to actually doing anything about the situation. One of the contractors who

---

3. Martha Mendoza & Margie Mason, *Hawaiian Seafood Caught by Foreign Crews Confined on Boats*, Associated Press, Sept. 8, 2016, http://www.ap.org/explore/seafood-from-slaves/hawaiian-seafood-caught-foreign-crews-confined-boats.html.

stay on the vessels for weeks at a time monitoring the catches to be in compliance with federal fishing laws told the AP journalists,

> "You get that sort of feeling that it's like gaming the system," said Forest O'Neill, who coordinates the boat observers in Honolulu. "It's a shock. It becomes normal, but it's like, 'How is this even legal? How is this possible?'... They are like floating prisons."[4]

The loophole in federal law that allows such conditions to persist exempts the Hawaiian fishing industry from the federal law that states that 75 percent of fishermen on commercial fleets operating in the United States must be Americans. The result is that an estimated 700 foreign workers, "who catch $110 million worth of seafood annually, lack certain labor rights most Americans take for granted."[5] Moreover, because US Customs and Border Protection officials require the boat captains to hold the passports and personal documentation of the foreign workers, conditions that essentially violate human trafficking law are present among the commercial fishing fleet. The foreign labor that ends up on American vessels under these arrangements are at the end of the labor pipeline that involves unscrupulous recruitment schemes, a shady network of labor brokers, and individuals who place profit far ahead of human rights. In addition, the economics of the fishing industry are such that profits are measured against costs and the risks and uncertainties that have been part of commercial fishing for millennia.[6]

While the foreign fishermen are not actual slave labor, they are paid wages far below American labor standards, and the fact that they are not allowed to step on shore constitutes a form of imprisonment throughout the typically 2 to 3 years that their labor contracts indenture them to boat captains. The Hawaiian government's response so far as of September 2016 was that signs are posted where the vessels moor offering a telephone hotline number for individuals to call if human trafficking is suspected. Tragically, nearly everyone involved in the fishing industry knows these conditions exist and yet do nothing about it. One wholesaler told the AP, "The owners are a bunch of leeches making money off these crews."[7]

Following publication of the AP report, barely a week later, Hawaiian state and federal authorities promised they would look into the matter and initiate significant reforms in the laws and the fishing practices of the industry. Major

---

4. *Id.*
5. *Id.*
6. *Id.*
7. *Id.*

buyers of the seafood have also reacted positively. Whole Foods halted buying seafood from the fleet until it can be shown that the workers are treated better, and the Hawaii Seafood Council announced that beginning on October 1, 2016, the Honolulu Fish Auction "will sell fish only from boats that have adopted a new, standardized contract aimed at assuring no forced labor exists on board."[8]

The other investigative report concerns a religious-based non-profit human trafficking rescue organization in central California in which the founder and director of the organization has been accused by former workers of engaging in several forms of fraudulent conduct, and violating the privacy of the rescued trafficking victims and using them as showpieces to gain financial contributions.[9] Jenny Williamson founded Courage House as a safe haven for women from sex trafficking in the Sacramento valley of California. Through aggressive marketing and public speaking and private fund-raising, she grew Courage House into a global brand that attracted celebrity recognition and wealthy, well-meaning donors.

In 2015, Courage House took in US$1.7 million in revenue, and Williamson drew a salary of US$115,000. Yet, staffers indicated that money never seemed to "trickle down" to the young women. Their needs were going unmet, and at times, the facility's beds were under capacity. The rescued women were known as Courage Girls, and they were exploited as such.[10] According to one staffer, residents were routinely forced to participate in speaking tours to a predominately white church to be displayed to the congregation in an effort to gain donations. "As nonwhite girls in a predominately white church, they stuck out like sore thumbs—it was very obvious that they were the 'courage girls,'" the staffer said.[11] This practice was also in direct violation of federal laws that protect the identities of trafficking victims. State inspectors also cited Courage House at least 16 times in 2016 for violations ranging from maintaining inadequate staffing, breaches of confidentiality, and infringement on the personal rights of residents.[12] Moreover, while the facility had no residents

---

8. Martha Mendoza & Margie Mason, *Hawaii Lawmakers Promise Reform for Confined Fishermen*, AP, Sep. 9, 2016, https://apnews.com/4c1f4af89db740cab9798a5fb401430d/hawaiian-lawmakers-promise-reform-confined-fishermen.

9. Steven Blum, *Non-Profit Accused of Exploiting Sex Trafficking Victims It Was Meant to Help*, Vice.com, Sept. 19, 2016, https://broadly.vice.com/en_us/article/non-profit-accused-of-exploiting-sex-trafficking-victims-it-was-meant-to-help.

10. *Id.*

11. *Id.*

12. *Id.*

in 2016, the organization "neglected to alert donors of this fact until after a wide-ranging exposé on the house was published in the *Sacramento Bee*."[13] Even as donors like the Rotary Club of Sacramento decided to withhold donations, Courage Worldwide's website announced grand plans to build new facilities to house 60 residents.

The characteristics of Courage House represent many practices HT NGOs use to gain support and funding that, not overtly corrupt, come very close to the line of misconduct, including:

- using grossly overinflated statistics about sex trafficking in the United States to help fundraising efforts, which impedes other organizations from assisting victims of less salacious forms of labor trafficking, which some experts consider to be more widespread than sex trafficking.
- stating that the organization was helping many families of trafficking victims, but providing no actual details.
- indoctrinating the women under the organizations' care into religious practices and kicking them out or forcing them to leave voluntarily when they did not comply with religious expectations.
- using promotional materials that violate the privacy of rescued individuals.[14]

These two journalistic reports provide the backdrop and the precedent for writing this book, in which we will strive through many examples and analysis of domestic and international legal instruments to advance our understanding of the links between human trafficking crimes and corruption in government, private, and non-government sectors, and to propose possible solutions to curb the temptation of actors to engage in corrupt and unethical practices that result in the continuing dehumanization, exploitation, direct victimization and re-victimization of human beings world-wide.

---

13. *Id.*
14. *Id.*

Acknowledgments

The author wishes to acknowledge the following individuals who have offered cogent suggestions and research support throughout the long and sometimes vexing course of writing this book: Australian attorney and legal scholar Dr. Anne Gallagher, a distinguished international authority on human trafficking; Mr. Ian McDougall, Executive Vice President and General Counsel at LexisNexis and a leading voice in combating global human trafficking and forced labor; Mr. Declan Croucher, Director of Business Development at Verité and an international expert on confronting human trafficking and forced labor in the private sector; Florida Attorney James Lake, a leading legal expert on libel law who offered critical objective input throughout the manuscript and particularly with regard to the chapter addressing non-government organizations; Professor Lucian Emery Dervan at Southern Illinois University School of Law, who provided excellent feedback on private corruption issues; Mr. Gerald Nagle, Law Librarian with the United States Court of Appeals for the Eleventh Circuit, who assisted in research and editing duties; Ms. Wanita Scroggs, Foreign and International Librarian at Stetson University College of Law; my Stetson colleagues Professor of Law Timothy Kaye and Associate Dean for Faculty and Strategic Initiatives and Attorneys' Title Insurance Fund Professor of Law Darryl Wilson, who provided additional sets of eyes and helpful comments; and my law student research assistants at Stetson University College of Law, Rachel Swanziger, Anna Pearl Kirkpatrick, Gina Cabrejo Perez, Natalia Reyna Forero, Chloe Wells, and Anna J. Liedl, who provided significant assistance with designing the figures and charts. I am also grateful to Stetson Law Dean Christopher M. Pietruszkiewicz, who provided vital support in the form of a faculty research grant and gave me constant collegial encouragement. This has been very much a collective effort involving many individuals who understand that the content presented in this book is sometimes of a difficult and frustrating nature, and I am deeply and gratefully indebted to all of you.

Finally, it must be understood that the topics I am addressing involve events happening in real time. Simply put, things change. Sources used in the early stages of research and writing may no longer be available due to the sometimes ephemeral nature of the world wide web. Cases that were pending in courts of justice while I was writing the book may have been resolved by the time this book comes to print. New laws may already have come on the books in some countries that alter the fight against both human trafficking and corruption such that issues that were a problem two years ago has since been resolved. Individuals cited or discussed may no longer be engaged in activities covered in the book. I ask forbearance and trust from the reader that I have done my best to address provocative and controversial topics in a fair and balanced manner. Any errors or omissions are inadvertent, and the expression of my own opinions do not represent any organization or the academic institution in which I teach and work.

Luz Estella Nagle
Professor of Law
Stetson University College of Law
St. Petersburg, Florida

Understanding Human Trafficking, Corruption, and the Optics of Misconduct in the Public, Private, and NGO Sectors

Chapter 1

Introduction: Understanding Human Trafficking

"Corruption is the lubricant that allows the wheel of human trafficking to adequately operate, embedding itself at all levels, from the planning to the aftermath of the actual trade."[1]

Summary: In this introductory chapter, we will look at the definitions of human trafficking and the international legal instruments and frameworks that establish human trafficking in its many forms as a pernicious criminal activity of global proportions. A brief introduction to the interconnection of human trafficking and corruption will follow. We will then look at how researchers, government and law enforcement officials, and non-government actors categorize human trafficking in a way that helps them understand its scope and characteristics.

Two decades ago, human trafficking made barely a ripple in the sea of constantly emerging domestic and international issues. By the late 1990s, policymakers, law enforcement officials, non-government organizations, the press, researchers, and academics began to take note that a sinister criminal enterprise was afoot that involved the dehumanization of people through a process that turned our fellow human beings into little more than chattel to be exploited

---

1. 14th Int'l Anti-Corruption Conference 2010, Bangkok, Thai., Nov. 2010, *Workshop Summary Corruption and Human Trafficking: Unraveling the Undistinguishable for a Better Fight*, at 1, http://14iacc.org/wp-content/uploads/ws1.2CamilleKarbassi_LR.pdf.

over and over again in various forms of sex and labor servitude. More shocking still was that children were the most vulnerable to becoming trafficking victims, and that human beings were being trafficked like cattle to an abattoir to provide body parts to meet a growing transborder black market demand.[2]

When we consider who exploits trafficking victims, we are influenced by the depiction of human trafficking in fictional movies and sensationalist interviews by trafficking survivors. We tend to conjure up images of brothel operators forcing vulnerable girls and young women to service clients against their will, or of men traveling to exotic destinations known for sex tourism to engage in illicit hookups with women and children. But we may be less aware that some of the worst forms of human trafficking and exploitation are not well-suited for sensational fictionalized representations.

Consumers who may not be very sophisticated about the world around them may not realize that the handwoven rug in one's living room was made by a small child tied to a hand loom for hours and hours, that the bedsheets and towels in a hotel room at a popular resort were tended to by someone who was tricked into a debt bondage arrangement by an unscrupulous labor broker, that the chocolate the world consumes in prodigious quantities each year was produced by multinational corporations using cocoa harvested by young children who are transported clandestinely across international frontiers to work as modern-day slaves on vast plantations in Western Africa, or that the farm-worker who picked the tomatoes in this evening's dinner salad is housed nightly in a primitive dormitory setting and has not been paid since his undocumented arrival in the United States months ago. We may not be aware that the canned fish we buy from Thailand was caught on factory ships far out to sea by Burmese fishermen working as de facto slaves who have not stepped foot on dry land in more than two years—and who will likely drown or simply disappear in the vast ocean. Nor might we realize that the kidney or cornea one

---

2. The 2012 Global Report on Trafficking in Persons identified the scope and scale of the crime. *See* United Nations Office on Drugs and Crime, Global Report on Trafficking in Persons 2012, at 38–39, U.N. Sales No. E.13.IV.1 (2012), http://www.unodc.org/documents/data-and-analysis/glotip/Trafficking_in_Persons_2012_web.pdf:

> Trafficking for the removal of organs may appear to be limited, as it accounts for less than 0.2 per cent of the total number of detected victims. Nonetheless, during the reporting period, cases or episodes of trafficking for organ removal were officially reported by 16 countries among those here considered. In addition, it appears that all regions are affected by trafficking for organ removal, which suggests that the phenomenon is not as marginal as the number of victims officially detected would suggest.

of our coworkers received was obtained through black-market arrangements overseas because the waiting time to receive a transplant was simply not viable for survival. All these human trafficking crimes have two related elements — first, they are economic crimes that satisfy some form of demand, and second, they cannot be perpetrated without acts of corruption involving either state actors or private entities, or both.

In an effort to articulate human trafficking and craft a multinational response to the trafficking in persons, the United Nations convened Member States in 2000 to draft the *Protocol to Prevent, Suppress and Punish Trafficking in Persons, Especially Women and Children,* which became known as the *Palermo Protocol,*[3] one of three protocols attached to the *United Nations Convention against Transnational Organized Crime* (UNCTOC).[4] Some 172 nations have signed onto the instrument, and many of that number have made it part of their domestic legislation since the *Palermo Protocol* took effect on December 25, 2003.[5]

In his address to the signing conference for the *United Nations Convention against Transnational Organized Crime* in 2000, then Secretary-General Kofi Annan stated:

> I believe the trafficking of persons, particularly women and children, for forced and exploitative labour, including for sexual exploitation, is one of the most egregious violations of human rights which the United Nations now confronts. It is widespread and growing. It is rooted in social and economic conditions in the countries from which the victims come, facilitated by practices which discriminate against women, and driven by cruel indifference to human suffering on the

---

3. Protocol to Prevent, Suppress and Punish Trafficking in Persons, Especially Women and Children, Supplementing the United Nations Convention against Transnational Organized Crime, Nov. 15, 2000, T.I.A.S. No. 13127, 2237 U.N.T.S. 319 [hereinafter Palermo Protocol].

4. United Nations Convention against Transnational Organized Crime, opened for signature Dec. 12, 2000, 2225 U.N.T.S. 209.

5. Palermo Protocol, *supra* note 3. As of June 25, 2016, 117 countries are signatories and 169 countries are parties. Some of the most recent countries to ratify, accept, approve, accede, or succeed to the Protocol include Afghanistan (2014), Barbados (2014), Czech Republic (2014), Eritrea (2014), South Korea (2015), Sierra Leone (2014), Singapore (2015), Sri Lanka (2015), and Sudan (2014). Note that some of this nations are origination countries for human trafficking. *See* Status as of June 25, 2016 at the United Nations Treaty Collection Depositary webpage, https://treaties.un.org/Pages/ViewDetails.aspx?src=IND&mtd sg_no=XVIII-12-a&chapter=18&lang=en.

part of those who exploit the services that the victims are forced to provide. The fate of these most vulnerable people in our world is an affront to human dignity and a challenge to every state, every people, and every community.[6]

The *Palermo Protocol* sets forth the first international legal definition on human trafficking. This definition is the generally accepted standard:

"Trafficking in persons" shall mean the recruitment, transportation, transfer, harbouring or receipt of persons, by means of the threat or use of force or other forms of coercion, of abduction, of fraud, of deception, of the abuse of power or of a position of vulnerability or of the giving or receiving of payments or benefits to achieve the consent of a person having control over another person, for the purpose of exploitation. Exploitation shall include, at a minimum, the exploitation of the prostitution of others or other forms of sexual exploitation, forced labour or services, slavery or practices similar to slavery, servitude or the removal of organs.[7]

Discerning the legal definition of human trafficking, the following elements emerge:

- Trafficking includes not only the movement of a person to be exploited but the maintenance of an individual in a condition of exploitation. Therefore, a trafficker can be a recruiter, a broker or transporter as well as a person or entity that sustains the exploitation.[8]
- Trafficking can be internal or transborder. Migrants and refugees can be trafficked within their country of destination.
- A human trafficking victims' consent is quashed by an assortment of means such as threat, force, coercion, abduction, fraud, deception, abuse of power or of a position of vulnerability, giving or re-

---

6. United Nations Office on Drugs and Crime, *The Secretary-General Address at the Opening of the Signing Conference for the United Nations Convention against Transnational Organized Crime, Palermo* (Dec. 12, 2000), http://www.unodc.org/unodc/en/about-unodc/speeches/speech_2000-12-12_1.html.

7. Palermo Protocol, *supra* note 3, art. 3(a).

8. Human Trafficking and Public Corruption: A Report by the IBA's Presidential Task Force Against Human Trafficking 8 (2016).

ceiving payments or benefits to attain consent of a person having control over another person.

- Under the *Palermo Protocol,* children (a person under 18 years of age) are trafficked when they are recruited, transported, transferred, harbored, or received in order to be exploited.

Figure 1: Trafficking Elements for Adults

Acts	Means *Quashed Consent*	Purpose: Exploitation *(At a minimum should include)*
· Recruitment · Transport · Tranfser · Harboring · Receipt of a person	· Abduction, fraud, deception, coercion, abuse of power or position of vulnerability, giving/receiving payment/benefits to attain consent of a person having control over another person	· Prostitution of others · Sexual exploitation · Forced labor or services · Slavery or similar practices to slavery, servitude · Removal of organs

Figure 2: Trafficking Elements for Children (under 18 years of age)

Act	Purpose of Exploitation *(At a minimum should include)*
· Recruitment · Transport · Transfer · Harboring · Receipt of a person	· Prostitution of others · Sexual exploitation · Forced labor or services · Slavery or similar practices to slavery, servitude · Removal of organs

1. Distinction between Trafficking in Persons and Smuggling

Human trafficking varies from smuggling of migrants. Smuggling is the "procurement, in order to obtain, directly or indirectly, a financial or other material benefit, of the illegal entry of a person into a State Party of which the person is not a national or a permanent resident."[9] While the essence of smuggling is a criminal act involving illegal border crossing, the core of human trafficking is a set of human rights violations, the most common being violations of the right to personal autonomy, the right not to be held in slavery or servitude, the right to liberty and security of person, the right to be free from cruel or inhumane treatment, the right to safe and healthy working conditions, and the right to freedom of movement.[10] Smuggling and human trafficking are not mutually exclusive, and at times may intersect, as illustrated in the following figure.

Figure 3: Trafficking and Smuggling

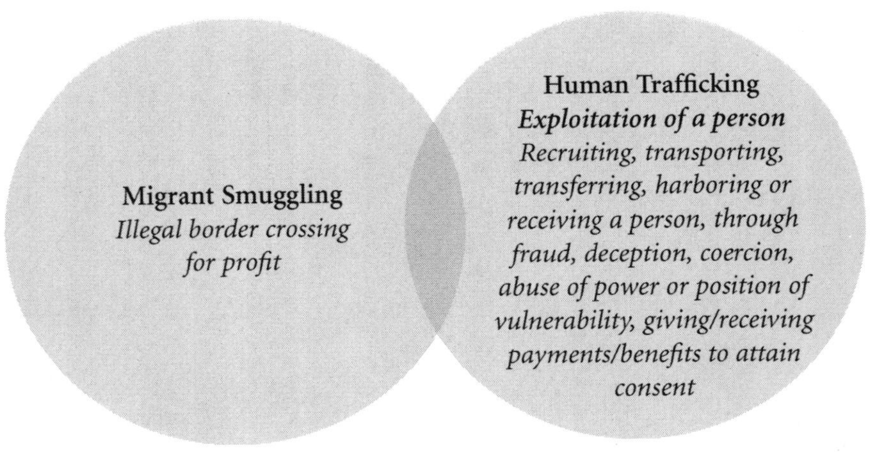

Migrant Smuggling
Illegal border crossing for profit

Human Trafficking
Exploitation of a person
Recruiting, transporting, transferring, harboring or receiving a person, through fraud, deception, coercion, abuse of power or position of vulnerability, giving/receiving payments/benefits to attain consent

---

9. UNITED NATIONS OFFICE ON DRUGS AND CRIME, PROTOCOL AGAINST THE SMUGGLING OF MIGRANTS BY LAND, SEA AND AIR, SUPPLEMENTING THE U.N. CONVENTION AGAINST TRANSNATIONAL ORGANIZED CRIME, G.A. Res. 55/25, U.N. Doc. A/55/383 (Nov. 15, 2000), art. 3(a), http://www.unodc.org/documents/treaties/UNTOC/Publications/TOC%20Convention/TOCebook-e.pdf.

10. Deutsche Gesellschaft für Technische Zusammenarbei (GTZ), *Trafficking in Persons as a Human Rights Issue* (2008), http://www.oecd.org/dac/gender-development/44896390.pdf.

2. Human Trafficking, Corruption, and the Millennium Development Goals

Corruption is a foremost obstruction to development, to combating human trafficking, and to reducing poverty. The interconnection of corruption and human trafficking is abundantly obvious. Corruption "keeps the machine up and running."[11] Human trafficking would not be at the current epidemic level if corruption did not provide momentous leverage. The partnership between corruption and human trafficking spans all levels of society, economic enterprise, and government affairs, and involves private and public actors in complicity, duplicity, and active engagement. It has become "a systemic predicament that needs to be stopped,"[12] to the point that gaining the upper hand on human trafficking simply cannot be accomplished without also confronting corruption.

This interwoven problem impedes the right of all human beings to reach their full potential and live a fulfilling life. It interferes with the attainment of the United Nations' eight Millennium Development Goals in several respects that are of critical importance to pursuing a holistic approach to combating human trafficking and corruption.[13] These goals are:

1. Eradicate extreme poverty and hunger;
2. Achieve universal primary education;
3. Promote gender equality and empower women;
4. Reduce child mortality;
5. Improve maternal health;
6. Combat HIV/AIDS, malaria and other diseases;
7. Ensure environmental sustainability;
8. Global partnership for development.

Notably, many of the goals identified by the UN are at the same time among the primary push factors that fuel human trafficking, specifically, but not exclusively:

- The desire to escape poverty and hunger;
- The quest for a better education and opportunity;

---

11. *Id.*
12. *Id.*
13. United Nations, *Millennium Development Goals and Beyond 2015: Background,* http://www.un.org/millenniumgoals/bkgd.shtml (last visited June 25, 2016).

- The hope to escape oppression by one gender over another;
- The urgency to move away from disease and environmental degradation.

In addition, the worldwide effort to combat HIV/AIDS is truncated by human trafficking, because trafficking victims are often at high risk of HIV infection, with women and young girls comprising the highest percentage of individuals infected.[14]

The "connectedness" also reaches to many of the ten principles articulated in the United Nations Global Compact for businesses,[15] specifically:

- Principles 1 and 2 addressing Human Rights;
- Principles 3–6 focusing on Labor, especially forced labor and child labor;
- Principle 10 pertaining to Anti-Corruption.[16]

This bundle of aspirations, rights, and principles forms a three-legged stool. As key stakeholders in achieving a sustainable future, corporate entities "must operate responsibly in alignment with universal principles and take actions that support the society around them."[17] Companies must be cognizant of embedded issues of corruption and human trafficking, develop procedures to

---

14. A compilation of findings from South Asia highlights the links between human trafficking and HIV and shows that the majority of victims are women and young girls from poor, illiterate families. *See* UNDP REGIONAL HIV AND DEVELOPMENT PROGRAMME FOR ASIA PACIFIC, HUMAN TRAFFICKING AND HIV, EXPLORING VULNERABILITIES AND RESPONSES IN SOUTH ASIA (2007), http://www.unodc.org/documents/hiv-aids/publications/human_traffick_hiv_undp2007.pdf. *See also* Amanda Kloer, *Sex Trafficking and HIV/AIDS: A Deadly Junction for Women*, 37:2 ABA HUMAN RIGHTS MAGAZINE (noting that sex trafficking is a "catalyst and facilitator of large-scale HIV transmission").

15. The United Nations Global Compact "is a leadership platform for the development, implementation and disclosure of responsible corporate policies and practices. Launched in 2000, it is the largest corporate sustainability initiative in the world." *See* UNITED NATIONS GLOBAL COMPACT, https://www.unglobalcompact.org/ (last visited June 25, 2015). The UN Global Compact's Ten Principles derive from fundamental universal documents such as the Universal Declaration of Human Rights; the International Labour Organization's Declaration on Fundamental Principles and Rights at Work; the Rio Declaration on Environment and Development, and the United Nations Convention against Corruption. *See The Ten Principles of the UN Global Compact*, UNITED NATIONS GLOBAL COMPACT, https://www.unglobalcompact.org/what-is-gc/mission/principles (last visited June 25, 2015).

16. *The Ten Principles of the UN Global Compact, supra* note 15.

17. *See generally Guide to Corporate Sustainability: Shaping a Sustainable Future*, UNITED NATIONS GLOBAL COMPACT, https://www.unglobalcompact.org/docs/publications/UN_Global_Compact_Guide_to_Corporate_Sustainability.pdf.

avoid contributing to the problem, and take steps to help combat it.[18] Government officials must be accountable to the people. The first priority must always be to preserve the rule of law and protect citizens from criminal conducts, including being vigilant against the corrosive influences of internal corruption and the debilitating effects of transborder criminality. The third leg of the stool is constituted by the nongovernment organizations that often have the capacity to work in an autonomous zone between government authority and corporate influence, and at least in theory, have the agility and flexibility to respond to critical needs of trafficking victims while at the same time serving as the voices of conscience in the public arena.

3. Gauging Human Trafficking Crimes Worldwide

Most researchers agree that human trafficking has for many years been among the fastest growing and increasingly debilitating criminal activities in the world.[19] We know that there are some communities that have been decimated by traffickers preying on vulnerable populations, and that some countries, due to conditions such as armed conflict, famine or other natural disasters, remain incapable of contending with human trafficking.

In an effort to understand the scope of human trafficking worldwide, a multitude of government bodies, non-government organizations, academics and

---

18. United Nations Global Initiative to Fight Human Trafficking (UN.GIFT), *Human Trafficking: Everybody's Business*, 9 IOM GLOBAL HUMAN TRAFFICKING DATABASE (October 2008), http://www.ungift.org/docs/ungift/pdf/Human_Trafficking_-_Everybodys_Business.pdf.

19. Press Release, Heinous, Fast-Growing Crimes of Human, Drug Trafficking Will Continue to Ravage World's Economies without Coordinated Global Action, Third Committee Told, U.N. Press Release GA/SHC/4039 (Oct. 11, 2012), http://www.un.org/press/en/2012/gashc4039.doc.htm. For several years during the 2000s, human trafficking was considered either the third largest criminal activity after drugs and weapons trafficking, or tied as the second largest criminal activity with weapons trafficking. Many organizations and government agencies used this oft repeated statement, but in reality it is extremely difficult to prove the statistic. The statement most cited is one that was issued in a 2006 Press Release by the United States Department of Health and Human Services. That release is certainly now somewhat long in the tooth but remains oft quoted. *See* U.S. Dep't of Health & Human Srvs, Fact Sheet Press Release, HHS Fights to Stem Human Trafficking, Aug. 15, 2006, http://archive.is/20131024051444/www.hhs.gov/news/factsheet/humantrafficking.html.

think tanks dedicated to combating human trafficking and studying its effects have produced a daunting amount of information that both corroborates and contradicts, and clarifies and confuses our current understanding of this global criminal enterprise. While much more is now known about human trafficking than a few years ago—its patterns, perpetrators, and victims at both the local level and internationally—less is known or understood about the nexus between human trafficking and corruption.

While we know that human trafficking and its related crimes are present at all points of the compass, there is much debate about the efficacy of crunching numbers to inform us about how widespread is human trafficking and how many people are affected worldwide. Precisely where does it rank alongside drug trafficking and weapons trafficking as the other two most serious global crimes, and does it even matter? Is it the second- or third-largest crime in terms of money generated? Is it the second- or third-largest crime because it impacts so many people worldwide? While the amount of illicit revenue generated by human trafficking is not known with any certainty,[20] the International Labour Organization (ILO) reported in 2014 (the most recent ILO statistics available) that forced labor in the private economy generates a staggering US$150 billion in illegal profits per year,[21] and that around two-thirds or US$99 billion comes from commercial sexual exploitation.[22]

Just as we do not have an accurate idea of the amount of profits generated from human trafficking, neither do we have precise numbers of trafficking victims worldwide—only rough estimates and educated guesses.[23] Yet, govern-

---

20. There is no accurate means to determine the amount of revenue generated by sex trafficking and other forms of trafficking-related exploitation because many victims, particularly in sex servitude, become reusable commodities that generate profits over and over again.

21. *Forced Labour, Human Trafficking and Slavery*, Int'l Lab. Org., http://www.ilo.org/global/topics/forced-labour/lang—en/index.htm (last visited May 20, 2016).

22. *ILO Says Forced Labour Generates Annual Profits of US$150 Billion*, Int'l Lab. Org, May 20, 2014, (referencing the ILO report, *Profits and Poverty: The Economics of Forced Labour*), *available at* http://www.ilo.org/global/about-the-ilo/newsroom/news/WCMS_243201/lang—en/index.htm.

23. *See* Anna Fletcher, *Government Complacency and Complicity in Human Trafficking*, Global Justice Blog, Nov. 24, 2014, http://www.law.utah.edu/government-complacency-and-complicity-in-human-trafficking/.

"In 2012, the International Labour Organization (ILO) estimated that an astounding 20.9 million people were victims of human trafficking worldwide. The 2014 report published by the Walk Free Foundation, an anti-trafficking NGO, estimated that 35.8 million men, women and children are living in modern slavery. Because it is so difficult to accurately measure the extent of human trafficking,

ments need to have some indication of how much human trafficking occurs within their borders and how many victims there are in order to dedicate precious resources to fighting the problem and providing for the basic human rights of its citizens and those souls who have been brought against their will to foreign lands. Policymakers spend thousands of man-hours attempting to compile criminal justice statistics and health and human services data. Nongovernment organizations dedicated to combating human trafficking and helping survivors of trafficking also produce or reuse statistics—some of which are suspect or known to be unreliable—in order to garner greater public and private financial support for operating expenses and programming.

How, then, do we obtain accurate numbers and useful data on this criminal enterprise? As one report indicated, gathering reliable numbers throughout the "murky world of human trafficking" is "notoriously hard to verify."[24] We cannot interview all the perpetrators and ask them to complete surveys, and for every trafficking victim we can verify and process, there may be many thousands who remain unknown. Moreover, there is a lack of uniformity among organizations tracking human trafficking about what is a trafficking activity, especially when some anti-trafficking NGOs (hereinafter HT NGOs) stridently promote a narrative in which *all* sex workers are trafficking victims even when they do not self-identify as such.

We can work with data collected by law enforcement agencies and the criminal justice system, but that data is subject to classification criteria and political manipulation that may vary from region to region. Moreover, too often a set of unreliable statistics begins circulating as "gospel" among very well-meaning individuals and reputable organizations, and while intentions are good, the misinformation is counterproductive to gaining a clear understanding of just how widespread are human trafficking and related crimes. For this reason, some of the leading organizations dedicated to combating human trafficking no longer attempt to collect numerical data, nor do they endorse some long-standing data. Instead, it becomes enough to know that human trafficking is a worldwide epidemic and that the focus needs to be on the three "P's"— prevention, prosecution, and protection of victims—as articulated throughout the *Palermo Protocol*.

NGOs have frequently been accused of artificially inflating the number of victims. Whether the number of victims is only a few thousand or several million, most victims are never identified and never receive justice."

24. Anne Elizabeth Moore, *Special Report: Money and Lies in Anti-Human Trafficking NGOs*, TRUTHOUT, Jan. 27, 2015, http://www.truth-out.org/news/item/28763-special-report-money-and-lies-in-anti-human-trafficking-ngos.

In the absence of statistics and agreement on the extent of human trafficking and the number of victims worldwide, we can at least strive to determine and agree upon one or more definitions of what is human trafficking. The most widely accepted working definition is that set forth in article 3 of the *Palermo Protocol*, which states that human trafficking is the:

> recruitment, transportation, transfer, harboring or receipt of persons, by means of the threat or use of force or other forms of coercion, of abduction, of fraud, of deception, and of the abuse of power or of a position of vulnerability or of the giving or receiving of payments or benefits to achieve the consent of a person having control over another person, for the purpose of exploitation.[25]

Consent of the trafficking victim is irrelevant, and child victims are anyone under the nearly universally accepted age of 18 years.[26] Human trafficking is also defined fundamentally as a crime against human rights that affects worldwide peace, security and development.

In comparison, the United States *Victims of Trafficking and Violence Protection Act of 2000* (known as the TVPA)[27] defines severe forms of human trafficking as:

> (A) sex trafficking in which a commercial sex act is induced by force, fraud, or coercion, or in which the person induced to perform such an act has not attained 18 years of age; or
> (B) the recruitment, harboring, transportation, provision, or obtaining of a person for labor or services, through the use of force, fraud, or coercion for the purpose of subjection to involuntary servitude, peonage, debt bondage, or slavery.[28]

The TVPA also provides detailed definitions of terms and meanings for human trafficking, and the United States Department of State provides these terms and meanings in order to measure and assess the capacity of other nations to combat all forms of human trafficking and modern-day slavery.

Most nations have now drafted domestic legislation to address human trafficking and related crimes that conform with their international commitments as States Parties to the *Palermo Protocol*. In the absence of specific human trafficking legislation, laws criminalizing certain acts have also been applied, such

---

25. Palermo Protocol, *supra* note 3, art. 3.
26. *Id.*
27. Pub. L. No. 106-386 of 2000, 114 Stat. 1464.
28. *Id.*, § 103(8).

as abduction and kidnapping, peonage, false imprisonment, falsification of documents, violations of immigration regulations and laws, and violations of labor practices and regulations. Some related crimes attendant to human trafficking include money laundering, tax evasion, racketeering, conspiracy, and corruption. It is the latter offense of corruption and its impact on human trafficking crime, and conversely, the impact of human trafficking crime on corruption, that one may argue warrants the greatest amount of attention.

The United Nations Office on Drugs and Crime (UNODC) relies on self-reporting by 128 member states to track human trafficking worldwide. In 2014, the UNODC issued its second *Global Report on Human Trafficking*. This comprehensive document attempts to show "patterns and flows" of trafficking at the local, regional, and international levels during a reporting period of 2010 to 2014.[29] While data takes time to compile and process and may not accurately reflect current conditions, the UNODC found that nearly every country has some kind of activity that could be construed as human trafficking.

The statistics presented in the *2014 Global Report* are sobering.[30] Among 80 countries reporting, more than 31,700 trafficking victims were detected. Of these, adult females constituted the largest number of trafficking victims, and minor females represented about 1/5 of the total number worldwide. As of 2011, of known trafficking victims globally, 48 percent were women, 18 percent were men, 12 percent were boys, and 21 percent were girls. Trafficking of males, both men and boys, rose significantly in 2012. The increase may have been due to more robust reporting of human trafficking related to labor exploitation. The number of women trafficked actually decreased over a longer seven-year period from 2004 to 2011, from 74 percent down to 49 percent. However, the number of minor females reported as trafficking victims during the same period doubled from 10 percent to 21 percent

Categorized by gender, between 2010 and 2012, 79 percent of women and children were trafficked for sexual exploitation while 83 percent of men were trafficked for labor exploitation.[31]

The UNODC then created a taxonomy of exploitation of human trafficking victims globally, broken down into the following 10 types:[32]

---

29. *See* United Nations Office on Drugs and Crime, Global Report on Trafficking in Persons 2014, U.N. Sales No. E.14.V.10) [hereinafter Global Report 2014], https://www.unodc.org/unodc/data-and-analysis/glotip.html.

30. *Id.*

31. *Id.*

32. *Id.* Types of exploitation as the "end purpose" continue to evolve. The European Commission Expert Group on Trafficking in Human Beings released a report finding that

- mixed exploitation and forced labor and sexual exploitation
- committing crimes
- begging and pandering
- pornography (including Internet pornography)
- forced marriages
- benefit fraud
- selling of infants
- illegal adoption[33]
- armed combat
- rituals

Among the data compiled for 2011, 53 percent of trafficking victims were subjected to sexual exploitation, 40 percent were exploited for labor, 0.3 percent were involved in voluntary or involuntary organ removal, and 7 percent were subjected to other forms of exploitation. While such data indicates the extent of exploitation, the manner in which human trafficking is reported makes some impact on percentages. For example, labor exploitation in some parts of the world may be underreported because the method of classification is imprecise or specific forms of what could be considered exploitation are not unlawful acts. This is particularly problematic in places like Western Africa, where unscrupulous labor brokers move hundreds of children across borders routinely, if often clandestinely, to provide field workers for cocoa plantations, and in the Middle East, where subcontractors recruit scores of improperly documented construction workers from Sub-Asian countries like India, Pakistan, and Sri Lanka to supply labor in Gulf State nations to work on building projects.

---

labor exploitation is reported for begging and criminal activity. *See Group of Experts on Trafficking in Human Beings of the European Commission, Opinion No. 7/2010,* 40–41, La Strada Int'l, http://lastradainternational.org/doc-center/2585/opinion-no-7-2010-of-the-group-of-experts-on-trafficking-in-human-beings-of-the-european-commission. *See also* Susan Kneebone and Julie Debeljak, Transnational Crime and Human Rights: Responses to Human Trafficking in the Greater Mekong Subregion 121 (2012) (noting that "servile marriage, commercial adoptions of children, sale of children into begging, and commercial arrangements involving the transfer of children from rural to urban areas for exploitation … are less acknowledged but highly prevalent.").

33. Under some circumstances, illegal adoption may be included when referenced to slavery and similar practices. *See* Report of the Ad Hoc Comm. on the Elaboration of a Convention against Transnational Organized Crime on the Work of Its First to Eleventh Sessions, Addendum, Interpretative Notes for the Official Records (Travaux préparatoires) of the Negotiation of the United Nations Convention against Transnational Organized Crime and the Protocols Thereto, ¶63, U.N. Doc. A/55/383/Add.1 (Nov. 3, 2000).

Similarly, the manner in which exploitation is categorized is rather broad, even with the help of the UNODC's taxonomy for guidance. For instance, forced labor includes many kinds of work, including servitude in various manufacturing settings like textiles and consumables, fisheries work (both catching and processing), agriculture (fields and processing), service sector jobs (hospitality, food preparation, personal care), and domestic servitude (childcare and maid service). Some forms of human trafficking are more prevalent in certain parts of the world than in other areas. For example, the number of children trafficked into being child soldiers appears to be greatest in sub-Saharan Africa where political violence is nearly constant, although it is nearly impossible to determine the total number of children trafficked into armed conflict. We do know, however, that conflict, including low intensity conflict, greatly increases the vulnerability of people who find themselves as refugees or internally displaced.[34]

In the Americas, for example, it is believed that 47 percent of trafficking victims are forced into labor servitude and 48 percent succumb to sexual exploitation. But in South America, fewer trafficking victims (40 percent) are forced into labor servitude. Also in South America, we see a higher percentage of men trafficked than women, 60 percent versus 40 percent and that 69 percent of trafficking victims are adults compared to 31 percent children. In South Asia, more than 80 percent of trafficking victims are trafficked for forced labor, while a roughly equal number of trafficking victims are exploited in both sex servitude and labor servitude in North America, Central America, and the Caribbean.[35]

Global reporting on the number of children being trafficked is suspect because crucial concepts presented in the *Palermo Protocol* are misunderstood and, hence, have been inconsistently "implemented and applied."[36] For instance, contrary to art. 3(b) of the *Protocol*, consent plays a role in several domestic legislations even when one of the means listed in the definition is employed (coercion, deception, etc.).[37]

---

34. *See for example* Luz E. Nagle, *How Conflict and Displacement Fuel Human Trafficking and Abuse of Vulnerable Groups: The Case of Colombia and Opportunities for Real Action and Innovative Solutions*, 1 Groningen J. Int'l L. 1 (2014); Luz E. Nagle, *Placing Blame Where Blame Is Due: The Culpability of Illegal Armed Groups and Narcotraffickers in Colombia's Environmental and Human Rights Catastrophes*, 29 Wm. & Mary Envtl. L. & Pol'y Rev. 1 (2004).

35. Global Report 2014 *supra* note 29, at 34.

36. United Nations Office on Drugs and Crime, The Role of "Consent" in the Trafficking in Persons Protocol 5 (2014) [hereinafter Role of "Consent"]. This UNODC study was issued to assist in understanding and implementing "difficult concepts" of the human trafficking definition.

37. The country survey done by the UNODC in preparation for its Issue Paper to clarify the concept of consent reflects how in practice, countries acknowledge consent in vio-

Moreover, in some Member States, there exists a conflict between the implementation of the *Protocol* and existing domestic legislation that allows the continuing exploitation of children. Under the *Protocol*,[38] as well as under other international instruments,[39] every person under 18 years of age is considered a child and therefore a minor's consent to any form of exploitation is irrelevant. In some countries' legislation, the minimum age for sexual consent is below 16 years and even 13 years.[40] Lower age is especially troublesome with regard to trafficking of a child for sexual exploitation. "The objective of the minimum age of sexual consent is to protect adolescents from sexual abuse and from the consequences of early activity on their rights and development."[41] Children 13 to 18 years of age residing in countries that do not recognize the *Protocol's* age standard fall into a gap that is something of a purgatory because they are not identified as victims,[42] and are presumed to engage willingly in prostitution, and therefore, are not protected.[43] More concerning is that some

---

lation of the *Protocol*. The questions posed by the survey are found in Role of "Consent," *supra* note 36, at 104–05.

38. Under the Palermo Protocol, art. 3(d), a child is defined as "any person under eighteen years of age." There is absolutely no ambiguity under the *Protocol*.

39. Under art. 1 of the United Nations Convention on the Rights of the Child, "a child means every human being below the age of 18 years unless, under the law applicable to the child, majority is attained earlier." *See* United Nations Convention on the Rights of the Child, G.A. Res. 44/25, 44 U.N. GAOR, Supp. No. 49, U.N. Doc. A/44/736 (1989). According to the International Labour Organization's 1999 Worst Forms of Child Labor Convention (No.182), "the term child shall apply to all persons under the age of 18." *See* Int'l Labour Organization, Convention Concerning the Prohibition and Immediate Action for the Elimination of the Worst Forms of Child Labour Convention, June 17, 1999, 2133 U.N.T.S. 161.

40. Across the Americas, the majority of the countries set the minimum age for sexual consent between 14 and 16 years, and a few have an age lower than 14. *See* UNICEF, *Legal Minimum Ages and the Realization of Adolescents' Rights*, http://www.unicef.org/lac/2._201 60308_UNICEF_LACRO_min_age_of_sexual_consent.pdf.

41. *Id.*

42. The UN High Commissioner for Human Rights recommends to nations that, "Children who are victims of trafficking shall be identified as such." Moreover, nations are to consider the best interests of a child paramount, and provide them with appropriate assistance and protection, considering their "special vulnerabilities, rights and needs." *See* Recommended Principle 10, addendum to the report of the United Nations High Commissioner for Human Rights (E/2002/68/Add. 1), http://www.unhcr.org/4963237811.pdf. "In accordance with the Palermo Protocol, evidence of deception, force, coercion, etc. should not form part of the definition of trafficking where the person involved is a child." United Nations Office on Drugs and Crime, Toolkit to Combat Trafficking in Persons, Guideline 8(1), at 361, U.N. Sales No. E.08.V.14.

43. In Colombia, the Child Welfare Institute identifies children as exploited in prostitution, but not as trafficking victims. Most of the children are sexually exploited in tourist

countries hide behind the age of sexual consent being under 18 in order to justify children and adolescents' status as sex workers, disregarding situations in which the minors are coerced or lured into sexual activity. Such consent becomes relevant when a child is sexually abused.[44]

More problematic is that what is considered the age of consent has deep social and historical underpinnings in some places on the globe, and this discontinuity impacts whether exploitative acts against adolescents can be criminalized. Such a troubling discrepancy has many implications for international enforcement and is also problematic for countries striving to be in full compliance with their obligations under the *Palermo Protocol*, particularly where tribalism or strict religious practices impede the best of government intentions.[45]

Trafficking for crimes such as begging and forced marriages are prominent in Europe, for example, while trafficking of babies for illegal adoption are a problem in Eastern Europe, the Middle East, Central Asia, and in Central America.[46] Even less data exists to give us a picture about groups of individuals exploited due to their social class characteristics. For example, the UNODC's *2014 Global Report* does not address the trafficking of persons due to their vulnerabilities as homosexuals (LGBTQ), indigenous groups (for example, Afro-Colombians or Burmese Padaung), or marginalized communities (for example, Roma communities throughout Europe or the Yazidis in the Middle East).

In any social studies discipline, facts and figures have long been used to press a point and underscore the severity of a social crisis. However, the statistics put forth by hundreds of anti-human trafficking organizations are all over the spectrum, and evoke incredulity in some cases. About this, one scholar stated:

> None of the trafficking claims—huge magnitude, growing problem, ranking among criminal enterprises, most prevalent type—have been substantiated. It is impossible to satisfactorily count (or even estimate) the number of persons involved in or the magnitude of profits within

---

and mining areas. *See* U.S. Dep't of State, The Trafficking in Persons Report 134 (2016) [hereinafter TIP Report 2016].

44. Consent of the victim is irrelevant when any of the "means" of art. 3(a) of the *Palermo Protocol* are present (threat or use of force or other forms of coercion, abduction, fraud, deception, abuse of power or position of vulnerability, and the giving or receiving of payment or benefits to achieve consent of a person having control over another person).

45. The differences in what constitutes a child for the purposes of combating human trafficking also create a conflict between domestic legislation and international legal obligations for some States Parties to the *Protocol*.

46. Global Report 2014, *supra* note 29, at 35.

an illicit, clandestine, underground economy at the macro level — nationally or internationally.[47]

Incorrect and even falsified statistics have been reported so often that the inaccuracies become widely circulated as factual information clothed in an aura of legitimacy, as if something said often enough will make it true. Yet, in the zeal to be proactive in combating human trafficking and to get the attention of the public, government authorities become susceptible to using unsupportable data because, in some cases, they have not taken stock of the validity of the information they embrace as fact.

This occurred in 2015 in the run-up to the iconic American motorsports event, the Indianapolis 500, when the Indiana Attorney General, Greg Zoeller, launched a billboard campaign near the race venue that stated: "13 is the average age kids are first used in the sex trade."[48] This statistic had already been considered debunked before the Attorney General used it for the public service campaign. Its origin was a 2001 report out of the University of Pennsylvania[49] that had not been peer-reviewed and was more than a decade out of date. But because it had been picked up by the FBI and a U.S. Senator, the statement was given legitimacy.[50] That same report included other false claims that also persisted in the mainstream, including an erroneous statement that more than 300,000 children were susceptible to being trafficked into commercial sex exploitation. The lead author of the report, Richard Estes, stated in 2015 that he no longer supported the content of the report, saying, "The world of the 1990s ... was quite a different one from that in which we live today."[51]

Absent any universal agreement on "how much" and "how many," we are left with three lessons about determining the scope of human trafficking worldwide. The first is that we simply do not know how to collect or report

---

47. Ronald Weitzer, *New Directions in Research on Human Trafficking*, in 653 ANNALS OF THE AMERICAN ACADEMY OF POLITICAL AND SOCIAL SCIENCE 13 (May 2014), http://www.researchgate.net/profile/Ronald_Weitzer/publication/273133970_New_Directions_in_Human_Trafficking_Research/links/54f8c97a0cf210398e96caa4.pdf.

48. Glenn Kessler, *Indiana AG Touts a Debunked and Rejected "Fact" on Sex Trafficking*, WASH. POST, June 8, 2016.

49. *See* Richard J. Estes & Neil Weiner, *The Commercial Sexual Exploitation of Children in the U.S., Canada, and Mexico*, Sept. 19, 2001, http://www.gems-girls.org/Estes%20Wiener%202001.pdf.

50. Kessler, *supra* note 48.

51. Statement by Estes to The Fact Checker, Glenn Kessler, quoted in Kessler, *supra* note 48.

accurate data about victims of transborder trafficking crimes because it is nearly impossible to sort fact from the chaff resulting from sensationalist tendencies to amplify an already horrible human tragedy. Therefore, our time and resources should be better put to use elsewhere for combating human trafficking.

The second lesson is that scholars and those who represent us in government, even when they have the best intentions to educate and inform, are fallible and susceptible to the same visceral reactions and repugnance most people feel about human trafficking and forced servitude. Was the Indiana Attorney General or his staff irresponsible for not fact checking sources before launching a high-profile public education campaign at a sports event that has worldwide coverage? Was the FBI remiss in perpetuating myths, later taken up by the Indiana AG and others, knowing that the Bureau's reputation for integrity is nearly sacrosanct? Surely, their intentions were admirable, but the result was unhelpful for fighting human trafficking because once the falsity of the information that has been out in the public comes to light, people can become skeptical of what they are being told by authorities, and less open to the message.

The third lesson is that the persistence of some HT NGOs to use "the sky is falling" narrative as a means to attract funding from private donors and government resources may have some short term value, but the long term benefits may be less productive and potentially detrimental to anti-human trafficking efforts. The conclusion about the extent of global human trafficking is that it simply needs to be enough to know that global human trafficking is widespread and impacts many people, many communities, across all cultures, and beyond international borders.

4. Characteristics of Trafficking Operations

There is no one face to the perpetrators of human trafficking worldwide. A trafficker can be a transnational criminal group, a gang member, a teenager, a government contractor, a diplomat, or the housewife next door. Traffickers are present in each stratus of society and they operate in both urban and rural landscapes. They penetrate inner city neighborhoods to prey on difficult socioeconomic conditions, and they harvest victims from remote villages in far-flung corners of the world by promising better lives for the children of parents who cannot afford to keep them. A trafficker can look like someone out of central casting in Hollywood, or s/he can be a nondescript, unassuming government worker or bureaucrat who one would never imagine is profiting on vulnerable individuals.

Because we cannot form a one-size-fits-all view of traffickers and trafficking organizations, we try to qualify and formulate categories to help us gain a handle on the criminal actors and organizations we are confronting. Establishing a typology helps guide us in understanding trafficking operations and determining the nature and scope of resources we must devote to confront particular trafficking situations. The UNODC has identified three "classes" of characteristics to help us in this task. These characteristics are: small local operations, medium sub-regional operations, and large transregional operations.

A. Small Local Trafficking Operations

Small local operations include trafficking crimes that are of a domestic and short distance character. Small local trafficking involves one or very few perpetrators, a small number of victims, and little investment. Profits are limited, travel documents are unnecessary because there are no border crossings, and the trafficking operations tend to be unsophisticated and unorganized. Small local operations may be a matter of an individual asserting control over another person or persons and subjecting them to sexual or labor exploitation. However, small local operations can often constitute some of the most brutal and abusive deprivations and violent conduct against victims. We see this in prostitution activities involving a single pimp (referred to as a third-party exploiter) who asserts control by force over one or a few individuals solely for his/her financial gain. Such an example would be the case of Aaron David George of Orlando, Florida, who was convicted and sentenced to life in prison on multiple counts for luring homeless and drug addicted girls, one as young as 16 years of age, into sexual servitude in an Orlando area motel and severely beating and emotionally tormenting them if they did not cooperate.[52]

In a 2005, the National Juvenile Prostitution Study (N-JPS) gathered statistics and identified several important characteristics of third-party exploiters that remain consistent eleven years later:[53]

---

52. *Convicted Sex Trafficker May Spend Life in Prison*, WFTV9 News, Jan. 1, 2015, http://www.wftv.com/news/local/convicted-sex-trafficker-may-spend-life-prison/69701308.

53. Kimberly J. Mitchell et al., Sex Trafficking Cases Involving Minors 3 (Crimes Against Children Research Center, University of New Hampshire, November 2013, *available at* http://www.unh.edu/ccrc/pdf/CV313_Final_Sex_Trafficking_Minors_Nov_2013_rev.pdf (noting that small and medium operations constituted 48 percent of pimping cases and larger well-organized operations 52 percent, respectively).

- 85 percent of exploiters were males;
- 27 percent of females involved in exploiting were older prostitutes who helped recruit and control juvenile victims;
- 44 percent of the exploiters were between age 20 to 29;
- 24 percent were age 30 to 39;
- 59 percent of exploiters were African-American and U.S. citizens.[54]

A small local trafficking operation may also involve a couple forcing an individual into labor servitude, as occurred in Houston, Texas, where a married couple, both naturalized U.S. citizens originally from Nigeria, were accused of coercing a 38-year-old Nigerian national with barely a fifth grade education into domestic servitude. Before the victim was able to escape, authorities claim, the couple subjected the woman to many depredations, physical abuse, and torment.[55] Until recently, a trafficker forcing one or more children into street begging in London, England, would also constitute a small local trafficking operations. However, the trafficking of children and other individuals for begging and committing crimes is becoming a lucrative large scale trafficking operation in which criminal gangs, working from Continental Europe, are running strings of more than 100 children to beg in London's streets.[56]

There is no accurate means to gauge how extensive and widespread are the trafficking crimes that fall within the small operations category. The fact that these cases turn up in the news media with growing frequency suggests that small local trafficking has reached alarming proportions and that perpetrators

---

54. *Id.*

55. *See* Kate Briquelet, *Houston Couple Forced Nanny into 'Slavery',* Daily Beast, Feb. 10, 2016, http://www.thedailybeast.com/articles/2016/02/10/houston-couple-forced-nanny-into-slavery.html. Chudy Nsobundu and Sandra Nsobundu faced multiple federal charges, including conspiracy to commit forced labor and unlawful conduct with respect to documents in furtherance of forced labor, forced labor and attempted forced labor, unlawful conduct with respect to documents in furtherance of forced labor, visa fraud, and harboring and introducing an alien to come to the United States. The case was filed in the United States District Court for the Southern District of Texas, case no. 4:26-cr-00089. As of this writing, the case is still ongoing.

56. Guy Adams, *Mafia Bosses Who Can't Wait to Flood Britain with Beggars: While Politicians Dither Over New Wave of Immigration from Eastern Europe, Ruthless Gangmasters Are Rubbing Their Hands with Glee,* Daily Mail, Feb. 18, 2013, http://www.dailymail.co.uk/news/article-2280294/The-mafia-bosses-wait-flood-Britain-beggars-While-politicians-dither-new-wave-immigration-Eastern-Europe-ruthless-gangmasters-rubbing-hands-glee.html (describing how one police investigation uncovered 103 Roma children "crammed into 16 houses in Ilford, East London," and authorities estimated that up to 2000 children from Eastern Europe may be forced to work as street pick-pockets nationwide.).

may have a false sense of impunity about the criminal conducts in which they engage because they believe that the odds of being caught are on their side.

B. Medium Sub-Regional Trafficking Operations

Medium sub-regional operations are characterized by trafficking activities that occur in what the UNODC characterizes as sub-regions or neighboring sub-regions around the world.[57] The operations involve a small group of traffickers controlling multiple victims. There is some form of investment involved in return for more robust profits gained from the volume of individuals being exploited. Moving trafficking victims across international borders with or without travel documentation is likely involved, and some organization needs to be established in order to sustain the operation. Examples of this type of operation may include situations in which traffickers collect trafficking victims through local advertising that deceives victims into involuntary forms of servitude, debt bondage arrangements, and "scouts" who sweep through impoverished areas preying upon vulnerable groups such as runaways, drug users, unemployed unskilled workers, and marginalized groups. An example of such traffickers would be labor brokers who transport illegal migrant workers across borders to work in the fields, or run groups of women in debt bondage arrangements to work in hotels and in service sector jobs. Another example would be kidney brokers in Nepal who trick poor villagers into going to India to sell their kidneys, using false documentation and identities to move them through the supply chain.[58] There is also a white collar criminal element involved in organ trafficking, and corruption is most certainly present that can involve a sophisticated network of government officials, accountants, doctors and other medical professionals, and unscrupulous staff working in nongovernment organizations.[59]

---

57. *Global Report 2014*, *supra* note 29, Executive Summary, at 14, https://www.unodc.org/documents/data-and-analysis/glotip/GLOTIP14_ExSum_english.pdf.

58. The scenario works like this: One victim was instructed by his broker to tell the doctors that he was a brother of the recipient, even though he could not understand the language being spoken. He subsequently received only a small portion of the agreed sum upon his return to Nepal. *See* Sugam Pokharel, *Nepal's Organ Trail: How Traffickers Steal Kidneys*, CNN Freedom Project, June 30, 2014, http://www.cnn.com/2014/06/26/world/asia/freedom-project-nepals-organ-trail/.

59. Organ trafficking involves criminal acts by administrators, medical professionals and in some cases, official representatives whose contribution to the criminality is often essential in terms of accessing the certification, approval and medical equipment necessary to set up a transplant clinic. *See 2013 Trafficking in Human Beings For the Purpose of Organ*

C. Large Transregional Trafficking Operations

Large transregional operations are considered major international human trafficking conspiracies. This is the domain of transborder organized crime. These operations involve multiples of victims drawn from all walks of life and social backgrounds. As the wife of a former Nigerian Vice-President stated more than a decade ago, "the dragnet of the traffickers is so wide that only God knows who is safe."[60] These groups use false advertising, deceit, coercion, local recruiting methods, and even family relationships, to funnel trafficking victims into well-traveled smuggling corridors around the world. These organizations operate in source, transit, and destination countries, and are the most responsible for elements of both public and private corruption in the human trafficking chain. Large transregional operations exploit conditions in weak and failing states and encourage corruption to persist. Significant investment is required in return for high profits, which is another reason that organized crime dominates this segment of human trafficking. These operations also require significant travel across national frontiers, across regions, and across continents. Because so much is required to make these operations profitable, endurance of the operations and the ability to sustain them are critical. Examples of these groups are various national and transnational mafias that rely on operatives all along the trafficking chain. Russian mobsters harvest trafficking victims throughout the Russian Federation and transport them into Europe where their operatives at destination points exploit the victims over and over until they are no longer able to generate profits. Asian crime gangs collect and move trafficking victims around the world to work in brothels, factories, and on fishing vessels on the high seas. Criminal organizations operating in Greece traffic Roma women from Albania and Bulgaria to be placed in "baby mills" where those who are not already pregnant are impregnated by gang members and forced to produce babies that are then sold through adoption agencies in Athens where private adoption arrangements are largely unregulated.[61] Nigerian gangs moving trafficking victims into Europe operate in

---

Removal in the OSCE Region: Analysis and Findings, at 6, Vienna: OSCE, Off. Spec. Rep. Coord. Combating Traffick. Hum. Beings.

60. Quote of Titi Atiku Abubakar, in Osita Agbu, *Corruption and Human Trafficking: The Nigerian Case*, 4 W. Africa Rev. 1 (2003), https://pdfs.semanticscholar.org/ab84/544291af64bdd21d4d99ea4e68ea4c7f26cd.pdf.

61. *See* Natalie Clarke, *The Shocking Truth about the Baby Factories*, Daily Mail, Dec. 22, 2006, http://www.dailymail.co.uk/femail/article-424450/The-shocking-truth-baby-factories.html; Juliana Koleva and Kostas Kallergis, *Lives for Sale: Booming Market for Bulgar-*

organized groups called confraternities.[62] The confraternities move mostly Nigerian women into sex servitude in Spain and elsewhere, where they are controlled and managed by confraternity associates that are mostly women.

---

ian Babies in Greece, EU OBSERVER, Dec. 22, 2015, https://euobserver.com/investigations/131625 (notably, this article was "produced as part of the Alumni Initiative of the Balkan Fellowship for Journalistic Excellence, supported by the ERSTE Foundation and Open Society Foundations, in cooperation with the Balkan Investigative Reporting Network, or, BIRN.").

62. *Global Report 2014*, *supra* note 29, at 56. Nigerians accounted for more than 10 percent of people trafficked into Central and Western Europe. The confraternities originated as groups of promising students operating as campus organizations in Nigerian universities beginning in the 1950s. Over time, the groups became radicalized and increasingly violent, until the 1990s, when the groups evolved into criminal organizations known as "campus cults." Female confraternities also formed during the 1990s and became known for running prostitution rings. *See also* Bestman Wellington, *Nigeria's Cults and their Role in the Niger Delta Insurgency*, 5 TERRORISM MONITOR 13, 6 July 2007, http://www.jamestown.org/single/?tx_ttnews[tt_news]=4288#.VT6Vj5MR8Xg.

Chapter 2

Key International Legal Instruments Regarding Human Trafficking

Summary: This chapter introduces the two primary international legal instruments created by the United Nations for addressing transnational organized crime and human trafficking worldwide: The Convention against Transnational Organized Crime (UNTOC) and its Optional Protocol to Prevent, Suppress and Punish Trafficking in Persons, Especially Women and Children, known as the Palermo Protocol. We will first look in detail at the UNTOC, its origin, its scope, and its goals for confronting international criminal organizations. We will then examine the Palermo Protocol as the primary instrument for defining human trafficking, addressing human trafficking crimes, and protecting victims of human trafficking. We will conclude with a discussion of the interrelationship between the two instruments.

1. UN Convention against Transnational Organized Crime and the Palermo Protocol

As an international agreement, the United Nations *Convention against Transnational Organized Crime* (UNTOC) and its supplementary instrument, the *Protocol to Prevent, Suppress and Punish Trafficking in Persons, Especially Women and Children* (*Palermo Protocol*), together constitute a unified body to combat transnational crimes, of which human trafficking constitutes a significant criminal activity.[1] Until the *Palermo Protocol* was drafted, there was no universal mechanism that addressed all aspects of trafficking in persons. Both instruments together create a framework for combating human trafficking at the international level and provide model language for creating domestic legislation and filling gaps in existing domestic legislation among States Parties.

A. UN Convention against Transnational Organized Crime (UNTOC)

The UN *Convention against Transnational Organized Crime* aims to promote cooperation among the international community in the fight against and effective prevention of transnational organized crime. The origin of the instrument arose from efforts within the United Nations in the early 1990s to develop a framework that became known as the *Naples Political Declaration* and *Global Action Plan against Organized Transnational Crime.*[2] Among the goals of the declaration were "closer alignment of legislative texts; greater international cooperation in investigations and prosecutions; agreement on modalities for cooperation at the regional and global levels; elaboration of international agreements on organized transnational crime; and development of

---

1. The three Protocols that supplement the Convention target specific types of organized criminal activity requiring specialized provisions. These are: The Protocol to Prevent, Suppress and Punish Trafficking in Persons, Especially Women and Children, supplementing the United Nations Convention against Transnational Organized Crime; The Protocol against the Smuggling of Migrants by Land, Sea and Air, supplementing the United Nations Convention against Transnational Organized Crime; and the Protocol against the Illicit Manufacturing and Trafficking in Firearms, Their Parts and Components and Ammunition, supplementing the United Nations Convention against Transnational Organized Crime. For full text of the Convention and its Protocols, see UNITED NATIONS OFFICE ON DRUGS AND CRIME, UNITED NATIONS CONVENTION AGAINST TRANSNATIONAL ORGANIZED CRIME AND THE PROTOCOLS THERETO, U.N. Doc A/55/383/Add.1 (Nov. 3, 2000), https://www.unodc.org/unodc/en/treaties/CTOC/#Fulltext [hereinafter UNTOC]. *See also* UNITED NATIONS OFFICE ON DRUGS AND CRIME, LEGISLATIVE GUIDES FOR THE IMPLEMENTATION OF THE UNITED NATIONS CONVENTION AGAINST TRANSNATIONAL ORGANIZED CRIME AND THE PROTOCOLS THERETO 269 (2004), http://www.unodc.org/pdf/crime/legislative_guides/Leg islative%20guides_Full%20version.pdf [hereinafter Legislative Guides].

2. The United Nations convened a World Ministerial Conference on Transnational Organized Crime in Naples in 1994. *See* Report of the World Ministerial Conference on Organized Transnational Crime: Report of the Secretary-General, U.N. GAOR, 49th Sess., Agenda Item 96, at 5, U.N. Doc. A/49/748 (1994).

strategies to combat money-laundering."[3] The *Global Action Plan* provided an important foundation setting forth critical components for the future *Convention against Transnational Organized Crime*. These components were:

- Agreement on a definition of organized crime;
- Adoption of national legislation dealing with organized crime;
- Using the model of more experienced states' laws;
- Development and improvement of bilateral and multilateral agreements on extradition and legal assistance;
- Strengthened regional initiatives, including technical assistance;
- Consideration of international instruments against organized transnational crime; and
- Anti-money laundering measures on the national and multinational levels.[4]

Throughout the 1990s, entities within the United Nations undertook efforts to develop a framework for an eventual draft for the convention, and the Government of Poland initiated a draft for comment by the General Assembly. During the process, recognition of a set of additional protocols evolved that concerned illegal trafficking of migrants, illicit manufacture and trafficking in firearms, and trafficking in women and children.[5]

In its completed form, the UNTOC covers among many other offenses, "offenses that facilitate the profit-making activities of organized criminal groups."[6] Specifically, the UNTOC "seeks to eliminate 'safe havens' where organized criminal activities or the concealment of evidence or profits can take place by promoting the adoption of base minimum measures."[7] States Parties are obliged to criminalize several offenses, "whether committed by individuals or corporate entities, including: participation in an organized criminal group, public corruption, laundering of proceeds, and obstruction of justice."[8] These offenses "shall be established in the State's domestic law independently of the transnational nature or the involvement of an organized criminal group."[9] For

---

3. CarrieLyn Donigan Guymon, *International Legal Mechanisms for Combating Transnational Organized Crime: The Need for A Multilateral Convention*, 18 Berkeley J. Int'l L. 53, 91 (2000).

4. *Id.* at 92.

5. *Id.*

6. Legislative Guides, *supra* note 1, at xviii.

7. Anne T. Gallagher, The International Law of Human Trafficking 74 (2010).

8. *Id.* at 75.

9. *Id.* at 79.

criminalization, neither transnationality nor organized criminal groups are to be made elements of the domestic offense.[10]

As the parent agreement to the *Palermo Protocol*,[11] the UNTOC contains significant provisions pertaining to victims of transnational organized crime, among them that victims are to be compensated when possible, including receiving the proceeds of crime and the return of property to rightful owners (art. 14(2)), and that States Parties will take all appropriate measures to protect and provide assistance to victims acting as witnesses (art. 24 and art. 25). The UNTOC also includes a provision requiring States Parties to consider establishing public corruption and *other forms of corruption* as a criminal offense,[12] specifying that a public official is "a person who provides a public service as defined in domestic law and as applied in the criminal law of the State Party in which the person in question performs the function."[13] Other forms of corruption can include private sector corruption, and participation as an accomplice in a criminal offense.

B. The Palermo Protocol

The *Protocol to Prevent, Suppress and Punish Trafficking in Persons, Especially Women and Children* (*Palermo Protocol*)[14] is the benchmark for defining human trafficking and serves as a model for global action against human trafficking. The *Protocol* is a critical instrument for law enforcement agencies to combat trafficking around the globe. The language that defines the foundation for understanding human trafficking, art. 3(a),[15] specifies human trafficking as comprising three separate but interconnected elements:[16]

---

10. UNTOC, *supra* note 1, art. 34(2). "In other words, in domestic law, the offences established in accordance with the Convention of participation in an organized criminal group, corruption, money-laundering and obstruction of justice and the Protocol offences of trafficking in persons, smuggling of migrants and trafficking in firearms must apply equally, regardless of whether the case involves transnational elements or is purely domestic." *See* Legislative Guides, *supra* note 1, at 10–11.

11. Anne Gallagher, *Human Rights and the New UN Protocols on Trafficking and Migrant Smuggling: A Preliminary Analysis*, 23 Hum. Rts. Q. 975, 978 (2001).

12. UNTOC, *supra* note 1, art. 8, subparts 1 and 2.

13. *Id.* art. 8(4).

14. Protocol to Prevent, Suppress and Punish Trafficking in Persons, Especially Women and Children, Supplementing the United Nations Convention against Transnational Organized Crime, Nov. 15, 2000, T.I.A.S. No. 13127, 2237 U.N.T.S. 319 [hereinafter Palermo Protocol].

15. The purpose of art. 3 is to define the term "trafficking in persons" in international law so as to provide some degree of consensus-based standardization of concepts.

16. As articulated in Gallagher, *supra* note 7, at 78.

1. An Action (recruitment, transportation, transfer, harboring, or receipt of persons)
2. A Means (threat or use of force or other forms of coercion, abduction, fraud, deception, abuse of power, abuse of a position of vulnerability, the giving or receiving of payments or benefits to achieve the consent of a person having control over another person)
3. A Purpose (exploitation)

According to the ILO, "any conduct that combines any listed action and means and is carried out for any of the listed purposes must be criminalized as trafficking."[17]

As a model global instrument, the *Protocol* sets forth three key goals in art. 2, known as the three "P"s in combating human trafficking—prevention, prosecution, and protection:

(a) to prevent and combat trafficking in persons, paying particular attention to women and children (prevention and prosecution);
(b) to protect and assist victims of sex trafficking, with full respect for their human rights; and
(c) to promote cooperation among States Parties in order to meet those objectives.[18]

Prevention is addressed in art. 9:

Article 9 (Prevention of trafficking in persons)
1. States Parties shall establish comprehensive policies, programmes and other measures:
(a) To prevent and combat trafficking in persons; and
(b) To protect victims of trafficking in persons, especially women and children, from revictimization.
2. States Parties shall endeavour to undertake measures such as research, information and mass media campaigns and social and economic initiatives to prevent and combat trafficking in persons.
3. Policies, programmes and other measures established in accordance with this article shall, as appropriate, include cooperation with non-

---

17. Int'l Labour Org., *The Cost of Coercion: Global Report Under the Follow-Up to the ILO Declaration on Fundamental Principles and Rights at Work* ¶ 30 (2009), http://www.ilo.org/wcmsp5/groups/public/---ed_norm/---relconf/documents/meetingdocument/wcms_106230.pdf [hereinafter *Cost of Coercion*].
18. Palermo Protocol, *supra* note 14, art. 2.

governmental organizations, other relevant organizations and other elements of civil society.

4. States Parties shall take or strengthen measures, including through bilateral or multilateral cooperation, to alleviate the factors that make persons, especially women and children, vulnerable to trafficking, such as poverty, underdevelopment and lack of equal opportunity.

5. States Parties shall adopt or strengthen legislative or other measures, such as educational, social or cultural measures, including through bilateral and multilateral cooperation, to discourage the demand that fosters all forms of exploitation of persons, especially women and children, that leads to trafficking.

Prosecution is addressed in art. 5:

Article 5 (Criminalization)

1. Each State Party shall adopt such legislative and other measures as may be necessary to establish as criminal offenses the conduct set forth in article 3 of this Protocol, when committed intentionally.

2. Each State Party shall also adopt such legislative and other measures as may be necessary to establish as criminal offenses:

(a) Subject to the basic concepts of its legal system, attempting to commit an offense established in accordance with paragraph 1 of this article;

(b) Participating as an accomplice in an offense established in accordance with paragraph 1 of this article; and

(c) Organizing or directing other persons to commit an offense established in accordance with paragraph 1 of this article.

Protection is addressed primarily under Section II of the *Protocol* in articles 6 through 8, and covers assistance to and protection of victims (art. 6); status of victims in receiving states (art. 7); and repatriation of victims to States in which the victim is a national (art. 8).

For all its distinction as a model international instrument, the *Protocol* fell short in several key areas, not the least of which is that it concerned only trafficking that is transnational in nature.[19] In the intervening years since its inception (as one United States Department of State analyst noted in recognition of the *Protocol*'s 10 year anniversary) States Parties have recognized that the term "trafficking" as set forth in the *Protocol*, "does not connote movement, but is instead a crime of compelled service, and that a significant number of traf-

---

19. *Id.* art. 4.

ficking victims never travel any distance or cross a border; governments are recognizing that their own citizens are trafficking victims within their borders."[20]

Another key shortcoming is that there is almost no precedent in international law, nor is there much national legislation, on the legal concept of exploitation—a key element of the *Protocol*.[21] The *Protocol* only lists some patterns of exploitation, and is "concerned only with prohibiting forms of dealing which facilitate or lead to exploitation."[22] At a minimum, a definition of exploitation should address exploitation of prostitution, other forms of sexual exploitation, forced labor or services,[23] slavery or practices similar to slavery,[24] servitude, or the removal of organs.[25]

Likewise, the *Protocol* does not define vulnerability.[26] The drafters might have attempted to do so, even though "vulnerability to trafficking is certainly

---

20. Kelly Hyland Heinrich, *Ten Years after the Palermo Protocol: Where Are Protections for Human Trafficking Victims?* 18 No. 1 Hum. Rts. Brief 2 (2008).

21. *Cost of Coercion, supra* note 17, at ¶ 29.

22. James C. Hathaway, *The Human Rights Quagmire of "Human Trafficking,"* 49 Va. J. Int'l L. 1, 10 (2008).

23. *Legislative Guides, supra* note 1, at 268, fn. 14.
"'Forced labour" is not defined in the Protocol. There are, however, several international instruments in this regard, for example: the 1930 Convention concerning Forced or Compulsory Labour (Convention No. 105) of the International Labour Organization; and the 1957 Convention concerning the Abolition of Forced Labour (Convention No. 105) of the International Labour Organization. "Slavery" is not defined in the Protocol, but numerous international instruments, as well as the domestic laws of many countries, define or deal with slavery and similar practices (*see for example*, art. 4 of the 1948 Universal Declaration of Human Rights; the 1926 Slavery Convention, as amended by the 1953 Protocol (United Nations, Treaty Series, vol. 212, No. 2861); the 1956 Supplementary Convention on the Abolition of Slavery, the Slave Trade, and Institutions and Practices Similar to Slavery (United Nations, Treaty Series, vol. 266, No. 3822); the 1999 Convention concerning the Prohibition and Immediate Action for the Elimination of the Worst Forms of Child Labour (Convention No. 182) of the International Labour Organization; article 11, paragraph 1, of the International Convention on the Protection of the Rights of All Migrant Workers and Members of Their Families (General Assembly resolution 45/158, annex); and article 4 (Prohibition of slavery and forced labour) of the 1950 Convention for the Protection of Human Rights and Fundamental Freedoms)."

24. Palermo Protocol, art. 3(a).

25. *Legislative Guides, supra* note 1, at 269.
"The removal of a child's organs for legitimate medical or therapeutic reasons cannot form an element of trafficking if a parent or guardian has validly consented."

26. Palermo Protocol, art. 3(a). *See* Gallagher, *supra* note 7, at 415–432.

not fixed, predetermined or even fully known."[27] The Group of Experts on Trafficking in Human Beings of the European Commission did, however, attempt to frame vulnerability of trafficking victims:

> Vulnerability factors that put people at risk of exploitation are linked to a number of issues including residency status, access to the labour market, language and cultural barriers, lack of awareness of rights and lack of information on possible resources, 'dependence on fellow-countrymen' or other intermediaries.[28]

According to Mark P. Lagon, current President of the NGO Freedom House, vulnerability befalls "those groups denied equal protection under the law in practice—minorities, migrants, women, or those who fall into more than one of those categories."[29]

---

27. There is not an agreed upon definition of vulnerability. *See* UNITED NATIONS OFFICE ON DRUGS AND CRIME, ABUSE OF A POSITION OF VULNERABILITY AND OTHER "MEANS" WITHIN THE DEFINITION OF TRAFFICKING IN PERSONS 13 (2012), https://www.unodc.org/documents/human-trafficking/2012/UNODC_2012_Issue_Paper_-_Abuse_of_a_Position_of_Vulnerability.pdf.

"In the context of trafficking, 'vulnerability' is typically used to refer to those inherent, environmental or contextual factors that increase the susceptibility of an individual or group to being trafficked. These factors are generally agreed to include human rights violations such as poverty, inequality, discrimination and gender based violence—all of which contribute to creating economic deprivation and social conditions that limit individual choice and make it easier for traffickers and exploiters to operate. More specific factors that are commonly cited as relevant to individual vulnerability to trafficking (and occasionally extrapolated as potential indicators of trafficking), include gender, membership of a minority group, and lack of legal status. Children have been identified as inherently vulnerable to trafficking."

See also U.N. High Commissioner for Human Rights to the U.N. Economic and Social Council [ECOSOC], *Report on the Recommended Principles and Guidelines on Human Rights and Human Trafficking*, Economic and Social Council E/2002/68/Add.1, 105–116 (May 20, 2002).

28. Group of Experts on Trafficking in Human Beings of the European Commission, *Opinion No 7/2010 of the Group of Experts on Trafficking in Human Beings of the European Commission Proposal for a European Strategy and Priority Actions on Combating and Preventing Trafficking in Human Beings (THB) and Protecting the Rights of Trafficked and Exploited Persons*, at 41 (2010), http://lastradainternational.org/lsidocs/EU%20experts%20group%20Opinion%20No%207.pdf.

29. *Get It Right This Time: A Victims-Centered Trafficking in Persons Report*: Hearing Before the Subcomm. on Afr., Global Health, Global Hum. Rts., and Int'l Orgs. of the H. Committee on Foreign Affairs, 114th Cong. 185 (2016) (statement of Mark P. Lagon, Pres-

The determination of age of trafficking victims is an additional vulnerability indicator. Cases tracked by the Human Trafficking Reporting System between January 2008 and June 2010 indicated that 85 percent of trafficking victims were under the age of 25 and 54 percent were under the age of 17.[30]

Gender is also a vulnerability factor identified in numerous studies. The Human Trafficking Reporting System data showed that 85 percent of victims of sex trafficking during the same period were females, while a study carried out by researchers at Baylor University indicated that 94 percent of child trafficking victims were female.[31]

Ethnicity or tribal membership may also be a notable factor, particularly in communities or societies in which an ethnic population is marginalized, disproportionately affected by environmental degradation and armed conflict, and susceptible to exploitation by another ethnic group.[32] We have seen this recently in Syria's civil conflict in which ISIS belligerents sell ethnic and religious minorities into forced servitude.[33]

Like many international instruments,[34] the *Palermo Protocol* determines its scope of applicability to all persons below the age of 18, labelling them

---

ident, Freedom House and others), *available at* http://docs.house.gov/meetings/FA/FA16/20160322/104725/HHRG-114-FA16-Transcript-20160322.pdf (last visited Nov. 9, 2016).

30. Chelsea Parsons et al., *3 Key Challenges in Combating the Sex Trafficking of Minors in the United States*, CTR FOR AM. PROGRESS, Apr. 8, 2014, https://www.americanprogress.org/issues/criminal-justice/report/2014/04/08/87293/3-key-challenges-in-combating-the-sex-trafficking-of-minors-in-the-united-states/.

31. Kimberly Kotrla & Beth Ann Wommack, *Sex Trafficking of Minors in the U.S.: Implications for Policy, Prevention and Research*, 2 J. APPLIED RESEARCH ON CHILDREN: INFORMING POLICY FOR CHILDREN AT RISK 1, 4 (2011).

32. *See* United States Department of State, Office to Monitor and Combat Trafficking in Persons, *Vulnerability of Indigenous Persons to Human Trafficking* (June 2014), https://2009-2017.state.gov/documents/organization/233942.pdf. *See also* Asia Indigenous Peoples Pact (AIPP), *Indigenous Women and Human Trafficking in the Mekong Region: Policy Overview and Community Response* (2015), http://aippnet.org/wp-content/uploads/2016/01/iva.aippnet.org_wp-content_uploads_2016_01_Final_Briefing-Paper-Indigenous-Women-Human-Trafficking_2015.pdf.

33. *ISIL's Persecution of Religious Minorities in Iraq and Syria*: Hearing Before the Subcomm. on Afr., Global Health, Global Hum. Rts., and Int'l Orgs. of the H. Committee on Foreign Affairs, 113th Cong. 211 (2014) (statement of Tom Malinowski, Assistant Secretary, Bureau of Democracy, Human Rights, Labor), http://docs.house.gov/meetings/FA/FA16/20140910/102642/HHRG-113-FA16-Transcript-20140910.pdf.

34. The following international instruments, for instance, consider a child as a person under the age of 18 years: Article 1 of the Convention on the Rights of a Child; Article 2 of the African Charter on the Rights and Welfare of the Child; Article 2 of the Inter-American Convention on International Protection of Minors; Article 9 of the Council of Europe

"child."[35] But it is silent with regard to the age of majority[36] and the age of legal sexual consent.[37] In fact, there is no international treaty establishing the age of majority and sexual consent, such that establishing these age markers is left to the individual states.[38]

Article 3(d) of the *Palermo Protocol* states that the designation "child" shall mean any person under 18 years of age,[39] and anyone under that age is a trafficking victim if s/he is recruited, transported, transferred, harbored or received for purposes of exploitation regardless of the use of the following illicit means: coercion, fraud, abduction, deception, abuse of power or of a posi-

---

Convention on Cybercrime; and Article 3(a) of the Council of Europe Convention on the Protection of Children Against Sexual Exploitation and Sexual Abuse [Lanzarote Convention].

35. According to the European Interagency Working Group, the international instruments do not "necessarily define who is a child but rather the scope of their applicability under international law." *See* Susanna Greijer & Jaap Doek, Terminology Guidelines for the Protection of Children from Sexual Exploitation and Sexual Abuse 5 (Interagency Working Group, Luxembourg, Jan. 2016), https://www.unicef.org/protection/files/Terminology_guidelines_396922-E.pdf [hereinafter Terminology Guidelines].

36. *Id.* at 6. The age of majority "is the legally defined age at which a person becomes an adult, with all the attendant rights and responsibilities of adulthood."

37. *Id.* at 9. The age at which criminal law recognizes the legal capacity of a young person to consent to sexual activity.

38. Article 18 of the Lanzarote Convention refers to the "legal age for sexual activities" (art.18(1)(a)), and leaves it up to the States Parties to the Convention to decide the age below which it is prohibited to engage in sexual activities with a child (art. 18(2)). Council of Europe Convention on the Protection of Children Against Sexual Exploitation and Sexual Abuse, Oct. 25, 2007, C.E.T.S. No. 201. Also, art. 2 of the European Union (EU) Directive 2011/93 on Combating the Sexual Abuse and Sexual Exploitation of Children and Child Pornography uses the expression "age of sexual consent," and means "the age below which, in accordance with national law, it is prohibited to engage in sexual activities with a child." Directive 2011/92/EU of the European Parliament and of the Council of 13 December 2011 on combating the sexual abuse and sexual exploitation of children and child pornography, and replacing Council Framework Decision 2004/68/JHA, OJ 2011 L 335 of 2011-12-17, p. 1-17, http://db.eurocrim.org/db/en/vorgang/204/.

39. One State Party, Saudi Arabia, practically accepts the age of majority as 18 years, but under the Shari'ah, the age of majority is established when puberty is attained together with evidence of the ability to make responsible decisions. According to Human Rights Watch, in November 2008, the government's Shura Council passed a measure raising the age of majority from 15 to 18 years, but the Saudi Cabinet did not pass the measure into law. In court proceedings, judges continue to determine majority on physical signs of puberty. *See Iran, Saudi Arabia, Sudan: End Juvenile Death Penalty*, Hum. Rts. Watch (Oct. 9, 2010), http://www.hrw.org/news/2010/10/09/iran-saudi-arabia-sudan-end-juvenile-death-penalty.

tion of vulnerability, giving or receiving payments or benefits to achieve their consent, and so forth. Most countries do not extend the scope of art. 3(d) to all persons under age 18. However, they do apply the age of majority and/or consent, which is below 18 years. The result is that many of the children within this age category are trafficking victims who fall through the cracks, and due to the age of majority and/or of consent, law enforcement fails to consider these children as trafficking victims. Instead, they are often treated as if they had consented to their own exploitation of abuse.[40]

When dealing with children, the *Palermo Protocol* is complemented by the main international legal instrument on the protection of children, the *Convention on the Rights of the Child* (CRC).[41] The *Protocol's* interpretation with regard to children "must be guided by applicable human rights standards and in particular by the principles of protection and respect for children's rights as set out in the CRC" and guidance provided by the Committee on the Rights of the Child.[42]

The CRC applies to persons under 18 years of age,[43] "unless, under the law applicable, majority is attained earlier,"[44] and embodies four general principles:

1. The best interests of the child shall be a primary consideration in all actions affecting children (Article 3).
2. There shall be no discrimination on the grounds of race, colour, sex, language, religion, political or other opinions, national, ethnic or social origin, property, disability, birth or other status (Article 2).
3. States Parties recognize that every child has the inherent right to life and shall ensure to the maximum extent possible the survival and development of the child (Article 6).

---

40. A child at or above the age of sexual consent may engage in sexual activities. However, under any circumstances, a child should "never be able to legally consent to her/his own exploitation or abuse." Terminology Guidelines, *supra* note 35, at 8.

41. Convention on the Rights of the Child, G.A. Res. 44/25, 44 U.N. GAOR, Supp. No. 49, U.N. Doc. A/44/736 (1989) [hereinafter CRC]. As of December, 2016 there are 196 State Parties. The United States is signatory but has yet to ratify.

42. UNICEF, GUIDELINES ON THE PROTECTION OF CHILD VICTIMS OF TRAFFICKING 10 (2006), https://www.unicef.org/ceecis/0610-Unicef_Victims_Guidelines_en.pdf [hereinafter Guidelines].

43. CRC, *supra* note 41, at art. 1.

44. Comm. on the Rights of the Child, General Comment No. 4 (2003): Adolescent Health and Development in the Context of the Convention on the Rights of the Child, 33rd session, Introduction, U.N. Doc. CRC/GC/2003/4 (1 July 2003) [hereinafter Adolescent Health].

4. Children shall be assured the right to express their views freely in all matters affecting them, their views being given due weight in accordance with the child's age and level of maturity (Article 12).[45]

Under the CRC, governments are obliged to bring their policy, legislation, and practice in conformity with the CRC.[46] Therefore, nations are to balance their duty to protect a child with the child's age-appropriate freedom for consensual activity, recognizing that a child's vulnerability and societal and peer pressure to adopt health risk behaviors pose new challenges to their health and development.[47] When majority is recognized before age 18,[48] the individual is deemed to have full capacity, and the CRC no longer applies. At that point, the right to protection from all forms of violence, and sexual abuse and exploitation under the CRC[49] shifts to protections accorded under the *Palermo Protocol*, in concert with the obligation of State Parties "to enact and enforce laws to prohibit all forms of sexual exploitation and related trafficking; to collaborate with other States Parties to eliminate inter-country trafficking; and to provide appropriate health and counseling services to adolescents who have been sexually exploited, making sure that they are treated as victims and not as offenders."[50]

For children whose age of majority falls below 18 years, the discrepancy among States Parties vis-à-vis the *Palermo Protocol* age mandate causes problems for cooperation, criminalization, and victim protection, particularly when

---

45. U.N. High Comm'r for Refugees, UNHCR Guidelines on Determining the Best Interest of the Child 14.

46. CRC, *supra* note 41, at art. 4.

47. Adolescent Health, *supra* note 44, at § 2.

48. Age of majority is a distinctive legal concept that (1) "signals the end of parental authority and responsibility, as well as the withdrawal of the state from its protective *parens patriae* role," and (2) confers on individuals "most of the legal capacities necessary to function as citizens and members of society." *See* Elizabeth S. Scott, *The Legal Construction of Adolescence*, 29 Hofstra L. Rev. 547, 559 (2000). In contrast, the age of sexual consent may be set lower than the legal age of majority, often at 16 years of age. Criminal violations of the age of sexual consent, in the form of statutory rape laws, "rely on the age differential between the victim and the perpetrator." *See* Vivian E. Hamilton, *Adulthood in Law and Culture*, 91 Tulane L. Rev. 55, 77 (2016). "In virtually all jurisdictions, the age of consent is the defining element of statutory rape law; it establishes the threshold age at which a person may lawfully choose to engage in sexual intercourse." *See* Nicole Phillis, *When Sixteen Ain't So Sweet: Rethinking the Regulation of Adolescent Sexuality*, 17 Mich, J. Gender & L. 271, 277 (2011).

49. CRC, *supra* note 41, at art. 19 and arts. 34–36.

50. Adolescent Health, *supra* note 44, at § 30.

dealing with the trafficking of children across borders.[51] Children in countries where the age of sexual consent is not pegged to the age of majority face additional challenges with protection from exploitation and abuse.[52]

One wonders if the legislators in countries setting the age of sexual consent below 16 years recognize and properly protect the rights of the child. The universal goal of a minimum age of consent is to protect minors from abuses and consequences when they are not fully aware of their rights and emotional development. Minors can be attracted to sexual activity from older individuals in exchange for favors, goods, and attention. Minors from marginalized and discriminated social groups, and minors living in stressful conditions (for example in armed conflict) are especially at risk. According to UNICEF, available data indicates that the sexual initiation of girls is often forced if occurring at an early age.[53] Therefore, national legislatures must become cognizant of the goals of having a minimum age of consent and should review their international commitments in order to protect minors and prevent impunity for violators. The Committee on the Rights of the Child has taken positive steps to encourage countries with a low legal age of consent to raise the age limit.[54]

---

51. Under UNICEF's Guidelines, identifying and providing assistance to someone as a child victim of trafficking does not depend on the child's willingness to cooperate with law enforcement investigations against suspected traffickers. If a minor victim's age is uncertain, then that victim shall be treated as a child and given all special protection measures until an actual age can be verified or reasonably determined to the satisfaction of a judicial authority. *See* Guidelines, *supra* note 42, at § 3.

52. Many countries set the age of sexual consent at 16 years, creating a troubling gap with protections afforded by the *Palermo Protocol*. In some countries, the age of sexual consent can be as low as 12 years, or when puberty is reached, according to examination by a judicial authority. The following sample of states set the age of sexual consent at or lower than 16 years: Angola (12), Burkina Faso (13), Canada (16), Comoros (13), Croatia (15), Iceland (15), Niger (13), Nigeria (11), Spain (13). The age of consent is 14 years in fourteen European states — states that also have a significant level of sex trafficking and sex tourism, for example, the former Yugoslavian republics, Denmark, France, Greece, and Romania. In the Americas, the average age of sexual consent in North and Central America is around 16, while in South America, the average is 14. In Argentina, the minimal age of consent is 13 years. In Asia, the average age of consent is around 16 years, although in the Philippines, the age of consent is 12 years.

53. In addition to emotional and developmental impacts, adolescents are particularly vulnerable to HIV and other sexually transmitted diseases. *See* UNICEF Fact Sheet, Edades mínimas legales para la realización de los derechos de los y las adolescentes, https://www.unicef.org/lac/2._20160308_UNICEF_LACRO_min_age_of_sexual_consent_esp.pdf.

54. For example, the Committee has pushed for México to reform its laws on the age of consent and marriage. *See* Comm. on the Rights of the Child, Observaciones finales

The failure to have a harmonized age of sexual consent with that of the *Palermo Protocol* becomes problematic for three reasons. First, adolescents falling between a lower age of consent and the age of majority at 18 years are essentially defenseless before individuals and criminal organizations involved in human trafficking.[55] Adults assert a high degree of control over children, and criminal organizations exploit this dynamic. This also renders police investigations highly problematic; traffickers and organized crime know it and exploit it.

Second, this "class" of children become easy prey in locations where sex tourism proliferates. The discrepancy among countries with regard to the age of consent has concerning parallels with travel patterns for sex tourism.[56] In

---

sobre México, E/C.12/MEX/CO/4, Documento de 9 de junio de 2006, párr. 40. The Committee has also addressed the age of consent in Spain. *See* Comm. on the Rights of the Child, Observaciones finales sobre España, CRC/C/OPSC/ESP/CO/1, Documento de 17 de octubre de 2007, párrs. 23 y 24.

55. For instance, Peruvian legal scholar Orlando Cubillas has criticized a 2012 decision of Peru's Constitutional Tribunal declaring unconstitutional the rape of minors between ages 14 and 18 when there is consent. One of his arguments is that the Tribunal's decision creates impunity for traffickers since the perpetrator can simply allege consent from the minor when in reality there was coercion, threat or violence. *See* Orlando Eduardo Cubillas Romero, *Opinión*, in *Tema: El Consentimiento sexual de menores de 18 años de edad* 2–3, CUADERNOS DE INVESTIGACIÓN, Universidad de San Martin de Porres, Año I, Núm. I (2013), http://www.derecho.usmp.edu.pe/instituto/cuadernos_investigacion_2013/El_Consentimiento_Sexual_de_Menores_de_14_a_18_de_edad.pdf.

56. In Latin America, as an example, Argentina, Brazil, Colombia, México, and Peru are at the forefront in child sex tourism in the hemisphere, according to UNICEF and Ecpat International. *See América Latina, a la cabeza del turismo sexual infantil*, INFOBAE AMÉRICA, Aug. 9, 2014, http://www.infobae.com/2014/08/09/1586472-america-latina-la-cabeza-del-turismo-sexual-infantil/. In Colombia, 2,135 children were rescued from sex tourism between 2011 and 2013. Of those rescued, children between 12 and 17 years of age were the main victims of sexual exploitation (1,174 cases), followed by "infants" ages 6 to 11 (648 cases), and "first infancy" comprising ages 0 to 5 years (313 cases). More troubling is that 45 percent of the victims were less than 11 years old. *See* ANÁLISIS DE LA SITUACIÓN DE EXPLOTACIÓN SEXUAL COMERCIAL EN COLOMBIA: UNA OPORTUNIDAD PARA GARANTIZAR LA PROTECCIÓN DE NIÑOS, NIÑAS Y ADOLESCENTES 44 (Instituto Colombiano Bienestar Familiar (ICBF), 2013, http://www.icbf.gov.co/portal/page/portal/Observatorio1/Archivo/2014/publicacion-51.pdf. In Argentina, child sex tourism is in high demand by tourists visiting the country for fishing and hunting, deploying from cruise ships, and staying as guests in prominent hotels. Regrettably, a woeful lack of statistics is due to government inaction. For an informed resource on human trafficking conditions in Argentina, visit the HT NGO Facebook page of anti-human trafficking activist Fernando Mao and RAAT Argentina, at https://www.facebook.com/rattentrerios/photos/pcb.946346842164705/946346815498041/?type=3.

many cases, children under the age of 18 have become a "commodity" for criminal syndicates to attract foreign "tourists" who know that having sex with a 12-year-old constitutes legal consensual sex in that destination country, and that even if coercion, fraud and force are used, the police will likely do nothing to protect the children or prosecute the offender.

Third, the lack of harmonizing the domestic legislation of many States Parties to the *Palermo Protocol* results in impunity and creates problems for co-operation, prosecution, and protection of adolescents, especially across international frontiers. The age incongruity for consenting to sex and being a minor creates a presumed shield of "protection" for abusers while failing to protect minors. In such instances, consent becomes a defense and safeguard for abusers. Tragically, the presumption by law enforcement and the justice system is often that the minors are "just prostitutes" and not victims.[57] We see this, for example, in Bosnia and Herzegovina's legislation that allows police to categorize minors between 14 and 18 years of age as "juvenile prostitutes" rather than as victims of rape or trafficking in persons.[58]

This entire issue of consent constitutes a serious gap in domestic legislation in dire need of attention and reform. It is also essential "to make a distinction between the age of sexual consent and the freedom to engage in prostitution."[59] While a piece of national legislation may recognize that a child between 16 and 18 years of age may lawfully consent to a sexual act, the age of consent should not vitiate the obligation of a State Party to the *Palermo Protocol* to prohibit the worst forms of child labor and sexual servitude

Accordingly, it is essential that States criminalize all forms of sexual exploitation of children under 18 years of age, regardless of the differential between the recognized age of majority and the recognized age of consent,[60] and

---

57. Interview with an intelligence official in the National Police in Medellín, Colombia. On file with the author.

58. Miscellaneous white paper on Bosnia Herzegovina, at 29, U.S. Dept. of State, 2015, https://www.state.gov/documents/organization/160181.pdf.

59. *See* ILO Observation (CEACR)—adopted 2013, published 103rd ILC session (2014), discussing Article 3 of the Convention concerning the Prohibition and Immediate Action for the Elimination of the Worst Forms of Child Labour, ILO Convention No. 182 (June 17, 1999), http://www.ilo.org/dyn/normlex/en/f?p=NORMLEXPUB:13100:0::NO:13100:P13100_COMMENT_ID:3145249:NO.

60. In the case of the *Federation of Catholic Family Associations in Europe (FAFCE) v. Ireland*, the European Committee of Social Rights held that: "Article 7 § 10 requires that all acts of sexual exploitation of children be criminalized," and that States "must criminalise the defined activities with all children under 18 years of age irrespective of lower national ages of sexual consent." *See* Complaint 89/2013, Decision of 12 September 2014, ¶ 58, *avail-*

affirm through legislation that any presumed "consent" to exploitative or abusive acts is null and void.[61]

1. Requirement to Criminalize

Under art. 5 of the *Protocol*, States Parties are required to criminalize human trafficking, "either as a single criminal offense or a combination of offenses that cover, at a minimum, the full range of conduct covered by the definition."[62] They are also required to criminalize organizing, directing, and participating as an accomplice in human trafficking.[63] Criminalization of such conducts is "a central and mandatory obligation of all States Parties to [that instrument]."[64] Of even greater significance, art. 5 shifts the duty to criminalize away from the trafficking victim and onto the trafficker, which then brings into play criminal proceedings as articulated in art. 6 that demand that the privacy and identity of victims must be protected, proceedings should be confidential, to the extent that they can be, and the victim should be fully informed to participate actively in the prosecution of the trafficker.[65]

2. Relationship between the UNTOC and the Palermo Protocol

The relationship between the UNTOC and the *Protocol* is established in art. 37 of the UNTOC and art. 1 of the *Protocol*, respectively. These articles un-

---

able at http://hudoc.esc.coe.int/eng/?i=cc-89-2013-dmerits-en. The decision was adopted by the Council of Europe's Committee of Ministers on Feb. 18, 2015.

61. ILO Observation (CEACR)—adopted 2009, published 99th ILC Session (2010), Worst Forms of Child Labour Convention, 1999 (No. 182)—Switzerland (Ratification: 2000), Art. 3(b), http://www.ilo.org/dyn/normlex/en/f?p=1000:13100:0::NO:13100:P13100_COMMENT_ID:2309396. The Committee of Experts on the Application of Conventions and Recommendations emphasized that it is necessary, "to make a distinction between the age of sexual consent and the freedom to engage in prostitution. Indeed, the freedom of sexual activity accorded to a young person by the law cannot include the freedom to engage in prostitution without being in violation of one of the objectives of the Convention, namely the prohibition of the worst forms of child labour."

62. Palermo Protocol, art. 5(1). *See also Legislative Guides, supra* note 1, at 267.

63. Palermo Protocol, art. 5(2)(b).

64. GALLAGHER, *supra* note 7, at 371 (citing *Legislative Guides, supra* note 1, at Part 2, para. 36). Art. 18 of the European Trafficking Convention is an identical provision. *See* Council of Europe, Convention on Action against Trafficking in Human Beings and its Explanatory Report, C.E.T.S. No. 197, at 16 (2005).

65. For a brief discussion, *see generally* Valsamis Mitsilegas, *Immigration Control in an Era of Globalization: Deflecting Foreigners, Weakening Citizens, Strengthening the State,* 19 IND. J. GLOBAL LEGAL STUD. 3, 7 (2012).

derpin the following rules: *First*, the *Protocol* supplements the UNTOC.[66] *Second*, the *Protocol* is not an independent treaty, but rather is connected to the UNTOC. Therefore, a State must be a State Party to the UNTOC to become a State Party to the *Protocol*.[67] *Third*, the UNTOC and the *Protocol* must be interpreted *together*, taking into consideration the purpose of the *Protocol*.[68] *Fourth*, the terms of the UNTOC apply *mutatis mutandis* to the *Protocol*.[69] *Fifth*, offenses under the *Protocol* are likewise offenses under the UNTOC.[70] Consequently, any State offense(s) criminalizing human trafficking will automatically be included within the scope of the UNTOC governing international cooperation.[71] *Also*, other mandatory provisions of the UNTOC apply equally to the offenses established in the *Protocol*.[72]

The UNTOC tackles "primarily crimes that play a facilitative role in the commission of other serious transnational crimes. The profit generating offenses of organized criminal groups are covered essentially by the offenses established in accordance with the *Protocols* and the serious offenses that States have defined."[73]

The following are some of the mandatory measures from the UNTOC that States Parties to the *Protocol* are required to take:

---

66. The UNTOC and the three Protocols "were drafted as a group." The basic relationship between the Convention and the Protocols is established by art. 37 of the UNTOC and art. 1 of each Protocol. Organized Crime Convention, art. 37(1). *See Legislative Guides, supra* note 1, at xviii.

67. UNTOC, art. 37(2). *See id.* at 253.

68. UNTOC, art. 37(4) and Protocol, art. 1(1). *See id.* at 253–255.

69. *See id.* at 254.

"With the necessary modifications" means that, in applying provisions of the UNTOC to the Protocol, "minor modifications of interpretation or application may be made to take account of the circumstances that arise under the Protocol, but modifications should not be made unless they are necessary, and then only to the extent that is necessary. This general rule does not apply where the drafters have specifically excluded it."

70. Protocol art. 1(3). This is "a critical link" between the Protocol and the UNTOC. *See id.* at 254.

71. This includes forms of international cooperation such as extradition and mutual legal assistance (UNTOC, art. 16).

72. Applicable UNTOC provisions include: money-laundering (art. 6), liability of legal persons (art. 10), prosecution, adjudication and sanctions (art. 11), confiscation (arts. 12–14), jurisdiction (art. 15), extradition (art. 16), mutual legal assistance (art. 18), special investigative techniques (art. 20), obstruction of justice (art. 23), witness and victim protection and enhancement of cooperation (arts. 24–26), law enforcement cooperation (art. 27), training and technical assistance (arts. 29–30). Implementation of the UNTOC (art. 34) applies equally to the offences established in the Protocol.

73. Legislative Guides, *supra* note 1, at 91.

(a) Criminalize the laundering of the proceeds.[74]
(b) Criminalize all forms of corruption when committed by public officials.[75]
(c) Liability must be established both for natural and legal persons.[76]
(d) Offenses must be "criminal offenses" for natural persons. For legal persons the offense can be criminal, civil or administrative.[77]
(e) "Asset confiscation. To the greatest extent possible, tracing, freezing and confiscation of the proceeds and instrumentalities of these offenses should be provided for in domestic cases and in aid of other States."[78]
(f) Criminalize obstruction of justice when performed with respect to human trafficking.[79]
(g) Protect victims and witnesses from potential retaliation or intimidation.[80]

---

74. *Id.* at 272–273.
75. UNTOC, art. 8, *supra* note 1.
76. *Id.* art. 10. *See* Legislative Guides, *supra* note 1, at 273.
77. UNTOC arts. 5, 6, 8, and 23, respectively.
78. *Id. See* Legislative Guides, *supra* note 1, at 273–4.
79. *Id. See* Legislative Guides, *supra* note 1, at 275–6.
80. *Id. See* Legislative Guides, *supra* note 1, at 275.

Chapter 3

Responding to Human Trafficking Crimes

Summary: This chapter examines the nature of human trafficking crimes and the three prongs used to combat human trafficking as articulated in the Palermo Protocol: Prevention, Prosecution, and Protection. Our discussion will include looking at several countries engaged in combating human trafficking, and we will look at some statistical data on prosecuting human trafficking internationally to determine if efforts are meeting with satisfactory outcomes. We will conclude with a look at what is being done or should be done to protect trafficking victims.

Combating human trafficking is based on three integral and interrelated prongs articulated in the *Palermo Protocol*: prevention of human trafficking crimes, prosecution of perpetrators, and protection of victims. Increasingly, each of the three components anchor domestic legislation and criminal enforcement policies in many countries.

1. Prevention

Article 9 of the *Palermo Protocol* addresses the prevention of trafficking in persons. Under art. 9, States Parties are to establish "comprehensive policies, programs and other measures to prevent and combat trafficking in persons."[1] States Parties are also committed to "endeavor to undertake measures such as

---

1. Palermo Protocol, art. 9(1)(a).

research, information and mass media campaigns and social and economic initiatives to prevent and combat trafficking in persons."[2] In addition, States Parties shall initiate policies and programs to strengthen cooperation between government and nongovernment organizations to protect the society from trafficking crimes, and create or strengthen measures to alleviate the factors that make persons vulnerable to trafficking, "such as poverty, underdevelopment and lack of equal opportunity."[3] Furthermore, States Parties "shall adopt or strengthen legislative or other measures, such as educational, social, or cultural measures, including through bilateral and multilateral cooperation, to discourage the demand that fosters all forms of exploitation of persons, especially women and children, that leads to trafficking."[4]

In many cases, people become trafficking victims due to being members of vulnerable groups—the impoverished, the displaced, the disaffected, the outcast, and the underrepresented.[5] The task of prevention becomes all the more challenging because too often vulnerable groups are hiding in the shadows or beyond the reach of social services and government assistance. According to TakingITGlobal!, "the prevention of human trafficking requires several types of interventions. Some are of low or moderate cost and can have some immediate impact, such as broad-based awareness campaigns that allow high risk individuals to make informed decisions. Robust laws that are enforced are an effective deterrent, however, serious law enforcement is expensive."[6] It is widely held that the most effective method for prevention is through the deployment of awareness campaigns targeting specifically vulnerable populations. These efforts are best accomplished through television and radio public service announcements and increasingly in social media venues like Twitter and various online communities.

On the law enforcement side, the confiscation of assets from the proceeds of trafficking crimes is believed to be an effective preventative measure. According to the UNODC, in addition to being an effective method of prevention, seizing the proceeds of crime also constitutes an appropriate punishment. "Confiscation is a deterrent for criminals who try to maximize their profits,

---

2. *Id.* art. 9(2).

3. *Id.* art. 9(4).

4. *Id.* art. 9(5).

5. For example, armed conflict creates displacements and refugee situations that render women and children particularly vulnerable to becoming trafficking victims. *See* Trafficking in Women and Girls, G.A. Res. 63/156, U.S. Doc. A/RES/63/156 (2009).

6. *Presentation on Human Trafficking*, TakingITGlobal!, http://webcache.googleusercontent.com/search?q=cache:bUXkL-JkqXcJ:www.tigweb.org/action-tools/projects/download/5044/PRESENTATION%2520ON%2520HUMAN%2520TRAFFICKING.doc+&cd=2&hl=en&ct=clnk&gl=us (last visited June 3, 2017).

and it also prevents illicitly acquired assets from being reinvested into the legitimate economy."[7]

Preemption is also a method for prevention. For example, classified advertising websites like Craigslist and Backpage have been used by traffickers to troll for victims and arrange sexual encounters between their victims and johns. Being able to engage such website owners to cooperate or self-police the activities of subscribers could help reduce trafficking crimes and is critical for effective law enforcement. For example, Craigslist relented to government pressure and banned advertisements for adult services in 2010.[8] When that occurred, advertising for such commercial sex services moved elsewhere, mainly to Backpage. In 2013, the classified advertising website Backpage, long known for being an Internet portal for individuals to engage in all kinds of commercial sex activities, was utilized by investigators to gather evidence necessary to conduct raids in 70 cities across the United States that resulted in the arrest of 159 pimps and the rescue of 105 teenagers.[9] While Backpage took credit for being a partner with law enforcement, such cooperation is usually forthcoming only upon request of law enforcement agencies, and not voluntarily given. The National Association of Attorneys General, for example, would like to fill a gap in existing federal law that would allow Internet service providers and websites like Backpage to face prosecution "by state and local governments for promoting prostitution and child sex trafficking, simply by running such ads."[10] Nevertheless, having preemptive access to sites utilized by human traffickers can lead to rescuing trafficking victims while at the same time keeping the heat up on traffickers who rely on social networking and digital media to ply their illicit trade.

Prevention is also achieved by deterrence through enacting legislation that makes punishments for human trafficking far more punitive. If a trafficker knows that s/he will lose everything and go to jail for a long time, then there may be less incentive to engage in trafficking, at least at the small and medium

---

7. United Nations Office on Drugs and Crime, Global Report on Trafficking in Persons 2014 53, U.N. Sales No. E.14.V.10) [hereinafter Global Report 2014], *available at* https://www.unodc.org/unodc/data-and-analysis/glotip.html.

8. William Saletan, *Pimp Mobile: Craigslist Shuts Its "Adult" Section. Where Will Sex Ads Go?* Slate, Sept. 7, 2010, http://www.slate.com/articles/news_and_politics/frame_game/2010/09/pimp_mobile.html.

9. Suzanne Choney, *Classified Ad Site Backpage in Crosshairs Over Child Sex Ads*, NBC-News.com, July 29, 2013, http://www.nbcnews.com/technology/classified-ad-site-back-page-crosshairs-over-child-sex-ads-6c10789250.

10. *Id.*

operations levels. Polaris Project, based in Washington, D.C., does a yeoman's job of tracking and analyzing anti-human trafficking laws and model legislation, accessible on the organization's website.[11] Several countries are also actively engaged in strengthening anti-trafficking laws. In April 2016, the German government took up debate on strengthening laws that are preventive in intention by punishing with prison sentences of up to five years anyone who engages prostitutes who are victims of human trafficking.[12] Regulated prostitution remains legal in Germany, however, anyone exploiting or violently forcing a person into prostitution would face harsher penalties up to 10 years in prison under the new legislation. Critics of the proposed law argue that there remain important gaps in the draft legislation that, in the words of one women's rights activist, keeps Germany's status as "Europe's brothel" intact.[13] One suggestion missing from the legislation is to set the minimum age for legal prostitution at 21 years, which some activists argue would have the effect of cutting down on the number of young women from Eastern Europe who are trafficked into Germany for prostitution.[14]

Border security, addressed in art. 11 of the *Palermo Protocol*, needs to be strengthened as an additional prevention measure. The *Protocol* sets forth the steps that States Parties should take to prevent cross-border human trafficking. Among them, transborder commercial carriers, whatever the means of transport, should be obligated to "ascertain that all passengers are in possession of the travel documents required for entry into the receiving State."[15] States Parties are also required to take necessary measures to provide for sanctions and to permit "the denial of entry or revocation of visas of persons implicated in the commission of offenses established in accordance with [the] Protocol."[16] In addition cross-border cooperation is key to preventing trafficking at the frontiers, and developing measures to secure the integrity, security, and con-

---

11. Polaris Project.org, http://polarisproject.org/state-laws-issue-briefs (last visited Oct. 1, 2016).

12. Reporting cases of sex trafficking would make a john exempt from prosecution. *See New German Draft Law Seeks Harsher Penalties for Pimps and Johns of Forced Prostitutes*, DW News, Apr. 6, 2016, http://www.dw.com/en/new-german-draft-law-seeks-harsher-penalties-for-pimps-and-johns-of-forced-prostitutes/a-19166326 (noting, "Critics of the draft law say that it will be hard to prove that a client knowingly went to a forced prostitute," although there are many circumstantial indicators that a prostitute may not be a willing sex worker.).

13. *Id.*

14. *Id.*

15. Palermo Protocol, art. 11(3).

16. *Id.* at art. 11(5).

trol of travel and identity documents is critical to sustaining prevention measures against transborder trafficking.[17] Prosecution for transnational offenses, however, must rest with national jurisdictions.[18]

Prevention concerns primarily law enforcement and community efforts to curtail human trafficking. But can the case be made that prevention should also extend to dealing with traffickers who have been brought into the criminal justice system? This notion seems to be overlooked in the literature, and warrants some brief discussion.

The visceral reaction by most people toward human traffickers is that the people who do these things are "sick" individuals. But what if such a clinical diagnosis could be used as a prevention tool? Focusing prevention efforts on the mental state of traffickers could accomplish three goals: (1) to understand better the patterns that compel traffickers to traffic and exploit human beings and how to short-circuit those patterns; (2) to introduce a mental health assessment as a way to keep traffickers off the street for a longer period of time, and (3) to reduce recidivism of traffickers through clinical treatments.

Under a mental health assessment protocol, traffickers could be subjected to mandatory psychological examination during detention to determine a diagnosis of antisocial personality disorder (or some other disorder or more serious psychosis). According to the definitive manual on mental disorders, the essential feature of antisocial personality disorder is "a pervasive pattern of disregard for, in violation of, the rights of others that begins in childhood or early adolescence and continues into adulthood."[19] The pervasive pattern of disregard for and violation of the rights of others is presented based on some of the following criteria:

- Failure to conform to social norms with respect to lawful behaviors, as indicated by repeatedly performing acts that are grounds for arrest.
- Deceitfulness, as indicated by repeated lying, use of aliases, or conning others for personal profit or pleasure.
- Irritability and aggressiveness, as indicated by repeated physical fights or assaults.
- Reckless disregard for the safety of self or others.

---

17. *Id.* at art. 12 and art. 13.

18. Pierre Hauck & Sven Peterke, *Organized Crime and Gang Violence in National and International Law*, 92 INT'L REV. OF THE RED CROSS 407, 420 (2010).

19. AMERICAN PSYCHIATRIC ASSOCIATION, DIAGNOSTIC AND STATISTICAL MANUAL OF MENTAL DISORDERS (DSM-V) 5th 659 (2013).

- Lack of remorse, as indicated by being indifferent to or rationalizing having hurt, mistreated, or stolen from another.[20]

Other traits presented include that the individual is at least age 18 years, shows evidence of the conduct disorder with onset before age 15 years, and that the occurrence of antisocial behavior is not exclusively during the course or episodes of schizophrenia or bipolar disorder.[21]

This bundle of traits closely describes the characteristics of many traffickers, and should be applicable to both sex traffickers and labor traffickers. The lack of regard for the welfare of others can also be described as sociopathic, evidenced by patterns of behavior "in which the basic rights of others or major age-appropriate societal norms or rules are violated."[22]

Providing a clinical diagnosis for the presence of antisocial personality disorder in traffickers could become an effective law enforcement and criminal justice tool, utilized not to *help* the trafficker per se, but to determine how to keep him or her away from trafficking in the future, if not also away from society for a longer period of incarceration based on a mental health expert's testimony/opinion. Extending the notion of prevention to dealing with the traffickers rather than only with the victims could become another important preventive mechanism for, if not preventing trafficking crime, then reducing the possibility of future occurrences.

2. Prosecution

The *Palermo Protocol* does not go into great detail about the prosecution of human trafficking offenses. Article 5 addresses criminalization, and in two brief subsections constrains States Parties to "adopt such legislative and other measures as may be necessary to establish as criminal offenses," the acts set forth in art. 3, including recruiting, transporting, using threats of force or other forms of coercion (no matter how subtle) that render people vulnerable to becoming trafficking victims, and subjecting persons to all forms of exploitation articulated throughout the *Protocol*. Organizing and directing other persons to commit trafficking offenses, or participating as an accomplice in such offenses are also subject to criminal prosecution.[23]

---

20. *Id.*
21. *Id.*
22. *Id.*
23. Palermo Protocol, art. 5(c).

States Parties to the *Protocol* undertake their commitments to prosecute human trafficking in many different ways. Some states have established special offices to coordinate human trafficking efforts. Specially trained prosecutors have been funded and vested with powers to investigate and prosecute trafficking operations, and punishments have been strengthened to give human trafficking crimes greater punitive effect.

A. Country Examples

Argentina's Office of Women in the Supreme Court and the National General Directorate on Institutional Relations in the Senate recognized that the country's human trafficking laws needed further strengthening, particularly with regard to the trafficking of women, and steps were undertaken in the new administration of conservative President Mauricio Macri to address critical gaps in domestic legislation. The result was *Ley 26.364 de 2008*,[24] which significantly modified sections of Argentina's *Penal Code* and introduced new penalties and protections critically needed to contend with a trafficking crisis that expanded greatly during the prior administration of Cristina Fernandez de Kirchner, who was subsequently indicted on corruption charges after leaving office at the end of 2015. Argentina also established special investigative units, task forces, and victim assistance networks to combat trafficking, including establishing the Procuraduría para Combate de la Trata y Explotación de Personas (PROTEX).

Article 3 of *Ley 26.364* specifically addressed the trafficking of minors under 18 years of age and defines child trafficking as the offering, acquisition, transport and/or transfer, either within the country or abroad, the receipt or acceptance of persons under the age of eighteen for the purpose of exploitation.[25] A distinguishing element of Art. 3 is that there is child trafficking even absent deception, fraud, violence, threat, or any means of intimidations or coercion, or abuse of authority, and that consent of the minor has no effect on perfection of the crime.

---

24. Ley 26.364 (9 abril 2008), Prevención y sanción de la trata de personas y asistencia a sus víctimas, http://www.infoleg.gov.ar/infolegInternet/anexos/140000-144999/140100/norma.htm.

25. In early 2016, Argentina enacted a new law against human trafficking that significantly modifies Ley 26.364 and various sections of Argentina's Penal Code. *See* Nueva Ley de Trata de Personas, https://www.mpf.gob.ar/protex/files/2016/06/nueva_ley_de_trata_de_personas.pdf.

In Denmark, which is considered a significant destination country for human trafficking, anti-human trafficking laws are set forth in section 260 et seq. of the *Criminal Code* as follows:

- § 260 prohibits coercion or threats of violence that force(s) a person to do, suffer or omit anything with regard to human trafficking.
- § 261 makes it illegal for anyone to deprive another person of freedom and carries a punishment of up to four years of imprisonment.
- § 262 bans recruiting, transport, transfer, housing, or receiving a person using unlawful coercion, deprivation of liberty, threats, unlawful exploitation, and other unseemly conduct. Punishment includes up to 8 years' incarceration.
- § 262(a) prohibits all forms of both sex trafficking and forced labour and prescribes punishments of up to 10 years' imprisonment.[26]

The *Consolidated Danish Working Environment Act No. 268 of March 18, 2005* addresses labor exploitation and defines working conditions for employees and establishes penalties for violations of specific working conditions. Section 26 of the Denmark *Liability for Damages Act No. 885 of September 20, 2005* holds liable any person who is found responsible for the unlawful violation of another individual's freedom, peace, honor, or person.

Although Denmark occupied the top tier in the United States State Department's *2014 Trafficking in Persons Report*, there have been concerns over the efforts of law enforcement to combat trafficking and to prosecute trafficking offenders. The TIP Report noted:

> The government increased the number of trafficking investigations in 2013, and investigated 20 trafficking suspects in 2013, charging 16 of these suspects under 262(a), compared with nine trafficking suspects investigated in 2012. The government initiated prosecutions of 16 trafficking offenders in 2013, an increase from 11 in 2012. It convicted three sex trafficking offenders in 2013, the same number it convicted in 2012. Sentences for the convicted trafficking offenders were 10 months', three years', and four years' imprisonment. The government launched its first prosecutions under 262(a) for forced labour during the reporting period. In March 2014, a court acquitted one suspect

---

26. Consolidation Act No. 909 of 27 September 2005, http://www.legislationline.org/documents/action/popup/id/6901.

in a forced labour case in which two alleged victims were forced to work in the cleaning sector.[27]

The *2015 Trafficking in Persons Report* for Denmark noted that that nation had implemented a more stringent penal code for human trafficking and that cooperation and collaboration with foreign officials had increased significantly.[28] Yet, in a bizarre, recent incident that calls into question the political ramifications of both anti-human trafficking laws and Denmark's *Aliens Act*,[29] a well-known Danish children's ombudsman and activist, Lizbeth Zornig, and her husband were convicted and fined over 2000 Euros in March 2016 for the simple act of giving a lift to a Syrian refugee family trying to make their way to Sweden.[30] The family was already on Danish soil and the Zornigs, trying only to perform an act of kindness, took the family from southern Denmark to the couple's home in Copenhagen, fed them, and then took them to a train station to continue on to Sweden. Under the *Aliens Act*, transporting people who do not possess residence permits is a crime. When interviewed, Zornig stated, "I thought smuggling was when you pass a border and when you take money or benefit from it—not driving inside the country," she said. "But unfortunately that seems to be the case in Denmark." The Zornigs' lawyer has appealed the conviction on the grounds that Denmark's people trafficking laws only apply when a border is crossed and monetary value is received, as articulated in art. 3(a) of the UN *Protocol against the Smuggling of Migrants by Land, Sea and Air*,[31] which along with the *Palermo Protocol* is one of the supplemental instruments of the UNTOC. More troubling is that between September 2015 and February 2016, a time period that corresponds with the Syrian refugee crisis in northern Europe, 279 other people were charged under the same offense with committing trafficking crimes that the accused individuals insist are acts of humanitarian assistance carried out presumably at their own expense.[32]

---

27. U.S. Dep't of State, The Trafficking in Persons Report 156 (2014).

28. U.S. Dep't Of State, The Trafficking In Persons Report 141 (2015).

29. Alien's (Consolidation) Act (No. 863 of 25 June 2013).

30. David Crouch, *Danish Children's Rights Activist Fined for People Trafficking*, Guardian, Mar. 11, 2016, https://www.theguardian.com/world/2016/mar/11/danish-childrens-rights-activist-lisbeth-zornig-people-trafficking.

31. United Nations Office on Drugs and Crime, Protocol against the Smuggling of Migrants by Land, Sea and Air, supplementing the U.N. Convention against Transnational Organized Crime, G.A. Res. 55/25, U.N. Doc. A/55/383 (Nov. 15, 2000).

32. Crouch, *supra* note 30.

One country at the forefront of prosecuting human trafficking cases in the Gulf States is the United Arab Emirates. Beginning around 2007, the Dubai police force established an anti-human trafficking unit, followed soon after by a similar special unit in the Dubai public prosecutor's office. By 2010, the UAE had established a specialized court to process human trafficking cases to help victims of sexual exploitation, becoming the first such court of special jurisdiction in the region.[33] The human trafficking court was established because human trafficking crimes place unique responsibilities on the UAE government. One responsibility is that the government bears the costs of caring for the victims while the case is adjudicated. Judge Ahmed Ibrahim Saif said the purpose of the court was to hear cases more quickly, to "protect the interests of the victims and to mitigate the damage inflicted upon them due to such crimes," and to assist victims in returning to their homelands.[34] Before creation of the human trafficking court, cases involving human trafficking could take up to three months in the criminal court system where the adjudication process involved several hearings and adjournments before reaching a verdict. The court is composed of a three-judge panel convening to hear cases twice weekly, and care is taken to ensure a suspect's right to a fair trial, including assigning defense lawyers to help move the adjudication process along. However, the court hears only cases involving sex trafficking, and not labor trafficking. Going one step further, the Dubai police more recently initiated a special diploma program in human trafficking. The four-month program, implemented and administered by the National Committee to Combat Human Trafficking (NCCHT) and the Dubai Judicial Institute (DJI) and the Human Trafficking Monitoring Centre at Dubai Police, is designed to enhance the professional skills of government officials "and parties concerned with combating human trafficking."[35]

B. The Bigger Picture

The United States State Department uses the annual *Trafficking in Persons* global reports (TIP Reports) to gather important composite data with regard

---

33. Nick Webster, *Battle to Beat Human Trafficking Being Won: Dubai Police*, Nat'l UAE, Oct. 21, 2015, http://www.thenational.ae/uae/battle-to-beat-human-trafficking-being-won-dubai-police.

34. *Dubai to Set Up Special Human Trafficking Court*, Emirates 24/7 News, Oct. 25, 2010, http://www.emirates247.com/news/emirates/dubai-to-set-up-special-human-trafficking-court-2010-10-25-1.308704.

35. Amira Agarib, *Dubai Police Introduce Diploma in Human Trafficking*, Khaleej Times, Nov. 16, 2015, http://www.khaleejtimes.com/nation/crime/dubai-police-introduce-diploma-in-human-trafficking.

to prosecutions and convictions worldwide.[36] But even the State Department concedes the caveat that "statistics are estimates only, given the lack of uniformity in national reporting structures."[37] In 2007, there were approximately 5,682 prosecutions with 3,427 convictions.[38] In 2014, the number of prosecutions rose to 10,051 with 4,443 convictions. In 2015, the number of prosecutions rose significantly to 18,930, while convictions showed a modest improvement to 6,609.[39] While the number of prosecutions more than tripled between 2007 and 2015, the increase in the number of convictions did not keep the same robust pace. The number of convictions was about 35 percent of prosecutions in 2015. This disappointing number may be attributed to not all of the prosecutions being adjudicated during the calendar year. On the labor trafficking side, of the approximately 857 prosecutions worldwide in 2015, about half or 456 resulted in convictions.[40]

Looking at these figures for the years reported in both the 2015 and 2016 TIP Reports raises some interesting questions. For instance, the conviction rate for labor trafficking cases during 2007 was 60 percent. But in 2015, when one would assume that the fortification process of new and amended anti-human trafficking laws were in place,[41] the prosecution-to-conviction rate remained static at around 52 percent.[42] This is in spite of approximately 14,262 labor trafficking victims having been identified—an increase of 2,824 victims over the prior year. The fact that there were only 857 prosecutions and 456 convictions out of more than 14,262 labor trafficking victims identified seems on the face to be shocking. What factors would contribute to so many fluctuations? With judicial systems logging a higher intake of cases, were prosecutors unable to handle the extra load? Is it the result of the judicial system not understanding the interpretation of labor regulations and criminal laws? Is it possible that some perpetrators of labor trafficking crimes are part of the political elites and have the leverage to influence proceedings against them? Or, if large groups of labor trafficking victims were named together in some of the prosecutions, would that not contribute to the number of prosecutions look-

---

36. U.S. Dep't of State, Global Law Enforcement Data, http://www.state.gov/j/tip/rls/tiprpt/2015/243364.htm.

37. U.S. Dep't of State, The Trafficking in Persons Report 40 (2016) [hereinafter TIP Report 2016].

38. U.S. Dep't of State, The Trafficking in Persons Report 48 (2015).

39. TIP Report 2016, *supra* note 37, at 40.

40. *Id.*

41. *Id.* Between 2007 and 2015, approximately 248 acts of legislation worldwide were enacted or amended for combating human trafficking.

42. *Id.*

ing smaller on the face? For instance, if 2,000 workers were named in a case brought against a labor broker, that would certainly skew the victims-to-convictions numbers. Could inadequate training of judicial officers and prosecutors also impact the conviction outcomes? Finally, is it possible that elements of corruption were present in the judicial processes that interfered with successful prosecution efforts?

3. Protection

At its core, the *Palermo Protocol* is intended as a mechanism to preserve the most fundamental human rights of individuals who are made vulnerable to human trafficking. Much of the *Protocol* is addressed specifically to protection, as articulated in section II. Under art. 6 (Assistance to and protection of victims of trafficking in persons) State Parties must commit to the following:

- Protect the privacy and identity of victims of trafficking in persons ... making legal proceedings relating to such trafficking confidential;
- Provide trafficking victims with information on relevant court and administrative proceedings;
- Give assistance and representation throughout all stages of criminal proceedings against offenders;
- Implement measures to provide for the physical, psychological and social recovery of victims of trafficking ... including "in cooperation with nongovernmental organizations, other relevant organizations and other elements of civil society. These measures can include (a) appropriate housing; (b) counseling and information, in particular as regards to legal rights in a language that the victims understand; (c) medical, psychological and material assistance; and (d) employment, educational and training opportunities."
- Consider the "age, gender and special needs of victims of trafficking in persons, in particular the special needs of children, including appropriate housing, education and care."
- Attend to the physical safety of trafficking victims "while they are within its territory."
- Ensure that "the domestic legal system contains measures that offer victims of trafficking in persons the possibility of obtaining compensation for damage suffered."

Article 7 (Status of victims of trafficking in persons in receiving states) obliges States Parties to adopt legislative and other appropriate measures that allow trafficking victims to remain in its territory on a temporary or permanent basis, as appropriate. Article 8 (Repatriation of victims of trafficking in persons) binds States Parties to facilitate the return of trafficking victims to their countries of origin. The return of trafficking victims to the territory in which they have a right of permanent residence should be effected with "due regard for the safety of that person and for the status of any legal proceedings related to the fact that the person is a victim of trafficking and shall preferably be voluntary."

Adequate protection of trafficking victims involves intensive and sustained cooperation between government and nongovernment organizations. Such cooperation is a result of preparation and practice. Law enforcement officers require specialized training to identify the telltale signs that an individual may be a victim of trafficking and take appropriate measures to isolate the individual as quickly as possible from trafficking situations. Victims' advocates work closely with law enforcement agencies to help determine whether someone who has been detained for some offense is actually a trafficking victim. HT NGOs must coordinate resources with law enforcement to get liberated trafficking victims into a safe environment and then utilize their professional capacities to address the physical, emotional, and often, financial needs, of a trafficking victim who must begin the transition to being a survivor.[43]

The criminal justice process may depend greatly on trafficking victims participating as witnesses in the prosecution of their traffickers. The challenge prosecutors face is that many victims come from places where government authority is not to be trusted, or the victims themselves have a troubling history of adversarial encounters with law enforcement. Added to this dynamic, the trauma they have experienced can amplify a sense of distrust that some law enforcement officials may perceive as irrational and uncooperative. Traffickers know that they can use this lingering fear to control and brainwash their victims into believing that the authorities do not care about them, will not help them, and instead will arrest and incarcerate them for engaging in the activities that are part of their exploitation. It is a delicate game of keeping control and breaking those bonds, and it is very often fraught with significant emotional conflict. In the case of transborder rescues, many victims are scared they will be deported to their nations of origin where the dire conditions and/or personal relationships that caused them to become vulnerable to being trafficked in the first place

---

43. This, however, should NOT include imposing behavior and conduct on a trafficking victim such as forcing them to pray or speak to potential donors about his/her trafficking experience, as has been reported in some faith-based anti-human trafficking organizations.

await them. Understandably, this can create conditions of high anxiety for trafficking victims and compel them essentially to "clam up."

Such intensive fears are not unfounded, as evidenced from what happened to a sex trafficking victim who was repatriated from the United Kingdom back to her native Moldova. Following the woman's detention for prostitution, a British court determined that while she was a trafficking victim, she would most likely be safe back home in Moldova. Once back in Moldova, she was located and tortured by her original traffickers before again being trafficked internationally, eventually ending up once more on British soil:

> "They took me to a forest and I was beaten and raped. Then they made a noose out of rope and told me to dig my own grave as I was going to be killed," Katya's court statement reads. "They tied the noose around my neck and let me hang before cutting the branch off the tree. I really believed I was going to die. They then drove me to a house where many men were staying. They were all very drunk and took turns to rape me. When I tried to resist, one man physically restrained me and pulled my front tooth out using pliers."

> The attack ended only when her trafficker told the men they needed to stop as Katya was to be sold in Israel. "I think maybe they did not kill me because I was more valuable alive," her statement reads.[44]

---

44. Amelia Gentleman, *Katya's Story: Trafficked to UK, Sent Home to Torture*, GUARDIAN, Apr. 19, 2011, http://www.theguardian.com/law/2011/apr/19/sex-trafficking-uk-legal-reform. Katya sued the British government, arguing that immigration solicitors "should have investigated evidence that she was a victim of trafficking and that their decision to return her to Moldova, where she ran the risk of retribution and retrafficking, was a violation of her rights under article 3 (the right to freedom from torture and inhumane and degrading treatment) and article 4 (the right to freedom from slavery and servitude) of the European Convention on Human Rights." She ultimately settled with the British government for an undisclosed sum.

Chapter 4

Monitoring Human Trafficking

Summary: In this chapter we will look in detail at how data about human trafficking is gathered and processed in such a way as to help researchers, law enforcement, policymakers, and victim advocates determine how best to confront human trafficking. We will also discuss the controversy around the United States Department of State's annual Trafficking in Persons country reports, which summarize the level to which nations are attempting to combat human trafficking crimes and influence United States foreign policy agendas.

1. How Data Is Gathered

Researchers and government officials rely on data supplied by government authorities and international organizations engaged in combating human trafficking to understand the scope of the problem and monitor trends and developments.[1] National and international entities such as the United States Department of State's Office to Monitor and Combat Trafficking in Persons, the United Nations Office on Drugs and Crime (UNODC), the International Organization on Migration (IOM), the Council of Europe's Group of Experts on Action against Trafficking in Human Beings (GRETA), the European Commission Migration and Home Affairs Department, and the International Labor Organization (ILO) all publish research and engage in awareness-raising ini-

---

1. *See* Virginia M. Kendall, *Greasing the Palm: An Argument for an Increased Focus on Public Corruption in the Fight Against International Human Trafficking*, 44 Cornell Int'l L.J. 33, 39 (2011).

tiatives against human trafficking. Both the United States[2] and the UNODC publish major reports on trafficking in persons, which are issued on an annual and biennial basis, respectively,[3] and for a decade, the IOM has maintained a database with primary data on victims of trafficking globally, known as the Counter-Trafficking Module.[4] The ILO recently developed a Data Initiative on Modern Day Slavery as part of its efforts to eradicate forced labor practices,[5] and the Protection Project at Johns Hopkins University, and the Human Trafficking Law Project database at the University of Michigan School of Law each maintains country reports and study trends in human trafficking.[6] Other valuable sources to understand human trafficking worldwide include articles and monographs published by HT NGOs and academics, news stories by the mainstream press, and blogs. These latter sources are particularly important for assessing the extent to which corruption, both state and private in nature, impact the sustenance and growth of human trafficking. Much of the data on local and regional human trafficking comes from law enforcement agencies and any HT NGOs that may attempt to keep statistical data, but this information can be a bit spotty and possibly unreliable. The reasons for unreliability at the regional or local levels may be due to a lack of financial resources to sustain statistical data gathering, or a lack of understanding or misinterpretation of acts that constitute human trafficking, or there may be an absence of legislation that criminalizes certain conducts that would otherwise constitute human trafficking crimes.

Most analysis relies on what is known and what may only be speculated. What is known includes actual data on numbers of prosecutions, numbers of reported cases, the existence or nonexistence of human trafficking-related crimes established by legislation, human trafficking police investigations, and government programs for police action or victim assistance. Such statistics either confirm or condemn efforts at local, regional, and national levels and provide useful common indicators to study a nation's fight against human trafficking. What is speculative emerges from suspicion that some statistics are manipulated, are prone to subjective elements that skew an accurate under-

---

2. Through the U.S. State Department.

3. *See* UNITED NATIONS OFFICE ON DRUGS AND CRIME, UNODC ON HUMAN TRAFFICKING AND MIGRANT SMUGGLING, http://www.unodc.org/unodc/en/human-trafficking/index.html?ref=menuside.

4. *See* Int'l Org. for Migration, Counter-Trafficking Database, http://www.iom.int/counter-trafficking.

5. *See* Int'l Lab. Org., ILO Data Initiative on Modern Slavery, http://www.ilo.org/global/topics/forced-labour/publications/WCMS_364025/lang—en/index.htm.

6. Unfortunately, the country reports are not updated regularly or consistently.

standing, or are produced by organizations or entities that may have hidden reasons to inflate or deflate data.

2. Challenges to Compiling Data

Even with the substantial resources devoted to monitoring human trafficking trends, there are multiple barriers to identifying accurately the numbers and characteristics of human trafficking victims globally. Primary among these challenges is the hidden nature of the crime. Victims may be unable to self-identify due to the coercive hold over them by their traffickers, or because they have no way to contact authorities, or because their fear of the authorities is greater than their fear of their traffickers.[7] They may not view themselves as trafficking victims, and they may be mistaken as criminals rather than victims by law enforcement authorities.[8]

In the United States, the *Trafficking Victim Protection Reauthorization Act of 2005* mandated that state and local authorities should begin collecting data on human trafficking.[9] At the same time, more than 40 law enforcement task forces were established across the United States and provided with generous federal funding. But nearly 3 years transpired before the task forces were required to provide any statistical data to the United States Bureau of Justice Statistics.[10]

In the last decade when public awareness of human trafficking was gaining world-wide momentum and eliciting outrage, strong emotions about egregious forms of exploitation often interfered with the reliability of statistical data collection. By the close of the decade, and after millions of dollars had been expended worldwide to fund various campaigns and public awareness efforts about human trafficking, little remained known about the extent of human traffick-

---

7. *See* U.S. Gov't Accountability Office, Human Trafficking: Monitoring and Evaluation of Int'l Projects Are Limited, but Experts Suggest Improvements 21 (2007), http://www.gao.gov/assets/270/264599.pdf [hereinafter GAO Report].

8. Johnny E. McGaha & Amanda Evans, *Where are the Victims? The Credibility Gap in Human Trafficking Research*, 4 Intercultural Hum. Rts. L. Rev. 239, 247–48.

9. *Id.*

10. *Id.* "The lack of accountability regarding data meant that the funds dispersed prior to January 2008 had very few restrictions on how they could be used. In essence, funds were being dispersed without accurate data on the number of victims involved in human trafficking.

ing, or what worked or did not work in combating it.[11] When the United States economy went into a tailspin beginning in 2008, funding for anti-human trafficking efforts was significantly curtailed, which added another layer of challenges for organizations to compile and retain useful data at local, regional, and national levels.[12] Despite literally hundreds of millions of dollars dedicated to date to fund a wide range of programs to combat human trafficking, one can argue that the statistical data collected remains problematic.

Because definitions of trafficking can vary from nation to nation, in spite of there being a model definition established in the *Palermo Protocol*, precisely what constitutes a trafficking victim can vary across jurisdictions (taking for example disagreement over the age of consent, or labor practices that may or may not constitute forced exploitation or the use of child labor). In addition, countries in which the greatest number of trafficking victims could be identified may have limited capacity to collect data on the crime due to the institutional and resource challenges that allow trafficking to flourish there in the first place.[13] These discrepancies, among others, further impede capacity to compile accurate data for empirical and long-term research.

3. United States Department of State Country Reports on Trafficking in Persons

Every year since 2001, the United States Department of State has issued the TRAFFICKING IN PERSONS REPORT (TIP Reports). The TIP reports are utilized by the United States as a foreign policy tool to encourage other nations to conform to their commitments to combat human trafficking, or risk sanctions, status, and the loss of foreign aid from the United States. Compiled by the Office to Monitor and Combat Trafficking in Persons, yet another layer of bureaucracy some have criticized for being prone to political influence, the TIP Reports present unique challenges to human trafficking researchers that warrant some discussion.

Each TIP report ranks nations into Tiers based on the extent to which countries comply with the minimum standards articulated in the United States *Trafficking Victims Protection Act* (TVPA). The ranking system is defended as "an essential tool for promoting protection for victims, prevention of trafficking,

---

11. *Id.* at 251–53.
12. *Id.*
13. GAO Report, *supra* note 7.

and prosecution of perpetrators."[14] However, the TIP country reports are controversial, in some cases unreliable, and in some instances elicit derision and contempt. In fact, a cadre of experts have expressed concern that the analysis in the reports is compromised and undermined by political influence and institutional tensions within the State Department, and that some of the data presented is simply wrong or protected in a veil of secrecy. As a former U.S. ambassador testified before Congress in 2013:

> [T]he State Department does a tremendous job in producing a report which tells it like it is, offering objective rankings. Yet at times it pulls punches, typically due to the urging of regional specialists rather than the TIP Office's dedicated experts on trafficking.[15]

We also saw similar skepticism more recently in testimony given during Congressional Foreign Affairs Sub-Committee hearings in March 2016 by several experts who lodged serious concerns about the integrity and accuracy of the 2016 TIP Report prior to its publication on June 20, 2016.[16]

The requirement that foreign governments must comply with United States domestic legislation alone raises criticism that the rankings are based more on geopolitical considerations and shifting alliances than on objective assessments. A 2013 report from the United States Congressional Research Service about the content of the TIP Reports noted that the "inconsistent application of the minimum standards [mandated by TVPA] and superficial country assessments have compromised their credibility," that it is "difficult to determine what standards make a country eligible for Tier 1," and that the Tier 2 and Tier 2 Watch List categories serve as little more than "catch-all" categories for countries that should be ranked in Tier 3.[17] Understandably, the influence of the TIP reports worldwide range from Tier 1 countries touting validation for their antitraf-

---

14. Human Trafficking Prioritization Act of 2015, H.R. 514, 114th Cong. § 2(4) (2015).

15. Mark P. Lagon, *Grading States for not Degrading People: Human Trafficking Assessments*, Hearing Before the Subcomm. on Afr., Global Health, Global Hum. Rts., and Int'l Orgs. of the H. Committee on Foreign Affairs, 113th Cong. (2013), http://docs.house.gov/meetings/FA/FA16/20130418/100697/HHRG-113-FA16-Wstate-LagonM-20130418.pdf.

16. To view a video recording of the hearing and read the statements given by a panel of human trafficking experts, *see Get It Right This Time: A Victims-Centered Trafficking in Persons Report*: Hearing Before the Subcomm. on Afr., Global Health, Global Hum. Rts., and Int'l Orgs. of the H. Committee on Foreign Affairs, 114th Cong. 185 (2016) http://docs.house.gov/meetings/FA/FA16/20160322/104725/HHRG-114-FA16-Transcript-201603 22.pdf.

17. Alison Siskin & Liana Sun Wyler, Cong. Research Serv., RL34317, Trafficking in Persons: U.S. Policy and Issues for Congress 33 (2013).

ficking efforts, to resentment and diplomatic tensions with countries ranked at the bottom. Moreover, while a government may be pleased to move up to Tier 1 status, HT NGOs working in-country may not agree with the elevation and cry foul because the change of status may mask serious problems that will continue to persist.

While the TIP Reports do provide a useful foundation for analyzing human trafficking problems and reviewing counter-trafficking efforts among the family of nations, objective, unbiased reporting constitutes a thorny issue for many States, particularly those nations closely aligned to the United States. Consequently, the matter of issues like corruption as it pertains to human trafficking may be underreported or unreported, which means that deciding not to report details on corruption constitutes a form of corruption, as well.

Let us assume that allies of the United States may continue to enjoy Tier 1 status in the annual TIP Reports as long as they remain on good terms with the United States. Or let us suppose that placing a country on a Tier 1 status is an incentive to do something the United States would like that country to do. If the United States needs cooperation from an ally state, it might overlook or gloss over unflattering data about that country's conditions. Some countries may be Tier 1 for reasons having to do with unrelated geopolitical, economic, and/or foreign policy considerations. Likewise, there may be states in the Second Tier that should be placed in the Tier 2 Watch List, but are not relegated there because that state holds some importance that affects United States foreign policy or status in the region.

One might argue that such is currently the case with Colombia, which moved to the top tier in the 2016 TIP Report, despite the fact that both sex trafficking and forced labor servitude persist and are flourishing throughout the nation (particularly in Cartagena and Medellín,[18] two prominent urban centers increasingly well-known for commercial sex tourism). In fact, all forms of human trafficking are increasing there, especially among vulnerable minority and indigenous communities. Forced sexual and labor servitude of young women and children continues at the hands of the leftist FARC rebels who, despite signing a dubious peace agreement with the government in 2016, have yet to change their violent and criminal conducts. Additionally, anti-human trafficking aid workers and activists continue to be targeted with violence by traffickers and by corrupt officials involved with traffickers.[19]

---

18. Anyone who may not believe this need only Google the words "Medellín" and "sex tourism" together.

19. This author spent several weeks in Colombia in 2015 and 2016 interviewing anti-human trafficking activists and community organizers. One activist was forced to flee

Governments and world bodies certainly cannot set policy, devote resources, and address the trafficking of human beings in a vacuum of data, and the TIP Reports do attempt to fill that purpose. Each year the pages of the TIP Report increase in number, and while it may take some checking and rechecking to overcome or mitigate shortcomings or disinformation in the data provided, the TIP Reports can be mined for useful content that will improve our understanding of (1) the push and pull factors that cause human trafficking (financial stress, armed conflict, rapidly growing economies, labor demands); (2) the steps governments are taking to contend with human trafficking within their borders; (3) the efforts governments are making for mutual assistance; and (4) the responses government agencies and nongovernment organizations are implementing to rescue and restore trafficking victims.

Colombia on one occasion due to death threats by traffickers and corrupt police officials, and during the writing of this book was awaiting the processing of a temporary visa to the United States in order to escape new threats and indifference by Colombian authorities who are not interested in doing anything to bring attention to the dire human trafficking conditions currently manifest throughout the country (because doing so might impact the Tier 1 ranking in the TIP Report).

Chapter 5

Corruption and
Human Trafficking

Summary: This chapter brings together our prior discussions and examines the connection or nexus between corruption and human trafficking. We will look at the links between both criminal conducts, examine the definition of corruption, and review the international legal instruments for combating corruption. We will then look more carefully at corruption in the context of human trafficking.

1. Intersection of Criminal Conducts

Criminalization and the internationalization of corruption are manifestations and outcomes of expanding commercial interests, transborder venture opportunities, and the competition-driven objective of "leveling the playing field in international business transactions."[1] While corruption has been addressed for the purpose of protecting financial interests when dealing with

---

1. The lifting of commercial barriers and the privatization of state companies opened opportunities for competition for new markets. Many corporations bribed public officials as a matter of doing business and gaining market advantages. In 1977, the United States was the first country to criminalize bribery of foreign officials by enacting the Foreign Corrupt Practices Act (FCPA), Pub. L. No. 95-213, 91 Stat. 1494 (codified as amended at 15 U.S.C. §§ 78m, 78dd-1 to 78dd-3, 78ff (2012)). To level the playing field for commercial transactions, bribery was subsequently addressed at the international level. For an excellent description and analysis of the various treaties against corruption, *see* JULIO BACIO TERRACINO, THE INTERNATIONAL LEGAL FRAMEWORK AGAINST CORRUPTION: STATES' OBLIGATIONS TO PREVENT AND REPRESS CORRUPTION 48–79 (2012).

bribery in international commercial transactions, only recently have we linked corruption to the protection of an individual's human rights.[2]

Specific cases of the intersection between corruption and human trafficking have not been well-analyzed or documented. However, the increasing frequency of cases coming to light, along with a growing number of victim accounts, indicate that corruption in both the public and private sectors facilitates and influences the domestic and transborder trafficking of persons at a level largely overlooked in the past.[3] Few studies focusing on the link between these two criminal activities currently exist.[4] In fact, only in 2008 did the United Nations begin paying closer attention.[5]

Corruption in human trafficking has been identified throughout the human trafficking chain, particularly in the recruitment, transportation, and exploitation stages, and often involves (and depends on) illicit transactions in the form of bribes and kickbacks between employers and labor intermediaries in the private sector (private-to-private corruption), and government officials and traffickers in the public sector (public-to-private corruption). For example, an all too typical pattern of trafficking-related corruption reported across countries and regions involves sex trafficking operations occurring with the complicity and collusion of law enforcement officials who receive monetary compensation and/or sexual favors, or in some cases have a stake in or run the operations outright.

In the context of human trafficking, corruption "creates the platform of trafficking. It violates human dignity and creates an insecure environment for vul-

---

2. *See* Terracino *supra* note 1, examining the chronology and evolution of anti-corruption instruments.

3. United Nations Office on Drugs and Crime, The Role of Corruption in Trafficking in Persons 4 (2011), http://www.unodc.org/documents/human-trafficking/2011/Issue_Paper_-_The_Role_of_Corruption_in_Trafficking_in_Persons.pdf [http://perma.cc/9NRZ-H7QR] [hereinafter Role of Corruption].

4. *Id.* at 3. Several authors mention corruption in human trafficking reports. However, very few "have explored factors and mechanisms behind this nexus." *See* Atanas Rusev, *Human Trafficking, Border Security and Related Corruption in the EU,* at 1 (DCAF Brussels, Migration and the Security Sector Paper Series, Oct. 2013). *See also* Philip Gounev & Tihomir Bezlov, Examining the Links between Organized Crime and Corruption 131–136 (European Commission, 2010).

5. *See* U.N. Global Initiative to Fight Human Trafficking, U.N. Office of Drugs and Crime, 020 Workshop: *Corruption: The Grease that Turns the Wheel of Human Trafficking,* Background Paper for 2008 Vienna Forum to Fight Human Trafficking, UN.GIFT B.P.:020 (2008), www.unodc.org/documents/human-trafficking/2008/BP020CorruptionandHuman Trafficking.pdf [hereinafter Vienna Forum].

nerable people who are on the move. Corruption causes or perpetuates trafficking, and trafficking causes human insecurity."[6] Corruption presents significant challenges to the prevention of human trafficking by hindering national and international efforts to prevent, investigate and prosecute trafficking crimes.[7] Combating it is, therefore, essential to any strategy to end human trafficking.[8]

One study shows a direct correlation between corruption and human trafficking, concluding that countries with high levels of institutional corruption are more likely to have high levels of human trafficking within its territory.[9] Moreover, regions of the world where there is a perception of impunity for corrupt acts and inefficiencies in the delivery of justice seem to become hot spots for trafficking in persons, as well.[10]

2. Corruption Defined

As no one size fits all universal definition exists, corruption is defined in several ways across nations and international agencies.[11] Efforts to develop a commonly accepted definition "invariably encounter legal, criminological and, in many countries, political problems."[12] Various social studies, legal, and al-

---

6. M. Bashir Uddin, *Human Trafficking in South Asia: Issues of Corruption and Human Security*, 2 INT'L J. OF SOC. WORK AND HUMAN SERVICES PRACT. 18, 24 (Feb. 2014), http://www.hrpub.org/download/20140305/IJRH3-19201859.pdf.

7. Role of Corruption, *supra* note 3, at 12.

8. *Id.* at 1.

9. Sheldon X. Zhang & Samuel L. Pineda, *Corruption as a Causal Factor in Human Trafficking*, in ORGANIZED CRIME: CULTURE, MARKETS AND POLICIES (Diana Siegel & Hans Nelen eds., 2008).

10. *WJP Rule of Law Index 2014*, at 38, WORLD JUSTICE PROJECT, http://worldjustice-project.org/rule-of-law-index.

11. *See FAQs on Corruption*, TRANSPARENCY INT'L, http://www.transparency.org/whoweare/organisation/faqs_on_corruption#defineCorruption [hereinafter FAQs]; *Helping Countries Combat Corruption: The Role of the World Bank*, 2. Corruption and Economic Development, WORLD BANK, http://www1.worldbank.org/publicsector/anticorrupt/corruptn/cor02.htm [hereinafter Helping Countries]; *and also* Miguel Schloss, *Luncheon Address*, 33 CORNELL INT'L L.J. 3 (2000), http://scholarship.law.cornell.edu/cilj/vol33/iss3/2 (identifying the "abuse of public office for private gain" as the commonly used definition of corruption).

12. Ministry for Foreign Affairs of Finland, Department for Development Policy, *Anti-Corruption Handbook for Development Practitioners*, 19 (2012) [hereinafter Finland Handbook], http://formin.finland.fi/public/download.aspx?ID=100254&GUID=%7B4E90D9A4-B5EE-4EB9-B823-CCA228632695%7D. A 2012 study by the United Nations Development Programme found that women living and working at the community level in poor and mar-

lied disciplines offer a dissimilar "perception of the problem and therefore generate different policies."[13] Some classify corruption by type, like political corruption, while others approach it by field of study, like economics, for instance.[14] But most definitions share an emphasis on the abuse of some form of power or position for personal advantage.[15]

The World Bank, as one example, defines corruption as "the abuse of public power for private gain"[16] and covers "most of the corruption that the Bank encounters," and the "ways in which corruption imposes costs on our borrowers."[17] In contrast, Transparency International describes corruption as "the misuse of entrusted power for private gain."[18] The former definition limits the bounds of corrupt activity to the public sector, while the latter "represents a broader phenomenon where private agents also share responsibility with public servants."[19] Despite both definitions, we still lack a definition or inclusion of elements necessary "to link corruption with human rights."[20] That is not to say that international instruments trying to do so do not exist.

---

ginalized rural and urban areas in parts of Africa, Latin America, and South Asia included in their definition of corruption "a wide range of exploitative practices, such as physical abuse, sexual favours, and both the giving and taking of bribes—all of which are perceived as strongly linked to non-delivery of services and poor leadership." The study also found that "[c]orruption surrounding documentation ... acts as a bottleneck preventing women from accessing other forms of services and opportunities," as women are asked to pay prohibitive amounts in bribes in order to access basic government services, such as obtaining identification documents. *See* U.N. Dev. Program, Seeing Beyond the State: Grassroots Women's Perspectives on Corruption and Anti-Corruption 2–4 (2012), http://www.undp.org/content/dam/undp/library/Democratic%20Governance/Anti-corruption/Grassroots%20women%C20and%20anti-corruption.pdf.

13. International Council on Human Rights Policy, Corruption and Human Rights: Making the: Connection 15 (2009).

14. *See, e.g.,* David Mills, *Corrupting the Harm Requirement in White Collar Crime*, 60 Stan. L. Rev. 1371 (2008).

15. Finland Handbook, *supra* note 12, at 19–20.

16. Helping Countries, *supra* note 11.

17. *Id.* A review of several public expenditure and a "survey data gathered in the course of private sector assessments" draw attention of corruption to the Bank and illustrate "the costs of bribery to entrepreneurs."

18. Transparency International further categorizes corruption as "grand," "petty," or "political." *See* FAQs, *supra* note 11.

19. Finland Handbook, *supra* note 12, at 19–20.

20. *See* Int'l Council on Human Rights Pol'y, *Corruption and Human Rights: Making the Connection*, at 16 (2009), http://www.ichrp.org/files/reports/40/131_web.pdf [hereinafter Connection].

3. International Legal Instruments against Corruption Applicable to Human Trafficking

Today we see that corruption affects a country's business, its social and economic development and its political systems, and presents "an enormous obstacle to the realization of all human rights—civil, political, economic, social and cultural, as well as the right to development."[21] Corruption is also an affront to the core human rights principles of transparency, accountability, non-discrimination, and meaningful participation in civil society.[22]

On January 5, 2015, the United Nations Human Rights Council (UNHRC) recognized the need for a broad definition of corruption that expresses "a human rights perspective." The UNHRC set out three key aspects. First, existent definitions exclude conducts that should also be characterized as corruption. The UNHRC stated:

> A common approach to the notion of corruption is the definition proposed by Transparency International. According to that definition, corruption is "the abuse of entrusted power for private gain". This, however, is a rather broad definition which encompasses a wide range of different behaviours. In contrast to the provisions typically included in criminal law, which determine specific offenses, the above-mentioned definition is more open. At the same time, a definition based on the three specific elements of "abuse", "entrusted power" and "for private gain" may exclude some conducts that should also be characterized as corruption. For example, the use (or abuse) of illegally claimed power can lead to corruption. This rather broad definition can, therefore, nevertheless be too narrow in respect of specific forms of misbehaviour that should also be regarded as corruption.[23]

---

21. Statement by UN High Commissioner for Human Rights, Navi Pillay, at a panel discussion on the negative impact of corruption on the enjoyment of human rights. Press Release, Office of the High Commissioner for Human Rights, The Human Rights Case against Corruption, http://www.ohchr.org/EN/NewsEvents/Pages/HRCaseAgainstCorruption.aspx#sthash.a5ok8kc0.dpuf.

22. *Id.*

23. Final Rep. of the Human Rights Council Advisory Comm. on the Issue of the Negative Impact of Corruption on the Enjoyment of Human Rights, at 3, 28th Sess., U.N. Doc. A/HRC/28/73 (Jan. 5, 2015).

Second, in differentiating between corruption by state and non-state entities, the UNHRC emphasized that non-State actors are accountable for any violation of human rights resulting from a corrupt conduct, and they are responsible for any corrupt acts in which they are involved, are subject to criminal and civil law, and are bound to all legal consequences.[24]

Third, the UNHRC addressed the duty of States to protect "against any adverse human rights impacts arising from acts of corruption by non-State actors, including corruption by the private sector." This duty to protect against human rights abuses by third parties obliges States "to take effective regulatory or other measures to prevent such acts by third parties, to investigate violations that occur, to prosecute the perpetrators as appropriate, and to provide redress for victims."[25]

International conventions against corruption follow diverse approaches and often neglect to define and criminalize corruption *per se*, instead grouping specific criminal acts that correspond to the "general notion of an abuse of entrusted power."[26] Some conventions use the term "corruption" interchangeably with "bribery".[27] Others set forth acts to be criminalized without stipulating that such acts constitute corruption.[28] Another group of instruments differentiates "corruption as a term to group criminal acts more explicitly from actual acts that involve corruption."[29] Still another body of

---

24. *Id.*

25. *Id.*

26. Connection, *supra* note 20.

27. *See, e.g.*, United Nations Convention against Transnational Organized Crime; the Council of Europe Civil Law Convention on Corruption; Convention on the Fight against Corruption Involving Officials of the European Communities or Officials of Member States of the European Union (EU); Council of the European Union's Framework Decision on Combating Corruption in the Private Sector (EU Decision on Corruption in the Private Sector); Council Framework Decision 2003/568/JHA of 22 July 2003 on combating corruption in the private sector; The Organization for Economic Co-operation and Development (OECD) Convention on Combating Bribery of Foreign Public Officials in International Business Transactions; Convention on Combating Bribery of Foreign Public Officials in International Business Transactions.

28. UNCAC, adopted by the General Assembly, resolution 58/4 on 31 October 2003, entered into force on 14 December 2005; The Council of Europe Criminal Law Convention on Corruption, *See* Chapter III of the Criminal Law Convention on Corruption, adopted by the Committee of Ministers of the Council of Europe on 27 January 1999, entered into force on 1 July 2002, European Treaty Series, No. 173.

29. The Economic Community of West African States (ECOWAS) Protocol on the Fight against Corruption (ECOWAS Protocol against Corruption), at ECOWAS Protocol on the Fight against Corruption, adopted by the Heads of State and Government of the ECOWAS on 21 December 2001, not yet entered into force; The Inter-American Convention against Corruption (IACAC), OEA/Ser. K/XXXIV.1, CICOR/doc. 14/96 rev. 2 (29 Mar. 1996), 35

instruments distinguishes more clearly between corruption and the acts that constitute it.[30]

Regardless of the various approaches international conventions and other multilateral instruments present, corruption is not an easily identifiable criminal act. Rather, in a "legal context, corruption is the generic heading for a cluster of different and specific criminal acts."[31] Although considering corruption as a bundle of criminal conducts makes sense in principle, this lack of specificity is troubling and needs to be addressed. There is no need for new international instrument addressing corruption and human trafficking together. We already have several that are applicable and that States must apply to human trafficking. The problem is not lack of instruments but the need to interpret corruption broadly within a human rights perspective. To effectively combat human trafficking, it is incumbent upon nations to address it together with corruption.

A. The United Nations Convention against Corruption (UNCAC)

In October 2003, the UN General Assembly adopted the landmark *Convention against Corruption* (UNCAC).[32] Among existing anti-corruption conventions, UNCAC has the "most extensive provisions on the ways, means and standards for preventive measures in the public and private sectors."[33]

ILM 724 (1996), entered into force Mar. 6, 1997. Both conventions list acts that constitute corruption. *See* Connection, *supra* note 20, at 17.

30. Article 1 of the African Union (AU) Convention on Preventing and Combating Corruption (AU Convention against Corruption) states that "[c]orruption means the acts and practices including related offences proscribed in this Convention". Subsequently, art. 4 lists acts of corruption, such as the bribery of a national public official, abuse of function and embezzlement. An even stronger difference is provided by the Southern African Development Community (SADC) Protocol against Corruption. This instrument separates corruption and the acts that constitute it, and provides a general definition of corruption. *See* Connection, *supra* note 20, at 18.

31. Connection, *supra* note 20, at 18.

32. United Nations Convention against Corruption, Dec. 14, 2005, 3249 U.N.T.S. 41 [hereinafter UNCAC]. The UNCAC was signed by 111 states. On September 15, 2005, it reached the 30 ratifications required for entry into force of the Convention, making the actual entry into force date December 14, 2005.

33. The General Assembly mandated the Ad Hoc Committee negotiating the Convention to "negotiate a broad and effective convention." *See* Terms of Reference for the Negotiation of an International Legal Instrument Against Corruption, G.A. Res. 56/260, U.N. GAOR, 56th Sess., Agenda Item 110, para. 2, U.N. Doc. A/RES/56/260 (2002), https://

Although UNCAC does not define corruption as such, criminal acts that constitute corruption are enumerated that should be considered in every jurisdiction covered by UNCAC, such as bribery, embezzlement of public funds, money laundering, and obstruction of justice.[34] Also included in this bundle are offenses relating both to public sector corruption and corruption within the private sector.[35]

UNCAC art. 9 includes mandatory preventive measures against corruption such as adopting legislative enhancements, "as appropriate and consistent with the legal system of the State," to promote integrity, prevent, detect and punish corruption of public officials, and ensure effective action by officials. It also requires States to provide anti-corruption authorities ample independence and autonomy to deter undue influence.

Under UNCAC, States Parties are required to establish the enumerated acts in their domestic law as criminal, civil, or administrative offenses. UNCAC also addresses various areas, including preventive measures, criminalization and law enforcement, international cooperation, recovery of corruption assets, and technical cooperation and information exchange. Some of UNCAC's provisions are mandatory, while others are either "strongly encouraged" or optional.

UNCAC also tackles the cross-border nature of corruption through provisions for international cooperation and for the return of the proceeds of corruption, and it obligates States Parties to help each other to prevent and combat corruption through technical assistance protocols.

---

www.unodc.org/documents/commissions/CCPCJ/Crime_Resolutions/2000-2009/2001/General_Assembly/A-RES-56-260.pdf.

34. The definition of "public official" is broad. Under UNCAC, art. 2(a), "Public official" shall mean: (i) any person holding a legislative, executive, administrative or judicial office of a State Party, whether appointed or elected, whether permanent or temporary, whether paid or unpaid, irrespective of that person's seniority; (ii) any other person who performs a public function, including for a public agency or public enterprise, or provides a public service, as defined in the domestic law of the State Party and as applied in the pertinent area of law of that State Party; (iii) any other person defined as a "public official" in the domestic law of a State Party. However, for the purpose of some specific measures contained in chapter II of this Convention, "public official" may mean any person who performs a public function or provides a public service as defined in the domestic law of the State Party and as applied in the pertinent area of law of that State Party. The Council of Europe Criminal Law Convention on Corruption follows a similar approach, at Chapter III of the Criminal Law Convention on Corruption, adopted by the Committee of Ministers of the Council of Europe on 27 January 1999, entered into force on 1 July 2002, European Treaty Series, No. 173.

35. UNCAC, *supra* note 32, art. 12.

B. The United Nations Convention against Transnational Organized Crime (UNTOC) and Corruption

Entered into force in September 2003, the *Convention against Transnational Organized Crime* (UNTOC) recognizes corruption as an integral component of transnational organized crime that must be addressed alongside any efforts to combat organized crime.[36] However, transnationality and "organized criminal groups" are not to be made elements of the domestic offenses.[37]

Under UNTOC art. 8, States Parties are required to "consider" establishing criminal offenses for forms of corruption beyond active and passive bribery. Although art. 8 stops short of defining corruption, it does establish a mandatory requirement to criminalize: (1) active bribery (the giving of bribes), (2) passive bribery (the acceptance of bribes), and (3) participation as an accomplice to bribery.[38] In contrast, UNCAC, as the more comprehensive and specific anticorruption instrument, *requires* States Parties to establish further mandatory offenses for *other* forms of corruption. Unlike UNCAC, which specifically addresses private sector corruption in its art. 12, UNTOC does not cover issues relating to corruption in the private sector. Additionally, UNTOC is among the group of international treaties that use the term "corruption" interchangeably with "bribery."[39]

---

36. U.N. Convention against Transnational Organized Crime, *opened for signature* Nov. 15, 2000, 2225 U.N.T.S. 209. The Convention along with its supplementary protocols are available on the UN treaties webpage at https://www.unodc.org/unodc/en/treaties/CTOC/. "If the enemies of progress and human rights seek to exploit the openness and opportunities of globalization for their purposes, then we must exploit those very same factors to defend human rights and defeat the forces of crime, corruption and trafficking in human beings." *See* UNCTOC, Foreword, at iii.

37. United Nations Office on Drugs and Crime, Legislative Guides for the Implementation of the United Nations Convention against Transnational Organized Crime and the Protocols Thereto 84 (2004), http://www.unodc.org/pdf/crime/legislative_guides/Legislative%20guides_Full%20version.pdf [hereinafter Legislative Guides].

38. *Id.* at 81–82, 84.

39. Connection, *supra* note 20, at 16–17. Other anti-corruption conventions that follow the same approach include: Council of Europe Civil Law Convention on Corruption (article 2), adopted by the Committee of Ministers of the Council of Europe on 4 November 1999, entered into force on 1 November 2003, European Treaty Series, No. 174; The Convention on the Fight against Corruption Involving Officials of the European Communities or Officials of Member States of the European Union (EU), drawn up on the basis of Article K. 3(2c) of the Treaty on European Union, adopted by Council Act of 26 May 1997,

Mandatory preventive measures against corruption are addressed in art. 9:

(a) Adoption of legislative or other measures, as appropriate and consistent with the legal system of the State, in order:
(i) To promote integrity;
(ii) To prevent, detect and punish corruption of public officials;
(iii) To ensure effective action by officials;
(b) Endowing anti-corruption authorities with sufficient independence to deter undue influence.

UNCAC and UNTOC are inter-related; the obligations under UNCAC are to be taken into account when UNTOC is to be implemented.

It is important to take the obligations under the United Nations Convention against Corruption into account as work to implement the Organized Crime Convention is carried out, as more comprehensive requirements are likely to be included in the former, which States parties will be obligated to implement.[40]

While UNTOC views corruption as a "tool" of organized crime, UNCAC is the "tool" used to deal with corruption in a comprehensive manner. Accordingly, as the work to implement UNCTOC is undertaken, it remains important to consider its relationship to UNCAC, which contains more comprehensive requirements.[41] In this manner, UNTOC art. 8 is complemented by the more comprehensive and specific anti-corruption UNCAC treaty. For instance, UNCAC's coverage of private sector corruption complements UNTOC's lack thereof.[42] As applied to corruption in trafficking in persons, while UNTOC does not address the corruption of public officials, it could

---

Official Journal C 195, 25 June 1997, pp. 1–11; The Council of the European Union's Framework Decision on Combating Corruption in the Private Sector (EU Decision on Corruption in the Private Sector), Council Framework Decision 2003/568/JHA of 22 July 2003 on combating corruption in the private sector, entered into force 31 July 2003, Official Journal L 192, 31 July 2003, pp. 54–56; and The Organization for Economic Co-Operation and Development (OECD) Convention on Combating Bribery of Foreign Public Officials in International Business Transactions, which follows the same line, although it is reflected in the title, Convention on Combating Bribery of Foreign Public Officials in International Business Transactions, adopted by the OECD on 21 November 1997, entered into force on 15 February 1999, DAFFE/IME/BR(97)20.

40. Legislative Guides, *supra* note 37.

41. *Id.*

42. UNCAC, *supra* note 30, art. 12 (bribery), art. 21 (embezzlement), and art. 22 (fraud).

extend to their peripheral involvement in corrupt private sector activities, such as crooked travel and marriage agencies, construction companies and non-governmental service providers.[43]

The UNCAC also has relevant articles that criminalize active and passive bribery,[44] obstruction of justice,[45] and money laundering.[46] All are criminal acts that can and do facilitate human trafficking.[47]

4. Corruption in the Context of Human Trafficking

Corruption has four goals in the human trafficking cycle: (1) to allow the crime to be invisible, (2) to facilitate the impunity once a case of human trafficking is detected, (3) to facilitate the different routes in the country, and (4) to assure the revictimization of the trafficked victims.[48]

The link between corruption and human trafficking appears conspicuous. "Corruption is the lubricant that allows the wheel of human trafficking to adequately operate, imbedding itself at all levels, from the planning to the aftermath of the actual trade."[49] What we do not yet understand clearly, however, is the magnitude of the role corruption plays in human trafficking activities.

For example, is a corrupt practice directly violating the trafficked person's human rights or is the corrupt practice *leading* to the violation of those rights,

---

43. International Anti-Counterfeiting Coalition, 14th IACC Conference Paper, Corruption, Gender and Trafficking in Women: Possible Correlations and Legal Solutions (2010), http://iacconference.org/en/archive/document/corruption_gender_and_trafficking_in_women_paper/.

44. UNCAC, *supra* note 32, art. 15 and art. 16.

45. *Id.* art. 25.

46. *Id.* art. 23.

47. Anti-Slavery, Transparency International & United Nations Office on Drugs and Crime, The Role of Corruption in Trafficking in Persons 12–16 (Nov. 11, 2009). *See also* V, Background Paper presented at the side event 'The Role of Corruption in Trafficking in Persons' at the Third Session of the Conference of State Parties to the UNCAC, 11 November 2009, *and also* Virginia M. Kendall, *Greasing the Palm: An Argument for an Increased Focus on Public Corruption in the Fight Against International Human Trafficking*, 44 Cornell Int'l L.J. 33, 34 (2011).

48. IACC (2010), WS#7 Corruption and Human Trafficking: unraveling the undistinguishable for a better fight. Long Workshop report, 14 the International Anti-Corruption Conference 2010, Bangkok, Thailand, 10–13 November 2010, at 1, http://www.sandrocalvani.it/docs/14th_IACC_Long_Workshop_report.pdf.

49. *Id.*

but does not in itself *violate* those rights? Nor do we understand the level of resolve governments have at present to address corruption in the context of human trafficking.[50] Most human trafficking analyses, whatever the purpose, rely on quantitative rather than qualitative statistics. The numbers of prosecutions, numbers of reported cases, the existence or nonexistence of human trafficking-related crimes in legislation, human trafficking investigations by police, and government budgets for police action or victim assistance are the most common indicators to study a nation's fight against human trafficking. Such statistics either confirm or condemn efforts at national levels, and some statistics are manipulated and prone to subjective elements and motivations that skew an accurate understanding. Moreover, the extent to which data mentions the nexus between human trafficking and corruption is often little more than anecdotal or is part of the description of particular cases and presented in limited context. While anecdotal information is better than no information at all, the manner in which it is generated can be disappointing.

The lack of attention to this nexus has not gone ignored, however. Academic papers have addressed this issue, even if it has not been broadly pursued as a central element of analysis in any major international context. A possible explanation is that investigating and prosecuting corrupt actors can interfere with government policies in multiple ways and erode public confidence in government institutions and officials, such that authorities are reticent to admit to corruption in the ranks.[51] Such admissions can also be bad for sustaining constituencies.

---

50. Connection, *supra* note 20, at 24. It cannot be concluded that a corrupt act automatically violates a human right. In order to apply the human rights framework "with potential legal effects," it is essential to differentiate "corrupt practices that directly violate a human right from corrupt practices that lead to violation of a human right (but do not themselves violate a right), and from corrupt practices where a causal link with a specific violation of rights cannot practically be established."

51. *See* Jan Van Dijk & Fanny Klerx-Van Mierlo, *Indicators of Corruption: Further Explorations of the Link between Corruption and Implementation Failure in Anti-Human Trafficking Policies* 17, University of Tilburg (2006?), http://lastradainternational.org/lsidocs/indicators%20of%20corruption.%20link%20between%20corruption%20and%20trafficking.pdf.

5. Types of Corruption Impacting and Impacted by Human Trafficking

Some researchers have established two "gateways" to corruption as it pertains to human trafficking.[52] The first corruption gateway entails the individual phases of trafficking: recruitment, procurement of documents, transport, asserting/maintaining control and exploitation of victims, and profit laundering. Corruption involved in this gateway typically entails the bribery of individuals such as police officers, border police, customs officers, immigration authorities, high-ranking officials, superiors, influential parties, and private sector entities involved in travel (travel agencies, transport companies, airlines, maritime shipping/transport, and financial institutions).[53]

> Corruption can emerge before, during and after the actual trafficking crime, which means that corruption is not limited to countries of origin and transit countries, but also facilitates the continued exploitation of trafficking victims once at their destination. Police officers, labour inspectors and others working in the field of administrative controls, health workers, NGO staff, and other actors may be prepared to turn a blind eye to trafficking situations that come to their attention for a 'small fee.'[54]

The second gateway pertains to phases of domestic legislation and its enforcement. Corruption influences the drafting of legislation, preliminary proceedings of investigations, asset seizures, prosecution, enforcement of sanctions, and protection of victims. Corrupt actors may be parliamentarians and executive officers, police, judicial officials, prosecutors, defense lawyers, prison personnel, and witnesses susceptible to bribery or coercion.[55]

> Corrupt practices may also play a role after the actual identification and rescue of a trafficked victim, e.g. before, during and after possible criminal proceedings. Such practices are applied by the traffickers to avoid conviction and otherwise obstruct the actions of those who

---

52. Bianca Schimmel & Birgit Pech, *Corruption and Gender: Approaches and Recommendation for TA* 14, Anti-Corruption Resource Center (2104), http://www.u4.no/recommended-reading/corruption-and-gender-approaches-and-recommendations-for-ta/.

53. *Id.*

54. Vienna Forum, *supra* note 5, at 3.

55. Schimmel, *supra* note 50.

should assist and protect the trafficked victims and investigate, prosecute and convict the traffickers. Traffickers often have the means and feel no inhibitions against bribing their way through the criminal justice system and investigators assigned to the case all too often fail to overcome the temptation. Corruption can establish close ties between traffickers and those who are actually charged with bringing them to justice.[56]

Labor trafficking may occur at the hands of a private individual or can rise to a macro level. Sex trafficking can be part of an international crime syndicate crossing continents and time zones, or it can be a local operation involving a single individual with the capacity to coerce and control another individual for personal gain. Corruption can also have different gradients along the human trafficking chain. For example, corruption is generally believed to be higher in source countries where trafficking victims originate and where some officials are actively engaged in trafficking conspiracies.[57] Corrupt state actors and business people in destination countries or at the point in which the servitude occurs may be involved in more passive roles, like political elites who benefit from labor trafficking and judges who are bribed or actively solicit payment to delay or disappear cases against traffickers.

When labor trafficking occurs on a large scale, it can be the result of a decision-making body; a board of directors, a CEO, a manager, lawyers/counselors—all can initiate and sustain the trafficking chain in direct and indirect ways. Corporate entities exist to make money and exploit markets. When competition is fierce, there may be a temptation and a tendency to place profit above moral responsibility. This can lead to engaging in corrupt acts, if not directly, then passively with a layer or two of separation between the corporate entity and the trafficking crimes.

At the same time governments that strive to stimulate economic development may inadvertently become enablers for labor trafficking. Government-sponsored programs like guest worker visas, for example, may influence companies to exploit the opportunities to improve the bottom line, including engaging in corrupt business practices if they think they can do so with impunity. In some cases, the penalty for getting caught might be considered lit-

---

56. Vienna Forum, *supra* note 5, at 3.

57. "Studies show that victims tend to come from countries where the public sector is perceived to be highly corrupt." *See Breaking the Chain: Corruption and Human Trafficking*, TRANSPARENCY INT'L, Sept. 1, 2011, https://www.transparency.org/news/feature/breaking_the_chain_corruption_and_human_trafficking.

tle more than the price of doing business, and fines for labor infractions may already be factored into the bottom line. Paying a fine while being allowed to accept no responsibility, as often happens when corporations settle disputes, further allows corruption to persist rather than be curtailed. Whereas sex trafficking is a matter of criminals exploiting gaps and weaknesses among government officials, labor trafficking by corporations becomes an extremely complex matter of exploiting loopholes, hiding in gray areas, and staying one step ahead of accountability. Labor trafficking can also be a matter of moral corruption in which an individual who feels s/he is above the law can exploit someone in forced servitude with impunity. Such acts constitute not only corruption and disregard for the rule of law, but are the workings of a depraved heart. Sex trafficking, in contrast, seems to have a more direct connection to corruption. There is a more visceral and collusive element at play. For instance, border patrol agents and law enforcement officials make individual decisions to accept bribes from sex traffickers or to accept favors that can include being serviced by the trafficking victims they are supposed to protect. They may also harbor misogynistic disdain for sex trafficking victims that is not present in labor trafficking.

Finally, we must consider that corruption is present among some of the non-government organizations that ostensibly exist to combat human trafficking. The zeal to do something about the trafficking in human beings has created an "industry" of sorts over the last two decades in which opportunists may corrupt the efforts of well-meaning individuals and organizations in order to make money off the misery of others. There is a growing number of documented instances of individuals who commit fraud, who depict themselves as victims when they are not, who use the fight against human trafficking for personal enrichment or to gain status in the community, or take advantage of the well-meaning intentions of people who want to learn about human trafficking and get involved in fighting it.

Chapter 6

Public Corruption and Human Trafficking

Summary: Chapter 6 introduces the topic of public corruption and its connection to human trafficking. We will first examine the challenges of defining public corruption, which is vitally necessary to understanding its impact and intersection with human trafficking. We will then break down the types of public corruption, looking at several examples relating to human trafficking crimes. The chapter will conclude with a provocative discussion of whether the government bureaucracy in place to study, fund, and fight human trafficking is inherently corrupt due to the complex relationships at play between government authorities and the agencies and entities that receive funding for anti-human trafficking programs.

1. Defining Public Corruption

Corruption in the public sector is the elephant in the room that few are willing to acknowledge.[1] There are several multilateral mechanisms against corruption ranging from binding legal instruments and policies to political declarations.[2] The *United Nations Convention against Corruption* (UNCAC)

---

1. M. Bashir Uddin, *Human Trafficking in South Asia: Issues of Corruption and Human Security*, 2 Int'l J. of Soc. Work and Human Services Pract. 18, 23 (2014), http://www.hrpub.org/download/20140305/IJRH3-19201859.pdf (noting that most people involved in combating human trafficking know about corruption but prefer not to discuss it).

2. *See for example* The Inter-American Convention against Corruption (IACAC), OEA/Ser. K/XXXIV.1, CICOR/doc. 14/96 rev. 2 (29 Mar. 1996), 35 ILM 724 (1996), entered into force Mar. 6, 1997, http://www.oas.org/en/sla/dil/inter_american_treaties_B-58_against_

depicts corruption as a force "undermining the institutions and values of democracy, ethical values and justice and jeopardizing sustainable development and the rule of law."[3] Corruption's corrosive effects include decreased access to public services and diminished public trust in governance. It discourages investment and creates market uncertainty.[4] In addition, although corruption appears in societies throughout the world, it is within the contexts of instability, weak institutions, and extreme poverty that corruption may be particularly caustic.[5] Because corruption both drives and results from a multitude of social forces, it has been assessed in the context of other governance maladies, such as politically motivated violence, impingements on freedom of expression, association, and the media; government incompetence, loss of government transparency; and diminishment of the "rule of law" and the enforcement of rights.[6]

Corruption.asp. *See also* Philippa Webb, *The United Nations Convention Against Corruption: Global Achievement or Missed Opportunity?* 8 J. OF INT'L ECON. L. 193 (2005).

3. G.A. Res. 58/4 (Oct. 31, 2003).

4. *See* UNITED NATIONS DEVELOPMENT PROGRAMME, CORRUPTION AND DEVELOPMENT: ANTI-CORRUPTION INTERVENTIONS FOR POVERTY REDUCTION, REALIZATION OF THE MDGs AND PROMOTING SUSTAINABLE DEVELOPMENT 25 (2008).

5. *See* WORLD BANK, HELPING COUNTRIES COMBAT CORRUPTION: THE ROLE OF THE WORLD BANK §2 (1997), http://www1.worldbank.org/publicsector/anticorrupt/corruptn/cor02.htm (noting that, "The causes of corruption are always contextual, rooted in a country's policies, bureaucratic traditions, political development, and social history. Still, corruption tends to flourish when institutions are weak and government policies generate economic rents. Some characteristics of developing and transition settings make corruption particularly difficult to control."). *See also* UNITED NATIONS DEVELOPMENT PROGRAMME, CORRUPTION AND DEVELOPMENT: ANTI-CORRUPTION INTERVENTIONS FOR POVERTY REDUCTION, REALIZATION OF THE MDGs AND PROMOTING SUSTAINABLE DEVELOPMENT 10, 16 (2008) (identifying "(1) the absence of rules, regulations, policies and legislation; (2) weak systems of enforcement; (3) weak systems of oversight; (4) lack of accountability; (5) lack of transparency; (6) lack of checks and balances in the system (e.g., institutional weaknesses in the legislative and judicial systems); (7) lack of integrity; (8) monopoly of power; (9) high degree of discretion; (10) low salaries; (11) high rewards compared to risks; and (12) low detection rate[s]" as commonly cited causes of corruption, and explaining that the United Nations Development Programme has also observed that "[c]ountries afflicted by structural poverty are likely to be suffering from systemic corruption because corruption is among the exacerbating conditions of poverty in countries already struggling with the strains of economic growth and democratic transition.").

6. The World Bank recently issued a report on "Worldwide Governance Indicators," assessing governance in 215 countries between 1996 and 2013, based on six dimensions of governance: Voice & Accountability; Political Stability and Absence of Violence; Government Effectiveness; Regulatory Quality; Rule of Law; and Control of Corruption. *See World Governance Indicators*, WORLD BANK GRP, http://info.worldbank.org/governance/wgi/index.

In sum, public sector corruption can be classified into the following elements:

- Collusion and active participation in human trafficking by public officials;
- Bribery of public officials who benefit by looking the other way; and
- Involuntary corruption by public officials who are coerced or black-mailed into participation in human trafficking.

2. The Corrosive Influence of Corruption on Government Institutions

Corruption can manifest in any branch of government and in any sector of governance. Because definitions of who is an "official" for purposes of corruption can include "any person who performs a public function"[7] and those who work for public entities, corruption can extend to unlawful influence sought or obtained from employees of state-owned companies as well.[8]

---

aspx#reports (last updated 2014). As with the Transparency International *Corruption Perceptions Index,* control of corruption is intended to "capture perceptions of the extent to which public power is exercised for private gain, including both petty and grand forms of corruption, as well as 'capture' of the state by elites and private interests." Each of these categories is also rich with detail. For example, the World Justice Project has developed an index assessing rule of law using 47 different indicators organized into eight themes: Constraints on Government Powers; Absence of Corruption; Open Government; Fundamental Rights; Order and Security; Regulatory Enforcement; Civil Justice; Criminal Justice; and Due Process of Law and Rights of the Accused. *See* WORLD JUSTICE PROJECT, THE WORLD JUSTICE PROJECT RULE OF LAW INDEX 2014 (2014), at 196, http://worldjusticeproject.org/sites/default/files/files/tables_methodology.pdf (last visited June 30, 2015) [hereinafter ROL Index]. The "Absence of Corruption" theme measures the extent to which officials in the executive, legislative, or judicial branches, or in the police or military, do or do not "use public office for private gain." *See* ROL Index, at 167.

7. United Nations Convention against Corruption, Dec. 14, 2005, 3249 U.N.T.S. 41, art. 2(a) [hereinafter UNCAC].

8. The United States Foreign Corrupt Practices Act, Pub. L. No. 95-213, 91 Stat. 1494 (1977), for example, prohibits certain persons and entities from providing benefits to a "foreign official" in order to "influence the foreign official in his or her official capacity, induce the foreign official to do or omit to do an act in violation of his or her lawful duty, or to secure any improper advantage in order to assist in obtaining or retaining business for or with, or directing business to, any person." *See Foreign Corrupt Practices Act: An Overview,* U.S. DEPT. OF JUSTICE, http://www.justice.gov/criminal/fraud/fcpa/ (last updated June 12, 2015). The Act defines a "foreign official" as "any officer or employee of a foreign government or any department, agency, or instrumentality thereof, or of a public international

Corruption may be present in the criminal justice system in the form of obstruction of investigations and interference in prosecutions of human trafficking cases. Corrupt acts include intimidation of a witness, delays in the investigation of human trafficking complaints, spoliation of evidence, procedural delays in the courts orchestrated by judges who accept bribes from traffickers (and conversely, judges who expect bribes from trafficking victims to make cases move forward),[9] and the imposition of entirely inadequate penalties when a conviction is achieved. These forms of corruption allow traffickers to control the outcomes of judicial investigations and to manipulate their victims into believing that no one is going to help them, and that their only option is to keep quiet and submit to continuing abuse and renewed exploitation.[10] Moreover, corruption in judicial institutions and along the chain of detection, investigation, evidence gathering, and bringing charges can also render national and international cooperation efforts impotent.[11]

Throughout the European Union, for instance, allegations persistent that corruption pervades the criminal justice system to a significant degree.[12] Corruption can attach to some political elites who are rendered vulnerable due to their proclivities toward the good life, or their interactions with wealthy businessman who are in some way connected to criminal networks.[13]

The types of public corruption present in relation to the sex industry may depend on the legal status of sex businesses. "Brothels, ideally, provide a covert environment where corrupt exchanges can take place."[14] Placing a targeted official in an environment that can compromise his/her integrity is a tried and true tactic, and it only takes one instance of poor judgment on the official's part to be tainted. At the same time, public officials who have no moral com-

---

organization, or any person acting in an official capacity for or on behalf of any such government or department, agency, or instrumentality, or for or on behalf of any such public international organization." 15 U.S.C. §78dd-1(f)(1)(A) (2012). Similarly, the United Kingdom's Bribery Act, enacted in 2010, criminalizes bribery of foreign officials and the failure of businesses to prevent bribery on their behalf (Section 6). *See* Bribery Act 2010, Chapter 23, http://www.legislation.gov.uk/ukpga/2010/23/pdfs/ukpga_20100023_en.pdf.

9. Uddin, *supra* note 1, at 23.

10. Anti-Slavery, Transparency International & United Nations Office on Drugs and Crime, The Role of Corruption in Trafficking in Persons 12 (Nov. 11, 2009).

11. Anne T. Gallagher, The International Law of Human Trafficking 444 (2010).

12. Philip Gounev & Vincenzo Ruggiero, ed., Corruption and Organized Crime in Europe: Illegal Partnerships 79 (2012).

13. *Id.* (noting how unscrupulous businessmen utilize high end prostitutes to compromise, corrupt and blackmail political figures in exchange for protection from investigation.).

14. *Id.* at 80.

pass may seek out the opportunity for personal enrichment and diversion by exploiting the criminal enterprises that occur around them. Whichever way the corruption flows, it is difficult to assess the extent to which corrupt acts corrupt officials or corrupt officials encourage corrupt acts.

Corruption and the challenges of fortifying ineffective criminal justice and judicial systems are endemic problems worldwide.[15] In Latin America, although legislation such as the *Inter-American Convention against Corruption*[16] and the UNCAC have been signed and ratified by almost every country in the region, little progress has been made in terms of advancing the fight against corruption. In the last few years, none of the countries in the region have escaped corruption scandals.[17] Indeed, the perception that impunity is rampant in the Americas encourages the establishment of extensive criminal organizations with tentacles in different criminal activities, including trafficking in persons. This issue, together with the fact that the criminal justice system in Latin America "is on average the least efficient in the world"[18] due to case backlogs and poor enforcement, has made the region a hot spot for the trafficking of persons.[19]

However, it is important to note that almost every Latin American government has tried to implement legislation and other instruments in order to curb corruption and hinder human trafficking. Chile, for example, boasts one of the best ratings scores for transparency and lack of corruption in the region,[20] and occupies a Tier 1 slot on the current United States State Department TIP Report.[21] Likewise, Ecuador's serious efforts to improve the prosecution of human trafficking cases and to curb corruption among public officials helped lift the country from Tier 3 to Tier 2,[22] and this occurred despite how low Ecuador is ranked on the Corruption Perception Index.[23]

---

15. ROL Index, *supra* note 6, at 38.

16. Inter-American Convention Against Corruption, OEA/Ser. K/XXXIV.1, CICOR/ doc. 14/96 rev. 2 (29 Mar. 1996), 35 ILM 724 (1996), entered into force Mar. 6, 1997.

17. Some of the most important scandals include Petrobras in Brazil, and the corruption of law enforcement and public officials in Mexico.

18. ROL Index, *supra* note 15.

19. CLARE RIBANDO SEELKE, CONG. RESEARCH SERV., RL 33200, TRAFFICKING IN PERSONS IN LATIN AMERICA AND THE CARIBBEAN 4 (2013), http://www.fas.org/sgp/crs/row/ RL33200.pdf.

20. Ranked 21 among 175 countries and number one in the region by Transparency International.

21. U.S. DEP'T OF STATE, TRAFFICKING IN PERSONS REPORT 128–29 (2016) [hereinafter TIP Report 2016]. *See also* Seelke, *supra* note 19, at 9.

22. TIP Report 2016, *supra* note 21, at 158–60.

23. Ecuador has been ranked 120 among 176 countries. *See Corruption Measurement Tools*, TRANSPARENCY INT'L (last updated 2015), http://www.transparency.org/country#

3. Collusion and Active Participation

Government officials are susceptible to making very bad choices.[24] Often the temptation of making fast money or receiving benefits from trafficking victims results in state actors colluding with traffickers and actively participating in trafficking conspiracies. Some officials do not become corrupted simply by one act involving the trafficking of a person; investigators can usually find a pattern of corrupt conduct occurring over time.

Such is the case involving an immigration official in New York City in 2003 who pleaded guilty to obstruction of justice for helping a private individual avoid prosecution for human trafficking by attempting to deport two trafficking victims who were preparing to testify against him and his wife.[25] The government official, Nisim Yushuvayev, conspired to use the color of his authority to force two South Korean women, Jane Doe 1 and Jane Doe 2, to leave the United States involuntarily. The event that led to his fall from government service began when Yushuvayev frequented a drinking establishment called the Renaissance Bar and Room Café located in Flushing, Queens, New York, which was owned by Mr. and Mrs. Kang, a married couple of South Korean origin.[26] The Kangs brought two young women into the United States under false pretenses and forced them to work as hostesses at their bar. Upon arriving in New York City, the women were told that instead of receiving $40 a day plus tips as promised, they were to work 6½ hour days, six days a week, for $35 a day plus tips. Their situation bore all the hallmarks of forced servitude:

> The women were informed that they each owed the Kangs approximately $20,000 for various travel-related expenses, and were forced to sign promissory notes in the amount of $20,000. They were not permitted to keep their wages or tips while working at Renaissance; rather, all of their income was taken by the Kangs and credited toward

---

ECU. *See Corruption Perceptions Index 2016*, https://www.transparency.org/news/feature/corruption_perceptions_index_2016#table.

24. "The mix of profit and impunity through easily 'bought' protection from law enforcers and politicians has created a 'high reward/low risk' scenario for human traffickers and their accomplices." *See Breaking the Chain: Corruption and Human Trafficking*, TRANSPARENCY INT'L, Sept. 1, 2011, http://archive.transparency.org/news_room/in_focus/2011/breaking_the_chain_corruption_and_human_trafficking [hereinafter Breaking the Chain].

25. *Yushuvayev v. U.S.*, 532 F. Supp. 2d 455 (E.D.N.Y. 2008).

26. William Glaberson, *Obstruction Is Charged in Sex Slavery Case*, NY TIMES, Feb. 2, 2004, http://www.nytimes.com/2004/02/03/nyregion/obstruction-is-charged-in-sex-slavery-case.html?_r=0.

their "debt." In addition, the women were not permitted to leave the house in which they were staying without the Kangs' permission, and, because all of their income was confiscated by the Kangs, were forced to borrow money from the Kangs when they wished to make any purchases outside the bar, thereby increasing their indebtedness.[27]

After also being sexually assaulted and physically abused by the Kangs, Jane Doe 1 managed to find her way to police and reported what was happening to her and Jane Doe 2. Mr. Kang was subsequently arrested and charged with forced labor, false imprisonment and assault. While awaiting trial, he approached Yushuvayev, knowing that he was an Inspector for United States Customs and Border Protection, and offered to pay him $10,000 to forcibly place Jane Doe 1 and Jane Doe 2 onto flights to South Korea to prevent them from testifying.[28] With airline tickets in hand that had been purchased by Mr. Kang, Yushuvayev went looking for the two women. When he found Jane Doe 1, he showed her his INS badge, accused her of working in violation of her visa, and instructed her to accompany him to the airport to be put on a flight to Seoul. Jane Doe 1 became suspicious and called an attorney acquaintance for help, which eventually led to Yushuvayev being exposed for his illegal conduct. Yushuvayev was initially arrested by federal authorities and charged with obstruction of a peonage investigation in violation of 18 U.S.C. § 1581(b).[29] He was ultimately charged with five counts: conspiracy to kidnap in violation of 18 U.S.C. § 1201(c); conspiracy to deprive or intimidate an individual in the exercise of her rights under the Constitution and laws of the United States in violation of 18 U.S.C. § 241; deprivation of rights under color of law in violation of 18 U.S.C. § 242; and two counts of obstructing enforcement of the peonage statute in violation of 18 U.S.C. § 1581(b).[30] Upon entering a plea agreement with the government, Yushuvayev was sentenced to 10 years in federal prison.

In determining the appropriate sentence, federal courts look at past criminal conduct to determine the extent to which a defendant is cognizant of the gravity of charges s/he faces. In the course of investigating Yushuvayev's past, it was discovered that while working as an Immigration Inspector in 2002 and 2003, he had committed fraud and misuse of visas in violation of federal law[31]

---

27. *Yushuvayev*, 532 F. Supp. 2d at 458.
28. Yushuvayev eventually agreed to do the deed for $4,000.
29. *Yushuvayev*, 532 F. Supp. 2d at 461.
30. *Id.*
31. 18 U.S.C. § 1546 (2012).

by selling fraudulent visas and immigration stamps[32] to aliens already in the United States in order to extend their stay,[33] that he frequented brothels and facilitated prostitution in violation of New York penal law, and that he showed a serious disregard for the law despite the fact that he had a bachelor's degree in criminal justice from a prominent New York college.

Travel document fraud in the furtherance of a human trafficking operation is a prevalent act of corruption worldwide. In Nepal in 2012, various levels of officials colluded with traffickers to provide fraudulent documents to trafficking victims. But because many of the perpetrators were politically connected, there were often no investigations, prosecutions, or convictions of government officials for complicity in trafficking.[34] An investigation in Belgium in the 1990s did lead to the conviction of a Belgian civil servant for forgery while working in the protocol service of the Ministry of Foreign Affairs. During his time there, the individual sold at least 300 residence permits to individuals associated with Russian organized crime and people known to be engaging in espionage.[35]

In 2011, a complex internal investigation by Cambodian national police led to the arrest of Police Colonel Eam Rattana, the former head of the Phnom Penh Municipal Police Department section for Anti-Human Trafficking and Juvenile Protection. According to an unclassified diplomatic report released by the United States State Department and the American Embassy in Phnom Penh,[36] Colonel Eam allegedly attempted to recruit an investigator from an NGO partner (the name of the NGO was redacted in the document) and two others within his anti-human trafficking group to serve as informants in a criminal network protecting those involved in human trafficking and sexual exploitation. Colonel Eam had reportedly been observed and recorded attempting to recruit an investigator into a network of informants to tip off corrupt police and brothel owners to upcoming anti-trafficking in persons operations, the diplomatic report stated. In the recording, Colonel Eam indicated that the network included informants within most HT NGOs operating in Cambodia as well as high ranking Cambodian officials who remained unnamed. During the course of the investigation, Colonel Eam allegedly ap-

---

32. Obtained from a corrupt United States Immigration and Customs Enforcement official.

33. *Yushuvayev*, 532 F. Supp. 2d at 464.

34. Uddin, *supra* note 1, at 24 (citing to U.S. Dep't of State, Trafficking in Persons Report 260–262 (2012)).

35. Felia Allum & Stan Gilmour, Routledge Handbook of Transnational Organized Crime 314 (2012).

36. Unclassified U.S. Department of State Case No. F-2014-21919 Doc. No. C05757413, 04/14/2015. On file with the author.

proached several other of his colleagues in an attempt to recruit them. The outcome of the investigation remains unclear, but the State Department made particular note of praising the Cambodian law enforcement community for stepping up efforts to uncover corruption. The report also emphasized that the investigation "speaks volumes about the protection individual officers expect from and within their own organization and illustrates how far the [Royal Government of Cambodia] and [Cambodian National Police] have to go in rooting out corruption."[37]

According to the 2016 State Department TIP Report on Cambodia, all of Cambodia's provinces are a source of human trafficking, and the same issues that were reported in the 2015 TIP Report appear to persist.[38] Nevertheless, Cambodia moved up from the Tier 2 Watch List in 2015 to Tier 2 for 2016.[39] What is startling about this case example, but not terribly surprising, is that not only is corruption present in law enforcement entities worldwide, but that it resides even within the very law enforcement special units dedicated to combating human trafficking. This underscores the reality that no agency is immune from corrupt elements and temptation, and that the solutions for stopping it remain uncertain.

In Bulgaria, a senior intelligence official had a side business as the owner of a travel agency that during the 1990s established close relations with a Western nation embassy in Sofia. Up until July 1996, the agency received and processed en masse official tourist visas, including one that was prepared for an individual who was convicted of sexually exploiting women, another that was prepared for an individual who was tied to a case involving Kurdish PKK child soldiers and weapons smuggling, and yet another processed for a known international car thief.[40]

In the Philippines, a judge was accused of corruption by acting improperly and in gross ignorance of the law.[41] The case involved a man's daughter who was recruited in Manila to work in a bar in the Oriental Mindoro town of Pinamalayan.[42] When the father filed a complaint with the authorities, a

---

37. *Id.*

38. TIP Report 2016, *supra* note 21, at 119.

39. *Id.* at 119–21.

40. Allum, *supra* note 35, at 314–15.

41. *Alejandro Gutierrez, PCI Antonio Ricafort, SPO4 Richardo G. Ong, and SPO1 Arnulfo Medenilla vs. Judge Godofredo G. Hernandez*, UNODC Human Trafficking Case Law Database, http://www.unodc.org/cld/case-law-doc/traffickingpersonscrimetype/phl/2007/psupt._alejandro_gutierrez_pci_antonio_ricafort_spo4_richardo_g._ong_and_spo1_arnulfo_medenilla_vs._judge_godofredo_g._hernandez.html?tmpl=old.

42. *Id.*

rescue operation was mounted and a total of five young girls were discovered in the home of a man holding the girls there for alleged "safe keeping."[43] Shortly thereafter, the judge assigned to the case issued an arrest warrant for the people who conducted the rescue mission, charging them with grave coercion and qualified trespass.[44] It was further alleged that the girls were taken to a beach resort by their suspected traffickers, and that the girls were coerced into signing a retraction of the complaint, as well as also signing a complaint against the men who rescued them.[45] While the girls were being re-victimized by their traffickers, the judge then allegedly showed up at the resort and conferred with the traffickers about the complaint he was going to file against the rescuers. His meeting with the traffickers involved drinking and "entertainment."[46] The judge was subsequently found guilty of corruption, but vehemently denied the accusation that he showed up at the resort.[47] This is an example of corruption at the criminal justice level in which a judge helped facilitate efforts to circumvent the legal system by filing false charges at the behest of the traffickers against the very people who helped rescue the girls. Moreover, the judge's actions eroded the integrity of the judicial process by allowing crimes to happen, by conspiring to commit additional crimes, and by contributing to the re-victimization of trafficked individuals. Such callous corrupt acts by a judicial official have a chilling effect on fighting human trafficking in the Philippines and contribute to the public perception that the government is inherently corrupt.

In another criminal case in the Philippines, Filipino victims were trafficked into Malaysia where they were forced into domestic servitude and told that after they completed their "employment contract," they would then be sent to work in a brothel.[48] This case demonstrated overt corruption because one of the co-conspirators was actually an immigration officer whose role in the trafficking chain involved passing for transit across the border, incident free, those trafficking victims whose passports had the letter "A" embossed on the back cover.

The border regions of Colombia, Ecuador, and Peru are also rife with transborder human trafficking operations dependent on the complicity of border

---

43. *Id.*
44. *Id.*
45. *Id.*
46. *Id.*
47. *Id.*
48. *Criminal Case No. 0310-2009*, UNODC Human Trafficking Case Law Database, http://www.unodc.org/cld/case-law-doc/traffickingpersonscrimetype/phl/2012/crim._case_no._0310-2009.html?tmpl=old.

officials in all three countries.[49] Among the criminal conducts being prosecuted in an increasing number in the region are charges of abuse of authority
by law enforcement agents,[50] transportation of victims across borders by immigration authorities,[51] and falsification of identification documents by public officials.[52] Statements taken from some of the trafficking victims in Ecuador
indicate that the owners of brothels and bars are routinely tipped off by corrupt law enforcement agents prior to raids and other operations. In exchange,
the officers are given monetary awards or receive sexual favors.[53] Moreover,
immigration officers have been identified by some of the trafficking victims as
prominent participants in the transportation of victims across the Ecuadoran
border. In one specific example, victims trafficked into Ecuador from Colombia identified a specific immigration officer as the person who actually drove
the car that took them across the frontier.[54] Other victims have testified that
they have crossed immigration check points between Ecuador and Colombia
without being required by immigration officials to produce proper identification documents.[55]

Another corrupt practice carried out by state actors in Ecuador concerns
the falsification of identification documents that allow minors to work in the
country as adults. Because prostitution is not penalized in Ecuador, false papers allow the traffickers to exploit their minor victims with impunity.[56] Many
of the false documents are obtained by brothel owners from criminal organizations, but some are also allegedly obtained through public officials working
for the Office of Civil Registry, the public institution in charge of issuing national identification papers. These officials are hardly ever prosecuted for their
conducts.[57] For example, a 2008 case decided by the Judge of First Instance in
the city of El Oro found girls between 12 and 17 years of age using false iden-

---

49. U.S. Dep't of State, Trafficking in Persons Report 161–162 (2014) [hereinafter
TIP Report 2014].

50. Causa Penal No. 2698-08, del Juzgado Décimo Octavo de lo Penal de Pichincha.

51. Causa Penal No. 604-09, del Juzgado Cuarto de lo Penal de Imbabura.

52. Causa Penal No. 012-08 del Tribunal Primero de lo Penal de El Oro.

53. Causa Penal No. 2698-08, *supra* note 50.

54. Causa Penal No. 604-09, *supra* note 51.

55. Causa Penal No. 1166-08 del Juzgado Décimo Segundo de lo Penal de Pichincha.

56. *See* Juan Carlos Corrales Sigcho, *Estudio Jurídico de la Normativa Penal Referente a
la Trata de Personas en el Ecuador*, 26, Facultad de las Américas (2011), http://dspace
.udla.edu.ec/handle/33000/336.

57. For a good analysis of the situation in terms of document fraud and the ability to
obtain false identification papers in Ecuador, *see Ecuador Zona Franca del Tráfico Humano*,
298 Revista Vanguardia 14 (2011), http://issuu.com/la_hora/docs/vanguardia298/15.

tification papers in order to be sex workers in a brothel. The papers were legitimate official papers and could have not been acquired without the help of officers in the Civil Registry. However, no investigation into this matter was ever launched.[58] Curiously, the Civil Registry is under the control of the Department of Telecommunications. It is possible that a disconnection between the policies of the Civil Registry and that of the Department of Telecommunications has allowed corruption to flourish within the former institution.[59]

Notwithstanding these instances, Ecuador has in recent years made a concerted effort to prevent human trafficking and to protect the victims.[60] However, the presence of generalized corruption in public institutions is a barrier to gain leverage in the fight against human trafficking, and while Ecuador ratified the UNCAC, and since 2009 has a designated council for coordinating the fight against corruption,[61] the ability of public officials to break the law with impunity persists and hampers the development and effective implementation of any anti-human trafficking policies in the country.

Across the Atlantic Ocean, the European Union has been plagued by involvement of police officers in prostitution rings that in some cases commit sex trafficking. Some police have also been found to be engaged in racketeering of prostitution in exchange for sexual favors or payments.[62] In France, the United Kingdom, Greece, and Bulgaria, some police officers have been directly involved in setting up and operating brothels and other sex businesses. In the UK, an investigation by *The Guardian* newspaper in 2012 revealed that sexual predators in the police force were abusing their authority to target the very victims of crime they were supposed to be protecting.[63] Between 2008 and 2011, 56 police and community support officers were found to have abused their position "to rape, sexually assault or harass women and young people or were investigated over such allegations."[64] The Independent Police Complaints Commission (IPCC) investigated corruption allegations and reported several

---

58. Causa Penal No. 012-08, *supra* note 52.

59. Ecuador Zona, *supra* note 56. Identification document fraud related to human trafficking in Ecuador also extends to different forms of organized crime, including drug cartels and terrorist organizations.

60. For more information regarding this point, *see* Informe Tematico de la Defensoria del Pueblo del Ecuador, Trata de Personas, Administración de Justicia, Impunidad y Derechos Humanos 28 (2010).

61. UNCAC, *supra* note 7.

62. Gounev, *supra* note 12, at 80.

63. Sandra Laville, *Revealed: The Scale of Sexual Abuse by Police Officers*, Guardian, June 29, 2012.

64. *Id.*

cases of police officers having sexual intercourse with vulnerable females while on duty and using access to official computer systems to gather information about vulnerable females.[65] The IPCC also noted that failures in the vetting process of police applicants during a large recruitment drive to increase manpower in the early 2000s allowed some bad apples to join the police ranks. The director of one watchdog organization, Wearside Women in Need, stated, "What you have here is the untouched tip of an iceberg in terms of sexually questionable behavior and attitudes. The police service ... has an incredibly macho culture and women are seen as sexual objects."[66] A key problem revealed by the report is that many of the officers accused of corruption never faced criminal charges, but instead were quietly dealt with through internal disciplinary proceedings.

In Albania, a number of former government security agents were recruited into one human trafficking organization for the purpose of training the traffickers in typical "intelligence" techniques to be applied to running internal secret communications within the criminal network.[67] An analysis of 43 criminal investigations indicated that former intelligence personnel actively played key roles in the activities of the criminal networks, working as freelance consultants to facilitate the exit, transit and entry of trafficking victims.

Law enforcement officials have also been found to be actively engaged in human trafficking crimes in the United States. In 2014, a former Washington, D.C. police officer was convicted of housing minors in his apartment and prostituting them.[68] The officer admitted to recruiting the girls from a shopping mall and bus stop with promises of modeling jobs and then forcing them to work as escorts.[69] His marketing strategy involved photographing the girls in the nude, providing them with clothing, shoes, and haircuts, and then adver-

---

65. *Id.*

66. Statement of Clare Phillipson. *Id.*

67. Johan Leman & Stef Janssens, *Albanian Entrepreneurial Practices in Human Smuggling and Trafficking: On the Road to the United Kingdom Via Brussels, 1995–2005*, Int'l Migration, doi:10.1111/j.1468-2435.2010.00654.x (2011), https://lirias.kuleuven.be/bitstream/123456789/358951/2/j.1468-2435.2010.00654.x.pdf.

68. Peter Hermann, *D.C. Police Officer Admits Prostituting Girls*, Wash. Post, June 20, 2014, http://www.washingtonpost.com/local/crime/plea-hearing-set-for-dc-police-officer-accused-of-running-underage-prostitution-ring/2014/06/19/d7dae1ea-f79e-11e3-8aa9-dad2ec039789_story.html. As a result, the officer would have to register as a sex offender, forfeit his property to the government, including eight cell phones, a laptop, and a Lincoln Navigator, as well as sacrifice his Freedom of Information Act rights so that he could not request information about the victims and witnesses who testified against him.

69. *Id.*

tising their services on the classified advertising website Backpage.com.[70] While he was not charged with human trafficking, his modus operandi is very similar to the actions undertaken by corrupt police officers elsewhere in the world.

In El Paso County, Texas, a juvenile probation officer was arrested and charged with conspiracy to commit human trafficking and trafficking of a minor in 2014.[71] The officer was convicted of collaborating with local gang members who forced teenage girls and women into prostitution.[72] In Chicago in 2012, a community-based organization called the Young Women's Empowerment Project conducted a youth-led research study on violence experienced by girls working in Chicago's sex trade.[73] Among the findings of the report, the group asserted that police officers were responsible for about 30 percent of violence perpetrated against young sex workers, while the local family services department was responsible for 6 percent of violent encounters. In contrast, pimps were responsible for 4 percent of violent encounters. The study also asserted that police officers were responsible for 11 percent of violent sexual encounters, a percentage nearly three times greater than similar encounters with pimps.[74]

Just as government officials and state actors should be accountable for corruption in their official capacities, they also have a duty to conduct their personal affairs ethically and with respect for the law. Unfortunately, some state actors believe their status places them above the law, and that they are unac-

---

70. *Id.*

71. Daniel Borunda, *El Paso County Juvenile Probation Officer Charged in Connection with Ex-Trafficking Gang*, El Paso Times, Jan. 22, 2014, http://www.policeprostitution-andpolitics.com/pdfs_all/COPS DAs JUDGES RAPE EXTORT PROSTITUTES RUN PROSTITUTION RINGS/COPS WHO RUN PROSTITUTION RINGS AND BROTHELS/2014 Timothy McCullouch Jr.| Juvenile Probation Officer El Paso TX/El Paso County juvenile probation officer charged in connection with sex-trafficking gang - El Paso Times.pdf, *and also* Daniel Borunda, *Convicted El Paso Sex Trafficker Get Three Life Sentences in Gang Case*, El Paso Times, June 25, 2015, http://www.elpasotimes.com/story/news/local/2015/06/25/convicted-el-paso-sex-trafficker-gets-three-life/71950152/.

72. *Id.*

73. C. Angel Torres & Naima Paz, *The Bad Encounter Line: A Project of the Street Youth Rise UP Campaign by the Young Women's Empowerment Project*, study posted on the webpage of the Chicago Taskforce on Violence Against Girls & Young Women at http://www.chitaskforce.org/occasional-papers-series/bad-encounter-line/. The .PDF copy of the full report can be viewed at http://www.chitaskforce.org/wp/wp-content/uploads/2011/07/YWEP-paper-7-11.pdf (copy on file with the author).

74. Mike Ludwig, *From Somaly Mam to "Eden": How Sex Trafficking Sensationalism Hurts Sex Workers*, Truthout, Jul. 9, 2014, http://www.truth-out.org/news/item/24827-from-somaly-mam-to-eden-how-sex-trafficking-sensationalism-hurts-sex-workers. Such findings might explain why some sex workers and trafficking victims are not always relieved when police stage raids to "rescue" them.

countable for engaging in or being complicit in acts of human trafficking and various forms of forced servitude.

Foreign diplomats and foreign service staff are a rather unique class of public officials engaged in human trafficking, often involving forced labor and other deprivations. Particularly egregious is that they have the capacity to hide behind their diplomatic immunity to escape accountability. In 2007 at least four members of the Indian Parliament were accused of involvement in human trafficking.[75] One of them, Babulal Katara (along with his real wife), was arrested when he tried to use his diplomatic status to smuggle a woman and a young boy posing as his wife and son through airport security to board a flight from India to Canada.[76] Authorities became suspicious when the photos on the red diplomatic passports of Katara's actual wife and son did not match the faces of the two individuals traveling with him. Katara was detained and arrested on human trafficking-related charges. The ensuing investigation revealed that not only had Katara trafficked two other individuals into the UK a year earlier, but that several other members of the Indian Parliament were also using their diplomatic status to traffic individuals into Canada and other countries. The investigation further revealed that the trafficking operation exploited security loopholes at the airport that allowed travelers holding diplomatic passports to process through separate and less stringent facilitation counters at both domestic and foreign airports.[77] The Indian MPs were believed to have been contacted by human traffickers to utilize their diplomatic passports to move trafficking victims in exchange for cash payments.[78]

In December 2013, India's Deputy Consul General in the United States, Devyani Khobragade, was arrested in New York City on allegations of visa fraud in obtaining a staff member's visa to work in her home as a domestic servant and nanny.[79] Her doings made international headlines and had a chilling effect on relations between the United States and India. What made Khobragade's arrest and the charges against her so egregious and notable is that she was in charge of women's affairs at the Indian consulate, and her female ac-

---

75. *BJP May Be Cornered in Parliament Over Human Trafficking*, Indo-Asian News Serv., Apr. 22, 2007.

76. Sandeep Unnithan & Saurabh Shukla, *The VIP Smugglers*, IndiaToday, May 7, 2007, http://indiatoday.intoday.in/story/human-trafficking-racket-exposed/1/155729.html.

77. The process apparently did not always involve matching the faces of the passport holders to the passports.

78. Unnithan, *supra* note 76.

79. Nick O'Malley, *Foreign Diplomats Accused of Human Trafficking, Assault in US*, Sydney Morning Herald, Dec. 31, 2013, http://www.smh.com.au/world/foreign-diplomats-accused-of-human-trafficking-assault-in-us-20131231-hv77g.html.

cuser was precisely the kind of individual Khobragade was supposed to help in her official capacity. While she was not charged with human trafficking offenses, Khobragade's conduct, as described in the legal complaint filed by her domestic servant, Sangeeta Richard, shows characteristics that can be construed as both corruption and human trafficking.

Richard alleged that in November 2012, Khobragade *verbally* agreed to pay Richard a starting salary in the United States of about $3.31 per hour (around Rs 30,000) for a 40-hour work week, plus overtime pay.[80] Khobragade presented to Richard a *written* contract to sign and take to the U.S. consular official, indicating that Richard's salary while in the United States would be $9.97 per hour for a 40 hour work week. Khobragade also instructed Richard not to say anything to the consular official about being paid Rs 30,000. Shortly before leaving for the United States, Khobragade had Richard sign another work contract for the initial rate of Rs 30,000, with no mention of any other benefits. Several months later, Richard fled the Khobragade residence and found refuge among strangers in New York City's Indian community. Eventually, Richard ended up at the anti-human trafficking organization Safe Horizon, which in turn took Richard and her allegations to the United States State Department. Khobragade was subsequently arrested, charged and later indicted by a grand jury with willful visa fraud under penalty of perjury along with an additional charge of submitting to the State Department a materially false and fraudulent employment contract for another individual. The Indian government, meanwhile, was allowed (with no reason given by the State Department) to transfer Khobragade to the United Nations in order for her to be covered by full diplomatic immunity. She subsequently returned to India, leaving behind her husband and two children, all of whom are United States citizens. Meanwhile, Richard's visa was cancelled by the Indian government, and she was repatriated back to India. She later returned to the United States under a non-immigrant status T visa, which is a special visa for trafficking victims and their family to come into the United States or remain in the United States in order to testify against individuals accused of trafficking crimes.

Despite some efforts to push for prosecution, Khobragade's fraud charge was eventually dismissed in February 2014. In an unexpected turn of events, the indictment against her was re-issued after the Indian government retaliated by expelling the very U.S. consular official who had assisted Richard

---

80. Colleen Long & Ashok Sharma, *Lawyer: Indian Housekeeper Did Not Extort Money*, AP, Dec. 19, 2013, http://news.yahoo.com/lawyer-indian-housekeeper-did-not-extort-money-203247611.html.

and her family with obtaining the T visa. Upon leaving the United States, Khobragade is said to have stated, "You have lost a good friend. It is unfortunate. In return, you get a maid and a drunken driver. They are in, and we are out."[81]

According to attorney Martina Vandenberg, the founder of The Human Trafficking Pro Bono Legal Center in Washington, DC, at least 21 civil cases and five criminal cases against foreign staff and officials were investigated in the United States over ten years leading up through 2013.[82] In many of the cases, the diplomats rendered their victims completely dependent on them by withholding the passports and visas (constituting false imprisonment under 22 U.S.C §7101(b)(1)), and threatening to expose them as illegal aliens facing deportation if they disobeyed (in violation of 22 U.S.C. §7101(b)(13)). Some of the reported cases against diplomats as summarized by Nick O'Malley in his article about the Khobragade case include:

- In June 2011, a former housekeeper had sued India's Consul General in New York, accusing him of intimidating her into a year of forced labor. A year later, he reportedly settled the case on undisclosed terms.
- In 2011, the director of the Taipei Economic and Cultural Office in Kansas City, Missouri, was deported from the United States after pleading guilty to enslaving two Filipina housekeepers. The two were made to work 16–18 hours a day, including weekends and holidays, and were paid only a quarter of their agreed wages. The victims received restitution of over $80,000 and were allowed to stay in the United States.
- In February 2012, a New York City Magistrates' Court judge fined a former press counselor for the Indian consulate $1.5 million for allegedly forcing an underage Indian girl to work without pay and meting out "barbaric treatment" to her. The counselor appealed the verdict but did not return to the US.
- In November 2012, a United Nations ambassador pleaded guilty to a misdemeanor charge of failing to pay his housekeeper the minimum wage in 2009. The ambassador did not invoke his diplomatic immunity and was ordered to pay a $5,000 fine and nearly $25,000 in back wages to the woman, whom he brought from the Philippines to take care of his home in New Jersey.

---

81. Ellen Barry & Benjamin Weiser, *As Indian Diplomat Exits After Arrest, a Culture Clash Lingers*, NY Times, Jan. 10, 2014.

82. O'Malley, *supra* note 79.

- In May 2012, United States officials rescued two Filipinas from a gated compound in northern Virginia owned by the government of Saudi Arabia. The compound had three gates and guards and one woman was reportedly trying to slip through the gates when she was rescued.
- The Minister of Consular affairs in the embassy of Tanzania and his wife were found guilty in January 2008 in federal district court of forcing a 20-year-old African woman into domestic slavery after bringing her to the country in 2000. Among many deprivations, the woman was forced to perform domestic service 112 hours per week for no pay.[83]
- In January 2007, three Indian women sued an attaché at the Kuwaiti embassy for paying them a fraction of their wages and submitting them to physical abuse and death threats after he brought them to the United States in the summer of 2005 to work as domestic servants.[84]

4. Bribery and Passive Participation

Bribery is an ancient means of corrupting any political system and debilitating the integrity of public officials. In many parts of the world, human traffickers establish ties to the political elites and state actors and pay them bribes to facilitate trafficking conspiracies. Corrupt public officials may have no direct participation in trafficking, but certainly benefit from illicit income. According to Transparency International, "Weak institutions offer weak protection. Pay-offs to police, courts, and other public sector officials result in state institutions being willing to turn a blind eye to trafficking gangs or even to participate in them."[85] Such activity is considered passive involvement.

An anonymous staffer working with an international non-government organization in Kolkata, India, explained to a researcher in 2011 that corruption exists from the top down and impedes the delivery of justice for victims of trafficking,[86] and that police officers are essentially indifferent toward Indian brothels suspected of trafficking in minors. In some cases, conditions for trafficked women and children actually worsen if the police take law enforcement action.

---

83. E. Benjamin Skinner, *Modern Day Slavery on D.C.'s Embassy Row?* TIME.COM, June 14, 2010, content.time.com/time/nation/article/0,8599,1996402,00.html.

84. *Id.*

85. *Breaking the Chain, supra* note 24.

86. Uddin, *supra* note 1, at 24

"Girls rescued from brothels are treated as criminals, and in many cases when they are kept in government remand homes, they face sexual abuse by the police and staffs."[87]

> In most cases brothel owners pay bribes to the authorities for returning the girls to the brothel. In such cases, the debt owed by the girls to the brothel owners and traffickers further increases as the costs of bribing is added to their labour debt.[88]

In 2011, officials of the Philippine Overseas Employment Administration (POEA) along with three private overseas work recruitment agencies were charged before the Philippine Department of Justice for human trafficking and violation of the country's *Anti-Graft and Corrupt Practices Act*.[89] The charges resulted from a whistleblower working in the POEA. Named in the criminal complaint were the Director IV for Adjudication; the Director II for Legal Research, Docket, and Enforcement Branch; Attorney V, of the Docket and Enforcement Division; an Administrative Aide VI (Sheriff); a POEA Web Administrator, and officers in three overseas work recruitment agencies in Manila.[90] According to the allegations, 100 Filipino workers were sent abroad by private recruitment agencies whose licenses POEA directors and staff knew had been canceled. In addition, high officials within POEA conspired to delay for long periods of time enforcing punitive orders to shut down agencies no longer licensed to do business due to recruitment violations:

> "There was human trafficking because OFWs were actually transported and recruited for overseas employment with the clear intent of exploiting them through forced labour and involuntary servitude as evidence by previous complaints against the same private respondents," the complaint read.
>
> "These OFWs were subjected to exploitation, forced labour, some of them to prostitution, they were not paid, not fed," said Assistant City Prosecutor Raymond Jonathan Lledo, National Task Force chairman of the Inter-Agency Council Against Trafficking (IACAT).[91]

---

87. *Id.*

88. *Id.*

89. Republic Act No. 3019 of August 17, 1960, http://www.lawphil.net/statutes/repacts/ra1960/ra_3019_1960.html.

90. Ina Reformina, *POEA Officials Charged with Human Trafficking, Corruption*, ABS-CBN News, Jan. 11, 2001, http://news.abs-cbn.com/globalfilipino/01/10/11/poea-officials-charged-human-trafficking-corruption.

91. *Id.*

The criminal complaint also alleged that the willful failure of POEA officials to execute signed orders against the unlicensed agencies resulted in exploitation in the commission of fraud.[92]

Halfway across the world in the European Union, corrupt police officials have likewise been found to engage in several different forms of bribery in relation to human trafficking. In EU states having liberal policies toward prostitution, police officers responsible for enforcing the licensing of prostitution are often bribed to 'turn a blind eye' to unlicensed, unregulated prostitution.[93] Bribery of police officers throughout the European Union is essential for providing protection for brothels and other sex businesses, and some police officers are also bribed by criminal organizations involved in human trafficking to leak information regarding ongoing police operations or to obstruct investigations.

Judicial officers are also pulled into involvement in human trafficking. In one such case in Spain, a judge was suspended from the General Counsel of Judicial Power after he was found to be engaged with a criminal network in prostitution and human trafficking.[94] In 2009, in Bratislava, Slovakia's Justice Minister dismissed the Chairwoman of the Bratislava I District Court on suspicion of influencing court proceedings in a case of human trafficking.[95]

In the Southern Hemisphere, New Zealand[96] has a thriving fishing industry within its 200 nautical mile exclusive economic zone (EEZ).[97] Following the implementation of a quota management system in 1986, many New Zealand com-

---

92. *Id.*

93. Gounev, *supra* note 12, at 80.

94. *Id.* at 81.

95. *Last Week's Major Political Happenings*, SITA SLOVENSKA TLACOVA AGENTURA, Oct. 4, 2009.

96. New Zealand took its first steps against human trafficking in 2002 when it ratified the *Palermo Protocol*. In 2009, the Department of Labour convened an Interagency Working Group on People Trafficking. In conjunction with a number of other government departments, the Working Group released The Plan of Action to Prevent People Trafficking. The Plan of Action to Prevent People Trafficking is "a proactive whole-of-government approach to people trafficking issues for New Zealand, outlining a comprehensive response to any future people trafficking cases." It also identified gaps in any government agencies with regard to protecting victims of human trafficking. In 2012, an inter-ministerial inquiry outlined specific steps for the government to take to prevent labor trafficking onboard FVCs. But these steps were not yet implemented as of 2013. *See Plan of Action to Prevent People Trafficking*, MINISTRY OF BUS., INNOVATION & EMP., LABOUR INFORMATION. (undated), http://evawglobaldatabase.unwomen.org/en/countries/oceania/newzealand/2009/plan-of-action-toprevent-peopletrafficking.

97. Established in 1997.

panies invested in fishing vessels, growing the industry from serving primarily domestic markets to become a global exporter with 90 percent of all fish landed being shipped abroad.[98] Many fishing vessels operating in the EEZ are foreign chartered (FCV) and crewed by foreign workers. While it is difficult to determine how much revenue is made from New Zealand waters, in 2009, the value of the nation's commercial fish stocks surpassed US$4 billion.[99]

Investigations into New Zealand's fishing industry have revealed that a significant amount of commercial fishing is done with slave labor, which directly and indirectly benefits New Zealand's economy. The Ministry of Agriculture and Forestry acknowledges the problem and has posited that roughly 40 percent of squid exported from New Zealand is caught on vessels using forced labor. It is also believed that 15 percent of New Zealand's exports of hoki (also known as blue grenadier or blue hake) and 8 percent of its southern blue whiting may be "slave-caught"[100] as well, despite the New Zealand government having a stated policy that an FCV worker must receive the same terms, conditions and protections from mistreatment and exploitation as a New Zealander.[101] The government has been aware of these conditions since at least the mid-1990s,[102] but FVC worker abuse went largely ignored by the authorities until the 2010 sinking of the Oyang 70, a South Korean fishing trawler contracted to a New Zealand-based company.[103] The crew comprised individuals from Indonesia, the Philippines, South Korea, and China. On August 18, 2010, the large ship suddenly sank, killing six crew members. The tragedy received significant media scrutiny over corruption in the fishing industry, and in the wake

---

98. *The New Zealand Fishing Industry*, MINISTRY FOR PRIMARY INDUS., Oct. 16, 2012, http://www.fish.govt.nz/en-nz/Commercial/About+the+Fishing+Industry/default.htm.

99. *Commercial Fish Stocks Valued at over $4 Billion*, STATISTICS N.Z., Feb. 24, 2010, http://www.stats.govt.nz/browse_for_stats/Corporate/Corporate/CorporateCommunications_MR2009.aspx.

100. E. Benjamin Skinner, *The Fishing Industry's Cruelest Catch*, BLOOMBERG BUS., Feb. 23, 2012, http://www.bloomberg.com/bw/articles/2012-02-23/the-fishing-industrys-cruelest-catch#p2.

101. *See* Christina Stringer, Glenn Simmons, & Daren Coulston, *Not in New Zealand's Waters, Surely? Labour and Human Rights Abuses Aboard Foreign Fishing Vessels*, N.Z. Asia Institute Working Paper Series, Working Paper No. 11-01 (2011), http://docs.business.auckland.ac.nz/Doc/11-01-Not-in-New-Zealand-waters-surely-NZAI-Working-Paper-Sept-2011.pdf.

102. In 1997 Russian owned vessel, *Udovenko, was forfeited to the Crown after* crew members complained of non-payment and alterations of hours worked. *See* Thomas Harré, *Human Trafficking in New Zealand: A Review of Recent Case Law*, NZ LAWYER MAG. ONLINE, Jan. 14, 2014, http://www.nzlawyermagazine.co.nz/sections/special-reports/human-trafficking-in-new-zealand-a-review-of-recent-case-law-183130.aspx.

103. *Id.*

of the sinking, crewmembers alleged physical abuse, non-payment and under payment of wages, a plethora of deprivations, and debt bondage.[104]

The New Zealand government launched an official inquiry, including interviews of fisheries observers.[105] One observer described abusive and slave like conditions and recalled seeing a South Korean officer hitting Indonesian workers in the head with a 26 pound pan, resulting in a profusely bleeding wound that required 26 stitches to close.[106] No criminal charges resulted from the Oyang 70 sinking; only recommendations regarding vessel safety that were submitted to the Minister for Primary Industries and the Minister of Transport. Among other findings, the report revealed that enforcement problems and lack of monitoring of the industry allowed the foreign operators of vessels working New Zealand waters to flout with impunity sec. 103 of New Zealand's *Fisheries Act of 1983*.[107]

In 2006 a *Code of Practice for Foreign Fishing Crew: Regulatory Framework* was introduced by New Zealand's Department of Labour.[108] But that amendment to the country's *Fisheries Act* did little to alter conditions in the industry at the time of the Oyang 70 sinking four years later, and while the widows of the lost crewmen were compensated by the Accident Compensation Corporation, no compensation was ever offered by the fishing company as required under New Zealand law.[109] Interestingly, Annex 3 of the official report from the Department of Labour was "heavily censored in the version released to the public."[110]

---

104. *Id.*

105. *Id.* Observers are not hired to "observe" abuse against people, but to "monitor the environmental impact of fishing activity and record accurate and reliable data relating to vessel catch and processing.

106. Skinner, *supra* note 100.

107. Jennifer Devlin, *Modern Day Slavery: Employment Conditions for Foreign Fishing Crews in New Zealand Waters*, 23 Australian & New Zealand Maritime L.J. 82, 88 (2009), http://www.austlii.edu.au/au/journals/ANZMarLawJl/2009/9.pdf.

108. *See* New Zealand Human Rights Lawyers Association, *Fisheries (Foreign Charter Vessels and Other Matters) Amendment Bill to the Primary Production Committee*, Mar. 25, 2013, at 3, fn.7.

"In 2006 the Code of Practice on Foreign Fishing Crew was introduced by the Department of Labour due to serious concerns about employment conditions in the fishing industry. The Code sets out minimum working and living conditions that need to be met before visas will be granted to foreign crewmembers. Notably, the code provides that crews must always be paid at least the minimum New Zealand wage. It also puts in place reporting and inspection requirements, and access to the relevant bodies established to resolve disputes arising under employment agreements."

109. Under the Minimum Wage Act 1983, and the Holidays Act 2003, respectively.

110. Devlin, *supra* note 106. "Concerns raised included: pay as low as US$140 per month

This case and others similar to it show that the New Zealand government is well aware of problems of serious abuse in the fishing industry, that the Department of Labour acknowledges abuse onboard FCV vessels, and that some awards have been made for financial, physical and sexual abuse. The New Zealand legal system appears to possess a clear understanding of "the parameters of forced labour,"[111] but lacks comprehensive anti-trafficking laws to protect the FCV workers and prosecute those who abuse them. The *Crimes Act of 1961* and the *Wages Protection Act of 1983* apply to FCV workers, but each law is limited in scope.[112] The *Crimes Act* criminalizes only some specific forms of forced labor while the *Wages Protection Act* prohibits fraudulent employment and recruiting practices and provides for penalties up to $250,000 and 20 years imprisonment.[113]

In 2012, a *Bloomberg Business Week* issue published the results of a half year investigation into FCV debt bondage and labor trafficking on at least ten fishing vessels operating under contract with New Zealand companies in territorial waters.[114] The report made a strong case for widespread fraud under both the *Crimes Act* and the *Wages Protection Act*. Yet, even in the face of documented, blatant human trafficking violations, complaints and reports, the government has as of this writing neither prosecuted any ship captains, nor tried to cooperate with worker source countries in shutting down disreputable private recruitment offices.[115]

Another wrinkle in the political arena regarding New Zealand's fishing industry is that the Maori native peoples control over 30 percent of the commercial fisheries, and as of April 15, 2014, the Ngāpuhi iwi, New Zealand's second largest Māori group, won a parliamentary amendment that would permit its fishing fleet to continue using FCV workers. The Ngāpuhi leadership argued that without such labor and large commercial vessels, New Zealand and the indigenous sector of the country would lose US$300 million annually.[116]

---

with heavy deductions making actual pay even lower; serious physical and mental abuse; working hours of 12 hours or more per day; denial of access to passports or fisherman's books; no washing or laundry facilities; no provision for differing religious or cultural needs; poor food and no food at all when fishing was poor."

111. Harré, *supra* note 102.

112. TIP Report 2014, *supra* note 49, at 291–93.

113. *Id.* at 161–62.

114. Skinner, *supra* note 100.

115. *Id.*

116. Other corporations apart from the New Zealand fishing industry have threatened to boycott, claiming that the "special treatment" toward the native tribe is a national scandal. *See* Michael Field, *Fishing Pay Fight Damaging NZ*, STUFF.CO.NZ, Apr. 8, 2015, http://www.stuff.co.nz/ business/industries/9943488/Fishing-pay-fight-damaging-NZ.

Conditions in New Zealand strongly suggest that the government is stuck in a cultural, ethical and business model conundrum. Perhaps because so much money is involved in the maritime industry, and because that industry is vital to the island nation's economy and to issues involving the rights of indigenous peoples and economic development, the government chooses passively to look the other way and allow trafficking and forced labor of foreign fishermen to continue—a textbook example of the end justifying the means.[117]

We see similar conditions persist in the commercial shrimping industry in Thailand, where multinational corporations involved in shrimp farming have been engaged in trafficking workers to farm and process shrimp that is sold cheaply in big-box stores worldwide, particularly in the United States. This form of human trafficking of workers to produce consumer goods to mass markets has become known as the Walmart Effect. Narong Seafood is a major supplier of cooked, peeled, frozen shrimp, and is considered a model company that enjoys a longtime supply arrangement with Walmart stores.[118] Thailand imports multitudes of foreign labor, including workers trafficked illegally from Myanmar, Cambodia, and Laos. Once in Thailand, they are subjected to horrible working conditions, "including under and nonpayment of wages, violations of minimum wage laws, long overtime hours, dangerous and unsanitary working conditions and the systematic denial of freedom of association and collective bargaining rights."[119]

Thailand's fishing industry has been under close "watchdog" scrutiny for several years going back to at least 2008 when the AFL-CIO Solidarity Centre released its report, *The True Cost of Shrimp*, focusing on conditions of exploitation faced by shrimp processing workers in Thailand.[120] Following release of the report, the Thai government and the Thai Frozen Foods Association introduced reforms to monitor shrimp processing facilities and enforce labor

---

117. *See* Harré, *supra* note 102. There is also evidence that organized crime has been involved in widespread forging of New Zealand passports for purposes of forced labor. Charges and convictions were brought against perpetrators in one case, but the court declined to address the issue of trafficking. *See R v Rahimi* CA4/02 (30 April 2002).

118. Briefing Paper: The Walmart Effect: Child and Worker Rights Violations at Narong Seafood, Thailand's Model Shrimp Processing Factory, Sept. 24, 2013, Laborrights.org, undated, http://www.laborrights.org/publications/walmart-effect-child-andworker-rights-violations-narong-seafood.

119. *Id.* at Briefing Paper, page 2.

120. *Id. See also* Solidarity Centre, The Degradation of Work the True Cost of Shrimp: How Shrimp Industry Workers in Bangladesh and Thailand Pay the Price for Affordable Shrimp (2008), http://www.solidaritycenter.org/wp-content/uploads/2014/12/pubs_True_Cost_of_Shrimp.pdf.

standards. Among the mandates were that shrimp producers exporting to the United States market must meet the Association's "membership criteria as well as the standards established by the Global Aquaculture Alliance's Best Aqua-culture Practices (BAP) certification system which includes provisions for fair treatment of workers."[121] As a major buyer of cheap shrimp from Thailand, Walmart, which has its own standards for suppliers, joined BAP, understand-ing that the Alliance conducts audits of the production facilities of its mem-bers. However, the audit process was discovered to be significantly flawed. But neither the BAP audits nor Walmart's audits are subject to public review or verification by outside organizations,[122] which essentially allows Walmart and its suppliers to maintain control of their own narratives about the conditions of workers who process products for consumers. Regardless, the Solidarity Centre's researchers discovered that Narong managers were given advance no-tice of audits and took evasive actions to be in compliance when inspectors ar-rived, practicing a de facto shell game with regulatory authorities. This included ensuring that inspections did not occur during the night shifts. Plant man-agers then staffed the night shifts with underage workers and undocumented migrant workers in order to avoid detection by inspectors that normally only come during the day.[123] One worker interviewed by Solidarity Centre re-searchers stated that auditors performed only cursory inspections and would "speak mostly to the management."[124] Some workers also reported that man-agers hand-selected workers to be interviewed by the auditors and instructed them on how to answer questions. They were also instructed to wear clean uni-forms on inspection days.[125] Widespread immigration documentation fraud and severe labor violations were also reported. The Solidarity Centre's re-searchers concluded that the auditing regimes have serious shortcomings and that the highly lucrative large-retail market, particularly in the United States, continues to encourage high volume suppliers like Narong Seafood to engage in corrupt practices. Ironically, despite evidence of several acts of corrupt con-duct, Narong Seafood was awarded for leadership and fair trade by the eco-nomic crime division of the Thai government.[126]

Point of contact with human trafficking at international border crossings creates constant temptations for border agents and supervisors to accept bribes

---

121. *Id.* at 2.
122. *Id.* at 3.
123. *Id.* at 5.
124. *Id.*
125. *Id.*
126. *Id.* at 1.

or to participate passively in criminal activities involving human trafficking. There is not a border in the world that corruption through bribery does not threaten. Along the United States-Mexico border, customs agents and border guards on both sides face a constant barrage of bribes and offers to engage in human trafficking operations. Often, the rewards to merely look the other way can far surpass a border agent's annual salary. Sometimes, government efforts to improve security by adding border personnel actually results in higher instances of corrupt acts. This is believed to have occurred along the United States-Mexico border in June and July 2006, when two brothers working at U.S. Border Patrol offices disappeared while being investigated for corruption.[127] During the same period, two U.S. Customs and Border Protection agents were indicted for taking bribes to allow illegal immigrants to cross the border, and two U.S. Border Patrol supervisors "pleaded guilty to accepting nearly $200,000 in payoffs to release smugglers and illegal immigrants who had been detained."[128] Investigators believed that the lowering of hiring standards to build up personnel numbers, along with an increase in the fees demanded by traffickers that led to more pressure to offer bribes, were contributing factors to corrupt acts occurring.[129]

5. Coercion and Blackmail

Like bribery, coercion and blackmail of law enforcement officers occur worldwide. Some police officers commit blackmail against sex workers to guarantee police protection and avoid raids, and traffickers blackmail and coerce police officers into allowing trafficking crimes to occur. This is a difficult problem in nations such as Argentina, where women may work legally as sex workers, but police corruption blurs the lines between those who choose sex work as a legal profession and those who are forced into involuntary prostitution.[130]

In the European Union, police officers can be corrupted with blackmail by prostitutes and organized crime syndicates engaged in human trafficking. One method is to record secretly police officers gambling and having sex with legal prostitutes. The recordings are then used at a later time to compromise the of-

---

127. John Pomfret, *Bribery at Border Worries Officials*, WASH. POST, July 15, 2006, http://www.washingtonpost.com/wp-dyn/content/article/2006/07/14/AR2006071401525.html.

128. *Id.*

129. *Id.*

130. Jason McNamara, *Let's Debate Human Trafficking without Judging Sex Workers*, BUENOS AIRES HERALD, May 11, 2014.

ficers and to exhort information from them about police operations.[131] Likewise, criminal organizations in several EU countries are known to use prostitutes (and human trafficking victims) to blackmail and compromise judges in order to avoid investigations, influence trials, receive lower sentences, and to divert sensitive cases involving political elites.[132]

6. Accountability and Transparency

The corrosive influence of corruption persists where there is little transparency and accountability for corrupt acts. Impunity breeds contempt for the law and misdirects an individual's moral compass. For some actors, engaging in corruption is a numbers game; they think that the legal system is in such a state of turmoil that the chances of being caught and held accountable for corrupt deeds are very slim.

Curbing corruption requires that many sets of factors be brought together in a coordinated manner.

First, education and training, and continuing education and training, are vital to deterring individuals from engaging in corrupt acts over the long term. The *Palermo Protocol* has been quite clear on this, directing States Parties to "endeavor to undertake measures such as research, information and mass media campaigns and social and economic initiatives to prevent and combat trafficking in persons,"[133] and to "adopt or strengthen legislative or other measures, such as educational, social or cultural measures, including through bilateral and multilateral cooperation, to discourage the demand that fosters all forms of exploitation of persons, especially women and children, that leads to trafficking."[134] The *Palermo Protocol* also directs States Parties to:

> [p]rovide or strengthen training for law enforcement, immigration and other relevant officials and the prevention of trafficking in persons. The training should focus on methods used in preventing such trafficking, prosecuting the traffickers and protecting the rights of the victims, including protecting the victims from the traffickers. The training should also take into account the need to consider human rights and child- and gender-sensitive issues and it should encourage

---

131. Gounev, *supra* note 12, at 81.
132. *Id.*
133. Palermo Protocol, art. 9(2).
134. *Id.* art. 9(5).

cooperation with non-governmental organizations, other relevant organizations and other elements of civil society.[135]

Among other things, this means that judges who serve on the bench should
be required to pass an education course, generally about human trafficking,
and specifically about human trafficking—related corruption. Law enforcement officials need to be trained by experts in combating human trafficking,
as well as by internal affairs personnel specially trained to monitor, investigate,
and address the many issues of corruption. State actors who assume positions
of diplomatic authority must be trained to understand that their high positions of public trust and the immunities that come with service abroad do not
give them carte blanche to engage in corrupt conduct or to take advantage of
loopholes and privileges for their own personal benefit.

Second, continual monitoring and vigilance to improve and sustain accountability are also necessary. Law enforcement and other state actors must
know that their conduct and work product are subject to constant review and
vetting. Establishing a "culture" of monitoring is expressed throughout the
Palermo Protocol, from obligations of States Parties to take measures to secure
the integrity of travel and identity documents,[136] for instance, to training law
enforcement, immigration or other relevant authorities to "cooperate with one
another by exchanging information, in accordance with their domestic law,"[137]
and to "strengthening cooperation among border control agencies by, inter
alia, establishing and maintaining direct channels of communication."[138]

Third, those who may be tempted to engage in corrupt activities must know
ahead of time that the system in which they work will bring the full force of
the law down upon them if they are caught engaging in corruption. Of course,
this is a difficult policy to enforce in weak and failing states, in places where
strong government authority is largely absent, or where a culture of profes-
sionalism among government workers and law enforcement is lacking. For individuals who are in situations where they may be blackmailed or coerced into
engaging in corrupt practices, there should be strategies in place to provide
some form of assistance to avoid or mitigate misconducts—something akin
to a diversionary program. Regardless, sanctions and punishments must have
teeth; penalties cannot continue to be of such a *de minimis* nature that state
actors are willing to risk getting caught.

---

135. *Id.* art. 10(2).
136. *Id.* art. 12.
137. *Id.* art. 10(1).
138. *Id.* art. 11(6).

Fourth, creating incentives within government service must, whenever possible, be of such a benefit to state actors that they will not feel the need to enrich themselves via corrupt practices. Professionalizing law enforcement by giving officers livable wages, bestowing benefits that extend to their families, and instilling in them a strong sense that they are stakeholders in their government and stewards of the rule of law, are all vital to reducing the pull of corruption.[139]

7. Is the "System" Corrupt?

One of the most increasingly assertive voices emerging in human trafficking issues comes from an unlikely coalition of organized adult sex workers who feel that anti-human trafficking crusaders who want to outlaw all forms of commercial sex have manipulated the laws, law enforcement, policymakers and public opinion to push morality agendas, and that in doing so, the anti-human trafficking movement has introduced and constitutes an element of corruption within the system. This is a particularly thorny and controversial allegation. However, this particular group of critics has raised legitimate questions, if perhaps in unorthodox ways, and has challenged the methods, motivations, and outcomes of the anti-human trafficking movement in both the public sector and among HT NGOs. Their unique perspective as outsiders to the establishment narrative, and the sometimes bold and brutally frank manner in which they challenge data and claims made by anti-human trafficking groups, legislators, and law enforcement raise the question of whether the "system" is inherently corrupt.

This is a concern not only for the United States, but in all countries where prostitution and escorting and various forms of sex entertainment are under attack from religious groups and conservative feminist movements. The underlying narrative asserted by these two groups, generally speaking, is that all forms of sex work is sex trafficking, and all adult sex workers are trafficking victims. Sex worker rights advocates bristle at the notion that the profession in which they choose to make a living is labeled as sex trafficking and slavery. They see such branding as a tactic to outlaw all adult prostitution, and label all men as sex offenders.

According to one advocate for sex workers rights, Christine Monfort, the zeal to label all consensual prostitution and adult entertainment as traffick-

---

139. Luz E. Nagle, The Search for Accountability and Transparency in Plan Colombia: Reforming Judicial Institutions—Again 27–8 (Strategic Studies Institute, United States Army War College, 2001).

ing "hurts any real victims because it labels all sex workers as victims."[140] Monfort argues that anti-human trafficking groups, particularly those that are conservative faith-based, misrepresent and falsify statistics and create false narratives knowing that no one bothers to check the veracity and accuracy of the claims they endorse. "A big reason they do this is because it provides high-paying jobs for them. They get big donations, and grants from the government, charity, churches, etc. to have these groups, and pay these high salaries of the anti-prostitution workers."[141] As Alex Andrews,[142] another advocate for decriminalization of sex work, put it, "The 'bad actors' have influenced the political process and created a stage where they can play out their moral outrage and collect ticket money from both the audience and the supporting cast."[143]

Complaints have also been raised that the laws against trafficking are written in such a way that unscrupulous individuals are able to use them for their personal advantage. Monfort asserts that if an illegal alien is taken in as a trafficking victim all s/he has to do is play the game to take full advantage of the United States antitrafficking prostitution laws, particularly the Trafficking Victim Protection Act. Undocumented individuals brought before the authorities as assumed trafficking victims know that they do not have to go to jail or be arrested, they get to stay in America and become United States citizens, and the government will provide housing, food, education, "and will cater to them since they will be considered victims."[144] This may seem to some as an allegation without merit, but it is a sentiment in circulation among individuals who are intimately familiar with these issues because they are among the population that the so-called rescue industry targets. These individuals' opinions and conclusions are valid, certainly among themselves, and their viewpoint and perspective must be taken into consideration. This also illustrates the level of vitriol present among the individuals and groups involved in confronting human trafficking issues.

If it is accurate that a system that has been set up to help trafficking victims becomes corrupted by unscrupulous individuals who see an opportunity to

140. Christine Monfort, *Stop Calling Adult Consensual Prostitution Human Trafficking!!!* Petition posted on the change.org webpage in 2012, https://www.change.org/p/stop-calling-adult-consensual-prostitution-human-trafficking.

141. *Id.*

142. Alex Andrews is an alias used to protect herself from possible retaliation from some faith-based organizations.

143. Email exchange with Alex Andrews and the author, June 19, 2016.

144. Monfort, *supra* note 140.

take advantage of it for personal gain, then how do we prevent this? Has the anti-trafficking movement become so big, so bureaucratic, and so controlled by special interests and moralistic agendas that the system itself has become inherently and unavoidably corrupt and unaccountable?

A. Follow the Money

As it turns out, some allegations of malfeasance leveled at the rescue industry by sex worker rights advocates have been substantiated. In 2008, the United States Department of Justice Office of the Inspector General's Audit Division released a report about publically funded anti-human trafficking programs and organizations, and the results were very troubling.[145] Among the findings were that despite the tremendous outlay of government funding to service organizations and U.S. Bureau of Justice Assistance (BJA) task forces, the reported number of trafficking victims assisted was underwhelming. The audit analyzed 19 service agreements and supplements awarded to seven service providers and found "a wide variation in the amount of funds awarded compared to the number of victims each agreement recipient anticipated serving."[146]

> For example, one service provider received $1,896,535 to supply services to an estimated 100 victims over the three-year agreement period, or $18,965 per estimated victim. Another provider received $490,829 to service an estimated 100 victims over the three-year agreement period, or $4,908 per estimated victim. For the 19 agreements and supplements we tested, the amount awarded per anticipated victim ranged from a high of $33,333 to a low of $2,500.

There were several inaccuracies discovered in the reporting processes by the service organizations and the BJA task forces. The auditors reviewed the records for 620 of the 2,128 reported victims and could verify only 234 of the 620 as being victims as defined by the Trafficking Victims Protection Act.[147] Further-

---

145. U.S. Dep't of Justice, Office of the Inspector General Audit Division, Management of the Office of Justice Programs' Grant Programs for Trafficking Victims, Audit Report 08-26, July 2008. The primary tasks of the audit were to: (1) assess the adequacy of the Office of Justice Programs' design and management of human trafficking grant program; (2) evaluate the extent to which grantees have administered the grants in accordance with applicable laws, regulations, guidelines, and terms and conditions of the grant awards; and (3) assess the effectiveness of the grant programs in assisting trafficking victims.

146. *Id.* at vii.

147. *Id.* at x.

more, the Office of Inspector General auditors uncovered serious deficiencies in how the service providers managed federal grants given to them during the grant period. The findings were considered to be systemic and warranted additional guidance and direction by the U.S. Department of Justice Office of Victims of Crime and BJA for all human trafficking program grantees. The deficiencies identified included:[148]

- Goals and accomplishments—Six of the seven grantees had not met or were not accomplishing one or more project goals.
- Reporting—Three of the seven grantees submitted Financial Status Reports containing inaccurate financial data, and three of the seven grantees had a significant problem in submitting program progress reports in a timely manner.
- Fund Drawdowns—Three of the seven grantees drew down funds too early to meet immediate needs, and one grantee did not maintain adequate accounting records to determine if the funds were drawn down appropriately.
- Local Match—Four of the seven grantees had significant deficiencies related to supporting matching funds claimed against the agreements.

The following two findings are particularly concerning:[149]

- Expenditures—Six of the seven grantees claimed expenditures totaling $1,488,956 that, at the time of the audits, were either not authorized; not properly classified and supported; not accurately recorded; not reasonable, allocable, or allowable; not necessary to the project; or not in accordance with applicable laws, regulations, guidelines, and terms and conditions of the cooperative agreements. As of June 19, 2008, the Office of Justice Programs and the grantees had completed actions to remedy only $56,710 of the $1,488,956 in questioned direct expenditures.
- Indirect Costs—At the time of the audits, three of the seven grantees claimed $271,071 in unallowable or unsupported indirect costs. As of June 19, 2009, the grantees had not provided documentation to support any of the questioned indirect costs.

Even more troubling is that the findings could suggest that the Office of Justice Programs grant managers seemed to be either mismanaging their responsibilities, inept, or incompetent, because the auditors found that the systemic

---

148. *Id.* at xi–xii.
149. *Id.*

deficiencies they identified persisted despite *past* Office of Inspector General reviews of Office of Justice Programs grant programs that found similar grant administration deficiencies.

Additional examination of some HT NGOs has revealed "a remarkable lack of fiscal accountability and organizational consistency, often even eschewing an open acknowledgement of board members, professional affiliates and funding relationships."[150] Even keeping track of an HT NGO can present a challenge because some "fold, move, restructure, and reappear under new names with alarming frequency, making them almost as difficult to track as their supposed foes."[151]

B. Bishops and Bureaucrats

At least one prominent public interest law organization has challenged the conduct of a prominent HT NGO. The American Civil Liberties Union (ACLU) filed a lawsuit on March 17, 2016, in Federal District Court for the Southern District of New York against the federal agency Administration for Children and Families (ACF), seeking records concerning the United States Conference of Catholic Bishops (USCCB).[152] The ACLU lawsuit filed under a Freedom of Information Act (FOIA) request[153] asks for production of agency records related to federal government funds awarded to the USCCB under the Trafficking Victim Protection Act (TVPA). The ACLU contends that in 2006, the Office of Refugee Resettlement (ORR), a subdivision of ACF, "provided a multi-year, multi-million dollar contract to USCCB to distribute funds as subcontracts to organizations that directly serve trafficked individuals,"[154] and permitted the USCCB "to prohibit all subcontractors from using federal funds to pay for abortion and contraception services and referrals, based solely on USCCB's religious beliefs."[155] Denying reproductive health services, the ACLU contends, can further victimize trafficked individuals, stressing that, "Victims of severe forms of human trafficking frequently need reproductive health care services and referrals to lead safe lives, become self-sufficient, and protect themselves

---

150. Anne Elizabeth Moore, *Special Report: Money and Lies in Anti-Human Trafficking NGOs*, Truthout.org, Jan. 27, 2015, http://www.truth-out.org/news/item/28763-special-report-money-and-lies-in-anti-human-trafficking-ngos.

151. *Id.*

152. *American Civil Liberties Union v. Administration for Children and Families*, No. 1:16-cv-01987 (S.D.N.Y.); amended complaint filed March 29, 2016 [hereinafter ACLU].

153. Filed under 5 U.S.C. §552 (2012).

154. ACLU, *supra* note 152, at ¶3.

155. *Id.*

and others." Such services include "emergency contraception, condoms, and in some cases abortion."

In a subsequent amended complaint, the ACLU asserts that the contract awarded to the USCCB included the disbursement of more than $15.9 million over the course of five and a half years and that USCCB kept over $5.3 million of the funds[156] for administrative services and expenses.[157] According to the complaint:

> The Freedom Network — a national coalition of antitrafficking organizations — raised concerns about the contract, stating: "[T]rafficked persons interested in avoiding sexually-transmitted diseases and pregnancy often approach social services agencies for contraception and referrals. Moreover, trafficked persons who have been raped by their traffickers often approach social service providers for information regarding abortion services."[158]

Based on these concerns, the ACLU filed a lawsuit in United States District Court in Massachusetts alleging that the government's ORR contract violated the Establishment Clause of the First Amendment of the United States Constitution. The District Court subsequently agreed, ruling that the government violated the establishment clause "insofar as they delegated authority to a religious organization to impose religiously based restrictions on the expenditure of taxpayer funds, and thereby impliedly endorsed the religious beliefs of the USCCB and the Catholic Church."[159] What is quite startling, however, is that in the course of overturning the lower court order, the United States Court of Appeals for the First Circuit wrote that this oversight by the ORR would not happen again in the foreseeable future, because "the defendants are high-ranking federal officials, including a cabinet member, who have, as a matter of policy, abandoned the prior practice and adopted a concededly constitutional replacement."[160]

Federal government grants to HT NGOs are awarded based on applications presented to the government in response to Funding Opportunity Announce-

---

156. A surprising 33 percent of the total award went to internal expenses. In a later response by the government to the ACLU's amended complaint, the ACF stated that the contract award was actually $18,839,323 and that the total administrative expenses were $5,929,425, "representing approximately 31% of the total costs. *See* Answer to the Complaint, filed by the US Attorney's Office for ACF on February 25, 2016 at ¶ 17.

157. ACLU, *supra* note 152, at ¶ 17.

158. *Id.* at ¶ 18.

159. *Id.* at ¶ 20.

160. *Id.* at ¶ 22.

ments (FOA). In 2015, ORR issued a new FOA, including language that was more mindful of potential *religious objections* (emphasis added) by providers to the Trafficking Victim Assistance Program's service and referral requirements.[161] That language states:

> If an organization has a religious objection to providing any of the services or referrals required in the program, it may propose an approach to meeting its grant obligations consistent with ACF's faith-based policy. The alternative approach must be one that accomplishes the goal of ensuring that trafficking victims understand the full range of services available to them, including reproductive health services, and that there is a mechanism by which victims requesting such services can receive appropriate referrals. If an alternative approach is proposed, ORR will decide whether to accept the alternative approach, based upon a determination of whether the alternative approach will ensure timely referrals to all services and/or referrals for which the individual is eligible, is not burdensome to the client, and is operationally feasible for ACF.[162]

Fast forward to September 2015, the USCCB applied for and was again awarded a grant from ACF, this time in the amount of $2 million, to provide comprehensive case management to foreign-born victims of trafficking as part of the Trafficking Victim Assistance Program. Not surprisingly, the USCCB has not changed its position on refusing services that it deems contrary to its religious beliefs. The ACLU filed a FOIA with ACF on November 13, 2015, and received no reply beyond confirmation of receipt of the request. According to the ACLU, "the records sought in the instant request will significantly contribute to the public understanding of the operations and activities of [Health and Human Services] and its grantees."[163]

As would be expected, the government rejected the ACLU's complaint on several grounds not germane to this present discussion, but on May 17, 2016, the Department of Justice attorney presented a letter to the court confirming that the FOIA request was being fulfilled by DHS and ACF. At the time of this writing, the litigation is ongoing. The ACLU sees the USCCB litigation as a case of a powerful constituent getting special treatment to receive funding at the taxpayers' expense under a contract that was found by a federal court to violate the Establishment Clause. This is analogous to someone having their

---

161. *Id.* at ¶ 24.
162. *Id.* at ¶ 24.
163. *Id.* at ¶ 36.

cake and eating it too. The ACLU's lead attorney for the lawsuit puts it quite succinctly: "We are shocked and deeply concerned to see history repeating itself with millions of taxpayer dollars funneled into the hands of a religious group that has a long history of refusing critical health care services to the most vulnerable people in their care."[164] Moreover, the government essentially gave special treatment to the USCCB, knowing that it would not provide all the services to trafficking victims that the Trafficking Victims Assistance Program mandates.

When the ACLU challenged this murky relationship, while the litigation arising from 2006 was underway, the government stated that the lawsuit was moot because it had ended its relationship with the USCCB and would not contract with the Catholic Bishops in the future. Yet, in 2015 the government again awarded a grant of more than $2 million to USCCB to assist trafficking victims. This litigation provides a striking example of the relationships between the government, which is mandated to fulfill programs created by federal law, and powerful nongovernment organizations that are positioned to gain the lion's share of funding with what appears to be very little monitoring or oversight. It takes a watchdog legal organization like the ACLU to challenge these relationships. We are then left to ask whether there is corruption on the part of the government that colludes with nongovernmental organizations to fill legislative mandates, or whether the corruption is on the part of the NGOs taking advantage of a system that for lack of a better description is susceptible to influential constituencies, or both. Is this also corruption when the government continues to fund a powerful constituent *knowing* that the constituent retains the right to refuse services that are anathema to its religious beliefs?

The ACLU is one of the most potent and vigilant legal organizations in the United States for monitoring and calling out unethical practices, misconduct, and corrupt acts. But the ACLU does not have the manpower to monitor an entire community of HT NGOs, large and small. It must pick and choose which groups to hold accountable to the taxpayers. This leaves a considerable void for monitoring conducts. Unethical and fraudulent actors within the rescue industry know that the chances of being caught are quite slim. For this reason, one might conclude that the rescue industry seems to attract dishonest individuals. Indeed, it is a community of nongovernment and nonprofit organizations that is ripe for the pickings by scam artists, grafters, and other individuals who may start out with noble intentions but gradually succumb to

---

164. *FOIA Lawsuit Demands Records on $2 Million Contract to U.S. Conference of Catholic Bishops*, ACLU Press Release, Mar. 17, 2016, https://www.aclu.org/news/aclu-sues-federal-records-grant-religious-group-obstructs-trafficking-victims-access.

the allure of personal enrichment from susceptible donors and government grants awarded by grant monitors who do not seem to look too carefully at the organizations being funded, or worse, have developed personal relationships with individuals running the organizations that constitute a conflict of interest that may result in corrupt acts occurring.

C. Come and Get It

In June 2016, Florida Governor Rick Scott announced the disbursement of more than $6.8 million in state government grants to a handful of HT NGOs to fund safe houses and other services for human trafficking survivors statewide.[165] Among eight organizations receiving funding, three received over $1 million and one of those three received over $3 million.

A review of the application of the organization receiving the highest award, Open Doors, raises some concerns about the vetting process undertaken by the state officials who granted nearly half of the available funding to an organization whose proposal was only to "provide a framework and program design to make better use of existing services and improve their delivery."[166] One might question whether a state government should divert precious resources from victim-centered programs to one that is merely placing another layer of bureaucracy between the problem and solution. Looking at Open Door's proposed budget also raises some questions. For example, of the $2.9 million requested for the budget, nearly half (approximately $1.5 million) seems to be going to pay staff salaries and compensation, and of that amount, it appears that $500,000 is being paid to the head of the organization who is listed as the Statewide Contractor, though this distinction is unclear. Equally perplexing, is the budgeted amount of $800,000 for rent and other office expenses and additional costs for anticipated travel.

While the Governor's intentions are in the right place as a matter of public policy, questions may arise about transparency in the process of determining which organizations get the funding. What is the vetting process and the criteria for selecting the recipients, and is the criteria easily available to the public for scrutiny? Do any of the beneficiary organizations engage in religious practices that would violate the separation of church and state? Do grant applicants have any kind of history of taking advantage of trafficking victims in

---

165. *Gov. Scott Highlights Efforts to Fight Human Trafficking in Florida*, WCTV EYE-WITNESS NEWS, June 28, 2016, http://www.wctv.tv/content/news/Gov-Scott-highlights-efforts-to-fight-human-trafficking-in-Florida-384672341.html.

166. Proposal on file with the author.

order to solicit donations in a manner that may violate privacy protections? Does the selection process create unnecessary animosity among competing HT NGOs that may feel that the "system" is politically motivated and unfair?

An investigative report by an ABC news affiliate in Tampa Bay raised these very questions in November 2016 regarding an HT NGO called Bridging Freedom.[167] Bridging Freedom received a $1 million grant from the state of Florida in 2015, ostensibly to be used for building a shelter for trafficking victims on a hundred rural acres complete with facilities for horses. In 2016, Governor Scott approved an additional $1.2 million as a recurring annual grant for Bridging Freedom. Yet, it is uncertain as of this writing whether ground has been broken on the project since Bridging Freedom was founded in 2011. According to a state court judge interviewed for the report, "I remember when the 1.2 million was awarded to a program that doesn't exist. I was horrified." Moreover, the judge added, "I have a problem with that amount of money! It seems exceedingly unwise when we have immediate services. It makes no sense to me."

Kathy Arnold, an HT advocate affiliated with another NGO in the area asked, "Where's the accountability?... There should be an accountability of where that money goes. We as taxpayers deserve it, we as survivors deserve it."[168] The reporters breaking the story noted that Bridging Freedom's president, Laura Hamilton, canceled a scheduled interview with them and then declined to reschedule. Nikki Cross, affiliated with STAAR Ministries, a competing HT NGO that had to shut down operations due to lack of funding, disputed Gov. Scott's explanation that holding HT NGOs accountable is a budget priority. Cross stated, "I don't question, I absolutely know that there are some that not only should not be receiving money but should not be open."[169]

Regardless of the good intentions that underpin government support for nongovernment organizations, citizens have a right to know how the recipients of their taxes are chosen, and they need to become more cognizant that the political connections and interpersonal relationships cultivated over time between a government's executive leadership and the founders and directors of beneficiary NGOs run deep and may create troubling conflicts of interest along the public funding-to-private beneficiary chain. Left unchecked, eventually public perception can result in public rejection of the programs that are intended to help vulnerable individuals — in this case victims of human traf-

---

167. Jarrod Holbrook, *I-Team: Controversy Over State Anti-Human Trafficking Money*, WFTS Tampa Bay, Nov. 4, 2016, http://www.abcactionnews.com/news/local-news/i-team-investigates/i-team-controversy-over-state-anti-human-trafficking-money?autoplay=true.

168. *Id.*

169. *Id.*

ficking. Government agencies dispensing funding to HT NGOs should be mindful of an oft-quoted saying of Ronald Reagan:

> Government is like a baby. An alimentary canal with a big appetite at one end and no sense of responsibility at the other.[170]

---

170. Quip reportedly made during Ronald Reagan's 1965 campaign for Governor of California.

Chapter 7

Private Corruption and Human Trafficking

Summary: Chapter 7 examines the elements of private corrupt and how corrupt acts occurring in the private sector sustain human trafficking crimes, specifically in the form of labor trafficking. We will first look at the definition and characteristics of private-to-private corruption, followed by a brief discussion of international legal instruments addressing private-to-private corruption, before moving on to review several case examples of private-to-private corruption and misconduct by various actors along the labor trafficking chain.

1. Corrupt Business Practices in Labor Recruitment

It should be no surprise that corruption also occurs in the private sector,[1] and that corruption fuels labor trafficking. The international labor and human rights monitoring organization Verité has documented thoroughly the high level of corruption by various means and avenues commonly present in the never ending demand for cheap labor. In its 2016 exploratory study on corruption in labor migration, Verité noted:

---

1. *See* THE WORLD BANK, HELPING COUNTRIES COMBAT CORRUPTION: THE ROLE OF THE WORLD BANK §2 (1997), http://www1.worldbank.org/publicsector/anticorrupt/corruptn/cor02.htm; UNITED NATIONS DEVELOPMENT PROGRAMME, CORRUPTION AND DEVELOPMENT: ANTI-CORRUPTION INTERVENTIONS FOR POVERTY REDUCTION, REALIZATION OF THE MDGS AND PROMOTING SUSTAINABLE DEVELOPMENT 7 (2008).

The myriad official approvals, documents, and associated fees—foreign worker quotas, job order attestations, exit and guest worker visas, medical certifications, police clearances, work permits etc.—required to deploy a migrant worker from one country to another mean the opportunities and incentives for employers and their recruitment agents to bribe civil servants have become a structural feature of the international labor migration process.[2]

Some large corporations exploit both complexities and gaps in guest worker visa programs by using middlemen/intermediaries (labor recruiters and brokers) to sign recruited workers to questionable labor contracts with the false promise of good paying jobs, benefits, and in some cases permanent residency leading eventually to citizenship. Some fraudulent labor unions have also been created as fronts for labor traffickers to move migrant workers from source to destination countries.[3] Once such a recruiting practice is in place, corporations submit official applications requesting permission to hire the workers, and governments then have the discretion to issue temporary work visas—which nearly always occurs. While there is little evidence of deception in the visa process on the part of companies per se, the money companies save by using independent contracts as labor recruiters is substantial—so much so that the debt bondage that results between the recruiters and the workers is de facto modern slavery.

Back in 1997, the ILO drafted the *Convention Concerning Private Employment Agencies, C-181*, which entered into force on May 10, 2000.[4] The primary intent of the Convention was to protect workers from depredations committed by private employment agencies and labor recruiters whose businesses are found worldwide.[5] Several provisions of the Convention are remarkable as they pertain to issues of labor trafficking. Among them:

- The legal status of private employment agencies shall be determined in accordance with national law and practice and must be in full compliance with licensing and certification requirements under the domestic law in which the agencies operate (Article 3);

---

2. Verité, An Exploratory Study on the Role of Corruption in International Labor Migration 1 (January 2016).

3. UNODC, *Issue Papers: The Role of Corruption in Trafficking in Persons* 14 (2011).

4. *Opened for signature* June 19, 1997, 2115 UNTS 249 (entered into force May 10, 2000).

5. The Convention does not apply to agencies that recruit seafarers (art. 2(2)). *See also* Adelle Blackett, *The Decent Work for Domestic Workers Convention, 2011*, 106 Am. J. Int'l L. 778, 788–89 (2012).

- Measures shall be taken to ensure that the workers recruited by private employment agencies ... are not denied the right to freedom of association and the right to bargain collectively (Article 4);
- Private employment agencies shall not charge directly or indirectly, in whole or in part, any fees or costs to workers (Article 7);
- Measures shall be taken to ensure that child labour is not used or supplied by private employment agencies (Article 9);
- Adequate protection of workers' rights shall include:
  - freedom of association;
  - collective bargaining;
  - minimum wages;
  - working time and other working conditions;
  - statutory social security benefits;
  - access to training;
  - occupational safety and health;
  - compensation in case of occupational accidents or diseases;
  - compensation in case of insolvency and protection of workers claims;
  - maternity protection and benefits, and parental protection and benefits.

Despite the efforts of the ILO to produce a comprehensive international instrument by which private agencies should conduct their affairs and recruited workers should be protected, it is discouraging to note that only 32 countries have ratified the convention to date.[6] Conspicuously absent are the United States, United Kingdom, Germany, and several developing countries where private recruitment agencies are intensely active, such as India, Pakistan, Bangladesh, Afghanistan, and Thailand, to name just a few.

Private worker recruitment agencies are responsible for a large proportion of the many acts of labor trafficking worldwide. These are not all small "mom and pop" operations; many are sophisticated trans-global contractors and subcontractors that scour Third World countries for tens of thousands of workers to fill skilled and unskilled positions in large multinational corporations and to fill civilian worker needs under government contracts, including military contracts worldwide.

---

6. For a list of nations that have ratified the Convention, visit the NORMLEX Information System on International Labor Standards Ratifications by Country, advanced search URL at http://www.ilo.org/dyn/normlex/en/f?p=1000:20020:0::NO:::.

A. Private-to-Private Corruption

Private-to-private corruption is defined as corruption that "occurs when a manager or employee exercises a certain power or influence over the performance of a function, task, or responsibility within a private organization or corporation, that is contrary to the duties and responsibilities of his position in a way that harms the company or organization in question and for his own benefit or the benefit of another person or organization."[7]

Corruption is not an exclusive practice of public officials abusing their position, but a practice solely within the business sector.[8] The traditional approach that corruption only involves the abuse of public office has evolved to a recognition of private-to-private corruption as another form of corruption.[9] This development is prompted by "the increasingly widespread privatization of government services, the blurring of the separation between private and public functions, and the growth of international business transactions."[10] Private-to-private corruption is now a common practice, and "is almost as high

---

7. Maíra Martini, *Regulating Private-to-Private Corruption*, Transparency International Anti-Corruption Helpdesk, http://www.transparency.org/files/content/corruptionqas/Regulating_private_to_private_corruption_2014.pdf, *citing specifically to* Antonio Argandoña, Working Paper No. 531, *Private-to-Private Corruption*, Universidad de Navarra, 2003, http://www.iese.edu/research/pdfs/DI-0531-E.pdf.

8. *See* Transparency International, Bribe Payers Index 2011, at 19, https://www.transparency.org/bpi2011 [hereinafter TI Index]. *See also* Julio Bacio Terracino, The International Legal Framework against Corruption: States' Obligations to Prevent and Repress Corruption 20 (2012).

9. For several years, the International Chamber of Commerce has called attention to the harm that private-to-private corruption causes to "the smooth functioning and credibility of free, open and global competition." Such corruption adds "an artificial and unwarranted element to the cost of business, it distorts the terms of exchange of international business transactions and penalizes loyal market participants." *See* International Chamber of Commerce, *Memorandum to the OED Working Group on Bribery in International Business Transactions, Recommendations by the International Chamber of Commerce (ICC) on further provisions to be adopted to prevent and prohibit Private-to-Private Corruption*, Sept. 13, 2006, https://cdn.iccwbo.org/content/uploads/sites/3/2006/06/Memorandum-tothe-OECDWorking-Groupon.pdf. *See also Private Commercial Bribery, A Comparison of National and Supranational Legal* Structures (Günter Heine et al., eds., Joint publication by Max Planck Institute for Foreign and International Criminal Law and ICC Publishing, Paris, 2003).

10. Terracino, *supra* note 8, at 20. Today, private sector corruption is generally accepted as "another of the types of corruption" and not as simply "corporate or commercial criminality."

as bribery of public officials across all sectors."[11] Private sector corruption can affect an entire supply chain, distort markets and competition, and penalize companies refusing to compete on those terms. Such corruption in the business sector undermines trust, confidence, and loyalty so "necessary for the maintenance and development of social and economic relations."[12] Companies recognized it as a serious threat as evidenced by a survey conducted in the last decade indicating that 90 percent of companies polled have "provisions on private-to-private corruption within their codes of conduct and compliance regimes."[13] However, self-regulation is not going far enough.

In recent years, anti-corruption regulations at the domestic and international levels have established specific legal frameworks covering corruption within the private sector.[14] The strongest international response has been at the European Union level.[15] At the national level, the United Kingdom sets a "new global standard" with its UK Bribery Act in which bribery between firms is a criminal offence.[16] Other countries lack specific laws and apply existing criminal and civil offenses using "abuse of trust, anti-competitive conduct and fraudulent behaviour." All are conducts that regulate other acts, and have different evidentiary and culpability standards that make it problematic to tackle private sector corruption in a coherent and effective manner.[17]

Countries could respond to private-to-private corruption by implementing some or all of the following recommendations. First, countries must enable specific legislation to punish private-to-private corruption. Such legislation would consider the following: (1) address passive and active corruption; (2) focus on a "broad scope of individuals" to include managers, staff, and independent professionals "who have specific duties and special responsibility to-

---

11. For the first time Transparency International's survey asked business executives how often they "pay or receive bribes from other firms." The responses reflected that such practice is common. *See* TI Index, *supra* note 8, at 14–19.

12. Council of Europe, Criminal Law Convention on Corruption, Explanatory Report (1999), art. 7, ¶ 52, European Treaty Series (ETS) no. 173, https://rm.coe.int/CoERM PublicCommonSearchServices/DisplayDCTMContent?documentId=09000016800cce44 [hereinafter Exploratory Report].

13. TRACE Int'l, *Commercial Bribery: No Government Officials in Sight*, Mar. 14, 2012, http://www.traceinternational.org/blog/485/Commercial_Bribery_No_Government_Officials_in_Sight.

14. Martini, *supra* note 7, at 1. Croatia, Italy, and the United Kingdom have reformed their domestic legislation to criminalize corruption in the private sector.

15. *Id.* at 4.

16. TI Index, *supra* note 8, at 19.

17. Martini, *supra* note 7, at 3–4.

wards society, above and beyond their responsibility toward a company (accountants, auditors, lawyers, consultants, brokers, etc.); (3) cover a broad scope of "undue advantage" and include persons taking "any kind of undue advantage" for oneself or for a third party; (4) include breach of duty to protect trust and loyalty as "a general obligation not to act in detriment of the interests of the company," as well as breach of duty required by the profession; (5) address the liability of legal entities, and; (6) mandate effective penalties.[18] Second, the UNCAC and the OECD Anti-Bribery Conventions should require States Parties to criminalize private-to-private corruption. Third, breaching one's duties should be included in the manifestations of private-to-private corruption.

B. International Instruments on Private-to-Private Corruption

There are several international instruments that address private-to-private corruption that warrant some brief discussion.

Article 8(1) of the United Nations *Convention against Transnational Organized Crime* (UNTOC)[19] provides for the criminalization of corruption of public officials, while art. 8(2) requires each State Party to consider establishing other forms of corruption as criminal offences.[20] This will include establishing criminal offences with regard to private sector corruption.

Article 12 of the United Nations *Convention against Corruption* (UNCAC)[21] addresses private sector corruption, but does not require States Parties to establish criminal offences in relation to such conduct. UNCAC only encourages States Parties to take measures to prevent private sector corruption, enhance accounting and auditing standards, encourage transparency, and put into place civil, administrative or criminal penalties for failure to comply. UNCAC also recommends criminalization of passive and active bribery in the private sector of "an undue advantage" to or by anyone working for a private

---

18. Martini, *supra* note 7, at 5.

19. United Nations Convention against Transnational Organized Crime, opened for signature Dec. 12, 2000, 2225 U.N.T.S. 209. Article 8 provides for the criminalization of corruption of public officials, while the 2nd indent of this article requires each State Party to consider establishing as criminal offences other forms of corruption.

20. *Id.* Under art. 8(2), each State Party "shall consider adopting such legislative and other measures as may be necessary to establish as criminal offences conduct referred to in paragraph 1 of this article involving a foreign public official or international civil servant.

21. United Nations Convention against Corruption, Dec. 14, 2005, 3249 U.N.T.S. 41.

sector entity in any capacity in order that the person "act or refrain from acting" in "breach of his or her duties."[22]

Article 29 of the *Treaty on European Union*[23] sets forth the basis for addressing private and public corruption in the EU. Article 29 specifically states that the EU's objective shall be "to provide citizens with a high level of safety within an area of freedom, security and justice by developing common action among the Member States in the fields of police and judicial cooperation in criminal matters.... That objective shall be achieved by preventing and combating crime ... in particular ... corruption."[24]

The Council of Europe *Criminal Law Convention on Corruption* imposes on States Parties the obligation to enact legislative and other measures criminalizing both active and passive bribery in the private sector (arts. 7 and 8).[25] Private bribery is restricted to "business activity," thereby excluding non-profit-oriented activities. However, a signatory country can implement provisions broadly to mean "any kind of commercial activity, in particular trading in goods and *delivering services including services to the public*" (emphasis added), therefore including non-profits.[26] The prohibition encompasses not only the employer-employee relationship, but also relationships with "partners, lawyers, clients," and anyone who can engage the responsibility of the company such as "consultants, commercial agents."[27]

Article 2 of the Council of Europe *Civil Law Convention on Corruption*[28] defines corruption broadly to include both public and private corruption. Specifically, corruption means "requesting, offering, giving or accepting directly or indirectly a bribe or any other undue advantage or the prospect thereof, which distorts the proper performance of any duty or behaviour required of the recipient of the bribe, the undue advantage or the prospect thereof."[29] This definition reflects the COE's "comprehensive approach to the fight against corruption as a threat not only to international business or to the financial in-

---

22. *Id.*

23. Treaty on European Union, Feb. 7, 1992, 1992 O.J. (C 191).

24. *Id.* art. 29.

25. Council of Europe, Criminal Law Convention on Corruption, Jan. 27, 1999, Europ. T.S. No. 173.

26. Exploratory Report, *supra* note 12, at §53.

27. *Id.*

28. Council of Europe, Civil Law Convention on Corruption, Nov. 4, 1999, Europ. T.S. No. 174.

29. Council of Europe, Civil Law Convention on Corruption, Explanatory Report, ETS No. 174, art. 2, ¶32 (1999), http://www.ethic-intelligence.com/wp-content/uploads/11_explanatory_report_civil_law.pdf.

terests but to the *democratic values, the rule of law, human rights and social and economic progress* (emphasis added)."[30] The *Convention* confronts corruption through civil law remedies by giving victims the option to safeguard their interests using civil law instead of criminal law. It also imposes on States Parties the obligation to provide effective remedies for persons who suffer damage due to corruption (art. 1).

The Institution of the European Union, or Council of the European Union presented its Framework Decision 2003/568/JHA on combating corruption in the private sector in 2003.[31] Article 2 requires all Member States to criminalize active and passive corruption in the private sector, and it extends the scope of passive and active corruption to business activities within profit and *nonprofit entities* (emphasis added).

Article 4(e) and (f) of the African Union *Convention on Preventing and Combating Corruption*[32] enumerates acts of corruption to include public and private corruption. These sections[33] address active and passive bribery in the private sector, while art. 11 provides mechanisms to combat corruption in and by "agents of the private sector."[34]

---

30. *Id.* art. 2, ¶ 33.

31. Council Framework Decision 2003/568/JHA of 22 July 2003, adopted by the European Council pursuant to Title VI of the Treaty on European Union, http://eur-lex.europa.eu/legal-content/EN/TXT/?uri=CELEX:32003F0568. For a text of the States' provisions incorporating into their national law the obligations imposed on them under this Framework Decision, *see* the Annex to the Report from the Commission based on Article 9, *available at* http://aei.pitt.edu/43086/1/SEC_(2007)_808.pdf, *and also* Martini, *supra* note 7, at 6–8.

32. African Union Convention on Preventing and Combating Corruption, July 11, 2003, 43 I.L.M. 5, http://www.eods.eu/library/AU_Convention%20on%20Combating%20Corruption_2003_EN.pdf.

33. Article 4(e) addresses the "offering or giving, promising, solicitation or acceptance, directly or indirectly, of any undue advantage to or by any person who directs or works for, in any capacity, a private sector entity, for himself or herself or for anyone else, for him or her to act, or refrain from acting, in breach of his or her duties."

34. Article 11 establishes that States Parties are to: (1) adopt legislative measures to prevent and combat acts of corruption and related offences committed in and by agents of the private sector; (2) establish mechanisms to encourage participation by the private sector in the fight against unfair competition, respect of the tender procedures and property rights, and; (3) adopt such other measures as may be necessary to prevent companies from paying bribes to win tenders.

C. Acts of Private-to-Private Corruption

The traditional view that corruption requires the presence of a public official and that corporate or private corruption are merely cases of corporate or commercial liability is "increasingly losing ground."[35] Corruption in the private sector corrodes commercial arrangements, suppresses fair competition, and adversely impacts the expectations that business is conducted in an ethical manner. For private-to-private corruption to occur, "an action must involve a corruptor who performs the action or a person who is corrupted by it."[36] This can be in the form of any of several acts like or similar to illicit acts identified by Transparency International, including:

- Bribery or kickbacks (commercial bribery), paid by employees of one company to another in order to obtain an advantage over competition. In labor trafficking, this can involve kickbacks by a labor broker who gains exclusive contracts to supply migrant labor to a business.
- Extortion or solicitation, occurs when an employee of a company requests a gift or an amount in cash in return for closing a deal.
- Conflicts of interest, become present when managers select a service provider because a relative has a financial stake.
- Gifts and hospitality, result when substantial gifts, such as luxury items, tickets to events or foreign travel to tourist locations are given to persuade employees to close a deal.
- Fees and commissions, prevalent in labor trafficking arrangements when fees and commissions for agents and intermediaries are paid not in line with the standard practices of the industry and the geographical region.
- Collusion, occurs when labor representatives and management exchange benefits or favors in order to gain some advantage that would be construed as falling outside standard practices of the industry and the geographical region.[37]

---

35. Terracino, *supra* note 8, at 20.

36. STANFORD ENCYCLOPEDIA OF PHILOSOPHY, entry on Corruption, http://plato.stanford.edu/entries/corruption/.

37. Martini, *supra* note 7, at 2–3.

2. Private-to-Private Corruption and Human Trafficking

Private-to-private corruption appears to be rampant and widespread in labor practices that involve trafficking of migrant workers. Verité has documented how labor migrants moving through trafficking corridors in Southeast Asia, namely Myanmar, Thailand, and Malaysia, are kept vulnerable to exploitation by being subjected to inhumane living conditions in work camps and dormitories, lack of access to health care, restricted movement, violence (including death), and recruitment fees that continue to be like anchors around laborers' necks as the costs to move the workers through the labor chain follow them from origination to destination.[38] The irony is that migrant workers resort to informal recruitment practices believing that the formal methods regulated by government officials are corrupt and costlier—only to find out that the informal recruitment and trafficking process is as costly, more dangerous, and far more exploitative.[39]

According to Declan Croucher of Verité, "The charging of recruitment fees and expenses to migrant workers is *the* most significant contributor to the shameful ongoing presence of debt bondage, human trafficking, forced labor, or modern slavery in global supply chains."[40] The following chart provides a sample of costs Asian laborers are assessed by recruitment agencies for jobs in the Persian Gulf States.

---

38. Verité, An Exploratory Study on the Role of Corruption in International Labor Migration 2–3 (January 2016).

39. *Id.* at 3.

40. On file with the author. Delcan Croucher is Director of Advisory Services at Verité and an international authority on private-to-private corruption in global labor markets.

Summary of Private Recruitment Agency Charges*

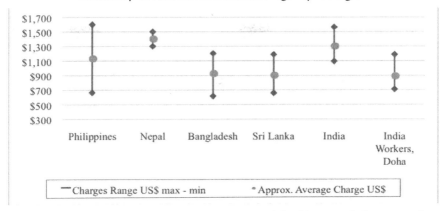

* Taken from only 15 recruitment agencies interviewed for this research due to very limited information.

In addition to going into debt bondage arrangements, laborers draw heavily from many sources in an effort to pay the recruitment costs. The following chart represents some of the typical sources used to enter into the labor migration chain.

Sources of Funds for Migration in %*

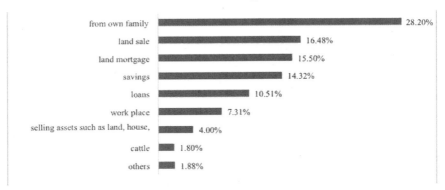

* A study by the IOM in Bangladesh 2002.

Employers rarely pay recruitment fees sufficient to cover intermediaries' costs (which include advertising, putting agents on the ground, transporting, housing, and paperwork), and agents recoup the shortfalls and legitimate expenses directly from the workers being recruited (or from their families, as well). Croucher notes that along the labor migration corridors, "employers or their duly appointed recruitment agents also pay bribes or un-receipted fees to government officials to fraudulently approve required formal applications or facilitate discretionary decisions (e.g., the provision of foreign worker quotas, demand letter attestations, exit and guest worker visas, medical certifications, police clearances, work permits)."[41] The sum of costs passed on to the recruited workers has been documented to range from US$1,500 to US$6,000 per worker, "depending on the country of origin of the workers as well as the type and location of the job."[42]

This additional burden can significantly extend the working contract by several years, resulting in a situation in which the workers are "essentially working for free—an improper benefit that accrues to their employer and indirectly to their employer's customers and clients."[43] It is hard to imagine that the companies employing migrant laborers are not aware of the corrupt practices of the labor agents with whom they do business. However, in addition to supplying a work force through whatever means, the recruiters/brokers, as private contractors to companies, provide the companies with a degree of separation from the labor trafficking operation.

Another act of private-to-private corruption noted by Verité is the practice of employers auctioning contracts out to labor brokers for the recruitment and selection of foreign migrant workers. According to Croucher, "Contracts are awarded to the agencies that can supply foreign contract labor at the lowest cost. In many cases the agencies do not charge the employers any fees for the recruitment and selection of foreign contract workers but offer a 'commission' in consideration for being given the 'demand letter' (purchase or work order to supply workers)."[44] In some instances, Verité investigators have found mid-level managers receiving kickbacks or direct payments from recruitment agents or brokers offering to gain an advantage over competition in offering their services as a contract labor provider. In one instance in Nepal, labor recruiters were charged US$300 per worker by labor brokers representing employers in Qatar in order to secure the demand letter or job order. "If the demand letter

---

41. Delcan Croucher, statement on file with the author.
42. *Id.*
43. *Id.*
44. *Id.*

comes directly from a Qatari employer the cost is frequently US$400 as the company human resources, contracts, or procurement representative also allegedly receives US$100," even though such "kickback commissions or 'pay to play' payments are illegal under Qatari law."[45] The following chart represents rough proportions of these costs.

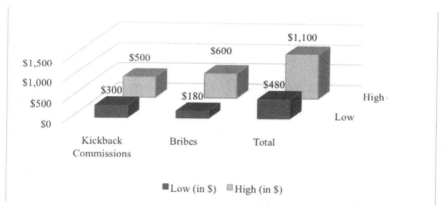

Corrupt or Improper Payments: Nepal to Qatar Labor Migration (in US$ per worker in 2015)

Moreover, the absence of a paper trail indicating that an employer is paying a recruitment fee presents a "red flag" that some form of a kickback or illicit payment is occurring between employers and recruiters/brokers.[46]

Private corruption and private-to-private corruption are the root causes of horrific labor trafficking depredations worldwide. For example, conditions for guest workers that fill jobs in construction in Abu Dhabi have found them-

---

45. An Exploratory Study on the Role of Corruption in International Labor Migration 8–9, report issued jointly by Verité and the Freedom Fund (Jan. 2016), https://www.verite.org/wp-content/uploads/2016/11/Verite-Report-Intl-Labour-Recruitment.pdf.

46. *Id.* For a detailed examination of how the kick-back schemes work in the labor recruitment process, *see* Ray Jureidini, Migrant Labour Recruitment to Qatar: Report for Qatar Foundation Migrant Worker Initiative 44–50 (2014), http://www.qscience.com/userimages/ContentEditor/1404811243939/Migrant_Labour_Recruitment_to_Qatar_Web_Final.pdf.

selves in the worst forms of labor trafficking. A 2013 investigation by the London *Guardian* newspaper uncovered deplorable conditions for workers brought to the United Arab Emirates over the span of several years.[47] The UAE's Tourism Development and Investment Company (TDIC), which manages commercial properties on Saadiyat Island (considered one of the crown jewels of development in Dubai), has routinely violated UAE labor and employment law. Workers are regularly left impoverished, confined to labor camps, and deported if they try to protest. In one case, migrant workers constructing New York University's Abu Dhabi campus on Saadiyat Island were found to be suffering serious mistreatment. The findings of the investigation revealed that:

- Companies confiscate and withhold migrant worker passports, making them de facto captives in the UAE.
- Thousands of workers live in substandard or squalid conditions elsewhere in the UAE in apparent breach of the Tourism Development and Investment Company's pledge to house all workers in its model Saadiyat accommodation village.
- Workers decorating the NYU university campus live in squalid conditions, with 10 men to a room, and no free healthcare.
- Many workers remain trapped in Dubai due to crippling debt bondage arrangements.
- Mobile-phone video footage of a riot at the Saadiyat accommodation village showed dozens of men roaming the camp armed with metal spears and planks spiked with nails. Men were seen jumping out of windows to avoid the conflict.
- A worker who claims he lost his leg while building luxury villas was forced to live on the top floor of a migrant camp for a year. He only received a prosthetic leg [a] month before the investigation and had been reliant on the Red Crescent for medical support. His claim for compensation and request for ground-floor accommodation were rejected.
- Workers on the Louvre project worked for nine months to a year just to pay back their recruitment fees. One worker who went on strike over poor wages was kept in his camp unpaid for three months and then sent back to Pakistan along with 19 others.

---

47. David Batty, *Conditions for Abu Dhabi's Migrant Workers 'Shame the West'*, THE GUARDIAN, Dec. 21, 2013, http://www.theguardian.com/world/2013/dec/22/abu-dhabi-migrant-workers-conditions-shame-west.

The *Guardian* report concluded that labor abuse is a systemic problem, even though the UAE is a prominent member of the International Labour Organization. Beyond the government needing to enforce its laws, however, companies doing business in the UAE also must take responsibility for the welfare of the workers employed there. It is also discouraging that such a prominent, iconic American institution of higher learning as New York University would be involved in the exploitation of workers to build a campus that is supposed to be a pillar of Western enlightenment in the Gulf States.

Qatar has also come under international scrutiny and criticism for corrupt labor practices impacting some 1.39 million foreign workers, that make up nearly 85 percent of Qatar's total population.[48] A report issued in 2014 by the law firm DLA Piper, commissioned by the Government of Qatar, found that migrant workers recruited primarily into the booming construction industry are subject to high levels of corruption and maltreatment by private corporations doing business there. Among the recommendations made by DLA Piper to address critical problems with corruption among the foreign recruited labor force were:

(1) that there be greater transparency and communication between the Qatari government, State of Origin countries, and the public and private sectors and companies doing business in Qatar;

(2) that there should be a strong focus on communication and information sharing with key non-government stakeholders and private contractors so as to address the many issues of concern regarding corruption and corrupt practices impacting the foreign workers being brought into Qatar and those already working there;

(3) that the Qatar government "adopt a comprehensive set of worker welfare standards setting out the minimum mandatory requirements for all public contracting authority construction projects in Qatar.[49]

Croucher and Verité assert that willful ignorance on the part of employers toward the labor recruitment supply chain is unacceptable and results in culpability:

If your company or contractors are not paying all of the recruitment related fees and expenses necessary to bring foreign workers to your project, then those costs are almost certainly being passed onto work-

---

48. DLA PIPER, IMMIGRANT LABOUR IN THE CONSTRUCTION SECTOR IN QATAR 3–5 (April 2014). Report on file with the author.

49. *Id.*

ers through a series of unethical and unscrupulous agents and corrupt government officials. Hoping that your recruitment agents adhere to whatever legal fee limits exist is not a sufficient safeguard as the actual hard costs of migration are far greater. Employers that do not pay all recruitment fees and expenses or ensure their recruitment agents conduct business ethically and lawfully, are complicit in exposing their workers to the risk of bonded labor and other exploitative practices.[50]

One obstacle to improving the conditions of global labor recruitment involves the cost of recruitment and supplying larger numbers of workers for an ever expanding global marketplace in which competition and profitability determine business success or failure. As such, "supply chain participants are rarely inclined to be transparent about their recruitment business model and practices."[51] What insights we have learned come from a relatively modest body of legal proceedings in the United States and abroad that shed important light on labor trafficking in the private sector. Let us turn to several examples.

A. *David v. Signal International LLC* (United States)

Following Hurricane Katrina, Signal International LLC, a marine and fabrication company based in Mobile, Alabama, used employment agencies in India as recruiting contractors to traffic approximately 590 men into the United States to work in its facilities in Texas, Louisiana, and Mississippi, under the United States H-2B guest worker program. The workers were recruited to fill skilled positions in welding, pipefitting and other activities to repair damaged oil rigs and related facilities.[52] The workers were allegedly told that if they qualified for jobs they would be on track for permanent citizenship in the United States. They were then charged a recruitment fee of around $2,000 to cover their transportation and accommodations.

The lead plaintiff in the lawsuit that brought all this to light, Kurian David, was working in construction in Abu Dhabi, United Arab Emirates, when he

---

50. Statement of Declan Croucher in EMMA CRATES, BUILDING A FAIRER SYSTEM: TACKING MODERN SLAVERY IN CONSTRUCTION SUPPLY CHAINS 22 (Chartered Institute of Building (CIOB), 2016), http://kj06q2hv7031ix2143c36tpx.wpengine.netdna-cdn.com/wp-content/uploads/2016/07/CIOB_Modern_Day_Slavery_WEB.pdf.

51. Croucher, statement on file with the author.

52. *Press Release: Cohn Reznick Pro-Bono Work Leads to a Settlement Agreement on Behalf of Exploited Indian Guest Workers*, July 14, 2015, https://www.cohnreznick.com/press-center/press-releases/2015/cohnreznick-pro-bono-work-leads-to-settlement-agreement.

responded to a newspaper advertisement to attend a worker recruitment seminar by Dewan Consultants and the Law Offices of Malvern C. Burnett. During the seminar, attendees were told that for $12,000 plus costs to pay recruitment fees for Burnett and a corporate employment recruiter called Global Resources, Inc, they could obtain an employment-based green card in the United States.[53] Plaintiff David subsequently signed a contract with Global Resources in Dubai. There, Dewan Consultants and attorney Burnett coached the workers on how to answer questions asked by American consular officers during their visa interviews, instructing them not to reveal how much money they had paid for the recruitment fees and not to mention the promise of green cards.[54] For unclear reasons, consular officials took the Plaintiffs' passports and returned them directly to the Dewan Consultants office, raising the question of what were the consular officials up to as well? At that point, Dewan Consultants withheld the passports until final installment payments were made by the workers, ostensibly to pay for medical testing to be performed by a physician chosen by Dewan Consultants.[55] David also testified that Dewan Consultants threatened to destroy workers' passports in retaliation if they tried to back out of their contracts.

After the workers arrived at Signal's facility in Orange, Texas, they were given a contract that dictated that their pay could be reduced after further skills testing, and they were also told that they were to be issued guest worker program visas that were temporary until the 24-month green card process was complete. The workers were then subjected to sundry abuses, threatened with deportation if they left their jobs, and housed in substandard work camps in which they were charged $35 a day for living costs. Signal told the workers that they could leave the camps, but that $35 would still be deducted from their daily pay. David and his fellow workers sued Signal and other parties for actions that constituted human trafficking,[56] claiming that Signal and its agents made false promises of "permanent work-based immigration to the United States," and that in order to take advantage of such a promising opportunity, the plaintiffs had "plunged themselves and their families into untenable debt bondage arrangements."[57] Signal denied any wrongdoing and denied that the

---

53. *David v. Signal Int'l, L.L.C.*, 735 F. Supp. 2d 440, 442 (E.D. La. 2010). Reconsideration of the case was denied, 2010 WL 4667972.
54. *Id.* at 442.
55. *Id.*
56. *David v. Signal Int'l, L.L.C.*, No 08-1220, 2012 WL 10759668 (E D. La. Jan. 4, 2012).
57. *Joseph v. Signal Int'l, L.L.C.*, No. 1:13-CV-324, 2015 WL 1262286 (E.D. Tex. 2015), at 2.

plaintiffs were subjected to forced labor, trafficking, or involuntary servitude. Nevertheless, the federal court in Louisiana eventually awarded the plaintiffs US$14 million in damages and compensation.[58]

Signal was also sued by the U.S. Equal Employment Opportunity Commission (EEOC) for violating Title VII of the *Civil Rights Act of 1964*. The company eventually settled the lawsuit in December 2015 by agreeing to pay an estimated $5 million to 476 of the Indian guest workers.[59]

B. Third Country Nationals and Military Contractors

Some of the most notorious cases of labor trafficking have occurred among government contractors and their sub-contractors working with the United States military under a program run by the Department of Defense's Logistics Civil Augmentation Program.[60] Over the last several years, more than 37,000 civilian laborers work or have worked for private contractors in military facilities under the administration of the United States Central Command, alone. Major corporations, including Fluor Corporation and DynCorp International, have utilized a shadowy network of overseas labor recruitment services engaged by dozens of spotty subsidiaries with names such as Ecolog International that are based in Persian Gulf States. The subsidiaries subcontract with hundreds of labor brokers, most unregistered, throughout India and Nepal to supply unskilled workers for menial jobs in food services, laundry services, and construction/maintenance for the United States military.

An investigation by *Aljazeera America* in 2014 uncovered dozens of cases of labor abuse of South Asian workers who were sent to military camps under entirely false pretenses after taking on crippling debt to be recruited (one worker paid US$4,000 to a recruitment agent).[61] Once in the camps, they found themselves at the bottom of the social ladder. They were forced to work 12-hour

---

58. Signal International LLC filed for bankruptcy protection in July 12, 2015.

59. U.S. Equal Employment Opportunity Commission Press Release: Signal International, LLC to Pay $5 Million to Settle EEOC Race, National Origin Lawsuit, Dec. 18, 2015, https://www1.eeoc.gov/eeoc/newsroom/release/12-18-15.cfm.

60. The program awarded more than $16.8 billion to just Dyncorp and Fluor, alone. *See* Jessica Schulberg, *The American Government if Funding Human Trafficking*, NEW REPUBLIC (undated), http://www.newrepublic.com/article/120269/contractors-violate-us-zero-tolerance-policy-human-trafficking (last visited Aug. 15, 2016).

61. Samuel Black & Anjali Kamat, *After 12 Years of War, Labour Abuses Rampant on US Bases in Afghanistan*, ALJAZEERA AMERICA, Mar. 7, 2014, http://america.aljazeera.com/articles/2014/3/7/after-12-years-ofwarlabourabusesrampantonusbasesinafghanistan.html.

shifts with little or no time off, were prevented from contact with the outside world, and were prohibited from communicating with military personnel.

This practice of labor recruitment is actually typical throughout Asia where hundreds of agents and sub-agents chum urban and rural areas looking for recruits. Individuals picked for jobs are told they can make as much as US$1,200 a month in nice hotels in safe areas, only to find out later that their destination is Afghanistan. Recruits nearly always pay a recruitment fee to the agencies of between US$1,000 and US$5,000, and then sent off like cattle to holding facilities, mainly in Dubai. Once there, they are told that their salaries are going to be considerably lower, but by then, it is too late to back out of their work arrangements because they have accrued so much debt during the recruitment process.

With regard to American companies engaging in such practices, the payment of recruitment fees is actually in direct violation of United States federal anti-human trafficking law. Under Title 22, §7104(g) of the United States Code:

> The President shall ensure that any grant, contract, or cooperative agreement provided or entered into by a Federal department or agency under which funds are to be provided to a private entity, in whole or in part, shall include a condition that authorizes the department or agency to terminate the grant, contract, or cooperative agreement, or take any of the other remedial actions authorized under section 7104b(c) of this title, without penalty, if the grantee or any subgrantee, or the contractor or any subcontractor, engages in, or uses labour recruiters, brokers, or other agents who engage in—
>
> (i) severe forms of trafficking in persons;
>
> (ii) the procurement of a commercial sex act during the period of time that the grant, contract, or cooperative agreement is in effect;
>
> (iii) the use of forced labour in the performance of the grant, contract, or cooperative agreement; or
>
> (iv) acts that directly support or advance trafficking in persons, including the following acts:
>
> (I) Destroying, concealing, removing, confiscating, or otherwise denying an employee access to that employee's identity or immigration documents.
>
> (II) Failing to provide return transportation or pay for return transportation costs to an employee from a country outside the United States to the country from which the employee was recruited upon the end of employment if requested by the employee, unless—

(aa) exempted from the requirement to provide or pay for such return transportation by the Federal department or agency providing or entering into the grant, contract, or cooperative agreement; or

(bb) the employee is a victim of human trafficking seeking victim services or legal redress in the country of employment or a witness in a human trafficking enforcement action.

(III) Soliciting a person for the purpose of employment, or offering employment, by means of materially false or fraudulent pretenses, representations, or promises regarding that employment.

(IV) Charging recruited employees unreasonable placement or recruitment fees, such as fees equal to or greater than the employee's monthly salary, or recruitment fees that violate the laws of the country from which an employee is recruited.

(V) Providing or arranging housing that fails to meet the host country housing and safety standards.

While it also clearly states in the 2009 rule book for contractors working in Afghanistan that labor brokering is prohibited, this regulation seems to be ignored. For example, in addition to using labor brokers to recruit workers:

- Workers have been forced to work under threats of punishment in situations in which they have no choice but to comply;
- Workers requesting to go home have been refused, particularly while being cloistered in the labor camps in Dubai;
- Workers have been recruited under false pretenses (in at least one documented instance a worker hired on after being promised he would not be sent to Afghanistan but was then sent there anyway);
- The recruiting fees are far in excess of "fees equal to or greater than the employee's monthly salary;"
- Housing in the holding camps are by many accounts entirely unsuitable and violate the living standards of the host country.[62]

During 2011, similar recruitment tactics came to light with regard to Fluor and DynCorp recruiting hundreds of women from the Philippines and from South Pacific islands who were told they would be given lucrative and high-paying jobs as hairstylists and staff in a luxury hotel in Dubai. Once they ar-

---

62. Sarah Stillman, *The Invisible Army*, New Yorker, June 3–6, 2011, http://www.new yorker.com/magazine/2011/06/06/the-invisible-army.

rived in Dubai, they were told that their final destination was actually to work on United States military bases in Iraq and Afghanistan. Once at these bases, the workers were known by military personnel as T.C.N.s (third-country nationals). Some of the women reported being "robbed of wages, injured without compensation, subjected to sexual assault, and held in conditions resembling indentured servitude by their subcontractor bosses."[63]

C. Adhikari v. Daoud & Partners

In one of the most egregious cases to date and one that was litigated before the United States District Court in Texas in 2013, Ramchandra Adhikari, a plaintiff from Nepal, and the surviving family members of 12 other Nepali men, sued two business entities, KBR and Daoud & Partners, under United States federal racketeering laws (RICO), the *Alien Tort Statute*, and the *Trafficking Victim Reauthorization Act*.[64] The Nepali men were recruited in 2004 by a Nepal-based recruiting firm called Moonlight Consultant Pvt. Ltd. (Moonlight) who told some of the recruits that they would be working in a luxury hotel in Amman, Jordan, and that others would be working at an American military base alluded to be in the United States. The workers were promised salaries of approximately US$500 per month and were led to believe that they would not be sent into any dangerous situations. All the men and their families incurred substantial debt to pay brokerage fees (again, a violation of federal law).

Moonlight then transferred the recruits to a job brokerage in Amman, Jordan, called Morning Star for Recruitment and Manpower Supply (Morning Star). After housing the men for a brief time in Amman, Morning Star transferred the men to agents of Daoud & Partners (Daoud). Once under Daoud's control, the Nepali men were forced to surrender their passports and informed that they were being sent to work in Al Asad, an area north of Ramadi, Iraq. They were also told that they would be paid only three quarters of what they were initially promised. The trial court's opinion states, "Although they wanted to return home to Nepal, rather than proceed into the Iraqi war zone, the men were compelled to proceed to Iraq because of the debts that their families had

---

63. *Id.*

64. *Adhikari v. Daoud & Partners*, 994 F. Supp. 2d 831, 834 (S.D. Tex. 2014). Summary judgment was ultimately awarded to the defendant because the violations occurred before the TVPRA was amended to grant federal courts extraterritorial jurisdiction. Motions for rehearing were also denied, 95 F.Supp.3d 1013 (S.D. Tex. 2015).

assumed to pay the brokers."[65] While in transit along a dangerous highway in Iraq, their vehicles were overtaken by members of an insurgent group known as the Ansar al-Sunna Army. What then ensued was captured on video, and later sent to the Foreign Ministry of Nepal, showing members of the Ansar al-Sunna Army executing the deceased plaintiffs. One victim was beheaded and the other eleven were executed by gunshots to the back of their heads. Their bodies were never recovered. The surviving plaintiff whose vehicle was not captured arrived at Al Asad where he was handed over to KBR, a military contractor, where for the next 15 months he worked in the supply warehouse. During his time there, he was frequently subjected to mortar fire without adequate protection. He was eventually permitted to return to Nepal.

D. *Affumicata a.s.* (Czech Republic)

Exploitation of workers by private companies is not just a problem that occurs in developing states and war zones. In 2009, several hundred workers from Vietnam, Romania, Slovakia, Moldova, Ukraine, Bulgaria, and Mongolia were recruited to work in the Czech Republic, harvesting wood on government-owned forestry land. Affumicata a.s., a Prague-based firm, recruited foreign workers who were promised between €400 and €600 per month to harvest timber under a government contract with Less & Forest a.s.[66] The laborers worked 10 to 12 hour days, seven days a week for several months and received basically nothing. Instead of the free lodging they were promised, they were forced to pay for their accommodations, which ranged from "local hostels to buildings near the forests."[67] To date, neither the Czech government nor the main contractors have accepted liability, instead placing responsibility for compensation on Affumicata.[68]

The murky world of contractors and subcontractors involved in labor exploitation remains a complicated and largely unregulated web of companies and shadowy managers and agents. Investigating allegations of exploitation is difficult, time-consuming, and costly. Even after the Czech forestry case attracted widespread attention from the prominent European antitrafficking or-

---

65. *Id.*
66. *Human Trafficking of Migrant Forestry Workers Exposed in the Czech Republic*, BWI Connect (Mar. 11, 2011), http://www.bwint.org/default.asp?index=3334.
67. *Id.*
68. *Id.*

ganization La Strada, as well as the Organisation for Security and Co-Operation in Europe, no action was taken by the Czech authorities.[69] The individuals behind the companies kept playing shell games to stay ahead of regulators and law enforcement, and because forestry is big business in the Czech Republic, there is very little impetus to investigate labor exploitation. This situation follows a similar pattern of exploitation in the forestry industry in Sweden, where Latvians have been recruited and exploited to work in Swedish forests by corrupt subcontractors.

The corporate sector is not the only private actor engaged in corruption and human trafficking. Corrupt travel agencies and transport firms are well known to collaborate with fraudulent employment agencies in furthering human trafficking conspiracies. Their involvement may be of a more passive character, although some travel agencies have been engaged in the sale of false identity and travel documents and working in collusion with crooked attorneys. Generally, the managers of these travel agencies and transport firms have no criminal record; their motivation is simply to maximize profits. From an organized crime point of view, engaging otherwise legitimate travel and transport companies renders it more difficult for law enforcement to identify the primary criminal elements in the human trafficking chain.

In the same way, indifferent property owners rent properties to traffickers to use as safe houses or for document forgery, and shopkeepers engage in laundering money and supplying consumables and necessities during transit and destination stages of human trafficking operations.[70] Such corrupt business entities in the labor trafficking chain are quite difficult, and costly, to investigate. In fact, case files reviewed by two researchers on Albanian human trafficking in Europe revealed that not one driver, not one manager of a travel agency or transport firm, and not one owner of a safe house was punished when the cases were brought to court.[71] Moreover, these pieces of the trafficking chain can remain in place even after a successful prosecution of traffickers or trafficking organization, ready to be exploited again by new sets of corrupt actors.

---

69. Martina Křížková & Marek Čaněk, *Czech State Forestry and Exploitation of Migrant Workers*, MigrationOnline.cz, Feb.23, 2011, http://www.migrationonline.cz/en/czech-state-forestry-and-exploitation-of-migrant-workers.

70. Johan Leman & Stef Janssens, *Albanian Entrepreneurial Practices in Human Smuggling and Trafficking: On the Road to the United Kingdom Via Brussels, 1995–2005*, Int'l Migration (2011), https://lirias.kuleuven.be/bitstream/123456789/358951/2/j.1468-2435.2010.00654.x.pdf.

71. *Id.*

3. Passive Involvement for Financial Gain

Some businesses use several degrees of separation from labor exploitation to try to avoid responsibility for trafficking crimes. Executives can claim that labor brokers and recruiters are to blame for occurrences of labor servitude and that the company is not responsible for the acts of independent contractors. For example, a major corporation may argue that given the size of its global operations, it is nearly impossible to vet the labor recruiting networks utilized to supply a workforce, that it is not responsible for aberrations that occur in subsidiaries in distant countries away from the main headquarters, or that it is not possible to monitor the labor practices of the suppliers of the raw goods that go into manufacturing finished products. Such plausible deniability constitutes a form of passive involvement.

Some corporations use uncertain government regulation of business to take advantage of the exploitation of workers and to shield themselves from any liability. The recruitment and exploitation of forestry workers by Affumicata in the Czech Republic is a case in point.[72] Despite criminal charges of human trafficking having been filed, police in Prague could not determine if any of the charges met the definition of human trafficking, and that until that definition could be satisfied, the authorities were prohibited from intervening in the business activities of the individuals involved in exploiting workers.

The international hospitality and travel industry is another business sector that benefits impassively from both labor servitude and sex tourism. While the industry is aware of the problem and executives have partnered with anti-human trafficking efforts to reduce abuses, it is difficult to police the entire industry, especially international hospitality corporations with properties all over the world. This became evident two years ago, when the United States White House found itself at the center of a scandal involving Secret Service agents bringing sex workers into rooms at distinguished Colombian hotels, including the Hilton Hotel in Cartagena, Colombia.[73] Although Hilton received stinging negative publicity, the fact that American Secret Service agents traveling to Colombia knew how to tap into the sex tourism underground would suggest that hotel chains utilized by government officials in many destinations are aware of what goes on in and around their properties, but do very little about it. Sex tourists know, through underground networks, that certain hotels, including upscale properties, are staging areas for sex tour operators to pick hotel

---

72. Křížková, *supra* note 69.

73. Carol D. Leonnig & David Nakamura, *Aides Knew of Possible White House Link to Cartagena, Colombia, Prostitution Scandal*, Wash. Post, Oct. 8, 2014.

guests up at the hotel to transport them to areas where they can engage in illicit sex acts. While corporate hotel chains would never openly accept such activities on or through their properties, it must be abundantly obvious to hospitality executives that sex tourism occurs around the world, that those engaged in sex tourism may very well be guests of their properties, and that their properties may be gathering and staging locations for sex tourists to pursue illegal acts. But on the other hand, such repugnant guests spend money for their rooms, eat there, drink there, and spread money around in the formal local economy. It may be an ugly business in many ways, but profit motive appears to trump best business practices and corporate governance.

Other corporate entities exist in a state of denial in order to maximize earnings, even amid growing criticism and attention to unsavory business practices. This has been the case for decades throughout the chocolate industry and involves children being trafficked from around Western Africa into the Ivory Coast to work in slave conditions on massive cocoa plantations. Chocolate is a major world commodity, controlled by a handful of multinational chocolate companies producing more than 60 million pounds of chocolate just for Valentine's Day alone each year.[74] "Big Chocolate" has long known that child labor exists in its industry, yet the trade association European Cocoa Association insists that assertions about labor trafficking and the use of child labor are false and excessive.

Amidst growing negative press and the threat of international boycotts against chocolate consumption in the late 1990s, the Chocolate Manufacturers Association, the World Cocoa Foundation, and its members, including Hershey, Kraft, Nestlé, and Cargill, convened in September 2001 to draft and sign the *Protocol for the Growing and Processing of Cocoa Beans and their Derivative Products in a Manner that Complies with ILO Convention 182 Concerning the Prohibition and Immediate Action for the Elimination of the Worst Forms of Child Labour,*[75] known as the *Harkin-Engel Protocol,* or the *Cocoa Protocol.* The primary goal of the *Cocoa Protocol* was to develop an action plan to address child labor in the industry and to rally the companies in mutual cooperation to improve working conditions on cocoa plantations. The members pledged to attempt to fulfill its commitments to the *Cocoa Protocol* by 2005. That date came and went, and one company, Hershey, put off meeting its commitments until at least 2017.

---

74. Leslie Hatfield & Dawn Brighid, *Where's the Love Hershey? On Chocolate and Labour (Part 2),* ECOCENTRIC BLOG, Feb. 11, 2014, http://gracelinks.org/blog/781/where-s-the-love-hershey-on-chocolate-and-labour-part-ii.

75. To view the Harkin-Engel Protocol, *see* http://www.cocoainitiative.org/wp-content/uploads/2016/10/Harkin_Engel_Protocol.pdf.

In 2011, independent filmmakers Miki Mistrati and U. Roberto Romano released a startling documentary, *The Dark Side of Chocolate*, which chronicles through a series of undercover reports, video footage, and interviews with government officials in the Ivory Coast, how children are trafficked to work on cocoa plantations. The film documents children between 10 and 15 years of age being subjected to brutal labor conditions that often involve beatings, injury, and no compensation. Many remain on the plantations and die there, never seeing their families or homelands again. The film also exposed how traffickers promise impoverished families that their children will be well paid and have a chance at a better life. The children are taken to a border town where another trafficker clandestinely takes the children by motorcycle across the border and into servitude. Another trafficker then takes the children and sells them to plantation farmers for around €250 each.

The two filmmakers met with Ivory Coast officials who were obviously aware of the trafficking operations, but refused officially to acknowledge conditions on the plantations. Later, when the documentary was brought to Nestlé's world headquarters in Switzerland, executives rejected the investigations and refused to look at the evidence documented in the film.[76] This was in 2010, years after Nestlé had signed onto the *Cocoa Protocol*.

The *Cocoa Protocol* is an important example of how good intentions and a public relations campaign can mask over passive involvement in corrupt practices. Mr. Romano opined during an interview that self-regulation could not work for these particular corporations because the places where the chocolate industry gets its raw product are often in weak and failing states where political corruption is high and enforcement of labor laws is nearly nonexistent. Passive involvement is sustained as long as the goal of a corporation's business model is constant growth of profit over the social impact of production.[77]

4. Accountability

In recent years, corporations have been called upon to adhere to rules of corporate governance and best practices. In fact, a thriving industry of consultants provide training and advice to companies large and small to reinforce how to manage business affairs and sustain positive public images. Corporate

---

76. When the filmmakers then showed the film on a large screen facing the Nestlé campus from across a street, Swiss police were summoned and told the filmmakers to shut it all down.

77. Hatfield, *supra* note 74.

governance is, in a manner, self-policing in many business sectors, and effective corporate governance can achieve incredible results in capitalist societies. Good governance and best practices can help raise employee wages and benefits, boost productivity, improve the environment, and strengthen conditions in the civil society in nations where the corporations do business. Corporate governance can also improve the dignity of human beings and can be an effective deterrent to both corruption and human trafficking.

On the other hand, corporations and business entities also have the capacity to bring formidable legal resources to bear to defend against charges of corrupt practices. As we know from reports and the outcomes of cases worldwide, all too often, individuals and entities with the means to refute allegations of wrongdoing often escape accountability and continue to engage with impunity in deprivations against individuals and the civil society at large. In many instances, punishments may be little more than a slap on the hand; large corporations can pay fines in the millions of dollars and write it off as little more than the cost of doing business in competitive global markets. On a smaller scale, affluent individuals who plead guilty to exploiting domestic staff are often first-time offenders and escape jail time by paying fines, being placed on probation, and providing some form of restitution to their victims—all consequences that may have little impact on their lives. Their punishments are never equal to the pain and suffering they had caused other human beings.

How then, can accountability acquire a meaningful deterrent effect? Nothing unsettles the corporate boardroom or a body of shareholders more than public criticism, bad press, and the potential loss of market share. The specter of boycotting products, reduced profits, and the possibility of losing access to resources and to markets generally gets the attention of corporate officers and directors. Public awareness campaigns such as film documentaries have the capacity to cause change, to improve working conditions, and to reduce the instances of exploitation and forced servitude. Increasingly, so does social media, especially when stories go viral. Powerful images of small children chained to looms all day weaving carpets, for instance, have led to the establishment of fair trade standards and the creation of labeling regimes such as Goodweave and Rugmark, which attempt to ensure that the rug a person buys is not made by child slaves.[78] We also see similar public awareness campaigns increasingly in other sectors, such as coffee growing and athletic apparel.

---

78. [Video] *Is Your Rug Slave-Free?* CNN Freedom Project, Apr. 18, 2011, http://the cnnfreedomproject.blogs.cnn.com/2011/04/18/is-your-rug-slave-free/.

Just as with private individuals, an effective means to get the attention of corporate entities seems to be through the pocketbook. Corporations and businesses should be subject to a zero tolerance policy. If they or their subcontractors and agents are caught using trafficked workers or caught engaging in corrupt acts related to human trafficking in the course of fulfilling a government contract, the corporation itself should bear the most responsibility and liability.

There has also been a growing effort to hold corporate officers and directors subject to criminal prosecution for human trafficking crimes and related acts of corruption that occur on their watch.[79] Doing so presents many challenges. In 2015, United States Deputy Attorney General Sally Quillian Yates presented a memorandum of legal arguments regarding the possibility of holding corporate officers individually responsible for wrongdoing.[80] The Yates Memo, as it is now known, stressed that individual accountability could achieve several goals: First, going after the executives could deter future misconduct and compel reforms in corporate behavior. Second, individuals responsible for illegal acts could no longer hide behind the corporate veil to escape accountability. Third, the possibility of wrongdoers rather than corporate entities being sanctioned could promote public confidence in the legal system. Yates proposed the following steps:

(1) that corporations must fully disclose all relevant facts relating to the individuals responsible for the misconduct;
(2) criminal and civil corporate investigators should target individuals from the "inception of the investigation";
(3) criminal and civil attorneys involved in investigations should coordinate and be in regular communication;
(4) culpable individuals should not be released from "civil or criminal liability when resolving a matter with a corporation";
(5) a clear plan should be in place to resolve individual cases related to a corporate investigation and to "memorialize any declinations as to individuals in such cases; and
(6) "civil attorneys should consistently focus on individuals as well as the company and evaluate whether to bring suit against an individual based on considerations beyond that individual's ability to pay."[81]

---

79. *See, e.g.*, Fred Fenster, *When Corporate Officers Are Personally Liable*, Greenberg Gluster webpage (Apr. 2012), http://www.greenbergglusker.com/news/articles/When-Corporate-Officers-Are-Personally-Liable-.

80. Memorandum of Sally Quillian Yates, U.S. Department of Justice, Sept. 9, 2015, on file with the author.

81. *Id.* at 2–3.

Corporations should also practice prevention and greater vigilance of their operations and how individuals in the ranks behave, especially at the point of production where problems of forced labor arise. For example, Big Chocolate punted on irrefutable evidence of child trafficking and child labor by saying that while the companies are aware of problems on cocoa plantations, they have so many cocoa producers that it is not practical to monitor every contracted plantation for labor violations and human trafficking. This is a feeble excuse. The chocolate industry earns billion in profits each year. Big Chocolate could easily field an army of inspectors to monitor what goes on in the cocoa plantations, and the cost to do so would have very little impact on the bottom line of profits.

It cannot be concluded, however, that corporations are evil by nature. Many corporate executives and businessmen want to do good in the world, and they ardently support anti-trafficking initiatives and the HT NGOs working to combat human trafficking and corruption. Some, like the founder of eBay, go so far as to establish well-funded and politically formidable foundations to combat human trafficking and to influence government policymaking to confront human trafficking.[82] The legal publishing and information services corporation LexisNexis has devoted a significant amount of resources to be at the forefront of business efforts to curtail all forms of human trafficking. Yet, despite the best of intentions, it can be a formidable ongoing challenge for many businesses to assert control over the subcontractors and middlemen they use.

---

82. Clare O'Connor, *Inside eBay Billionaire Pierre Omidyar's Battle To End Human Trafficking*, Forbes online, Nov. 8, 2012, http://www.forbes.com/sites/clareoconnor/2012/11/08/inside-ebay-billionaire-pierre-omidyars-battle-to-end-human-trafficking/.

Chapter 8

Trafficking in People to Harvest Their Organs: Where Private and Public Corruption Intersect

Summary: Our discussion of trafficking in persons for organ removal in this chapter is in many ways a difficult topic to address. Trafficking of persons to harvest their organs (as well as tissue, cells, and other body parts) brings together all the forms of corruption addressed in previous chapters. We will examine the international legal instruments and some domestic laws in place to combat this pernicious criminal enterprise and look at several case examples from around the world. We will conclude the chapter with a discussion of recommendations to confront and reduce the growing practice of trafficking in persons for removal of body parts.

Nancy Scheper-Hughes, a UC Berkeley anthropologist and co-founder of Organs Watch,[1] well describes the crime of trafficking of human beings for purposes of removing their organs and body parts (THB/OR):

Of the many field sites in which I have found myself, none compares with the world of transplant surgery for its mythical properties, its se-

---

1. Professor Scheper-Hughes co-founded Organs Watch with three other colleagues in 1999 to raise awareness and develop resources for confronting the growing illegal trafficking in human organs. It does not appear that Organs Watch is currently active as of 2016, but Professor Scheper-Hughes' work and writing remain seminal to the understanding and investigation of international trafficking in persons for organ removal.

crecy, its impunity, and its exoticism. The organ trade is extensive, lucrative, explicitly illegal in most countries, and unethical according to every governing body of medical professional life. It is therefore covert. In some sites the organs trade links the upper strata of bio-medical practice to the lowest reaches of the criminal world. The trans-actions can involve the police, mortuary workers, pathologists, civil servants, ambulance drivers, emergency room workers, eye bank and blood bank managers, and transplant coordinators.[2]

As Scheper-Hughes alludes, the illegal trade in organs and body parts is unique from other forms of human trafficking in that corrupt public, pri-vate, and non-government actors may all be co-conspirators in the same criminal act. There is some confusion over the difference between traffick-ing of human organs and body parts[3] and trafficking in human beings for organ removal. A significant amount of attention has been focused on or-gans (and other body parts) as an illicit commercial commodity, but not enough attention has been paid to the "box" in which the organ is trans-ported — the human being trafficked as a "donor" or host.

Like other forms of human trafficking, obtaining reliable data and statis-tics for THB/OR is difficult.[4] Part of the problem with data collection concerns the veil of secrecy over black market organ transplantation that persists due to: (1) organ sales being illegal in most countries, with steps taken to hide the transactions;[5] (2) hospitals and clinics disguising and concealing illegal trans-

---

2. Nancy Scheper-Hughes, *Global Traffic in Human Organs*, 41 Current Anthropol-ogy 1, 4 (2000).

3. Under United States federal law, the term "human organ" means the human kidney, liver, heart, lung, pancreas, bone marrow, cornea, eye, bone, and skin, and any other human organ specified by the Secretary of Health and Human Services by regulation." National Organ Transplant Act of 1983, Pub. L. 98-507, 98 Stat. 2343, sec. 301(c)(1).

4. *See* United Nations Assessment Toolkit: Trafficking in Persons for the Pur-pose of Organ Removal 12 (2015), https://www.unodc.org/documents/human-traffick-ing/2015/UNODC_Assessment_Toolkit_TIP_for_the_Purpose_of_Organ_Removal.pdf [hereinafter Toolkit].

5. Organization for Security and Co-operation in Europe (OSCE), Office of the Spe-cial Representative and Co-Ordinator for Combating Trafficking in Human Beings, Occa-sional Paper Series no. 6 *Trafficking in Human Beings for the Purpose of Organ Removal in the OSCE Region: Analysis and Findings*, at 28, SEC.GAL/123/13/Rev.1 (July 2013), https://ec.europa.eu/anti-trafficking/sites/antitrafficking/files/osce_organ_removal_1.pdf [here-inafter OSCE Analysis] (noting that "Fraudulent written consents and declarations are pre-pared with contents to comply with local legal requirements, such as disavowals of financial consideration for the organ, assertions of family relations, or assertions of informed and voluntary consent.").

plants as noble and selfless donations,[6] (3) criminals and health care professionals associated in organ trafficking networks hiding behind principles of confidentiality in the medical profession,[7] and;(4) victims and organ recipients desiring to keep their involvement a secret, perhaps out of fear of persecution or "feelings of shame and guilt."[8]

What we do know is that the present popularity and global reach of organ sales from commercial living donors or through organ brokers are well known.[9] We know that desperate wealthy patients now travel the world to bypass waiting lists and purchase a life-saving organ from vulnerable in impoverished individuals.[10] This trend has created the terms "organ tourism" and "transplant tourism,"[11] and "medical value travel" by insurance companies that encourage such a practice.[12] The emergence of transplant tourism began in the 1980s as a form of global trade in kidneys from living persons to supply the needs and demands of transplant recipients in the Middle East, Latin America, and Asia. In 1990, the medical journal *The Lancet* published what is considered the first scientific report on transplant tourism, recounting the transplant journeys of 130 renal patients from the United Arab Emirates and Oman who travelled with their private doctors to India. Once in India, the patients received kidneys provided by living "suppliers" recruited from local organ brokers. The report discussed the post-operative complications to the recipients,[13] but provided

---

6. *Id.* at 20.

7. *Id.*

8. *Id.*

9. This reality is well researched and documented. *See* D.A. Budiani-Saberi & F.L. Delmonico, *Organ Trafficking and Transplant Tourism: A Commentary on the Global Realities,* 2008 Am. J. of Transplantation 925 (May 2008) (describing organ trafficking known to them through their visits to several countries); *and also* G.M. Danovitch et al., *Organ Trafficking and Transplant Tourism: The Role of Global Professional Ethical Standards—The 2008 Declaration of Istanbul,* 2013 Transplantation 1306 (2013).

10. The financial gain, sale and purchase of organs are prohibited by various international instruments such as the WHO Guiding Principles on Human Cells, Tissue and Organ Transplantation in Guiding Principle 5. *See* Council of Europe Convention on Human Rights and Biomedicine, CETS 165 (4 April 1997).

11. Budiani-Saberi, *supra* note 9.

12. The economic term "value" is "the additional temptation of financial incentives offered by employers for their workers to participate in overseas healthcare programs that have been on the rise during the last decade. *See* K.A. Bramstedt & Jun Xuc, *Checklist: Passport, Plane Ticket, Organ Transplant,* 2007 Am. J. of Transplantation 1698 (2007).

13. The survival rate of the patients at one year was 81.5 percent. The most common complication was infection, although the report noted that, "Patients were not properly instructed about their treatment, and little or no information was given to doctors following

no information on or discussion of possible adverse effects on the kidney donors/sellers, who remained anonymous—like deceased donors.[14]

Of the nearly 100,000 known organ transplant operations undertaken worldwide annually at the end of the last decade,[15] between 5 percent and 10 percent of all kidney transplants were the result of organ trafficking in some form (or somewhere between 3,400 and 6,800 kidney transplants per year),[16] and that the retail value of illegal kidney transplants (including broker fee plus medical and transportation expenses) was between US$514 million and US$1 billion per year."[17]

1. Lack of THB/OR Cases and Data Renders Corruption Invisible

The arrangements behind THB/OR is rarely unmasked, and therefore, the magnitude has yet to be fully grasped. Several factors affect the insufficiency of cases and sound data and impede our ability to grasp the nature and modus operandi of this crime. This lack of clarity also obscures the link between the trafficking and organ removal acts and the unethical and corrupt practices of

---

up the patients, criteria of suitability for transplantation were not strict, and patients were exposed to serious infections (including human immunodeficiency virus infection)." A.K. Salahudeen, et al., *High Mortality among Recipients of Both Living-Unrelated Donor Kidneys*, 336 LANCET 8717, 8725–28 (1990).

14. The kidney sellers received between US$2,000 and US$3,000 for a 'spare' organ. *Human traffic: Exposing the Brutal Organ Trade*, NEW INTERNATIONALIST, May 2014, https://newint.org/features/2014/05/01/organ-trafficking-keynote/.

15. JEREMY HAKEN, TRANSNATIONAL CRIME IN THE DEVELOPING WORLD 21 (Global Financial Integrity, 2011), http://www.gfintegrity.org/wp-content/uploads/2014/05/gfi_transnational_crime_high-res.pdf. The approximate breakdown of transplants is as follows: Kidneys (68,500); livers (20,100), hearts (5,200), lungs (3,250), and pancreases (2,800) (citing as a source: Dr. Luc Noel, MD. Coordinator of the Clinical Procedures team, World Health Organization (July 29, 2009)).

16. *Id.* (citing to ARTHUR CAPLAN ET AL., COUNCIL OF EUROPE/UNITED NATIONS STUDY: TRAFFICKING IN ORGANS TISSUES AND CELLS AND TRAFFICKING IN HUMAN BEINGS FOR THE PURPOSE OF THE REMOVAL OF ORGANS 58 (2009), http://www.ont.es/publicaciones/Documents/OrganTrafficking_study.pdf).

17. *Id.* (citing to Jeneen Interlandi, *Organ Trafficking Is no Myth*, NEWSWEEK, Jan. 10, 2009, http://www.newsweek.com/organ-trafficking-no-myth-78079); *and also* Susan Scutti, *Organ Trafficking: An International Crime Frequently Unpunished*, MEDICAL DAILY.COM July 9, 2013, http://www.medicaldaily.com/organ-trafficking-international-crime-infrequently-punished-247493.

professionals and middlemen instrumental to carrying out THB/OR conspiracies, which Scheper-Hughes has labeled "neo-cannibalism" and "bio-terrorism."[18] So far, we have spent few investigative resources to focus on "the web" of actors underpinning each THB/OR exploitation,[19] and we have been largely unable to expose anyone involved in abetting THB/OR through corrupt acts and punish them.

A. Facts that Impede the Investigation of THB/OR

Investigating commercial organ trafficking crimes and adjudicating them present several challenges for law enforcement and government monitoring entities. These factors include:

(1) Confusion between THB/OR and trafficking for organ trade or organ trafficking;

(2) The clandestine character of this crime is exacerbated by the privacy requirements in the medical profession and the difficulty in identifying "donors/victims" due to "anonymity, fear, social stigma, and guilt."[20]

(3) Failure of governments to criminalize THB/OR in their domestic legislation;[21]

(4) Lack of investigations to corroborate credible information published by academics, physicians, investigative journalists, and NGOs that THB/OR has occurred;[22]

---

18. Nancy Scheper-Hughes, *Mr. Tati's Holiday and João's Safari—Seeing the World through Transplant Tourism*, 17 Body & Society 55, 58 (2011), https://www.sss.ias.edu/files/pdfs/Nancy%20Scheper-Huges,TATI's%20Holiday%20in%20BodSoc-2.pdf.

19. The Convention against Organ Trade uses the expression "the web of activity underpinning each trade" in reference to recruits, solicitors, doctors, hospital officials, and others that are overlooked in most of the laws of the countries that already prohibit the selling and buying of organs. Convention, http://www.coe.int/en/web/secretary-general/-/council-of-europe-convention-against-trafficking-in-human-organs.

20. In many countries, there are cultural and religious prohibitions and taboos to organ donation. So when vulnerable individuals resort to selling an organ, they often hide their actions, even from family members. This also makes investigating commercial organ sales problematic. The Bellagio Report, https://www.icrc.org/eng/resources/documents/article/other/57jnyk.htm.

21. The failure to recognize THB/OR as a domestic criminal offense denies these victims, the services and protections available to the other victims of human trafficking.

22. Several doctors, human rights groups, social scientists, and the media have issued reports on the human rights violations, suffering, and social, health and psychological consequences afflicting many donors as a result of their organs being harvested. In one inter-

(5) The nature and broad diversity of actors involved in this crime (transplant recipients, organ brokers, recruiters, medical specialists and hospitals, insurance companies, and public officials and/or law enforcement);

(6) Transplantations derived from illegal acts remain a financially rewarding practice for nearly everyone involved—except the victim.

Even though the buying or selling of organs is unethical, illegal, and universally vilified, researchers, social scientists, and human rights activists are divided on the issue of organ sale. The opposing view is rooted in social justice, the foundations of bioethics, and unease about health consequences of both donors and recipients. Opponents look at the setting of a market price for parts of the human body as exploitation of the desperate poor who "turn their suffering into an opportunity."[23] They also believe that (1) regulation of organ transfer will not work due to complex "social and medical realities in many parts of the world, especially in Second and Third World nations,"[24] and (2) that medical institutions established to monitor organ harvesting and distribution are often dysfunctional, corrupt, or compromised by the power of the commercial demand for organs and the impunity of the organ brokers who often seem to stay one or more steps ahead of the law. Moreover, to some surgeons an organ is little more than a tangible commodity used in their line of

---

view of a nephrologist in private practice in Rio de Janeiro, Brazil, Scheper-Hughes discovered that organ trafficking was "practically legalized" since it was done in several types of hospitals without regard to its illegality, and that many doctors simply "tolerate" the commercial transactions between live donors and recipients. Notable writings by Scheper-Hughes include, *Global Traffic in Human Organs*, 41 CURRENT ANTHROPOLOGY 191, 208 (2000); *Theft of Life: Globalization of Organ Stealing Rumors*, 12 ANTHROPOLOGY TODAY 3 (1996); and *Organ Trade: The New Cannibalism*, NEW INTERNATIONALIST (1998), https://newint. org/features/1998/04/05/trade/. Other authors writing about commercial organ transplantation include: M. Goyal et al., *Economic and Health Consequences of Selling a Kidney in India*, 288 JAMA 1589 (2002); A. Naqvi, *A Socio-Economic Survey of Kidney Vendors in Pakistan*, 20 TRANSPLANT INT'L 934 (2007); D. Budiani-Saberi & F.L. Delmonico, *Organ Trafficking and Transplant Tourism: A Commentary on the Global Realities*, 2008 AM. J. OF TRANSPLANTATION 925 (2008); Vivek Chaudhary, *Organ Trade Investigators Seize Hospital Record*, GUARDIAN, June 22, 1994; Hugh Hebert, *Victims of the Transplant Trade*, GUARDIAN, June 24, 1994; R. Chengappa, *The Organs Bazaar*, INDIA TODAY, July 31, 1990, and; Tsuyoshi Awaya, *The Human Body as a New Commodity*, 51 REV. OF TOYUYAMA U. 141 (1999).

23. Tarif Bakdash & Nancy Scheper-Hughes, *Is It Ethical for Patients with Renal Disease to Purchase Kidney's from the World's Poor?* SOCIAL SCIENCE IN THE 21ST CENTURY, iMedPub Thematic Collections Vol. 1, at 5.

24. *Id.* at 4.

work for achieving an outcome for which they are then compensated. The social and human rights elements of organ trafficking are irrelevant for some doctors engaged in THB/OR.[25]

Those in favor of commercializing organ transplantation argue that an individual has an autonomous right to sell one's organs in a marketplace that exists entirely due to the scarcity of human organs worldwide.[26] This position is sharply disputed. According to Scheper-Hughes, "the demand for human organs—and for wealthy transplant patients to purchase them—is driven by the medical discourse on scarcity."[27] Deconstructing the word "scarcity," Scheper-Hughes has asserted that organ scarcity represents an artificial need that is invoked "like a mantra in reference to the long waiting lists of candidates for various transplant surgeries.[28] In reality organs made available due to "high rates of youth mortality, accidental death, homicide, and transport death that produce a superabundance of young, healthy cadavers" simply go to waste.[29] Scarcity, according to Scheper-Hughes, is due to the lack of "well trained organ-capture teams in hospital emergency rooms and intensive care units, rapid transportation, and basic equipment to preserve" organs.[30] The true "scarcity is not of organs but of transplant patients of sufficient means to

---

25. See generally Scheper-Hughes, supra note 2.

26. The 2013 Global Observatory on Donations and Transplantation's informs us that there were 117,733 solid organs reported to be transplanted worldwide. This is a 2.6 percent increase over 2012, but the number of transplants may have met only about 10 percent or less of the global needs. See Global Activity in Organ Transplant: 2013 Estimates, https://view.publitas.com/ont/20151215_basic_slides_2013_con_datos_de_libya_de_2011/page/2. According to the Joint Study between the European Union and the United Nations, "the most serious consequence of the shortage of organs to meet the demand for transplantation is the fact that many patients will never be placed on the waiting list." The Study does a very comprehensive analyses of organ shortages as a universal problem and the consequences. See Council of Europe and United Nations, Joint Study on Trafficking in Organs, Tissues and Cells and Trafficking in Human Beings for the Purpose of the Removal of Organs 19–23 (2009), https://www.edqm.eu/medias/fichiers/Joint_Council_of_EuropeUnited_Nations_Study_on_tra1.pdf [hereinafter Joint Study on Trafficking in Organs]. The United States Department of Health & Human Services maintains national data on the Organ Procurement and Transplantation Network. In the United States, as of July 29, 2016, there were 131,098 patients registered on the waiting list for all types of organs, with 107,292 for kidneys. See National Data website https://optn.transplant.hrsa.gov/data/view-data-reports/national-data/#.

27. Scheper-Hughes, supra note 2, at 198.

28. Id.

29. Id. at 198–99.

30. Id. at 199.

pay for them,"[31] which in turn spurs a black market where organs can be obtained for a "pittance" from the abundant poor and desperate.[32]

The shortage of organs, regardless of the reasons, particularly from an "indigenous supply,"[33] has created a robust black market system by which government officials, health care practitioners (which Scheper-Hughes refers to as outlaws and vultures[34]) and medical facility administrators engage in unethical conduct in order to be rewarded financially. Illegal organ harvesting can also be construed as a form of neo-feudalism by which the social elites, either remaining in their home countries or traveling abroad, assert complete physical control over the poor and destitute who live in desperation so acute that they are forced to sell their organs as an act of survival.[35]

B. International Repudiation of Commercial Organ Transplantation

The commercialization of human organs has been repudiated by countries world-wide[36] and in several declarations, recommendations and guidelines of

---

31. *Id.*

32. *Id.*

33. Another researcher, Yosuke Shimazono, wrote in 2007 that the "shortage of an indigenous supply of organs has led to the development of the international organ trade, where potential recipients travel abroad to obtain organs through commercial transactions." *See* Yosuke Shimazono, *The State of the International Organ Trade: A Provisional Picture Based on Integration of Available Information*, 85 BULLETIN OF THE WORLD HEALTH ORGANIZATION (2007), http://www.who.int/bulletin/volumes/85/12/06-039370/en/. Nations are challenged by the fast increase in the number of patients on transplant waiting lists and the number of patients dying while waiting. In the U.S. in 2006, the amount of patients on the waiting list rose to "over 95,000, while the number of patient deaths was over 6,300." *See* G.M. Abouna, *Organ Shortage Crisis: Problems and Possible Solutions*, 40 TRANSPLANTATION PROCEEDINGS 34 (2008), http://www.ncbi.nlm.nih.gov/m/pubmed/18261540. The Global Observatory on Donations & Transplantation (GODT) tracks organ transplantation activities in its 112 Member States. The information is "confirmed by official national sources" and in "some instances, there are still provisional estimates" so data "may be modified without prior notice."

34. Scheper-Hughes, *supra* note 18, at 57.

35. Francis Delmonico & Alexander Capron, *Our Body Parts Shouldn't Be for Sale*, WASH. POST, Dec. 29, 2015, https://www.washingtonpost.com/news/in-theory/wp/2015/12/29/our-body-parts-shouldnt-be-for-sale/.

36. In Iran the organ trade is legal only among Iranian citizens and regulated through a government-sponsored paid living donor (LD) kidney transplant program. *See* WORLD HEALTH ORGANIZATION, GUIDE TO WORLD HEALTH ORGANIZATION, AGENDA-ILLEGAL ORGAN TRADE 8, Rhetorica Mun Conference 2015, http://rhetoricamun.weebly.com/up-

various international organizations going back to the late 1980s when the World Health Organization's World Health Assembly convened in 1987 to address the trade for profit in human organs.[37] Acknowledging the broad differences between countries in the level of "safety, quality, efficacy of donation and transplantation of human cells, tissues and organs," the WHA identified that ethical aspects of transplantation are foremost among issues of international organ transplantation, and that the failure to meet the needs of organ transplant patients and the conditions that cause a shortage of organs leads to the temptation to engage in THB/OR. Four years later in 1991, WHO issued *Resolution 44.25*, called the *Guiding Principles on Human Cell, Tissue, and Organ Transplantation*.[38] This resolution "urged states to ban the sale of human organs" and practices such as all types of advertising, "soliciting, or brokering for the purpose of transplant commercialism, organ trafficking, or transplant tourism." It also urged states to "include penalties for acts such as medically screening donors or organs, or transplanting organs—that aid, encourage, or use the products of, organ trafficking or transplant tourism."

The *Guiding Principles* underwent several subsequent modifications, including in 2004, when the WHO passed *Resolution 57.18* urging states "to take measures to protect the poorest and vulnerable groups from 'transplant tourism' and the sale of tissues and organs, including attention to the wider problem of international trafficking in human tissues and organs." In 2008, WHO revised the *Guiding Principles* again, clarifying the prohibition of organ commercialization, and stressing the link between organ sales and human trafficking. Donations from the living were allowed "if donors were given the necessary care." The Guiding Principles established requirements that there be a "genetic, legal, or emotional relationship between the donor and recipient" in order to combat the practice of transplant tourism.[39] Then, in 2010, the WHO issued *Resolution WHA63.22* revising the *Guiding Principles* by calling special attention to the international trafficking in human organs and tissues, and embracing "measures to protect the poorest and vulnerable groups from transplant tourism and

---

loads/5/3/4/7/53474781/new_study_guide_of_who.pdf [hereinafter WHO Guide]; *and also* A.J. Ghods, *Changing Ethics in Renal Transplantation: Presentation of Iran Model*, 36 Transplantation Proceedings 11 (2004). For a discussion on Iran's paid living donor program, *see* Nasrollah Ghahramani, *Paid Living Donation and Growth of Deceased*, 2016 Transplantation 1165, http://www.ncbi.nlm.nih.gov/pubmed/27203584.

37. *See* Transplantation of human cells, tissues and organs on the WHO website, http://www.who.int/transplantation/en/.

38. WHO Guide, *supra* note 36.

39. *Id.* at 12.

the sale of organs and tissues."[40] The Resolution contains 11 principles outlining the voluntary, non-monetary nature of organ donation.

Another organization that was an early advocate for ethical standards in human organ transplantation was the World Medical Association (WMA). In 1985, the WMA issued its *Statement on Live Organ Trade* condemning the "purchase and sale of human organs for transplantation" and calling on all governments "to take effective steps to prevent the commercial use of human organs."[41] In 2000, the WMA issued a more detailed statement on the prohibition of commercial organ trafficking, stating that a "financial incentive compromises the voluntariness of the choice and the altruistic basis for organ and tissue donation," and that any "access to needed medical treatments based on ability to pay is inconsistent with the principles of justice." Under this WMA statement, transplant centers and surgeons have an obligation not to accept for transplantation any organs "suspected to have been obtained through commercial transaction," and that the advertisement of organs should be prohibited.[42] However, the WMA accepts and considers permissible the "reasonable reimbursement of expenses such as those incurred in procurement, transport, processing, preservation, and implantation."[43]

In 2014, the WMA rescinded some sections of the *Statement on Live Organ Trade*, and amended it to reiterate the prohibition for organ payment by adding: (1) that "access to needed medical treatment based on ability to pay is inconsistent with the principles of justice"; (2) that doctors should refuse to transplant organs obtained through a commercial transaction; and (3) that advertisement of organs in exchange for money should be prohibited. The WMA also emphasized that individuals deemed to be "incapable of making informed decisions should not be considered as potential living donors except in extraordinary circumstances and in accordance with ethics committee review or established protocols."[44]

---

40. World Health Organization, Revised Guiding Principles on Human Cell, Tissue and Organ Transplantation, WHO Res. WHA63.22 (2010), http://apps.who.int/gb/ebwha/pdf_files/WHA63/A63_R22-en.pdf?ua=1.

41. Adopted by the 37th World Medical Assembly of the World Medical Association at Brussels, Belgium, October 1985," http://hrlibrary.umn.edu/instree/organtrade.html.

42. World Medical Association, Statement on Human Organ and Tissue Donation and Transplantation (adopted by the 52nd WMA General Assembly, Edinburgh, Scotland, October 2000), https://www.scribd.com/document/149834770/WMA-Statement-on-Human-Organ-Donation.

43. *Id.*

44. World Medical Association, Statement on Human Organ Donation and Transplantation, 65th WMA General Assembly, Durban, South Africa, October 2014, https://www.wma.net/

Two international organizations, the Transplantation Society and the International Society for Nephrology (ISN) responded to a call by the WHA to its members to take measures to protect the poor and vulnerable from transplant tourism and to address the problem of international trafficking of human organs and tissue. The result was an important international instrument known as the *Declaration of Istanbul* (DOI),[45] which is intended to guide physicians and healthcare providers on ethical issues with organ donations and transplantations and to protect the poor and vulnerable from transplant tourism.[46] The DOI was adopted in May 2008 by both organizations along with several government representatives.[47] Among its provisions, the DIO defines travel for organ transplantation as "the movement of organs, donors, recipients or transplant professionals across jurisdictional borders for transplantation purposes."[48] According to the DIO, travel for transplantation becomes transplant *tourism* when it includes: (1) organ trafficking and/or (2) transplant commercialism, or (3) the resources (organs, professionals and transplant centers) devoted to providing transplants to patients from outside a country that undermine the country's ability to provide transplant services for its own population.[49] The DOI also addressed unethical practices and the "undesirable consequence of the global shortage of organs for transplantation," and urged members to prohibit organ trafficking and transplant tourism because they violate "the principles of human dignity."[50] Moreover, transplant commercialism "leads inexorably to inequity and injustice" because it "targets impoverished and otherwise vulnerable donors."[51]

Another important international document to emerge in the late 1990s is *The Bellagio Task Force Report on Transplantation, Bodily Integrity, and the International Traffic in Organs,* known as the *Bellagio Report.* In 1997, the scarcity of human organs for transplant and growing concern over the sale

---

policies-post/wma-statement-on-human-organ-donation-and-transplantation/ [hereinafter WMA Statement 65th].

45. The Declaration of Istanbul organization webpage and related information can be found at http://www.declarationofistanbul.org/.

46. *See The Declaration of Istanbul on Organ Trafficking and Transplant Tourism,* Indian J. Nephrol. 18, no. 3 (2008): 135–140, http://www.ncbi.nlm.nih.gov/pmc/articles/ [hereinafter Declaration of Istanbul].

47. The list of government and non-government organizations endorsing the Declaration makes for interesting reading.

48. Declaration, *supra* note 46.

49. *Id.*

50. Declaration, *supra* note 46.

51. *Id.*

of organs in black market networks were conveyed to the international community by a multidisciplinary group of experts (transplant surgeons, organ procurement specialists, human rights activists, academics, and social scientists) tasked with defining ethical standards for the international practice of organ donation in light of the abuses of organ donation affecting the "socially disadvantaged" and interfering with the trust that must be integral to donation.[52] The result was the *Bellagio Report*, named for Bellagio, Italy, where the group convened.

The Bellagio group determined that organ shortages in many countries incentivise medical professionals and government officials "to pursue ethically dubious strategies for obtaining organs."[53] They also understand that foreign nationals in urgent need of an organ transplant have the financial resources to tender certain premium payments, which often take preference over any noble or altruistic "desire to meet the need of their country's patients."[54]

In addition to raising awareness of commercial organ transplantation as another form of exploitation of human begins, the *Bellagio Report* was important for identifying and articulating some of the factors that encourage transborder and transregional THB/OR, such as religious and cultural taboos in one part of the world that compel organ transplant patients to seek operations where such prohibitions are not recognized. The *Bellagio Report* also set the groundwork leading to a more focused international front against commercial organ trafficking by identifying travel patterns in which residents from Middle East Gulf States tended to go to India for transplants while residents from Taiwan, Hong Kong, Korea, and Singapore traveled to China for transplants.[55]

Yet another important report to emerge more recently is a document produced by the European Parliament called the *Trafficking in Human Organs* study, which found that "the financial aspects of organ trafficking has made it clear that the criminal proceeds from trafficking and illegal transplants are considerable [and] demonstrates that money is the ultimate driving force behind this crime."[56] The Parliamentary Assembly of the Council of Europe also is-

---

52. David J. Rothman et al., *The Bellagio Task Force Report on Transplantation, Bodily Integrity, and the International Traffic in Organs*, 29 TRANSPLANTATION PROCEEDINGS 2739 (1997), https://www.icrc.org/eng/resources/documents/article/other/57jnyk.htm.

53. *Id.*

54. *Id.*

55. *Id.*

56. *See* MICHAEL BOS, STUDY: TRAFFICKING IN HUMAN ORGANS 9, prepared for the European Parliament Directorate-General for External Policies Policy Department, 2015, http://www.europarl.europa.eu/RegData/etudes/STUD/2015/549055/EXPO_STU(2015)549055_EN.pdf.

sued *Recommendation 1611 of 2003* in which the Council identified the following compelling ethical questions regarding organ trafficking in Europe:

- Should the poor provide for the health of the rich?
- Should the price of alleviating poverty be human health?
- Should poverty compromise human dignity and health?
- And in terms of medical ethics, should help to recipients be counterbalanced by neglect of, and harm to, donors?[57]

The Recommendation also recognized that serious loopholes exist in the domestic legislation of Member States that allow trafficking in organs to occur, and that criminal responsibility must be specified in national criminal codes.

> Criminal responsibility should include brokers, intermediaries, hospital/nursing staff and medical laboratory technicians involved in the illegal transplant procedure. Medical staff who encourage and provide information on "transplant tourism" should also be liable to prosecution. The medical staff involved in follow-up care of patients who have purchased organs should be accountable if they fail to alert the health authorities of the situation.[58]

National level organizations have also turned their attention to commercial organ transplantation. For example, the Institute of Medicine in the United States officially opposes organ commercialization, declaring, "Every society draws lines separating things that are treated as commodities from things that should not be treated as 'for sale.' The committee believes that there are powerful reasons to preserve the idea that organs are donated rather than sold, even in a regulated market."[59]

2. Organ Trafficking and THB/OR: Two Different and Distinct Crimes

While THB/OR certainly does occur in Third World settings in less than pristine clinical conditions, THB/OR also takes place in the shadows—and some-

---

57. COE Recommendation 1611, article 7, https://search.coe.int/cm/Pages/result_details.aspx?ObjectId=09000016805dca9a.

58. *Id.* art. 12.

59. F. Delmonico et al., Letter to the Editor: *"Proposed Standards for Incentives for Organs Donation" Are Neither International nor Acceptable*, 2012 Am. J. of Transplantation 1954 (2012).

times openly—in the formal, licit First and Second World medical facilities.[60] Illegal organ removal meets a critical demand by affluent patients who when faced with long waiting lists or lack of donors in their home countries can travel abroad and pay out of pocket for a fast track transplant procedure via black market sources. It also meets the demands for transplants by individuals in some countries who cannot afford a legally allowed transplant, but can cobble together enough funds to travel abroad, even at great distances, to acquire a transplant organ.[61] THB/OR can also be a means for some governments to supplement their national health care systems through nefarious conduct,[62] and often this crime is disguised in the form of transplant tourism.[63] In fact, transplant tourism has become so lucrative that state-of-the-art medical centers are now built quite literally within a stone's throw of international airports, and surgical arrangements can include not only the medical costs, but also five-star accommodations with concierge services and guaranteed discretion and privacy.[64]

People frequently confuse the crime of organ trafficking[65] with the crime of trafficking in human beings for organ removal. Much of the literature uses the terms interchangeably, and incorrectly, or groups organ trafficking and trafficking of human beings for organ removal together. A policy report issued by the European Parliament in 2015 does not help the confusion over terminology and distinction, when the authors incorrectly treat both acts as sub-classes under the umbrella of trafficking in organs.

> The term 'trafficking in organs' groups together a whole range of illegal activities that aim to commercialise human organs and tissues

---

60. Scheper-Hughes, *supra* note 2, at 193. Globalization exposes every country to a capitalist economy in which everything is "reduced to commodities," including human beings and their organs. Today we now see how "the flow of organs follows the modern routes of capital: from South to North, from Third to First World, from poor to rich, from black to brown to white, and from female to male."

61. *Id.*

62. WHO Guide, *supra* note 36. The United Nations acknowledged that health is "paramount to the stability of mankind," it is essential in "allowing human beings to reach their full potential," and improving health "will help strengthen economic growth."

63. Shimazono, *supra* note 33. Shimazono defines transplant tourism as "when a patient obtains an organ through the organ trade or other means that contravene the regulatory frameworks of their countries of origin."

64. Scheper-Hughes, *supra* note 18.

65. Trafficking in organs is not recognized as an offence in many jurisdictions. There is a link between organ trafficking and THB/OR. *See* Alireza Bagheri, ed. Global Bioethics: The Impact of the UNESCO International Bioethics Committee (Springer International, 2016); *and also*, Rothman, *supra* note 52.

for the purpose of transplantation. It encompasses the trafficking of persons with the intent to remove their organs (THBOR); transplant tourism where patients travel abroad seeking an (illegal) transplant with a paid donor; and trafficking in organs, tissues and cells (OTC), which refers to commercial transactions with human body parts that have been removed from living or deceased persons.[66]

The problem with this ambiguity is that it hinders implementing proper policies for prevention, and for programming victim protection and assistance. Moreover, it impedes effective cooperation across international borders, and allows culprits and co-conspirators to go unpunished and unaccountable.

For instance, the *Declaration of Istanbul,* which declares, "Organ trafficking and transplant tourism violate the principles of equity, justice, and respect for human dignity and should be prohibited,"[67] merges organ trafficking and THB/OR into the same definition. This creates some unnecessary confusion. The DIO description of organ trafficking, modeled on Article 3(a) of the *Palermo Protocol,* defines organ trafficking as:

[t]he recruitment, transport, transfer, harboring or receipt of living or deceased persons or their organs by means of the threat or use of force or other forms of coercion, of abduction, of fraud, of deception, of the abuse of power or of a position of vulnerability, or of the giving to, or the receiving by, a third party of payments or benefits to achieve the transfer of control over the potential donor, for the purpose of exploitation by the removal of organs for transplantation.[68]

The confusion occurs when the DOI joins both organ trafficking and trafficking of a person for organ removal as a single criminal act involving (1) trafficking of living *or deceased* individuals and/or (2) trafficking of organs borne by them (inside of them). THB/OR should be defined as a distinct crime because it requires the *movement* of a *living* person through the threat or use of force or other forms of coercion, of abduction, of fraud, of deception, etc., to effect an organ removal. In contrast, organ trafficking entails the removal of organs attained through a commercial transaction in which abuse, coercion, etc. are *absent,* for example, removing organs and body parts from prisoners executed by the state and selling them on the black market.

---

66. Bos, *supra* note 56, at 2.
67. Declaration of Istanbul, *supra* note 48, at *Principle 6.*
68. Declaration of Istanbul, *supra* note 48, at *Definitions.*

The correct clarification of the distinction is put forth in a joint study on the trafficking of organs, tissues, and cells (OTC) conducted by the Council of Europe and the United Nations in 2009, which sought to address, "serious confusion in the legal and scientific communities" over the difference between trafficking in OTC and trafficking in human beings and to clarify the solutions:

> [T]he solutions for preventing both types of trafficking should necessarily be different because the "trafficked objects" are different: in one case the "organs tissues and cells" and in the other case the "person himself/herself" who was trafficked for the specific purpose removing his/her organs. To express this idea in legal terms, it could be said that trafficking in OTC differs from trafficking in human beings for the purpose of organ removal in one of the constituent elements of the crime — the object of the criminal offense. In the former case, the object of the crime is the organs, tissues and cells, while in the latter case it is the trafficked person.[69]

The United States State Department annual TIP Reports appear to have overlooked this critical distinction and actually perpetuate the confusion year after year and from country to country. There is a significant problem with consistency in TIP Report "observations" that criticize countries for criminalizing trafficking in persons for the purpose of organ removal, even though criminalization is *required* by the *Palermo Protocol*.[70] In other instances, the TIP Reports address organ trafficking as if referencing human trafficking for organ removal. Some of the country narratives manifest a misunderstanding or even ignorance of the forms of exploitation under the *Protocol*. When addressing organ harvesting as a form of exploitation, TIP Reports overlook the fact that organ removal does not always take place through threats, use of force or coercion, but is in most cases effected through more deceitful means such as fraud, deception, the giving of payments or benefits, the abuse of power, or the exploitation of some vulnerability.

For example, the 2010 TIP Report acknowledges organ removal as a form of exploitation, but appears to ignore or lack knowledge that most of the organ removal is achieved through nonviolent means. In describing trafficking in Sudan, the Report erroneously implies that organ harvesting is not a stand-alone form of exploitation when it states, "Government authorities reported efforts to investigate cases of organ harvesting. It is not clear that the victims

---

69. Joint Study on Trafficking in Organs, *supra* note 26.
70. Palermo Protocol, article 3(a).

of these crimes were subjected to forced labor or sex trafficking." The Report further confuses matters by stating:

> The trade in human organs—such as kidneys—is not in itself a form of human trafficking. The international trade in organs is substantial and demand appears to be growing. Some victims in developing countries are exploited as their kidneys are purchased for low prices. Such practices are prohibited under the Palermo Protocol, for example when traffickers use coercive means, such as force or threats of force to secure the removal of the victim's organs.[71]

The confusion continues in the 2015 TIP Report, in which the State Department errs with the statement that Bolivian and Peruvian law "diverges from the 2000 UN TIP Protocol ... by penalizing *non-trafficking crimes*, such as ... the removal ... of organs, as human trafficking."[72] Also, the same 2015 TIP Report contradicts itself when describing Moldova's approach to investigating and prosecuting trafficking crimes by focusing, among other things, on organ removal.[73] On the narrative about Mozambique's 2008 anti-trafficking law, the TIP Report not only contradicts its own conclusion on Peru's and Bolivia's law, but erroneously describes that the law includes a prohibition against organ trafficking.[74]

Given that the United States is a prominent party to the *Palermo Protocol,* one wonders why the investigators writing the TIP Reports do not seem to discern that the *Protocol* is the first international legal instrument to define and criminalize trafficking for purposes of organ removal.[75] Nor do they seem to refer to other important international instruments that make a clear distinction about THB/OR that could provide an abundance of guidance during the research stage of preparing the Reports. For example, the *Optional Protocol to the Convention on the Rights of the Child on the Sale of Children, Child Prosti-*

---

71. U.S. Dep't of State, Trafficking In Persons Report 318 (2010).

72. U.S. Dep't of State, Trafficking In Persons Report 94, 278 (2015). The TIP Report's narrative erroneously states that Peruvian law focuses only on the sale of organs when it addresses both organ removal and sale. *See* Peru's Law against Human Trafficking and Trafficking of Migrants, Article 153, of Law against human trafficking and trafficking of migrants. Ley No. 28950 de 2006 Ley contra la trata de personas y el tráfico ilícito de migrantes, https://www.hsph.harvard.edu/population/trafficking/peru.traf.07.pdf.

73. *Id.* at 248.

74. *Id.* at 254–55.

75. Toolkit, *supra* note 4.

tution and Child Pornography defines and criminalizes the transfer of organs for profit.[76] The 2014 Council of Europe's *Convention against Trafficking in Human Beings* (ECAT)[77] states in article 4(a) that exploitation resulting from the trafficking of human beings shall include the removal of organs. A 2011 *Directive* issued by the European Parliament greatly expands criminal acts that constitute human trafficking, including the trafficking in human beings for the purpose of the removal of organs, "which constitutes a serious violation of human dignity and physical integrity."[78]

These confusions and misstatements by the TIP Report, a publication that has so much influence and power, is worrisome. Perhaps this may be due in part to the fact that the United States does not criminalize THB/OR,[79] as is required by Article 5 of the Protocol.[80]

---

76. *Optional Protocol to the Convention on the Rights of the Child on the Sale of Children, Child Prostitution and Child Pornography*, G.A. Res. 54/263, U.N. Doc. A/RES/54/263 (May 25, 2000), art. 3(b).

77. Council of Europe, Convention on Action Against Trafficking in Human Beings and its Explanatory Report, C.E.T.S. No. 197 (2005).

78. Directive 2011/36/EU of the European Parliament and of the Council of 5 April 2011, on preventing and combating trafficking in human beings and protecting its victims.

79. The removal of organs is not present in the United States description of severe forms of human trafficking. Federal statutes do not formally define human trafficking or trafficking in persons. Instead, Section 103(8) of the Trafficking Victim Protection Act defines "severe forms of trafficking in persons" to mean:

    (A) sex trafficking in which a commercial sex act is induced by force, fraud, or coercion, or in which the person induced to perform such act has not attained 18 years of age; or

    (B) the recruitment, harboring, transportation, provision or obtaining of a person for labor or services, through the use of force, fraud, or coercion for the purpose of subjection to involuntary servitude, peonage, debt bondage, or slavery.

80. Article 5. Criminalization

    1. Each State Party shall adopt such legislative and other measures as may be necessary to establish as criminal offences the conduct set forth in article 3 of this Protocol, when committed intentionally:

    2. Each State Party shall also adopt such legislative and other measures as may be necessary to establish as criminal offences:

        a) Subject to the basic concepts of its legal system, attempting to commit an offence established in accordance with paragraph 1 of this article;

        b) Participating as an accomplice in an offence established in accordance with paragraph 1 of this article; and

        c) Organizing or directing other persons to commit an offence established in accordance with paragraph 1 of this article.

See United Nations Office on Drugs and Crime, United Nations Convention against Transnational Organized Crime and the Protocols Thereto, at 43, U.N.

3. Trafficking in Organs

In THB/OR, the aim of criminalization is to protect vulnerable persons from all aspects of exploitation, as set forth throughout the Preamble of the *Palermo Protocol*,[81] while with trafficking in organs, criminalization aims toward outlawing the commercialization of human organs and tissues for the purpose of transplantation. There *can* be a link between one and the other, since the crime of trafficking in organs may originate in cases of THB/OR, such as when an individual's position of vulnerability is manipulated and controlled in order to extract his/her organ.[82]

A. Convention against Trafficking in Human Organs

As we have seen in our discussion of the definitions for corruption, as of 2016, there is no international consensus on a definition for trafficking in organs. The only international treaty specifically addressing and defining trafficking in human organs is the Council of Europe's *Convention against Trafficking in Human Organs* (CTHO),[83] which was the result of a joint effort between the Council and the United Nations beginning in 2008.[84] The Joint Study identified a number of issues related to the trafficking in human organs, tissues and cells which deserved further consideration, in particular the need to distinguish clearly between trafficking in human organs per se (OTC), and trafficking in human beings for the purpose of the removal of organs (THB/OR); the need to uphold the principle of prohibition of making financial gains with the human body or its parts; the need to promote organ donation; the need to collect reliable data on trafficking in organs, tissues and cells, and the

---

Doc A/55/383/Add.1 (Nov. 3, 2000), https://www.unodc.org/unodc/en/treaties/CTOC/#Full text.

81. The Preamble clearly states that vulnerable persons will not be protected in the absence of a "universal instrument that addresses all aspects of trafficking in persons."

82. An organ sale can be considered trafficking when a person is received for the purpose of an organ removal by way of payment or benefits to achieve the consent of a person.

83. COUNCIL OF EUROPE, CONVENTION AGAINST TRAFFICKING IN HUMAN ORGANS, CETS No. 216 (2015), https://www.coe.int/en/web/conventions/full-list/-/conventions/treaty/216 [hereinafter COE Convention]. This Convention was adopted on July 9, 2014 by the Committee of Ministers in Strasbourg and opened for signature on March 25, 2015. *See also* Toolkit, *supra* note 4.

84. Joint Study, *supra* note 26, at 11. There were fourteen original State signatories in 2008.

need to reach international agreement on a definition of trafficking in organs, tissues and cells.

The CTHO states that the trafficking in organs shall mean the intentional removal of human organs from a living or deceased person, "where the removal is performed without the free, informed and specific consent of the living or deceased donor, or, in the case of the deceased donor, without the removal being authorized" under the domestic law of the State Party.[85] Such removals will establish criminal intent for the purposes of establishing domestic legislation of States Parties.[86]

The CTHO also defines the human organ as, "a differentiated part of the human body, formed by different tissues, that maintains its structure, vascularisation and capacity to develop physiological functions with a significant level of autonomy. A part of an organ is also defined to be an organ if its function is to be used for the same purpose as the entire organ in the human body, maintaining the requirements of structure and vascularisation."[87]

The United Nations groups the *crime* of organ trafficking into three general categories:

(1) Traffickers force or deceive the victims into giving up an organ;
(2) Victims "agree to sell an organ and are cheated because they are not paid for the organ or are paid less than the promised price;" and
(3) Vulnerable persons are treated for an illness that "may or may not exist and thereupon organs are removed without the victim's knowledge.[88]

For comparison, the World Health Organization[89] recognizes two types of trafficking in organs:

(1) When the trafficker forces or cheats victims into donating an organ; and

---

85. COE Convention, *supra* note 83, art. 4(1)(a).

86. Criminal intent is discussed in articles 4, 5, 7, 8, and 9, respectively.

87. COE Convention, *supra* note 83, art. 2(2).

88. *Trafficking for Organ Trade*, 2016, UNODC. Gift.Hub, http://www.ungift.org/knowledgehub/en/about/trafficking-for-organ-trade.html.

89. *See* Peter Hummel, *Kidneys on Special Offer*, DW.COM, July 31, 2012, http://www.dw.com/en/kidneys-on-special-offer/a-16134667 (noting, "The WHO Resolution WHA63.22 of 2010 contains 11 principles outlining the voluntary, non-monetary nature of organ donation. Three years prior to that, 150 experts and government representatives from all over the world had already adopted the Declaration of Istanbul on Organ Trafficking and Transplant Tourism. The Council of Europe and the World Medical Association have also outlawed organ trafficking.").

(2) When "donors agree either formally or informally to sell an organ and are underpaid by brokers or duplicitous doctors."[90]

The WHO then divides the organ trade into two main subcategories, which "can be classified as transplant tourism:"

(1) Moving the recipient to another country for the operation; and
(2) Moving both the donor and the recipient to a different country.[91]

Organ trafficking researcher Yosuke Shimazono goes further by establishing four "modes" of organ trade and trafficking:[92]

- Mode 1: OTC recipient travels from home country to the country in which the donor and transplant center is located.
- Mode 2: OTC donor travels from home country to the country in which the recipient and transplant center is located.
- Mode 3: OTC donor and recipient travel from home country to the country in which the transplant center is located.
- Mode 4: OTC donor from one country and OTC recipient from another country travel to a third country where the transplant center is located.

However, the CTHO emphasizes that organ trafficking can occur with no link to human trafficking.[93] While some countries "criminalize the sale and purchase of organs, as well as certain irregularities in the conduct of organ transplants, a key challenge to countering THB/OR is ensuring that THB/OR

---

90. WHO Guide, *supra* note 36, at 5.
91. WHO Guide, *supra* note 36, at 5–6.
92. OSCE Analysis, *supra* note 5, at 27.
93. Joint Study, *supra* note 26. This conclusion was reached by the Joint Study, noting that "the extent of the relationship between trafficking in organs and trafficking in persons (and other forms of organized crime) is unclear." *See also* Report of the Secretary-General to the Commission on Crime Prevention and Criminal Justice, on Preventing, Combating and Punishing Trafficking in Human Organs ¶ 81, February 21, 2006, E/CN.15/2006/10 [hereinafter Secretary-General Report]. https://documents-dds-ny.un.org/doc/UNDOC/GEN/V06/513/17/PDF/V0651317.pdf?OpenElement. The groundwork for the Joint Study was laid out on December 20, 2004, when the UN General Assembly requested the Secretary-General to prepare a study on the extent of organ trafficking. *See* Resolution 59/156 "Prevention, combating and punishing trafficking in human organs." The study was to be submitted to the Commission on Crime Prevention and Criminal Justice.

is indeed charged as a trafficking offence, which generally carries more severe penalties, but is also more difficult to investigate and prosecute."[94]

The reality is that many donors travel for surgery without being threatened or physically coerced. Such consensual removal of organs "for financial gain, or comparable advantage and/or outside of the approved domestic systems," was not included in any international legal instrument.[95] Notwithstanding the existence of international legal instruments and many regional and sub-regional action plans and declarations against human trafficking for organ removal, these instruments possess significant "loopholes, that are not sufficiently addressed by these instruments," and that "continue to exist in the international legal framework."[96]

The CTHO is currently the only criminal law convention against trafficking in human organs, and while it is an instrument of the Council of Europe, it is open to nations outside of Europe. Under articles 4 through 9 of the CTHO, any of the following acts when committed intentionally constitutes the crime of trafficking in human organs:

1. The illicit removal of organs:
   a. In the case of a living donor, removal without the free, informed and specific consent, or,
   b. in the case of the deceased donor, without the removal being authorized under its domestic law, or
   c. where, in exchange for the removal of organs, the living donor, or a third party, has been offered or has received a financial gain or comparable advantage, or—
   d. where in exchange for the removal of organs from a deceased donor, a third party has been offered or has received a financial gain or comparable advantage.
2. The use of illicitly removed organs.

---

94. OSCE Analysis, *supra* note 5, at 14.

95. COE Convention, *supra* note 83, adopted by the Committee of Ministers on July 9, 2014 and opened for signature March 25, 2015.

96. Additional Opinion of the Steering Committee on Bioethics (CDBI), the European Committee on Crime Problems (CDPC), the European Committee on Transplantation of Organs (CD-P-TO), Identifying the Main Elements That Could Form Part of a Binding Legal Instrument against the Trafficking in Organs, Tissues and Cells (OTC), article 5. The Committee also recognized in article 6 "the transnational dimension of trafficking in organs, tissues and cells and the need to combat the criminal acts related thereto at international level."

3. The illicit solicitation or recruitment (of organ donors or recipients), or the offering and requesting of undue advantages.
4. The preparation, preservation, storage, transportation, transfer, receipt, import and export of illicitly removed human organs.
5. Aiding or abetting and attempt.[97]

Accordingly, the CTHO criminalizes organ trading in cases where there has been *no human trafficking*; that is, in cases in which the consent to remove the organ is valid because the consent was not obtained through "threat or use of force or other forms of coercion, of abduction, of fraud, of deception, of the abuse of power or of a position of vulnerability or of the giving or receiving of payments or benefits to achieve the consent of a person having control over another person" as set forth in article 3 of the *Palermo Protocol*. To distinguished these two crimes requires careful, conscientious and proper identification and investigation with focus on the absence or existence of valid consent, deception, abuse, and so forth.

4. Trafficking in Human Beings for Organ Removal (THB/OR)

Trafficking for the removal of body organs only occurs if a person is transported in order to remove his/her organs. Because the *Palermo Protocol* does not cover the transportation of the organs alone, for the act to be considered a crime under the *Protocol*, it has to be connected to the recruitment, transportation, transferred, harbored or receipt of a person through any of the conducts enu-

---

97. States Parties to the CTHO are also required to take the necessary legislative or other measures to: ensure corporate liability if certain conditions are met (the offense is committed by a person in a leading position); punish the offenses described in the CTHO through sanctions which are effective, proportionate and dissuasive; consider a set of circumstances as aggravating, such as:
- The offense caused the death of, or serious damage to the physical or mental health of the victim;
- The offense was committed by persons abusing their position;
- The offense was committed in the framework of a criminal organization;
- The perpetrator has previously been convicted of offenses established in accordance with the Convention;
- The offense was committed against a child or any other particularly vulnerable person.

merated in article 3 of the *Protocol*. Also under the *Protocol*, "organ removal is one of the forms of exploitation that characterize trafficking in human beings."[98]

There are presently three constituent elements that comprise THB/OR:[99]

(1) recruitment,[100] transportation, transfer, harbor or receipt, of a person

(2) by means of the threat or use of force or other forms of coercion, of abduction, of fraud, of deception, of the abuse of power or of a position of vulnerability or of the giving or receiving of payments or benefits to achieve the consent of a person having control over another person,[101]

(3) for the exploitative purpose of removal of organs.

Recruiting techniques are similar to those applied in other forms of human trafficking such as false promises of employment abroad, withholding of passports, use of threats and physical abuse.[102] Recruiters resort to several methods to convince a potential donor to give up an organ. They conceal the health risks and long-term consequences, emphasizing that the donor will have a better life. They say that a kidney will grow back in place of the one removed, "that two kidneys are not foreseen by nature, that there are two kidneys, a smaller and a bigger one and that only the small one would be removed."[103] Recruiters try to seal the deal by telling a donor that once the contract has been arranged, it cannot be revoked. All decisions are final "once costs have been incurred from medical examinations and expectations on the part of the buyer

---

98. Secretary-General Report, *supra* note 93, at ¶ 5. According to Dr. Anne Gallagher, "a proposal to include organ removal as an end purpose of trafficking was made very late in the negotiations and survived despite rather curious objections that the protocol was dealing with trafficking in persons, not organs." Moreover, "It is widely accepted that trafficking in organs necessitates the trafficking of the organ's host." *See* Anne Gallagher, *Human Rights and the New UN Protocols on Trafficking and Migrant Smuggling: A Preliminary Analysis*, 23 Hum. Rts. Q. 975, 988 (2001), *and also* Revised Draft Protocol to Prevent, Suppress and Punish Trafficking in Persons Especially Women and Children, supplementing the United Nations Convention against Transnational Organized Crime, U.N. Doc. U.N. Doc. A/AC.254/4/Add.3/Rev.6 (2000), and U.N. Doc. A/AC.254/4/Add.3/Rev.7 (2000).

99. Palermo Protocol, art. 3(a).

100. Recruiting techniques are similar to those applied in other forms of human trafficking such as false promises of employment abroad, withholding of passports, use of threats and physical abuse. *See* Toolkit, *supra* note 4, at 29.

101. Toolkit, *supra* note 4, at 29.

102. *Id.* at 27.

103. *Id.* at 29.

have been raised."[104] Recruiters also take advantage of social and economic vulnerabilities of target donors, as well as of their lack of education and awareness. Deception regarding health care support also occurs when donors do not receive the post-operative and longer-term care, as promised, or in some cases, as never promised. Negative health impacts are not discussed and recruiters used a donor's lack of sophistication to mislead them about long term risks and the psychological and physical impact organ removal has on everyday life.[105]

A. Issues of Consent and Disclosure

As with other forms of trafficking, the problem of consent can arise in THB/OR cases. Questions may stem from donors/victims signing consent forms required under organ transplant regulations. However, under the *Palermo Protocol*, consent can be voided when one or more "means" of crime are present, such as the use of force, coercion, abduction, or exploiting a position of vulnerability.[106] Moreover, any apparent consent may be vitiated where the victim has been defrauded or been deceived as to the nature of organ removal surgery or its consequences.

An organ sale constitutes a human trafficking offence, irrespective of consent if:

- A living donor is received for the purpose of organ removal by means of payment or benefits to achieve the consent of that person.[107]
- An organ is removed[108] when there is a position of vulnerability on the part of the donor, and knowledge of that vulnerability is abused by another in order to recruit, transport, transfer, harbor or receive the donor for the purpose of removing his/her organ.[109]

---

104. *Id.*

105. *Id.*

106. OSCE Analysis, *supra* note 5, at 14.

107. Palermo Protocol, art. 3(a).

108. Removal of an organ is not per se a form of exploitation, yet, it is exploitive to remove an organ when a position of vulnerability is present.

109. For a detailed discussion of the meaning of abuse of position of vulnerability, *see* UNODC, *Guidance Note on 'abuse of a position of vulnerability' as a means of trafficking in persons in Article 3 of the Protocol to Prevent, Suppress and Punish Trafficking in Persons, Especially Women and Children, supplementing the United Nations Convention against Transnational Organized Crime* (2012), https://www.unodc.org/documents/human-trafficking/2012/UNODC_2012_Guidance_Note_-_Abuse_of_a_Position_of_Vulnerability_E.pdf.

The living donor's freedom of choice is protected by his/her consent if that individual is:

- Competent,[110]
- Willing to donate (voluntary nature),[111]
- Free of having been coerced,
- Medically and psychosocially suitable to be a donor,[112]
- Fully informed of the risks and benefits as a donor, and
- Fully informed of risks, benefits and alternative treatment available to the recipient.[113]

There are additional factors that should be included, but are not. A consensus statement on life donors issued in the *Journal of the American Medical Association* (JAMA) in 2000 stressed that prospective donors should be healthy individuals at least 18 years of age, and who are declared suitable as donors only after having been carefully evaluated and approved by a multidisciplinary team of doctors and medical professionals.[114] In addition, in 2004, the Ethics Committee of the Transplantation Society convened the Amsterdam Forum "to develop an international standard of care with a position statement of the Transplantation Society defining and affirming the responsibility of the transplantation community for the live kidney donor."[115]

---

110. Competency requires that the donor is "able to assimilate accurate information regarding the risks and benefits to themselves." *See* Harald Jung et al., *Forensic Psychiatric Evaluation of the Capacity to Donate an Organ for Transplantation: Case Presentations*, 13 Romanian J. of Psychiatry 76, 78 (2011), http://www.romjpsychiat.ro/uploads/revista/2-2011/5.pdf.

111. Voluntary nature is defined as the "freedom to choose to proceed with donation or decline." *See Consensus Statement on the Live Organ Donor*, 283 JAMA 2919, 2920 (2000), https://www.kidney.org/sites/default/files/docs/jama_article.pdf [hereinafter JAMA].

112. *Id.* at 2923. Psychosocial assessment also allows "the opportunity to evaluate the competence of the donor to give informed consent," as well as any "possibility of coercion," and of a "position of vulnerability" such as a "potential subservient relationship between potential donor and recipient (e.g., employer and employee).

113. *Id.* at 2920. A consensus statement applicable to ALL living donors was formulated in June 2000 by attendees of The National Conference on the Live Organ Donor. The group of experts "reexamine[ed] the medical and ethical issues involving live organ donors," and "evaluate[ed] the practices of living donor transplantation." The consensus statement would ensure that "the welfare of potential and actual donors remains preeminent in the process of live organ donation." Attendees included several healthcare practitioners, "lawyers, scientists, social workers, transplant recipients, and living donors."

114. *Id.* at 2922.

115. *See* Anthony P. Monaco & Peter J. Morris, *Care of the Live Kidney Donor: Consensus on the Ultimate Gift*, 79 Transplantation S51 (2005).

The standard should include a psychosocial evaluation of the donor, addressing indicators such as an evaluation to determine the presence of financial hardship, vulnerabilities to coercion, clarification of the relationship between donor and the transplant recipient, and the potential benefits received by the donor. As to the psychosocial assessment, the Amsterdam Forum stressed that, "the opportunity to evaluate the competence of the donor to give informed consent," as well as determining any "possibility of coercion," and of a "position of vulnerability" such as a "potential subservient relationship between potential donor and recipient (e.g., employer and employee)" should be part of the analysis.[116]

Full disclosure of what is to occur in a transplant operation and the aftermath must accompany obtaining proper consent from an organ donor. Disclosure affords the donor "a "cooling off period" between giving initial consent and undergoing the operation in order for the donor to have sufficient time "to reconsider the decision to donate." The disclosure process, as framed by the Authors for the Live Organ Donor Consensus Group[117] should include:

- Description of the evaluation, the surgical procedure, and the recuperative period;
- Anticipated short-term and long-term follow-up care;
- Alternative donation procedures, even if only available at other transplant centers;
- Potential surgical complications for the donor, citing the reports of donor deaths (even if never experienced at that transplant center);
- Medical uncertainties, including the potential for long-term donor complications;
- Any expenses to be borne by the donor;
- Potential impact of donation on the ability of the donor to obtain health and life insurance;

---

116. JAMA, *supra* note 111, at 2923.

117. JAMA, *supra* note 111, at 2929. The Live Organ Donor Consensus Group resulted from the efforts of an executive group representing the National Kidney Foundation, and the American Societies of Transplantation, Transplant Surgeons, and Nephrology. The group convened a steering committee of "12 members to evaluate current practices of living donor transplantation of the kidney, pancreas, liver, intestine, and lung. The steering committee subsequently assembled more than 100 representatives of the transplant community (physicians, nurses, ethicists, psychologists, lawyers, scientists, social workers, transplant recipients, and living donors) at a national conference held June 1–2, 2000, in Kansas City, Mo."

- Potential impact of donation on the life-style of the donor, and the ability of the donor to obtain future employment;
- Information regarding specific risks and benefits to the potential recipient;
- Expected outcome of transplantation for the recipient;
- Any alternative treatments (other than organ replacement) available to the recipient; and
- Transplant center-specific statistics of donor and recipient outcomes.

B. Proliferation

Most if not all regions of the world are affected by trafficking for organ removal in one form or another, from "South to North, from poor to rich, from black to brown to white, and from female to male bodies,"[118] and it occurs as both a domestic[119] and transborder crime.[120] According to the UNODC, THB/OR was detected in 16 countries in 2012 and in 12 countries in 2014.[121] Of the cases reported in 2014, 80 percent of persons trafficked for organ removal were males in Europe and Central Asia.[122] As would be expected, trafficked donors originated from less-developed countries to supply organs to recipients in the so-called industrialized nations. The trafficking brokers and recruiters were not so tied to a country of origin or a country of destination, and there is an

---

118. Nancy Scheper-Hughes, *Commodity Fetishism in Organs Trafficking*, in Commodifying Bodies 45 (Nancy Scheper-Hughes & Loic Wacquant, eds., 2001).

119. Neither transnationality nor organized criminal groups are elements of a domestic offense of human trafficking. Those are elements for a triggering of the parent convention and requirements of international cooperation. United Nations Office on Drugs and Crime, Legislative Guides for the Implementation of the United Nations Convention against Transnational Organized Crime and the Protocols Thereto ¶ 18 (2004), http://www.unodc.org/pdf/crime/legislative_guides/Legislative%20guides_Full%20version.pdf.

120. Under UNTOC, Article 3 (2) an offence is transnational in nature if:
   a. It is committed in more than one State;
   b. It is committed in one State but a substantial part of its preparation, planning, direction or control takes place in another State;
   c. It is committed in one State but involves an organized criminal group that engages in criminal activities in more than one State; or
   d. It is committed in one State but has substantial effects in another.

121. United Nations Office on Drugs and Crime, Global Report on Trafficking in Persons 2012, at 35, U.N. Sales No. E.13.IV.1 (2012), https://www.unodc.org/documents/data-and-analysis/glotip/ Trafficking_in_Persons_2012_web.pdf.

122. *Id.* at 68.

established pattern that some broker-recruiters often move from one country to another to avoid investigation or detention by the authorities, or to follow trending in the international black markets of organs and body parts.

Figure 1: Stakeholders in THB/OR Operations

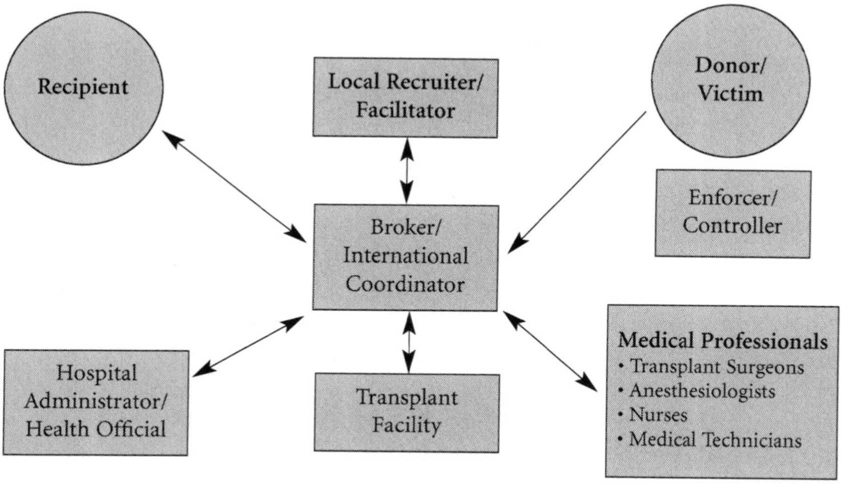

5. Corruption as Facilitator

THB/OR transnationally "would not be possible without the assistance of corrupt police officials, customs officers, officials giving out visas and travel documents, and sometimes officials in the health administration who issue false licenses to hospitals and doctors."[123] Corruption is a prominent element in THB/OR given that the main actors in destination transplant centers within countries and across borders are health professionals,[124] administrators of hospitals, transplant centers, or clinics, and at times, public officials. These white collar criminals play a crucial role in facilitating the crime through issuing licenses, falsifying documents, and "accessing the certification, approval and medical equipment necessary to set up a transplant clinic."[125] Corruption is

---

123. Bos, *supra* note 56, at 21.

124. Medical professionals such as nurses, surgeons, anesthesiologists, nephrologists, and medical technicians. OSCE, *supra* note 5, at 6.

125. *Id.* at 6–7.

also present in countries of origin through the acts of the recruiters, brokers, organizers, facilitators, and public officials.[126] The role of corrupt brokers and health professionals, specifically, is essential "to the 'success' of the trafficking network."[127]

A. Corrupt Actors

If there are indications that corrupt and unethical healthcare providers, hospital administrators, and government officials are linked to THB/OR, why is it apparently difficult to generate evidence about their involvement? If journalists and scholars working in various fields, including in medicine, have documented the illicit selling of organs, why in the course of many investigations has no one "followed the body" to corroborate allegations raised, and bring to light the culprits?[128] We know anecdotally that many thousands of illegal organ transplants have occurred, yet where are the prosecutions? Is it due to a lack of political will, or is it the affirmation of a cynical capital market system in which the human body of vulnerable individuals is treated as just another commodity to export and harvest for profit?

The following actors, engaged at different levels in what some have termed deliberate, silent bioviolence,[129] sustain a trade grounded in the exploitation

---

126. In Latin America, the transplants are usually arranged by unlicensed brokers, and the surgeries are performed for a fee by accredited surgeons, some of whom have trained at the world's leading medical schools. *See* Michael Smith, *Desperate Americans Buy Kidneys from Peru Poor in Fatal Trade*, BLOOMBERG.COM, May 12, 2011, http://www.bloomberg.com/news/articles/2011-05-12/desperate-americans-buy-kidneys-from-peru-poor-in-fatal-trade.

127. Bos, *supra* note 56, at 9.

128. In his article, Fr. Mathew Abraham, narrates how India remains a hub for "organ selling," that is, THB/OR, and nearly all of it happens in "five-star hospitals." It is a lucrative market that benefits brokers, doctors, transplant centers and drug companies. *See* Mathew Abraham, *Trafficking of Human Organs in India*, Paper presented at The Pontifical Academy of Social Sciences, Human Trafficking: Issues Beyond Criminalization, April 2015, http://www.endslavery.va/content/endslavery/en/publications/acta_20/abraham.html.

129. Monir Moniruzzaman defines bioviolence as "an act of inflicting harm and intentional manipulation to exploit certain bodies as a means to an end." The term refers to both, "the act itself (i.e. extracting organs from the physical body)" and also to "the process involved (i.e. deception and manipulation for organ procurement) in the exploitation of bodies, mostly of impoverished populations." *See* Monir Moniruzzaman, *"Living Cadavers" in Bangladesh: Bioviolence in the Human Organ Bazaar*, 26 MED. ANTHRO. Q. 69, 72 (2012). In Bangladesh, Moniruzzaman observed not only the practice of organ sales, but heard the donors' accounts of how they were tricked and deceived into selling their organs and their extreme suffering afterwards. Moniruzzaman posited that "organ commodification is both

of organ harvesting, and rationalize the illicit and unethical methods to obtain organs. To these facilitators along the THB/OR chain, obtaining a human organ from a vulnerable person, even if proper paperwork is forged and visas are bought, justifies the means (which often seems to be solely to prolong the life of a desperate wealthy individual).

Figure 2: Parties Involved in THB/OR

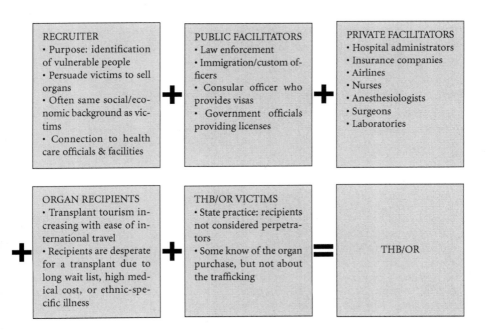

Recruiters can engage in multiple roles. They serve as "talent scouts," organizers, coordinators, and screeners. They can be local facilitators who know very well the social conditions and the vulnerabilities of targeted communities, preying on the poor, the ill-informed, and the desperate who can be easily lured by fraudulent promises of financial rewards.[130] Recruiters scour slums,

---

exploitative and unethical, as organs are removed from the bodies of the poor by inflicting a novel form of bioviolence against them."

130. According to Dr. Syed Adibul Hasan Rizvi, most Pakistani kidney donors sell one because they have few other options to make money and extricate themselves from "bonded labour." *See Dilemma Over Live-Donor Transplantation*, 85 Bulletin of the World Health

"army barracks, jails and prisons, unemployment offices, flea markets, shopping malls and bars."[131] They have no difficulty drafting the potential donors through "subtle means of control" such as deception,[132] and/or through the application of "abuse of a position of vulnerability and/or fraud."[133] Their methods include persuading donors into selling one of their organs with false promises of employment abroad, visas and easy money with little risk or no risk in exchange for a kidney," or using not-so-subtle means of withholding of passports and using threats and physical abuse.[134] In certain countries, recruiters employ debt bondage arrangements in which the organ is the collateral or the organ is exchanged as a gift by domestic workers and by hopeless prisoners in exchange for secure work and reduction in prison sentences.[135] Recruiters maintain a well-developed network for identifying vulnerable people. Recruiters can be recruiting potential donors from a continent away by utilizing social media to attract vulnerable individuals.

Brokers are the dealmakers. They ply their trade across international borders, and when the authorities close in, they shut down their operations and relocate to another location in another country, change the name or entity of their operations, and resume business as usual. They are predatory transborder white collar criminals. Brokers are the puppet masters for affecting, sustaining, supplying, and lubricating the THB/OR chain. They recruit recruiters,

---

ORGANIZATION 1 (Jan. 2007), http://www.who.int/bulletin/volumes/85/1/07-020107/en/. Academic David Rothman describes how in India, "physicians and brokers bring together the desperately poor with the desperately ill." The donors/sellers are "impoverished villagers, slum dwellers, power-loom operators, manual laborers, and daughters-in-law with small dowries." The recipients/buyers are from "Egypt, Kuwait, Oman, and other Gulf States, and from India's enormous middle class." *See* David J. Rothman, *The International Organ Traffic*, at 8, paper presented at the 10th Annual Conference on "The Individual vs. the State", Central European University, Budapest, 14–16 June 2002, on file with the author.

131. Nancy Scheper-Hughes, *Parts Unknown: Undercover Ethnography of the Organs Trafficking Underworld*, 5 ETHNOGRAPHY 64 (2004). Scheper-Hughes interviewed kidney sellers in the Philippines, Moldova, Turkey, Brazil, Iran, Israel, and the United States.

132. Toolkit, *supra* note 4. Donors are victims of deception "in terms of health support" because many "do not receive the promised post-operative and longer-term care.

133. OSCE Analysis, *supra* note 5, at 6–7.

134. Moniruzzaman describes how organ buyers in Bangladesh seize the donors'/sellers' passports to "ensure that the sellers cannot return to Bangladesh until their kidneys are removed." He also describes how a 22-year-old college student, who decided not to donate, was assaulted and beat up by thugs when he asked for his passport to return to Bangladesh. *See* Moniruzzaman, *supra* note 129, at 78. Recruiting techniques are similar to those applied in other forms of human trafficking, such as "false promises of employment abroad, withholding of passports, use of threats and physical abuse." *See* Toolkit *supra* note 4, at 29.

135. Scheper-Hughes, *supra* note 118.

they pay off corrupt officials, they arrange passports when necessary, they forge whatever legal documents and medical releases are required, including, in some instances, falsifying documents attesting that the trafficked donor is a family relation of the recipient and that the organ donation is being undertaken for altruistic reasons.[136] They advise the trafficked donors, often under subtle or flagrant threats, not to divulge their true identities to anyone.[137] Brokers engage in nefarious activities with nongovernment organizations when necessary, they cut deals with the medical professionals who perform the transplants, make arrangements with the medical clinics and hospitals involved in the conspiracy, and they nurture a network of transportation actors necessary to move THB/OR victims. Brokers may also set the prices for the trafficking transaction.[138] They are surprisingly easy to find, often by making inquiries around a hospital, and they are also very skilled at avoiding arrest or accepting any type of accountability.

Medical professionals involved in the trafficking chain can include all the members of the medical team or practice group. They are surgeons, nephrologists, neurologists, anesthesiologists, pharmacists, the nursing staff, and medical technicians. In some cases, physicians double as travel agents connecting transplant patients to hospitals in other countries or cities were black market transplants are performed. Some physicians think they are providing a valuable service when they are able to assist a patient in desperate need of a transplant by eliminating a long or futile waiting period for them and sending them to a location where the supply of organs can satisfy demand. Some physicians willingly engage in black market organ transplants believing that the illicit fees they collect will improve conditions and services in their hospitals. However, one investigation indicated that doctors involved in illegal organ transplantation are not altogether altruistic, and one doctor questioned did not want to admit any information about how much of the illicit money doctors keep themselves.[139]

In some countries, the additional financial incentive to treat foreign transplant patients can be intoxicating, especially where doctors earn significantly more money moonlighting at private hospitals that cater to affluent patients.

---

136. Abraham, *supra* note 128.

137. Moniruzzaman, *supra* note 129, at 77.

138. According to the experts at UNODC's expert group meetings, to obtain organ suppliers, brokers would do so directly, or hire recruiters to post newspaper ads to attract donors. *See* Toolkit, *supra* note 4, at 28.

139. One of the transplant surgeons interviewed in Russia referred to helping his hospital, but at the same time is well known for "his vast estate and passion for horses." *See* Rothman, *supra* note 130, at 15–16.

Some doctors readily acknowledge that they are engaged in illicit transplant operations, but choose to turn a blind eye to the telltale signs, for instance, a large number of "highly suspect cousins, godchildren, in-laws, nieces, and nephews" being processed as donors.[140] One transplant surgeon's justification for continuing to engage in illicit donor transplants was to say, "I am a doctor, not a police man."[141] Moreover, in some countries, legislation intended to prohibit the commercialization of medical procedures allows a loophole for transplants between unrelated individuals in the case of "medical need."[142] Equally repugnant is that the doctors and the medical teams performing the transplants can hide behind principles of confidentiality in the medical profession, and they can justify their involvement by insisting that the illegal trafficking of organs benefits their hospitals, biomedical businesses, and related businesses that benefit from the so-called transplant tourism.[143]

Private and public sector facilitators include administrators and managers working in hospitals, transplant centers, laboratories, and their staff members. In developing countries where public hospitals struggle to provide services to the community, the allure of bringing in significant income through black-market transplantations is too profitable to ignore. Hospital administrators and their staff do not feel it is incumbent upon them to determine what is legal or illegal. That determination, they feel, should be left to the judicial system and government officials. They rely on the veil of confidentiality in the medical profession to keep their involvement in illegal organ trafficking a secret. Hospitals also know that if they are in a destination country, competition to engage in transplant tourism means that if they do not reap the benefits of servicing affluent patients in obtaining organ transplants, some other facility will to the point where that facility prospers and expands while the other one goes broke and closes its doors.

THB/OR has become such big business, especially in border towns between source countries and destination countries, that a large number of private backstreet clinics where such clandestine transplants are performed by unscrupulous doctors have opened. The fact that many of these clinics lack the most basic sanitary facilities but are still busy and making money is an indication that desperate recipients and desperate hosts will take any risks to sustain their lives. In reality, such clinics are part of a market that some describe

---

140. Scheper-Hughes, *supra* note 2, at 208.

141. *Id.*

142. *Id.*

143. *Id.* In Brazil, for example, keeping the many transplant clinics in business has meant "greater tolerance for various informal incentives to encourage organ donation."

as a "marriage bureau of sorts, bringing desperately ill buyers and desperately poor sellers together in a temporary alliance against the wolves at their doors."[144]

Corruption among these private and public facilitators occurs in manipulating the paper trail that is always a part of medical procedures. Disclosure forms, treatment for services contracts, releases from liability, and falsification of medical records are all within the purview of hospital administrators and their staff. Just as with the doctors who perform the surgeries, administrators may also be entitled to a cut of the fees, and they may realize that the ongoing payday from illegal organ transplants is more personally satisfying than following the law.

Others in this category can include insurance companies and their agents, travel agents, airlines and their staff, security guards, drivers, service sector providers, law enforcement officials, translators, and members of various nongovernment organizations. While they may not have direct contact with a trafficked donor, their involvement is vital to the successful commercial transaction of bringing the donor to the recipient.

Finally, there are the **organ recipients** (patients/buyers) who may knowingly be involved in THB/OR. Their motivations are driven by human instincts to stay alive (involving the transplant of organs), or motivations to seek physical procedures to have a better life (corneal transplants, for instance). In their quest to stay alive they are complicit in the exploitation of the vulnerable, and this motivation is at the core of THB/OR crimes. They are willing to risk being exploited by unscrupulous organ brokers who place profit above the health concerns of the recipient and end up exposing the recipients to diseases and illnesses carried by the trafficked donor.

6. Case Examples

The UNODC maintains the Human Trafficking Case Law database, accessible online.[145] The database attempts to track human trafficking cases reported by courts around the world, including statistics on the numbers of prosecutions and convictions as well as important details about the trafficked persons as documented by the courts.[146] Of the many hundreds of cases reported in

---

144. *Id.* at 195.
145. UNODC Human Trafficking Knowledge Portal, https://www.unodc.org/cld/v3/htms/cldb/index.html?lng=en.
146. *Id.*

the database, only a scant 12 cases concerning exploitation for the removal of organs were cataloged as of mid-2016. What cases are extant can be broken down into rough categories to help us understand the level of corruption involved in THB/OR crimes. The most significant involve the exploitation of the donors/suppliers through fraud, coercion, and another means.

A. *State v. Netcare Kwa-Zulu Limited* (South Africa)

In November 2010, a healthcare company, Netcare Kaw-Zulu Limited (Netcare),[147] operating several private hospitals in South Africa pleaded guilty to more than one hundred counts related to charges that the facilities and staff members were engaged in illegal kidney transplant operations. The plea agreement emphasized especially violation of the public trust, noting that:

> ... a company, such as the accused company, guilty of an offence such as this, should be convicted and punished and more particularly, that that conviction and punishment should take place in open court for society as a whole to come to know and understand that the prosecuting authorities and the Department of Health will not tolerate breaches of the code of conduct and standards of ethics and compliance with the law required in a civilised society.[148]

The Netcare case was international in scope and involved Israeli citizens in need of kidney transplants, South African doctors, and Israeli, Brazilian, and Romanian donors trafficked to South Africa to undergo 109 transplant operations between 2001 and 2003 in violation of South Africa's *Human Tissue Act of 1983* and the *Prevention of Organized Crime Act of 1998*. The scheme was orchestrated by one Ilan Perry, an Israeli organ broker who charged a brokerage fee of between US$100,000 and US$120,000 to organ recipients and paid between US$6,000 to Romanian and Brazilian donors, and US$20,000 to Israeli donors.[149] Perry used overseas agents as recruiters who would undertake

---

147. *The State v. Netcare Kwa-Zulu (Proprietary) Limited*, Agreement in Terms of s105A(1) of Act 51 of 1977, Netcare Kwa-Zulu (Proprietary) Limited and the State, Commercial Crime Court, Regional Court of Kwa-Zulu Natal, Durban, South Africa, Case No 41/1804/2010, 8 November 2010.

148. *Id.*

149. Jean Allain, *Trafficking of Persons for the Removal of Organs and the Admission of Guilt of a South African Hospital*, unpublished article, http://www.repository.up.ac.za/bitstream/handle/2263/17030/Allain_Trafficking(2011).pdf?sequence=1 (last visited Dec. 11, (2016).

the preliminary medical screenings in the source countries to find suitable donors before sending them on to South Africa for surgery.[150]

Once in South Africa the donors were accommodated and kept under control and forced to sign documents that they were related to the transplant recipients. According to the court, this fraudulent activity was intended to bypass the requirements to gain prior government approval for transplants of unrelated principles. Netcare was paid upfront for its participation in the illegal operations and the donors were paid in cash after the fact. The company then paid surgeons and staff out of payments received by the broker. Among the charges admitted to by Netcare without minors were involved as donors (in violation of both national and international law), and that it knowingly engaged in activity that it knew was unlawful, and also that it knew that the proceeds gained were from unlawful activities.

The South African government sought to make an example of Netcare and its subsidiary hospitals where the transplants occurred by insisting that the proceedings occur in open court in order "for society as a whole to come to know and understand that the prosecuting authorities in the Department of Health will not tolerate breaches of the code of conduct and standards of ethics and compliance with the law required in a civilized society."[151] Netcare was ordered to pay a fine to the government in the amount of the approximate profits made from the illegal operations plus a monetary penalty.[152] Ilan Perry, however, escaped without accountability and continued his international kidney brokering elsewhere, including colluding from within Israel with a Jewish Orthodox rabbi from New York who became the first organ trafficker convicted in the United States.[153]

---

150. Susanne Lundin, Organs for Sale: An Ethnographic Examination of the International Organ Trade 75–79 (2015).

151. *The State, supra* note 147, and Summary of Substantial Facts. *See also* Allain, *supra* note 149.

152. The penalty was approximately US$466,839 plus a fine of approximately US$493,875.

153. Organ trafficking involving compensation was not illegal in Israel until passage of the Organ Transplant Act of 2008, http://www.declarationofistanbul.org/resources/legislation/267-israel-transplant-law-organ-transplant-act-2008. Section 2: Prohibited Activities, states, "No person shall receive a reward for an organ removed from his body or from the body of another person, or designated to be so removed, regardless of whether the removal be performed during the lifetime of the person or after his death" (Section 2(3)(a)), and, "No person shall give a reward for an organ transplanted into his or another's body, or that is designated to be so transplanted" (Section 2(3)(b)).

B. *United States v. Rosenbaum* (United States)

Between December 2006 and July 2009, Rabbi Levy Izhak Rosenbaum of Brooklyn, New York, acted as an international broker to match individuals in need of a kidney transplant in the United States with donors from Israel. Rosenbaum became the first defendant to be tried under the *National Organ Transplant Act*,[154] that makes it "unlawful for any person to knowingly acquire, receive, or otherwise transfer any human organ for valuable consideration for use in human transplantation if the transfer affects interstate commerce."[155] The case was part of a larger corruption probe, and court records reveal intriguing insights into the world of THB/OR and provides scenarios, statements and fact patterns that mirror the activities of organ brokers around the world.

Rosenbaum conducted his criminal activity out of his home in New York, where he met with three transplant recipients who would provide blood samples which Rosenbaum then sent on to recruiters in Israel to match blood types with potential donors. He would then make arrangements to bring the Israeli donors to the United States where the transplants were performed in prestigious hospitals, including the Albert Einstein Medical Center in Philadelphia, Pennsylvania.[156] While Rosenbaum was charged for arranging transplants for four individuals, including a government informant, prosecutors asserted that he had made millions of dollars arranging transplants for many recipients over a ten-year period. Rosenbaum charged $120,000 to the first recipient, $150,000 to the second recipient, and $140,000 to the third recipient.[157] He then paid the donors "paltry sums"[158] and hid the money in the bank accounts of several bogus charitable organizations. He informed the recipients that it was illegal to buy or sell a kidney in the United States, but that he would devise a cover story in an attempt to mislead hospital personnel into believing that the donation of the kidney was a purely voluntary act and not a commercial transaction whereby the donor was being paid.[159] In the course of the investigation,

---

154. National Organ Transplant Act, *supra* note 3.

155. *Id.* at sec. 301(a). *See also* Samantha Henry, *Brooklyn Man Sentenced 2½ Years in Fed Organ Trafficking Case*, NBCNEWYORK.COM, July 11, 2012, http://www.nbcnewyork.com/news/local/Kidney-Organ-Trafficking-Levy-Izhak-Rosenbaum-Brooklyn-Federal-Conviction-Sentencing-162046565.html (noting that Rosenbaum "was among more than 40 people arrested in the dual-track investigation into money laundering and political corruption. Defendants included politicians and rabbis in New Jersey and Brooklyn.").

156. Henry, *supra* note 155.

157. *United States v. Rosenbaum*, indictment charge sheet, 4, (also on file with author).

158. Henry, *supra* note 155.

159. *Rosenbaum, supra* note 157.

Rosenbaum told the undercover agent and an informant who pretended to be the organ recipient, "Let me explain to you one thing. It's illegal to buy or sell organs ... So you cannot buy it. What you do is, you're getting the compensation for the time ..." About fabricating the story, Rosenbaum told the agent that they would put something together about the relationship to satisfy the hospital, saying, "So we put in a relationship, friends, or neighbor, or business relations, any relation." When the informant suggested claiming that the donor and the recipient were cousins or third cousins, Rosenbaum rejected the idea of being cousins because the hospital investigates the donor, not the recipient, "So if, if you start with family, it's really easy to find out if he's not ... it's not the family, because the names and the ages and who is who ... it doesn't work good."[160] Rosenbaum indicated that creating the fictitious relationship and putting it together was actually the easy part. He said that he put the story together by observing the recipient and depending on what he sees the donor could be portrayed as neighbors, the synagogue friends from the community, or friends of the recipient's children. When asked about how the donor would be located in Israel, Rosenbaum explained the process of finding a donor, stating that "[t]here are people over there hunting ... One of the reasons it's so expensive is because you have to shmear (meaning pay various individuals for their assistance) all the time."[161]

As it came time to make payments, Rosenbaum instructed the undercover agent to fill out several bank checks payable to a charitable organization set up as a front by the rabbi.[162] Additional payments were made to two different charitable organizations.[163] Rosenbaum indicated that the money was used to pay for the donor and the doctors in Israel who would examine the donor, and further added that there would be expenses incurred for preparing the Visa work and paying the donor's expenses while in the United States.[164] Rosenbaum also stated during the course of the investigation that he had an associate based in Brooklyn who took blood samples on behalf of an insurance company for whom he worked and that he would pay the individual in cash for handling blood samples of would-be recipients of organs.[165]

---

160. *United States v. Rosenbaum*, 2:09-mj-03620, Mag. No. 09-3620, Criminal Complaint, filed July 21, 2009, ¶ 8.
161. *Id.* at ¶ 10.
162. *Id.* at ¶ 16.
163. *Id.* at ¶ 20.
164. *Id.* at ¶ 11.
165. *Id.* at ¶ 15.

The conspiracy was repeated for each organ recipient and the transactions were not undertaken until Rosenbaum had received cash payments in advance. Once a donor was located in Israel, Rosenbaum arranged for his travel to the United States where he would make arrangements for the donor to be housed. Rosenbaum's criminal conspiracy was foiled by an undercover FBI agent who portrayed herself as the niece of a man needing a kidney transplant.

The rabbi was charged in federal district court in New Jersey (because the organ recipients were New Jersey residents) with four counts, including one count of conspiracy to acquire or receive human organs for use in interstate commerce in violation of 18 USC § 371, three counts of acquiring or receiving human organs for use human transplantation affecting interstate commerce in violation of the 42 USC § 274e, and conspiracy to defraud the United States in violation of 18 USC § 371.

Rosenbaum pleaded guilty to the four counts on October 27, 2011. He was sentenced to 30 months in prison for each of the four counts, which he served concurrently, was ordered to forfeit property of $420,000 (the amount approximately equal to what he charged his three victims),[166] and he was charged a special assessment of $400 for each count. He served his sentence at the minimum — medium security Federal Correctional Institution in Otisville, New York, which is notable for having one of the largest and most active religious programs for Jewish inmates in the Federal Bureau Prisons.[167]

Rosenbaum's trafficking network crossed international boundaries, and involved the actions of corrupt medical professionals in Israel. Doctors directing the kidney center at the Einstein Medical Center expressed shock that Rosenbaum was involved in illegal conduct, testifying that Rosenbaum always seemed like a legitimate facilitator between kidney donors and transplant recipients.[168] Yet, between 1999 and 2002, Rosenbaum brought some 15 pairs of donors and transplant patients to Einstein's kidney center, alone. Given the scarcity of kidneys and extremely long waiting list in the United States, it is difficult to believe that the doctors involved in processing Rosenbaum's transplants in the United States had no inkling that he was engaged in illegal activities. While we do not know what transpired in Israel, Rosenbaum alludes to having to pay individuals off in Israel, which suggests that individuals who had an obligation to report the conspiracy to the authorities did not

---

166. *United States v. Rosenbaum*, 2:09-mj-03620, Plea Agreement, May 9, 2011, page 3.

167. ALAN ELLIS, FEDERAL PRISON GUIDEBOOK § 14:24 (2012–2014 Edition).

168. Samantha Henry, *Illegal Kidney Broker Faces Sentencing in NJ*, WASHINGTON TIMES.COM, July 11, 2012, http://www.washingtontimes.com/news/2012/jul/11/illegal-kidney-broker-faces-sentencing-in-nj/.

do so and therefore engaged in at least passive forms of corrupt conduct. While there is no mention about the process of how the donors were able to obtain travel visas from Israel to the United States, one must wonder to what extent United States visa officials in Israel were aware or should have been aware of Rosenbaum's THB/OR operation, especially since this was occurring after other international organ trafficking operations were well known to be run from Israel for several years prior to Rosenbaum's scheme, not to mention that in her own investigation of Rosenbaum, Professor Scheper-Hughes established links between Rosenbaum and Ilan Perry,[169] who should have been very well known to authorities in Israel and among consular staff in the US Embassy.

C. *Medicus Clinic* (Kosovo)

Several years ago, another Israeli national, one Moshe Harel (aka The Fixer), was involved in an international THB/OR network run through the Medicus medical clinic in Pristina, Kosovo, in spite of kidney transplantation being illegal in Kosovo.[170] Suspicious activities regarding the Medicus Clinic began coming to the attention of Kosovo police and immigration officials in October 2008 when foreigners began arriving into Pristina's international airport carrying letters of introduction to the Medicus Clinic to be treated for heart conditions even though that clinic was not "particularly renowned for treating this disease."[171]

---

169. Dan Pine, *Berkeley Professor Told FBI about Illegal Organ Trafficking*, JWEEKLY.COM, July 30, 2009, http://www.jweekly.com/article/full/39403/berkeley-professor-told-fbi-about-illegal-organ-trafficking/. Perry is just one of many suspected Israeli organ brokers known to international law enforcement. Other notable alleged Israeli brokers include Avigad Sandler, a former insurance agent long suspected of trafficking, Boris Volfman, a Ukrainian émigré working for Sandler, and Yaacov Dayan, a real estate and marketing businessman, according to a 2015 *New York Times* investigation involving organ trafficking in Costa Rica and based on a *Times* analysis of "major trafficking cases" from 2000 to 2014 suggesting that "Israelis have played a disproportionate role" in international organ trafficking. *See* Kevin Sack, *Transplant Brokers in Israel Lure Desperate Kidney Patients to Costa Rica*, NY TIMES, August 17, 2014, http://www.nytimes.com/2014/08/17/world/middleeast/transplant-brokers-in-israel-lure-desperate-kidney-patients-to-costa-rica.html?smid=tw-share&_r=4.

170. *Key Suspect in Kosovo Organ Case 'Arrested in Israel,'* BBC NEWS.COM, May 22, 2012, http://www.bbc.com/news/world-europe-18203920. *See also* Danna Harman, *Israeli Involved in Kosovo Organ Trafficking Case on Run from Interpol*, HAARETZ.COM, Dec. 20, 2010, http://www.haaretz.com/israeli-involved-in-kosovo-organ-trafficking-case-on-run-from-interpol-1.331544.

171. Bos, *supra* note 56.

Then in November 2008 police responded to a Turkish national in medical distress at the airport in Pristina while awaiting his flight back to Istanbul. The donor was in the company of an Israeli national (assumed to be Moshe Harel, but this is unclear), and the brother of the kidney recipient. During the examination, the Turkish national told authorities that he had his kidney recently removed at the Clinic.[172] Kosovo police, investigators from the Department of Organized Crime, and United Nations Interim Administration Mission in Kosovo (UNMIK) International police descended on the clinic and discovered the kidney recipient still in recovery. The director and owner of Medicus, urologist Lutfi Dervishi, and his son, Arban Dervishi, were arrested and clinic records confiscated. Investigators learned that at least 24 and as many as perhaps 30 kidney removals and transplants were performed at the clinic in 2008 by a Turkish doctor, Yusuf Ercin Sonmez, and were apparently sanctioned under a license issued to the clinic by the Ministry of Health, in violation of Kosovo law.[173] "The donors were recruited from poor Eastern European and Central Asian countries who were promised about 15,000 euros ($19.500) for their organs, while recipients would pay up to 100,000 euros each."[174] They were coerced to sign a document stating that they had donated their kidneys voluntarily to a family relation or "altruistically to a stranger, without any payments."[175] "They were given only a short time to agree and had to sign false declarations in the local language without explanation of the content."[176] Moreover, some of the donors later reported they did not receive the entire "fee" they were promised, or were not paid at all. Some testified that they would receive the balance of payment due to them "on condition that they themselves would recruit other 'donors.'"[177]

In 2013, the European Union Rule of Law Mission (EULEX) took over the prosecution, seating a tribunal of European judges in the Pristina Basic Court in Kosovo.[178] The tribunal tried the clinic owners for organized crime, engag-

---

172. *Id.*

173. *Id.*

174. *Defendant Admits Illegal Organ Harvesting in Kosovo Hospital,* EUBUSINESS.COM, Apr. 5, 2013, http://www.eubusiness.com/news-eu/kosovo-organ-trial.nrw. Court documents indicate that the donors came from Moldova, Kazakhstan, Russia and Turkey and were promised payments of about €15,000, and the recipients were from Israel, Canada, Germany, Poland, other locations. *See* Harman, *supra* note 170.

175. Bos, *supra* note 56.

176. *Id.*

177. *Id.*

178. Defendant, *supra* note 174. "The case is being tried by EULEX, the European rule of law mission in Kosovo, set up to help the local judiciary to handle sensitive cases after the territory declared independence from Serbia in 2008."

ing in illegal kidney transplants, document fraud and forgery, and inflicting grievous bodily harm,[179] and the former Ministry of Health general secretary Ilir Rrecaj, and another ministry official, Driton Jilta, for abuse of their official positions and falsifying official documents related to medical licenses.

During the course of the trial, the Health Minister admitted to writing a letter to the Medicus clinic in May 2008 informing the owner that the ministry "approved in principle the possibility" of performing a kidney transplant from a living donor, but he insisted that "it was a memo, a correspondence, not approval, decision or a licence."[180] He also admitted that he was aware of the illegal kidney transplants at the Medicus clinic, but denied concealing them, and he denied abusing his official position and falsifying documents.

In April 2013, Lufti and Arban Dervishi and three clinic staffers, including the head anesthetist, Sokol Hajdini, were found guilty of trafficking in persons for organ removal, organized crime, and unlawful exercise of medical care, and sentenced to up to 8 years in prison and fined.[181] Rrecaj was acquitted of abuse of official position. His ministry colleague, Jilta, pleaded guilty "to charges of abusing his official position or authority and the unlawful exercise of medical activity."[182] The Israeli broker, Harel, and the Turkish doctor, Sonmez, were not tried at all since they had left Kosovo in 2008.

In early 2016, the Kosovar appellate court issued new rulings in the case. The convictions of two assistant anesthetists were overturned for lack of evidence to prove their involvement in THB/OR.[183] The convictions of the father and son owners were upheld and they were ordered to prison to serve eight years for organized crime in connection with organ trafficking. Hajdini's con-

---

179. Bos, *supra* note 56. *See also* U.S. Dep't of State, *Country Report on Human Rights Practices 2013—Kosovo*, Ecoi.net, Feb. 24, 2014, https://www.ecoi.net/local_link/270751/400858_de.html.

180. Defendant, *supra* note 174.

181. Charges of inflicting grievous bodily harm, fraud and forging documents were rejected. Lutfi Dervishi, the director and owner of the Medicus clinic, received eight years in prison, a fine of €10,000, (US$14,000), and a ban from practicing his profession of urology for two years. His son, Arban Dervishi, received a sentence of seven years and three months in prison, plus a fine of €2,500 (US$3,400). The court ordered both to pay €15,000 (US$20,000) to each of seven organ-trafficking victims. *See* Country Report, *supra* note 179.

182. Defendant, *supra* note 174.

183. Petrit Collaku, *Convicted Kosovo Organ Trafficker Dodges Jail*, Balkin Transitional Justice.com, March 25, 2016, http://www.balkaninsight.com/en/article/convicted-kosovo-organ-trafficker-dodges-jail-03-25-2016.

viction was also upheld and he was sentenced to five years in prison.[184] The son did not surrender to the authorities on his appointed date in March 2016; his lawyer said he was out of the country but would return. Sonmez was eventually convicted in the Medicus case, arrested in Istanbul, but allowed bail. In fact, Dr. Sonmez was arrested and released in Istanbul at least six times according to one newspaper report, and he made quite a show of flaunting his freedom and his accomplishments as the self-described greatest kidney transplant surgeon in the world with more than 2,400 kidney transplant operations by his count.[185] He dropped later out of sight and then turned up in The Netherlands in September 2014.[186] Sonmez is also wanted in connection to kidney trafficking operations in Ecuador and Azerbaijian.[187] Since 2014, Sonmez has been wanted by the Serbian Prosecutor's Office for War Crimes in connection with his alleged role in taking part in organ transplantations harvested from Serbs, Roma and ethnic Albanians by the Kosovo Liberation Army in the later 1990s.[188]

As of summer 2016, Moshe Harel and Yusuf Sonmez both remain at large, wanted under two Interpol warrants each; one by Russian authorities for prosecution and to serve a sentence for intentional infliction of grave injuries and human trafficking, and the second warrant to be returned to Kosovo to face charges of human trafficking, organized crime, and unlawful exercise of medical activity.

D. Costa Rica Organ Transplant Tourism

THB/OR is due primarily to two factors: a critical shortage of organs through regulated, legal means,[189] and the highly lucrative profits that can be

---

184. *Id.*

185. He was interviewed at his seaside villa on the Asian side of Istanbul in 2011. According to the article, Sonmez at the time kept friends and investigators informed of his activities and affluent lifestyle via a blog and posting on a website. *See* Doreen Carvajal, *Trafficking Investigations Put Surgeon in Spotlight*, NY Times, February 10, 2011, http://www.nytimes.com/2011/02/11/world/europe/11organ.html?_r=0.

186. *Organ Trafficking in Kosovo: Yusuf Sonmez Found in the Netherlands*, InSerbiaNetworkFoundation.com September 2, 2014, http://inserbia.info/today/2014/09/organ-trafficking-in-kosovo-yusuf-sonmez-found-in-the-netherlands/.

187. Les Blough, *Organ Smuggling: Turkish Hospitals Traffic Injured Syrian Citizens' Organs*, GlobalResearch.ca, February 8, 2014, http://www.globalresearch.ca/organ-smuggling-turkish-hospitals-traffic-injured-syrian-citizens-organs/5367869.

188. *Prosecutors in Contact over Yusuf Sonmez*, InSerbia, Sept. 4, 2014, https://inserbia.info/today/2014/09/prosecutors-in-contact-over-yusuf-sonmez/.

189. Sack, *supra* note 169 (noting that the World Health Organization estimates that

generated through the black market. It is a classic supply and demand situation that is easily exploited by criminal actors. Certain cities have gained ignominy as centers for THB/OR operations, and Israel is well known for having several organ trafficking syndicates originating there, in part because the commercial trade in organs was not illegal there until 2008 and religious beliefs discourage organ donations.[190]

The rapid growth of transplant tourism is something of a subcategory of the growth in international medical tourism over the last two decades, in which foreign travelers can undertake a litany of medical and dental procedures often at a fraction of the cost to have the same treatments done in their home countries. Costa Rica has been a desirable destination for medical procedures for many years. The Costa Rican government encourages this inflow of medical tourists when it established the Council for the International Promotion of Costa Rica Medicine (PROMED). The PROMED webpage states that the Council was created "to ensure that international patients visiting Costa Rica receive consistent, high-quality medical and dental services from our members and to consolidate and promote Costa Rica as a leader in medical tourism, healthcare and wellness travel."[191] Its convenient proximity to the United States and Canada makes Costa Rica a desirable destination due to its ease of access from North American cities and because the medical professions are highly trained and capable. The PROMED webpage indicates that in 2012, nearly 50,000 medical tourists visited Costa Rica for various procedures that cost on average between 40 percent and 70 percent less than in the United States. There is little wonder then that since Costa Rica was already marketing itself as a destination country for medical tourism, unscrupulous organ brokers would find Costa Rica fertile ground for carrying out illegal commercial organ harvesting and transplantation. All that was necessary was to find a few doctors interested in making some extra money under the table by performing organ transplants resulting from illegal commercial transactions.

The THB/OR operation carried out in Costa Rica that was uncovered by the *New York Times* investigation conducted in 2014 bears all the hallmarks of

---

the supply of available organs meets somewhere around 10% of the need).

190. Israel had also become a commercial trafficking center due to Jewish religious prohibitions against allowing organs of dead relatives to be donated. *See* Judy Siegel-Itzkovich, *Israel Is Set to Outlaw Trafficking in Human Organs*, BMJ, December 1, 2007, http://www.ncbi.nlm.nih.gov/pmc/articles/PMC2099532/.

191. PROMED, http://www.promedcostarica.org/. The webpage also includes a section on Medical Tourism, including several paragraphs discussing Myths of Medical Tourism.

sophisticated international organized criminal enterprise. The investigation followed the path of one Israeli patient traveling to Costa Rica for organ transplant conducted by unscrupulous doctors who were paid a large medical fee.[192] According to journalist Kevin Sack, the international organ trafficking operation was "built by a cast that included high-rolling Israeli brokers, a prominent Costa Rican nephrologist and middlemen who recruited donors from the driver's seat of a taxi and the front counter of a pizzeria." While the Costa Rican government was unable to determine precisely how many foreign organ recipients had traveled to Costa Rica for kidney operations, at least 11 individuals (six Israelis, three Greeks, and two Americans) made arrangements with an Israeli organ broker named Yaacov Dayan who Israel Tax Authority investigators described as the manager of Ad-Al Holdings, a business entity believed to be engaged as an intermediary facilitator between people needing kidney transplants and donors willing to sell a kidney.[193]

According to Sack's investigation, the international transaction to travel abroad from Israel to Costa Rica to receive a kidney went like this:

> A meeting was arranged with Mr. Dayan, who explained that a transplant in Costa Rica would cost $175,000, Ms. Dorin said. He was careful not to specify that the package would include a kidney. "But it was understood," Ms. Dorin recalled, "that the payment was for everything, including the organ."
>
> She said that some of the money was wired to a hospital in San José, and that she delivered a payment to Dr. Francisco José Mora Palma, the kidney specialist who oversaw her transplant. Dr. Mora then paid the equivalent of $18,500 to an unemployed 37-year-old man for his kidney, according to a confidential Costa Rican court document.
>
> Just hours after Ms. Dorin arrived in San José in June 2012, Dr. Mora met with her and the donor at her hotel. There, she said, they signed affidavits in Spanish, a language she could not read, swearing that money would not change hands.[194]

---

192. Sack, *supra* note 169.

193. Shimon B. Lifkin, *Tax Authority Goes After Private Surgery*, Hamodia.com, September 2, 2013, http://hamodia.com/2013/09/02/tax-authority-goes-after-private-surgery/ . *See also* Sack, *supra* note 169 (reporting that Dayan has been described as a scheming businessman indicted by the Israeli government in 2013 for tax fraud in connection to setting up several bogus foreign companies to hide more than US$30 million—some of that money being the proceeds from his organ trafficking business).

194. Sack, *supra* note 169.

Ms. Dorin went on to have kidney transplant surgery and she returned to Israel. Other cases like hers follow the activities of similar criminal syndicates, and in one case a Costa Rican police officer was involved. That officer, Maureen Cordero Solano, moonlighted as a taxi driver where she would solicit potential individuals in economic need willing to donate a kidney for good money. Cordero had donated a kidney to the same Dr. Mora in 2009. She was subsequently paid US$1,000 by Mora for every donor she recruited.[195] Mora was arrested June 18, 2013, along with three other doctors, two staffers, and the owner of the pizzeria across the street from the hospital where some of the trafficking is alleged to have taken place. At the time of his arrest Mora was the head of nephrology at Rafael Ángel Calderón Guardia Hospital in San José, one of the largest government-run medical facilities in Costa Rica.[196] In announcing the arrest, Costa Rica's Attorney General stated that the conspiracy involved transplant patients in Israel receiving kidneys from Costa Rican donors who either had their kidneys removed in Costa Rica or traveled to Israel to have their kidneys removed there. Costa Rican authorities believed that one person died after being operated on in Israel.[197] The illegal operations were believed to have taken place in the Calderón Guardia facility and in a private medical facility called Clínica Biblica.[198]

Mora was charged under Costa Rica *Penal Code* § 172 with 14 counts of human trafficking for the purpose of illegal organ harvesting, with each count carrying a sentence of 10 years of imprisonment.[199] He was also charged with 16 counts of corruption by embezzlement. In March 2014, Costa Rican authorities announced that Ms. Cordero reached a plea arrangement with prosecutors to testify against her co-conspirators, including Dr. Mora.[200]

---

195. *Id.*

196. *Medical Chief at Costa Rica State Hospital Arrested as Part of Organ Trafficking Investigation*, ICRNews, June 19, 2013, http://insidecostarica.com/2013/06/19/medical-chief-at-costa-rica-state-hospital-arrested-as-part-of-organ-trafficking-investigation/.

197. *Id.*

198. Zach Dyer, *Costa Rica Prosecutors Charge 5 Members of Alleged Organ Trafficking Ring*, Tico Times, February 9, 2016, http://www.ticotimes.net/2016/02/09/prosecutors-charge-5-in-costa-rica-organ-trafficking-ring.

199. *Costa Rica Court Postpones Case against Alleged Organ Traffickers until End-Of-Year*, ICRNews, July 27, 2015, http://insidecostarica.com/2015/07/27/costa-rica-court-postpones-case-alleged-organ-traffickers-end-year/.

200. The details of the plea agreement were not made public. *Police Officer Arrested for Organ Trafficking to Turn Star Witness*, ICRNews, Mar. 25, 2014, http://insidecostarica.com/2014/03/25/police-officer-arrested-organ-trafficking-turn-star-witness/.

For reasons that remain unclear, the trial was delayed several times, but was finally scheduled to begin in the First Circuit Criminal Court of San José in November 2015. But in a tragic twist of events, the trial for Mora and his co-defendants was postponed until December 2015 after the lawyer for two of the defendants was assassinated by unknown gunmen while traveling in a taxi on October 1, 2015. Authorities believed the assassination may have been related to the lawyer representing drug traffickers.[201] Interestingly, the doctors had been released from custody after their arrests and allowed to resume their medical duties at the hospital where they worked with the only prohibitions being that they must report to the judicial authorities on a regular basis and that they could not leave the country.[202] Also released and allowed to return to work was the owner of the pizza shop across the street from the hospital who was accused of recruiting kidney donors.

For reasons that were never made clear, the trial was again postponed until February 2016. On February 8, 2016, prosecutors formally charged Mora and four accomplices with human trafficking for the purpose of organ extraction.[203] At this time of writing, it does not appear that the case has moved forward.

Kidney trafficking and the corruption related to the illegal enterprise are not the only issue Costa Rican authorities are fighting. In 2014 the Costa Rican Prosecutor's Office investigated the theft of 20 donated corneas from the government eye bank run by the Costa Rican Social Security System.[204] Authorities believe that a former employee of the eye bank took the corneas to a private eye clinic supposedly for research sometime between 2012 and 2013. That employee was unable to provide any documentation that the corneas were to be used for research, and suspicion mounted that the body parts would be used for illegal transplantation. Corneas in Costa Rica are worth around US$2,000 and the transplant procedures cost around US$5,000.[205]

---

201. *Abogado visitó la cárcel antes de ser asesinado a balazos*, ICRNews, Oct. 2, 2013, http://www.crhoy.com/abogado-visito-la-carcel-antes-de-ser-asesinado-a-balazos/.

202. *Doctors Accused of Organ Trafficking Are Released—and Back on the Job*, ICRNews, Oct. 17, 2013, http://insidecostarica.com/2013/10/17/doctors-accused-organ-trafficking-released-back-job/.

203. Dyer, *supra* note 198.

204. Zach Dyer, *Authorities Have Eyes Peeled Over Case of Stolen Corneas*, Tico Times, April 2, 2014, http://www.ticotimes.net/2014/04/02/authorities-have-eyes-peeled-over-case-of-stolen-corneas.

205. *Id.*

E. China's Lucrative Prisoner Organ Market

The Chinese government has long been implicated in organ trafficking schemes that involve the execution of prisoners to supply organs to recipients who are referred to China by corrupt doctors in Japan, Hong Kong, Singapore, and Taiwan. The doctors arrange for patients to undergo transplant surgeries in Wuhan, Beijing, and Shanghai.[206] Once in China, the foreign organ recipients wait only as long as it takes for executions timed to meet market demand are carried out and an organ becomes available. There are no reliable figures to determine how many prisoner executions are conducted in China each year, but Amnesty International suggests the number may be as few as 4,500 and possibly 3 to 4 times that number. The money paid by organ recipients enriches Chinese doctors and sustains several dozen medical facilities.

China's practice of using executed prisoners to meet demand for commercial transaction of organs can be traced to a confidential 1984 regulation entitled *Temporary Rules Concerning the Utilization of Corpses or Organs from the Corpses of Executed Prisoners*, which provided that organs from executed prisoners could be used for transplants if the prisoner agreed, if the family agreed, or if no one came to claim the body.[207] Although the Chinese government does not acknowledge that prisoners are executed specifically to harvest organs for commercial sale, supposed witnesses assert that prisoners set to be executed have blood taken from them the night before the execution and are then put to death with one bullet to the head in order to minimize tissue damage to the organs being harvested from the corpse.[208] The procedure is thought to be similar to executions conducted in Taiwan in the 1990s, which were described in great detail by David Rothman[209] in his influential report on international organ trafficking presented at the 10th Annual Conference on The Individual vs. the State, held in Budapest, Hungary in 2002:[210]

> Immediately before the execution, the physician sedates the prisoner and then inserts both a breathing tube in his lungs and a catheter in

---

206. Rothman, *supra* note 130, at 8.

207. Human Rights Watch, *China: Organ Procurement and Judicial Execution in China,* Sec. III (1994), https://www.hrw.org/reports/1994/china1/china_948.htm [hereinafter Organ Procurement].

208. *Id.*

209. Bernard Schoenberg Professor of Social Medicine at Columbia University.

210. Rothman, *supra* note 130.

one of his veins. The prisoner is then executed with a bullet to his head; the physician immediately moves to stem the blood flow, attach a respirator to the breathing tube, and inject drugs into the catheter so as to increase blood pressure and cardiac output. With the organs thus maintained, the body is transported to a hospital where the donor is waiting and the surgery is performed. The physicians have become intimate participants in the executions; instead of protecting life, they are manipulating the consequences of death.

Much has been written about conditions in Chinese prisons. Families of prisoners are often held responsible for the financial maintenance of imprisoned family members. It is said that in executions, the family of the prisoner must even pay for the bullet used.[211] Such a practice suggests that prisoners become little more than a commodity to be used and exploited by the state, which goes against international concepts of human rights. The Chinese government does not acknowledge executing prisoners for commercial organ harvesting, possibly to avoid additional criticism of the country's dismal human rights record. Moreover, since wealthy Chinese and foreigners pay more than US$30,000 for the organs of prisoners, there is little incentive to poke the cash cow. China has a long history of ignoring international pressure to fix its human rights abuses and corrupt practices, so it is reticent to heed to demands by other governments or organizations, such as international medical associations that decry Chinese organ harvesting practices.

As far as the element of corruption is concerned, the Chinese government's direct involvement in prisoner organ harvesting for commercial exploitation raises the question of whether such a practice can be considered corrupt if the government condones the practice. Does it become only become corrupt when the Chinese organ trade crosses international borders, for example, when Chinese organ brokers are discovered in places like New York and throughout Europe and Asia to be arranging organ transplants? This is a perplexing issue for governments and non-government organizations trying to stop THB/OR at the international level.

---

211. Organ Procurement, *supra* note 207.

7. Recommendations to Reduce Corrupt Practices in Organ Transplantation

A. For Governments

Organ traffickers exploit loopholes and gaps in domestic legislation. They also take advantage of poor mutual cooperation protocols and arrangements between countries when the organ trafficking is a transborder operation. In addition, the criminal code in some countries where THB/OR occurs is ineffective and punitive measures are weak, which hampers prosecution and achieving convictions with significant sentences that would have a deterrent effect on traffickers.

Strengthening the rule of law is the first defense against THB/OR. First, laws need to be strengthened to meet international standards for combating THB/OR, and to protect the "rights of organ donors, living and dead, as well as organ recipients."[212] National anti-corruption programs must also be implemented.[213] International legal cooperation and extradition procedures must be initiated, and training for effective investigation and prosecution in both domestic and transnational cases must be established and routinely reinforced and updated. This is particularly important when the transnationality of so many THB/OR cases require timely investigation and speedy arrests. International cooperation and interdiction at borders could be enhanced by providing special facilities and investigators for identifying potential donor victims or intercepting recent foreign organ recipients.[214]

Laws should also be in place that allow for law enforcement to undertake effective seizures of all relevant documents such as operation logs from hospitals and specialists involved in the transplant procedures. Promptness of arrest operations is key to prevent key players from escaping jurisdiction and shifting their criminal operations to other countries.

States governments should "take measures to protect the poorest and vulnerable groups from transplant tourism," seek the assistance of international organizations such as the WHO in drafting guidelines to protect such groups from THB/OR,[215] and implement the *Guiding Principles on*

---

212. Scheper-Hughes, *supra* note 2, at 34.
213. COE Recommendation 1611, *supra* note 57, at Article 14.3(i).
214. *Id.* at Article 14.3(h).
215. States also should "cooperate in the formulation of recommendations and guide-

Human Organ Transplantation issued by the WHO[216] and the Declaration of Istanbul.[217]

Countries should establish uniform guidelines on "informed donor choice."[218] A national donor registry source should be established, as well as a registry for nonresident donors and recipients. Primary prevention through public awareness campaigns and peer education should include "partnership with NGOs, the media, and relevant international agencies."[219]

Quality control and performance standards need to be in place and enforced for all transplant centers and hospitals where transplants occur, and all transplant facilities should be monitored and audited regularly. Medical professionals and healthcare facilities should be held accountable by governments for failing to maintain ethical standards. Likewise, they should also be held responsible "for ensuring that both organ donors and recipients receive equal care."[220]

---

lines to harmonize global practices in the procurement ... of human organs." WHA Resolution 57.18 (57th World Health Assembly 2004).

216. In Resolution WHA 44.25 of May 1991, the WHA adopted several guiding principles on human organ transplantation, including calling on nations to prevent the commercialization of human organs for transplantation, and to ban "all types of advertising, soliciting, or brokering for the purpose of transplant commercialism, organ trafficking, or transplant tourism." This resolution also called on governments to include "penalties for acts-such as medically screening donors or organs, or transplanting organs that aid, encourage, or use the products of, organ trafficking or transplant tourism." Among the Guiding Principles updated by WHA 57.18, the WHA declared that "transplantation encompasses not only medical but also legal and ethical aspects, and involves economic and psychological issues." In addition member States should:

- Authorize xenogenic grafts only when effective national regulatory control and surveillance mechanisms overseen by national health authorities are in place;
- Assure the traceability of human organs and tissues;
- Set out an appropriate mechanism for the authorization of health care facilities carrying out organ transplantations;
- Establish a national transplant system;
- Strictly regulate organ donation in order to protect both donors and recipients.

See MICHEL BELANGER, GLOBAL HEALTH LAW: AN INTRODUCTION 117–8 (2011).

217. Declaration of Istanbul, *supra* note 48.

218. For some ethical considerations for living donors, *see* NATIONAL ACADEMIES INSTITUTE OF MEDICINE, LIVING DONATION IN ORGAN DONATION: OPPORTUNITIES FOR ACTION 263 (2006), *Ch. 9 Ethical Considerations in Living Donation*, http://www.nap.edu/read/11643/chapter/11. *See also* A. Schulz-Baldes & F.L. Delmonico, *Improving Institutional Fairness to Live Kidney Donors: Donor Needs Must Be Addressed by Safeguarding Donation Risks and Compensating Donation Costs*, TRANSPLANT INT'L, 20:11:940–946, November 2007, http://www.ncbi.nlm.nih.gov/pubmed/17711405.

219. COE Recommendation 1611, *supra* note 57, at Article 14.3(a).

220. WHO Guide, *supra* note 36, at 10.

Any efforts undertaken by governments to increase organs for transplantation must have a method guaranteeing that the process of harvesting organs and distributing them for transplant surgery is fair, equitable, just, and ethical.[221] Implementation of such a system is up to the "gatekeepers," the transplant centers that decide who would or would not be accepted as a donor or transplant candidate.[222] From a bioethical perspective it is vital that the selection criteria is transparent, and that the hospital and medical members will reject donor's organ if the living donor's consent is found to be vitiated (out of fraud, coercion, or physical threat). Fairness and ethics demand standards of due diligence and knowing the patient on the part of hospitals and doctors when evaluating both living donors and recipients.[223]

If possible, governments should offer some form of financial support to poor living donors to help them defray expenses incurred throughout the donation process. Policies should also be established prohibiting insurance companies from denying coverage to donors for operative and post-operative care.[224]

The issue of consent must be addressed by governments where THB/OR is known to occur. Guidelines on what constitutes consent should be established and disseminated in all transplant facilities. At a minimum, consent information should be written in simple language and displayed prominently and provided in writing to potential donors. Illiterate donors should have consent information read to them in the language they speak. Those facilities that do not provide such public information should be fined and sanctioned up to and including closure. The consent information provided should be thorough and

---

221. In order to increase organ supply, several countries have implemented presumed consent laws. These laws make every citizen a donor unless they "opt out" by declaring themselves "no donors" while alive. "These laws have been tried in Spain, Italy, Austria, Belgium and Singapore." *See* Joint Study on Trafficking in Organs, *supra* note 26, at 32. In Brazil, there is resistance to presumed consent, and the lack of trust in the system has encouraged many to opt out and to conclude that regulation is driven by profit motives. *See* Scheper-Hughes, *supra* note 2, at 210.

222. Joint Study on Trafficking in Organs, *supra* note 26, at 32.

223. *Id.*

224. In order to encourage organ donations, the United States government, through the Department of Health and Human Services (HHS), made "more financial support available to low-income living donors to help cover expenses like travel and lodging costs that are incurred throughout the donation process." Moreover, the government prohibited insurers from denying health coverage under pre-existing condition to someone who donated an organ. Presidential Proclamation: National Donate Life Month, 2016 | whitehouse.gov, https://www.whitehouse.gov/the-press-office/2016/04/01/presidential-proclamation-national-donate-life-month-2016.

comprehensive with regard to the risks of the procedure and post-operative concerns.

Guidelines should include that the donor understands the information given and has formed a rational judgment based on the potential consequences of the decision. Donor's consent was given free of undue influence, duress and coercion.[225]

The government should establish a list of medical facilities approved for organ transplantation, and those facilities should be ranked. High ranking hospitals would be those that follow and develop procedures in accordance with the recommendations issued by a government authority having oversight of public health standards. This is a recommendation that was proposed in the *Consensus Statement* by the Ethics Committee of the Transplantation Society at its Amsterdam Forum on the Care of the Live Kidney Donor in 2000.[226]

---

225. WMA Statement 65th, *supra* note 44. The WMA calls it "informed donor choice."

226. Even though the recommendations were done for the care of the live kidney donor, the international standard of care should be applicable to all organ transplantations. The following recommendations include:

1. Prior to a live kidney donation to a potential recipient (known by the potential donor or not known in the circumstance of anonymous donation), the donor must receive a complete medical and psychosocial evaluation to include:
   - Quantification (as available) and assessment of the risk of donor nephrectomy on the individual's overall health, subsequent renal function, and any potential psychological and social consequences (including employability);
   - Assessment of the suitability of the donor's kidney for transplantation to the recipient (anatomy, function, and risk for transmissible disease).
2. Prior to donor nephrectomy, the potential donor must be informed of:
   - The nature of the evaluation process;
   - The results and consequences/morbidity of testing, including the possibility that conditions may be discovered that can impact future healthcare, insurability and social status of the potential donor;
   - The risks of operative donor nephrectomy, as assessed after the complete evaluation. These should include, but not be limited to: the risk of death, surgical morbidities, changes in health and renal function, impact upon insurability/employability and unintended effects upon family and social life;
   - The responsibility of the individual and health and social system in the management of discovered conditions (for example, if the donor is discovered to have tuberculosis, the donor should undergo treatment, the community has a responsibility to help the donor secure proper care with referral to an appropriate physician);
   - The expected transplant outcomes (favorable and unfavorable) for the recipient and any specific recipient conditions which may impact upon the decision to donate the kidney;
   - Disclosure of recipient specific information which must have the assent of

Governments must invest in the technical capacity of medical facilities to maintain donated organs and body parts, and promote proper training and continuing education for transplant specialists in order to ensure that organs from cadaveric donors are safe for transplant.[227]

Government should undertake efforts to encourage organ donation after death "in order to increase the availability of organs and tissues obtained post mortem."[228]

With regard to THB/OR, governments must offer some level of financial, medical, and mental health support to victims to assist them in recovering financially and emotionally from the impact of being exploited.

Insurance companies bear responsibility in some cases for tacitly encouraging THB/OR. Government authorities with oversight over the insurance industry should establish policies prohibiting insurance companies from

---

the recipient.

3. The potential donor should be informed of alternative renal replacement therapies available to the potential recipient.

4. The potential donor should be capable of understanding the information presented in the consent process.

5. The decision to donate should be voluntary, accompanied by:
   - The freedom to withdraw from the donation process at any time;
   - Assurance that medical and individual reasons for not proceeding with donation will remain confidential.

6. After kidney donation, the transplant center is responsible for:
   - Overseeing and monitoring the postoperative recovery process of the donor until that individual is stable, including provision of care for morbidity that is a direct consequence of donor nephrectomy;
   - Facilitating the long-term follow-up and treatment of the kidney donor with preexisting or acquired conditions (related to uninephrectomy) that are thought to represent a health risk such as—but not exclusive to—hypertension, obesity, diabetes, and proteinuria. In the absence of an established follow-up process for individuals with preexisting conditions that may possibly place the donor at health risk, organ donation should be avoided;
   - Identifying and tracking complications that may be important in defining risks for informed consent disclosure;
   - Working with the general healthcare community to provide optimal care/surveillance of the living kidney donor.

See JAMA, *supra* note 111, at 2922.

227. There seems to be trepidation about contracting AIDS or hepatitis from cadaveric organs, especially among wealthy patients. According to a nephrologist in Brazil, only the poor organ recipients accept a cadaveric kidney. *See* Scheper-Hughes, *Global Traffic in Human Organs*, 41:2 Current Anthropology 191, 210 (2000).

228. COE Recommendation 1611, *supra* note 57, at Article 14.3(e).

denying coverage for transplants and should also ensure that coverage include care from pre-operative to post-operative procedures.[229] Governments should also deny medical reimbursements for illegal transplants undertaken abroad.[230]

Governments that are far behind in living donor registries should make establishing and improving registries a high priority. The registry should include "demographic, clinical, and outcome information on all living organ donors."[231]

B. For Transplant Centers and Hospitals

Facilities must be required to obtain express and informed consent for all living donors, especially the poor, illiterate, foreign (particularly those from less developed countries), and those who lack any family relation to the organ recipient. Obtaining organs must be accomplished using appropriate safeguards to protect the weak, and any altruistic system of organ donation cannot equate to exploitation of vulnerable individuals. Moreover, eliminating organ shortages by taking advantage of the defenseless is unethical and criminal, and must not be tolerated.

Transplant institutions should establish proper screening procedures to "verify the donor's freedom from coercion."[232] In addition to recording health information, the screening team should keep complete and careful data on transplant donors and recipients having to do with (1) the recipient's relationship to the living donor; (2) details on how the donor came to know about the recipient, particularly if the transplant involves a foreign donor; (3) veri-

---

229. In order to encourage organ donations, the U.S. government, through the Department of Health and Human Services (HHS), made "more financial support available to low-income living donors to help cover expenses like travel and lodging costs that are incurred throughout the donation process." Moreover, the government prohibited insurers from denying health coverage under pre-existing condition to someone who donated an organ. Presidential Proclamation: National Donate Life Month, 2016 | whitehouse.gov, https://obamawhitehouse.archives.gov/the-press-office/2016/04/01/presidential-proclamation-national-donate-life-month-2016.

230. COE Recommendation 1611, *supra* note 57, at Article 14.1(b).

231. The justifications for such a registry includes: "concern for donor well-being, limitations of current knowledge regarding the long-term consequences of donation, the potential to evaluate the impact of changes in criteria for donor eligibility on the outcome of donors, and the need within the transplant community to develop mechanisms to provide for quality assurance assessments." *See* JAMA, *supra* note 111, at 2926.

232. *Id.* at 2921.

fiable economic status of both the donor and the recipient; (4) who recruited the donor and how the donor traveled to the facility, and; (5) who is responsible for the care of the donor. All such data should be audited and verified by an independent third party. The WMA *Consensus Statement on the Live Organ Donor* mandates:

> [D]ocuments in living donor transplantation should include not only the usual informed consent releases but also documentation of the disclosure process, the donor's capacity to balance risk and benefit, freedom from coercion and that the donation is not conditioned on direct monetary compensation. The documentation also should demonstrate that the recipient is aware of and accepts the risks (and benefits) that have been determined for the potential donor. The donor should have a medical record separate from the recipient's medical chart to maintain and protect donor confidentiality.[233]

In addition, transplant facilities should minimize any potential "conflict of interest"[234] and provide health care to the done by professionals "not involved in the care of the recipient."[235]

Transplant centers must have properly trained employees to inform and explain to the donor the need for a high standard of postoperative care. There should be a system in place that would reflect that the donor has understood and has consented freely to the risks and that s/he has the means to pay for the post-operative care. Transplant institutions must also offer qualified "unbiased and independent" interpreters/translators to donors who do not speak their language. Such interpreters must be trained on human trafficking and corruption, and understand the ethical demands of their role.[236]

Transplant centers should provide an independent advocate team for the donors with the only focus being the "best interest of the donor."[237] It should

---

233. *Id.*

234. *See* WMA Statement 65th, *supra* note 44. According to Principle 11 of the 2014 Statement of the World Medical Association, "In order to avoid a conflict of interest, the physician who obtains informed consent from the living donor should not be part of the transplant team for the recipient."

235. JAMA, *supra* note 111, at 2923.

236. *Id.* at 2921. The involvement of translators/interpreters should facilitate donors in expressing "hesitations, concerns, or health problems that the donor may wish to discuss."

237. For an interesting and complete discussion on living donor advocacy, *see* Part II of Jennifer Steel, Living Donor Advocacy: An Evolving Role Within Transplantation 103 (2013).

be a multidisciplinary team that includes a psychologist (different from that of the recipient care team), and a social worker or advocate from non-government groups trained (including trained about human trafficking) to provide an additional layer of information, assessment, and counsel to the donor. The independent living donor advocates should be given clear guidelines for conducting their assessments and monitoring responsibilities.[238] This additional involvement of professionals may ensure that the donor attains information and understanding on informed consent, the transplant procedure, risks, and post-surgery follow ups, and the donor advocates "should be empowered with full veto authority if they believe donation to be ill advised."[239] If confidentiality is a concern, then transplant facilities should establish a protocol that multidisciplinary professionals must follow in order to protect donor confidentiality.

Transplant centers must ensure that the donor's decision to consent to the procedure is based on the following elements:

1. *Understanding*

    Donors must be able to understand: (a) "accurate information regarding the risks and benefits to themselves," and (b) the benefits to the recipient as well as any "alternative treatments available to the recipient."

    This information must be given in a way that "the donor … can readily understand," therefore, delivery ought to take into consideration the donors' "educational background." "All donors should demonstrate capacity to understand the essential elements of providing consent to live donation, with information presented at a level of medical sophistication suitable for that individual."[240]

---

238. For a discussion of recommendations for the development of practice guidelines, *see* Jennifer Steel, *The Development of Practice Guidelines for Independent Living Donor Advocates*, 2013 Clinical Transplantation 178–184 (2013), http://www.ncbi.nlm.nih.gov/pmc/articles/PMC3623012/. The University of Texas Southwestern Medical Center's Independent Donor Advocacy team provides a useful model for a donor advocacy team, including its composition, role in patient care, and ethical obligations. This particular team is comprised of "physicians, surgeons, psychologists, medical ethicists, medical anthropologists, former living donors, living donor transplant recipients, and a chaplain." *See* Devasmita Choudhury, *Independent Donor Ethical Assessment: Aiming to Standardize Donor Advocacy*, 24 Progress in Transplantation 2 (2014), http://www.smu.edu/-/media/Site/Dedman/Departments/Anthropology/pdf/Smith-Morris/ChoudhuryFINAL.ashx?la=en.

239. JAMA, *supra* note 111, at 2921.

240. *Id.* at 2929.

2. Disclosure

Transplant centers have an obligation to give potential donors "full and accurate disclosure of all pertinent information regarding risk and benefit to the donor and recipient."[241]

International and national medical organizations and associations need to issue clearly defined codes of conduct for health care facilities and medical professionals regarding unregulated, paid organ donations.

C. For Physicians

Medical professionals must guard against being participants in an illegal activity involving coercive or compensated transplantations.[242] They need to try their best to be certain that the organs they transplant have been obtained in a legal and ethical manner, and they should desist from transplanting organs that they know or suspect have not been procured in such way.[243] If medical professionals are properly informed and encouraged, they can also assist law

---

241. Disclosure affords the donor a "cooling off period" between consent and the operation in order for the donor to have sufficient time "to reconsider the decision to donate." Such a disclosure process should allow the donor to have a clear understanding of the following issues:
- Description of the evaluation, the surgical procedure, and the recuperative period;
- Anticipated short- and long-term follow-up care;
- Alternative donation procedures, even if only available at other transplant centers;
- Potential surgical complications for the donor, citing the reports of donor deaths (even if never experienced at that transplant center);
- Medical uncertainties, including the potential for long-term donor complications;
- Any expenses to be borne by the donor;
- Potential impact of donation on the ability of the donor to obtain health and life insurance;
- Potential impact of donation on the life-style of the donor, and the ability of the donor to obtain future employment;
- Information regarding specific risks and benefits to the potential recipient;
- Expected outcome of transplantation for the recipient;
- Any alternative treatments (other than organ replacement) available to the recipient;
- Transplant center-specific statistics of donor and recipient outcomes.

See Id. at 2921.

242. WHO Guide, *supra* note 36, at 10.

243. WMA Statement, *supra* note 44.

enforcement in combating THB/OR. Ultimately, medical professionals must uphold ethical standards. Such cooperation of transplant surgeons and doctors and medical professionals engaged in transplant operations could weaken the illegal organ trade significantly.

D. For Insurance Companies

Insurance companies need to change coverage policies regarding the transplantation of organs and other body parts. The culpability of the medical insurance industry was raised in a 2007 article in the *American Journal of Transplantation* in which the authors wrote that insurance companies encourage transplant tourism without taking into consideration the health and ethical issues that arise with commercial transplantation.[244] For the insurance companies, it appears to be a matter of using transplant tourism for the sole purpose of addressing "the problems of organ availability, long waiting times, and high medical and surgical costs."[245] For corporate partners that sign up with insurance industry transplant tourism businesses, called medical travel program administrators, the motivation is lower employer health care costs and the ability for participants to receive care more quickly and at less cost by going overseas. One such medical travel program administrator, IndUSHealth, states that its programs allow "corporate self-insured health insurance plans to offer participants a way to obtain affordable, high-quality medical care overseas. We offer comprehensive personalized travel and treatment programs for Americans desiring care in world-class hospitals in Costa Rica, Cayman Islands, and India as an alternative to what has become oppressively expensive care in the U.S."[246] IndUSHealth asks potential corporate clients, "Are health care costs taking a toll on your bottom line?" The response states:

> Today's global marketplace is imposing new cost pressures on every company, large or small. And chances are they're taking a big bite out of yours.
> To make matters worse, these expenses are rising dramatically each year, with no end in sight.
> A growing number of U.S. companies are now taking advantage of a global health care option, seeking quality medical care in other coun-

---

244. Bramstedt, *supra* note 12.
245. *Id.*
246. *See* About IndUSHealth, http://www.indushealth.com/about/.

tries that offer top-notch physicians, services and facilities at a fraction of the cost. In fact, companies can expect to reduce hospital-related health care benefit expenses by 15–20% per year or more.[247]

Health professionals, government authorities, and ethicists should have some alarm over the growth of the medical health tourism industry. The foremost question should be, how has healthcare in first world countries like the United States become so prohibitively expensive that companies now look to health care overseas to reduce costs? Of greater concern is the ethical questions raised about these programs. Bramstedt and Xuc point out in their article on transplantation tourism that while programs like IndUSHealth may "make transplantation available in a manner that is faster (shorter waiting times) and cheaper, they are ethically troublesome in that they may create a coercive environment to patients and foster the practice of transplant tourism (which exploits living donors and disregards the needs of resident patients in foreign countries)."[248]

> Faced with the prospect of clinical deterioration, death, and high costs, transplant tourism could be enticing to some US patients. When employers add financial bonuses, this can increase the temptation to participate. Another concept to consider is pressure (subtle or not) placed on employees by their employers to participate in organ tourism as a condition of retaining employment and/or insurance coverage. It remains to be seen how employees who reject organ tourism are treated by their employers with regard to employment, promotions, and compensation.[249]

We as a society need to ask if this is what we want the future of medical care to be. Do we want our domestic medical arts to be exclusively for the affluent while others who are insured by employers are sent abroad for medical procedures because it is cheaper for the company where they work to engage in such a health program? This business practice also seems to contradict the WHO *Guiding Principles on Human Organ Transplantation* that include the notion that in the interest of "distributive justice and equity, donated organs should

---

247. *See* Corporate Programs, http://www.indushealth.com/about/.
248. Bramstedt, *supra* note 12, at 1700.
249. *Id.*

be made available to patients on the basis of medical need and not on the basis of financial or other considerations."[250]

---

250. WHO Draft Guiding Principle 9, Guiding Principles on Human Organ Transplantation, http://www.who.int/ethics/topics/transplantation_guiding_principles/en/index1.html.

Chapter 9

The Profusion of Anti-Human Trafficking Organizations

Summary: This chapter examines how efforts to confront human traf-ficking have resulted in the rapid growth of non-government organiza-tions (HT NGOs) dedicated to combating trafficking at the local, regional, and international levels. Some have labeled these organizations collec-tively, and at times pejoratively, as the "rescue industry." Others have de-rided the largely laissez faire environment among HT NGOs as akin to the Wild West, where monitoring is problematic and accountability for misconduct is nearly non-existent. Among the organizations that are doing vital, good works there lurk unscrupulous people who exploit for personal gain political and social instability, government resources, well-meaning private benefactors and corporate partners, competing NGOs, and the very victims the organizations are supposedly trying to help.

We will first look at the characteristics of HT NGOs, the goals and tactics of organizations to establish a presence in the rescue industry, and how the zeal and necessity to distinguish and create a "brand" can lead to individuals and organizations crossing the line separating appropri-ate conduct and behavior that does not pass the "smell test." We will then examine specific cases that illustrate the ways in which individuals in the rescue industry have engaged in conduct or display the optics of miscon-duct in a way that diminishes the credibility of all organizations in the anti-trafficking movement, and we will also look at efforts by an inter-esting assortment of individuals to monitor the rescue industry and de-velop ways to vet and hold HT NGOs accountable for their conduct. We will conclude with a discussion about the prospect of creating a mem-bership organization for HT NGOs as a means to clean up the rescue in-

dustry and that such membership would require adherence to a code of conduct and a willingness to be vetted and monitored in order to maintain good standing.

1. Types and Characteristics of Human Trafficking NGOs

To suggest that there may be many hundreds of HT NGOs dedicated to combating human trafficking, modern day slavery, and various forms of human exploitation and servitude is not necessarily a sweeping generalization or exaggeration. In the United States alone, there are dozens of HT NGOs dedicated to anti-human trafficking efforts, as of this writing.[1] The rapid growth of HT NGOs began in the late 1990s after human trafficking, especially sex trafficking, became a cause célèbre around the world. According to one human rights advocate, the visceral response of the public to images of women and children being exploited in horrific forms of servitude and exploitation allowed the antislavery movement, and particularly the anti-sex trafficking movement, to morph into a behemoth referred to by some as the "rescue industry."[2] This phenomenon of startup HT NGOs all dedicated to combating human trafficking is now a crowded field of organizations operating at the local, regional, and global level, and all are zealously competing for financial resources from both the government and private sectors.

Generally speaking, HT NGOs are of three types. The majority are established as nonprofit or not-for-profit organizations that enjoy tax-exempt status and the benefits that come with the status. These organizations rely primarily on private donations, government grants and contracts, corporate sponsorships, and partnerships with larger entities. Fundraising accounts for around 10 percent or more of operating expenses, and NGOs that spend between 80 to 97 percent of funds on programs and services are considered to be highly responsible.[3]

---

1. The HT NGO, A Heart for Justice, hosts an interactive webpage listing anti-human trafficking organizations. *See* Organizations Working to End Human Trafficking and Modern-Day Slavery, http://aheartforjustice.com/organizations/ (last visited June 3, 2017).

2. Stephanie Hanes, *Human Trafficking: A Misunderstood Global Scourge*, Christian Sci. Monitor, Sept. 9, 2012, http://www.csmonitor.com/World/Global-Issues/2012/0909/Human-trafficking-a-misunderstood-global-scourge.

3. This assessment results from reviewing a sample of HT NGOs that provide annual reports, tax filings, and other data collected and analyzed by GuideStar.org, the leading source for information on non-profit organizations.

The second type are faith-based organizations that may or may not be affiliated with established churches that already have tax-exempt status and therefore are not required to file annual tax returns. Examples would be Covenant House, which was founded by a Franciscan priest in the early 1970s to shelter homeless children around New York City, but has since expanded worldwide and includes combating human trafficking as part of its mission. Another example is the Lutheran Immigration and Refugee Service, founded in 1939, which works on human trafficking issues as just one of several programs and services.

The third type of HT NGO is comprised of entities arranged as public-private partnerships. This last type may not necessarily have tax-exempt status. An example of these organizations would be the partnership formalized in 2009 between LexisNexis and the Washington, DC-based HT NGO Polaris Project to develop a new web-based system that allows Polaris staff manning its crisis hotlines to access critical information in real time.[4] LexisNexis provides direct financial support, legal and technical advice, and research services to Polaris Project to meet "the company's significant commitment to combating human trafficking and advancing the Rule of Law around the world."[5] Google has also been heavily invested in partnerships with HT NGOs. In late 2011, Google disbursed US$11.5 million in grant funding to Polaris Project, Slavery Footprint, and the International Justice Mission to "support new initiatives utilizing technology to combat human trafficking."[6] Google, along with other corporations, has sponsored several summits, symposiums, and conferences to address combating human trafficking worldwide.[7]

2. The Best of Intentions

Most of the founders and the officers managing HT NGOs are well-meaning and singularly dedicated to the task of rescuing, counseling and accommodating trafficking victims, advocating for them, raising public awareness, and working to curtail and eradicate human trafficking and modern day slavery. But

---

4. *Polaris Project and LexisNexis Form Public-Private Partnership*, RELXGROUP.COM, May 27, 2009, http://www.relxgroup.com/mediacentre/pressreleases/2009/Pages/PolarisProjectandLexisNexisFormPublic-PrivatePartnershiptoFightHumanTrafficking.aspx.

5. *Id.*

6. *Private Sector Initiatives, Technology & Human Trafficking*, A Project of the USC Annenberg Center on Communication Leadership & Policy, University of South Carolina, http://technologyandtrafficking.usc.edu/private-sector-initiatives/.

7. *Id.*

establishing an organization, getting the public's attention, and securing steady funding require an understanding of public relations and branding. Many human trafficking organizations have names intended to evoke emotional responses from the public. The names are chosen with great care not only to distinguish the organizations and focus on the intensity of the work they do, but to help benefactors and donors feel good about their sponsorships. Polaris Project, for instance, is named after the North Star "that guided slaves towards freedom along the Underground Railroad."[8] Other symbolic names for organizations from around the world include: Children of the Night, The Emancipation Network, Eve, Hope for Justice, Half the Sky Movement, Break the Chain Campaign, Shared Hope International, Free the Slaves, Fair Girls, Passport 2 Freedom, and Called2Rescue. These entities that comprise the anti-trafficking/rescue milieu are a subgroup of human rights organizations and movements that University of Chicago Law Professor Eric Posner has referred to as an "exploding franchise" of organizations operating outside traditional government and institutional structures worldwide, and the operating revenues that some of these organizations have compiled are quite astonishing.

While some organizations get by on grassroots funding and operate on shoestring budgets to address local problems in partnership with local stakeholders, larger HT NGOs have become multi-million-dollar operations of national and international scope, supported by a continuous stream of celebrities, corporate sponsors, and affluent philanthropists who promote and sustain the organizations. In the United States alone, as of 2015, 50 of the most prominent HT NGOs shared a pool of funding of around US$686 million, "an amount that would place them approximately 184th on the UN's ranking of nations by GDP."[9] This amount does not include any additional available funds from the United States government of upwards of US$1 billion awarded in the form of grants each year.[10]

3. Transparency, Accountability and the Optics of Misconduct

So much money inevitably raises some concern about transparency and accountability and how such considerable revenues are managed and utilized.

---

8. Polaris Project webpage, http://www.polarisproject.org/.

9. Anne Elizabeth Moore, *Special Report: Money and Lies in Anti-Human Trafficking NGOs*, TURHOUT.ORG, Jan. 27, 2015, http://www.truth-out.org/news/item/28763-special-report-money-and-lies-in-anti-human-trafficking-ngos.

10. *Id.*

Human nature being what it is would suggest that misconduct of varying degrees would find its way into the anti-human trafficking movement, and it takes but a few irresponsible acts by a few bad actors to damage the integrity and reputations of other HT NGOs. As the founder of one HT NGO observed, how can the grant providers, donors, and benefactors be substantively advised about the specifications, resources and objectives of the organizations seeking support, especially when the HT NGOs are controlling their own narrative largely without scrutiny? Absent standards, validations and quality review of results, how can one discern objectively what is fulfilling public need or fomenting private gain? Valid and verifiable truth must be the "key hallmark for all programs serving in this difficult social, political, human arena."[11]

A. Finding Need and Opportunity

There are believed to be more than 3,000 NGO's of various types currently operating in Phnom Penh,[12] earning the Cambodian capital a reputation as a wild frontier for relief organizations. The extreme violence and genocide carried out by the Khmer Rouge in the late 1970s and the regime's subsequent overthrow rendered Cambodia a failing state without adequate infrastructure to support the surviving civil society, revitalize services, and reform the rule of law. Those who survived genocide and mass displacements became highly vulnerable to all forms of human exploitation and abandonment. Children were especially at risk, and many aid workers flocked to Cambodia during the last three decades to help rebuild the nation and its people.

Unfortunately, among the thousands of individuals who went to Cambodia were those who saw opportunities to game the system and enrich themselves under the color of operating as non-government and tax exempt organizations. Notes one reporter covering NGOs there, "In Cambodia, where the rule of law is frail and bureaucracy impenetrable, no story is straightforward."[13] One egregious act by a corrupt individual running a corrupt NGO can badly damage the image of many people and organizations trying to do good works in Cambodia. "It's outrageous," wrote Rob Jamieson, founder of PenhPal.com, an online guide for expats living in Phnom Penh, "that we for-

---

11. Comments of Mary Elizabeth McIlvane, a Florida expert on child sex abuse and founder of the Center for Truth and Trust in Central Florida.

12. Stephanie Wood, *Dodge City*, SYDNEY MORNING HERALD (Australia), Feb. 15, 2014, at Good Weekend 14.

13. *Id.*

eigners come here, criticise the government for lack of governance and transparency, then turn around and behave the same way."[14]

Among the first cadre of NGO's to establish facilities in the capital were orphanages and residential care centers. The number of such operations experienced a growth spurt of 70 percent between 2005 and 2010, according to UNICEF.[15] But the problem with the narrative of doing incredible works that accompanies so many of these organizations is that there are more orphanages than orphans, and the orphan children the world envisions from the Cambodian genocide, images long used to solicit funding for the NGO's working there, are now adults.[16] Taking their place in the orphanages are not necessarily actual orphans, but children who have been given up or sold by family members who cannot care for them. According to an Australian journalist who investigated the murky world of NGOs in Phnom Penh in early 2014, "The myth of the Cambodian orphan is a powerful marketing tool for child speculators who exploit the abundant supply of small cute faces from destitute families. For every reputable operation, there are many more of doubtful worth or worse."[17] The journalist went on to quote Sebastien Marot, Executive Director of Friends International, who noted, "Kids are the item on sale, if you want, or exhibition." Marot's organization campaigns to end "orphanage tourism," a repugnant practice to take "visitors' cash for cuddles with children who might have been collected by 'child recruiters' to fill facilities falling way below legislated minimum standards."[18]

Investigative journalist claims of orphanage tourism impacted one NGO called Love in Action, run by a female Australian national, whose 12-year-long unlicensed operation was shut down in 2013 for maintaining facilities that fell below legal standards, and for suspicion of human trafficking.[19] The raid on her facilities was allegedly orchestrated by a competing NGO called SISHA International, founded in 2007 by another Australian expat and retired police officer named Steve Morrish.[20] The tangled web of events that fol-

---

14. *Id.*
15. *Id.*
16. *Id.*
17. *Id.*
18. *Id.*
19. *Cambodia Shuts Australian-Run Orphanage Called Love in Action*, NEWS.COM.AU, Mar. 25, 2013, http://www.news.com.au/world/cambodia-shuts-australian-run-orphanage/story-fndir2ev-1226605864587.
20. SISHA, which has since ceased operations, claimed as of August 2013 to have assisted more than 860 victims, initiated 147 prosecutions and delivered practical training for 540 police officers over the prior seven years.

lowed the raid on Love in Action turned the spotlight back on Morrish and resulted in unsubstantiated allegations of misconduct and mismanagement of his own organization.

The Financials section on the SISHA website, since removed, stated that, "SISHA International adheres to the highest standards of governance and accountability, working in a diligent manner to ensure that funds and resources are always allocated to provide services to women and children who are abused and come to us for help."[21] Even so, the *Sydney Morning Herald* investigated Morrish and detailed a colorful individual whose personal charm and sometimes larger-than-life conduct enabled him to build an HT NGO funded by more than AU$1 million from private benefactors. The tone and unconventional methods of his organization were unapologetic and may have ruffled some feathers of competitors, particularly after using the crass slogan "Bugger a Pedophile" to get attention for his organization's work.[22] Morrish came under closer scrutiny in the early 2000s when he became affiliated with International Justice Mission. While it is irrefutable that SISHA did do good works, Morrish was criticized for pursuing a lavish lifestyle on a salary of more than AU$80,000 annually, while not paying staff members. He also was suspected of misappropriating earmarked funds by applying them to programs and services, including more than AU$1 million donated by one benefactor whose donation was reportedly intended for a SISHA scholarship fund. Additionally, a donation of AU$440,000 set for establishing and funding a crisis center was possibly sidetracked to cover administration expenses and salaries, "including more than $70,000 for Morrish's back pay."[23]

The combined weight of so many unproven allegations, many made by a former intern according to a statement released on the SISHA USA webpage, compelled Morrish to step down as Executive Director of SISHA in August 2013, until such time as his name and the good name of the organization could be cleared by independent audits and investigations. A review was subsequently done by KPMG Cambodia Limited, a professional services firm, finding that most of the allegations were unsubstantiated and wrong, although KPMG did determine that some earmarked funds had been mismanaged.[24]

---

21. SISHA INT'L, at http://www.sisha.org/what-we-do/financials/. Webpage no longer available.

22. Wood, *supra* note 12. Other SISHA promotional material features an Asian pop star wearing a revealing, bondage-style dress.

23. *Id.*

24. Key findings from the KPMG investigation, which have since been removed from

While it cannot be said that SISHA and Morrish engaged in corrupt practices, the optics of misconduct arising from questionable activities do not
cast the organization's work and the work of other HT NGOs in a very favorable light. Morrish's circumstances also suggest a less than transparent.
world of HT NGOs that rely on sensationalism and hyperbole to promote a
narrative that is attractive to media consumption and potentially lucrative
for the organizations. One seasoned aid worker with a solid background
working with HT NGOs going back 30 years became something of a whistleblower in late 2013 when he was interviewed for an article that appeared in
the *Cambodia Daily* on human trafficking organizations fabricating stories
about trafficking victims.[25] The aid worker, Dr. Pierre Fallavier, opined that
fabricating stories about the beneficiaries of aid organizations is an approach
that all major international NGOs employ worldwide: "They take bits and
parts of life stories of different beneficiaries and make up a 'typical' sob story
that they use to raise funds with."[26] He considered the practice unethical and
was compelled to leave one of the NGOs where he worked because of it. He
asserted that the NGOs need money and they are unapologetic about the
false narratives they create. "This is marketing," he explains. The groups "need
to raise money, and it is only with extreme stories that they will get people
to give the cash they need to undertake their work. In fact, in many cases,

---

the Internet, included:
   • Morrish did not steal or misappropriate funds and did not make inappropri-
     ate payments to relatives.
   • SISHA's board of directors instructed Morrish to reduce the liability for his de-
     ferred salary (which had accumulated over a period of four years) as soon as
     SISHA's financial position allowed.
   • The CamKids and Hope Scholarship programs were on track and operating as
     envisaged.
   • Some funds earmarked for these programs were used to support core opera-
     tions of SISHA via intra-program loans. No intentional mishandling of the
     funds was detected.
   • Limited progress was made on a proposed Women's Crisis Centre, and fund-
     ing earmarked for this Centre was used for operational expenses within SISHA.
     The Board recommended discontinuing the programs.
Original source was http://sishausa.org/sisha-announces-investigation-results-2/. For an
alternative source to the story, *see* Laignee Barron, *SISHA Internal Audit Identifies No
Wrongdoing*, PHNOM PENH POST, Dec. 6, 2013, http://www.phnompenhpost.com/na-
tional/sisha-internal-audit-identifies-no-wrongdoing.
   25. Simon Marks, *Aid Worker Claims Fabricated Stories Are Common*, CAMBODIA DAILY,
Nov. 7, 2013, https://www.cambodiadaily.com/archives/aid-worker-claims-fabricated-stories-
are-common-46708/.
   26. *Id.*

back home, private marketing companies are in charge of the advertising, and they sell NGO work in the same way they would with any other service."[27] Understandably, the organizations mentioned in the article refuted Dr. Fallavier's claims by attempting to minimalize his level of association with the organizations.

Accusations of misconduct by nongovernment organizations involved in combating human trafficking have emerged in other parts of the world, and some of the charges are quite perplexing. In 2007, a French organization working in Chad called Zoe's Ark (L'Arche de Zoé) was accused by Chadian officials of attempting to traffic 103 children from Chad into France.[28] The organization refuted the claim, saying that in fact it was taking it upon itself to take injured and sick children out of war-torn areas of Chad to France in an effort to literally save their lives. The Chad government responded, accusing Zoe's Ark of being in blatant violation of adoption laws and insisted that the organization had no such authorization to remove children from the country. Members of Zoe's Ark were formally charged with child trafficking.[29] The defendants claimed that the children were orphans from Darfur, Sudan, but United Nations officials determined that many of the children were actually Chadian, and not orphans at all. The defendants also claimed that tribal leaders in Sudan said that all the children were Darfuri orphans. Moreover, Zoe's Ark insisted that the operation was a medical evacuation and not an adoption operation.[30] Chadian prosecutors alleged that six of the Zoe's Ark members "used deception to persuade villagers on Chad's eastern border with Darfur to part with their children, promising education and care in local Chadian centres but without mentioning any plan to fly them to Europe."[31] They were also accused of using fake blood and bandages on the children to effect a ruse. The trial became an international media sensation, and even included a hunger strike by the Zoe's Ark defendants, and demands by affected families for more than €300,000 in compensation for each child taken.[32] Also, the criminal pro-

---

27. *Id.*

28. *CHAD: French NGO Accused of Trafficking Children*, IRIN, Oct. 26, 2007, http://www.irinnews.org/report/75019/chad-french-ngo-accused-of-trafficking-children.

29. *Profile: Zoe's Ark*, BBC NEWS ONLINE, Oct. 29, 2007, http://news.bbc.co.uk/2/hi/europe/7067374.stm.

30. *Id.*

31. Moumine Ngarmbassa, *Families Weren't Duped, Zoe's Ark Duo Tell Court*, SYDNEY MORNING HERALD, smh.com.au, Dec. 24, 2007, http://www.smh.com.au/news/world/families-werent-duped-zoes-ark-duo-tell-court/2007/12/23/1198344884621.html.

32. *Chad Kidnap Families Want Millions in Compensation*, LIVELEAK.COM, Dec. 24, 2007, http://www.liveleak.com/view?i=6b1_1198531211.

ceedings had a chilling effect on foreign relations between Chad and France. Then-French President Nicolas Sarkozy intervened and managed to have charges dropped on several defendants. However, six Zoe's Ark members were convicted in December 2007 and sentenced to six years of hard labor and ordered to pay substantial fines.[33] Their sentences were transferred from Chad to France, where they served only a few months of minimal confinement before being released in March 2008, after Chad President Idriss Deby signed a pardon.[34]

There is also an overabundance of NGOs working in various sectors of relief work in Nepal, where the hundreds of millions of aid dollars entering the country each year constitute a substantial "pillar of the economy."[35] With so many NGOs present in such a relatively small nation, it is nearly impossible for the government or watchdog groups to monitor illicit or corrupt activities.

For example, in early 2014, the Thomson Reuters Foundation reported on how the HT NGO Next Generation Nepal (NGN) received a tip about a problem with an orphanage operating outside Kathmandu.[36] Upon investigating, NGN staff discovered nearly 20 trafficked children living in squalor. The children were found not to be orphans, but victims of child traffickers who "tricked their parents with promises to educate their kids and keep them safe."[37] Once the children were placed in the orphanage, they were forced to pose for tourists and foreign donors in order to bring funds into the orphanage. The investigation brought attention to the intersection of orphanages and child trafficking in Nepal. According to the Thomson Reuters Foundation, NGN has attempted to investigate and close unscrupulous HT NGOs suspected of child trafficking through unregulated orphanages that take advantage of "the inefficiency and corruption that permeate Nepal's bloated aid sector."[38]

Another fundamental problem that the Thomson Reuters Foundation reported concerns the fact that Nepal's formal private sector is quite small.

---

33. *Zoe's Ark Workers Get Hard Labor*, CNN.com, Dec. 26, 2007, http://www.cnn.com/2007/WORLD/africa/12/26/chad.children/index.html.

34. *6 French Charity Workers Released*, UPI.com, Mar. 31, 2008, http://www.upi.com/Top_News/2008/03/31/6-French-charity-workers-released/UPI-85581207020691/?st_rec=55581256847123.

35. Rachel Browne & Alia Dharssi, *Some NGOs in Nepal Do More Harm than Good Say Experts*, Thomson Reuters Found., May 7, 2014, http://www.trust.org/item/201405072 13441-lnbvr/.

36. *Id.*

37. *Id.*

38. *Id.*

"The only place to make money is through civil society. This is where the income is in the country. People set up NGOs as a business," according to NGN's director Martin Punaks.[39] Researchers working outside Nepal have also noticed the challenges there. "Right now, everybody is just doing their own thing, following the money, and it's very sensationalised and it really causes more chaos than help in a lot of ways," said Michelle Kaufman, a professor at Johns Hopkins University who has studied anti-trafficking programs in Nepal.[40]

Nepalese children appear vulnerable to being trafficked through illegal adoption operations due to significant gaps in government policies and procedures that may involve some official collusion. A report issued by a technical assistance mission to Nepal in November 2009 found the procedures for inter-country adoptions woefully lacking and in noncompliance with the *Hague Convention of 29 May 1993 on Protection of Children and Co-operation in Respect of Intercountry Adoption.*[41] Nepal is a State Party of the *Convention*, and like other countries that are parties, the purposes, principles, and safeguards of the *Convention* must be incorporated into each country's domestic law "and made effective through a strong legal and administrative framework."[42]

Implementing legislation for Nepal's adoptions procedures are controlled by a protocol called the *Terms and Conditions 2008*. According to the *Convention's Guide to Good Practice, Guide No. 1 (2008)*,[43] compliance with the *Convention* requires that a specific set of essential elements must be present in a country's adoption protocols and legal framework. Included among these elements are: to establish minimum standards for the protection of the children; to develop safeguards to prevent the abduction, the sale of, or traffic in children; and to engage in adoption practices that are in the best interests of the child, that first take into account national solutions for adoption, adhere to safeguards articulated in the *Convention*, and ensure that competent national authorities are involved in the adoption procedures.[44]

---

39. *Id.*

40. *Id.*

41. Hague Conference on Private International Law, Intercountry Adoption Technical Assistance Programme Report of Mission to Nepal 23–27 November 2009, Feb. 4, 2010, https://www.brandeis.edu/investigate/adoption/docs/INTERCOUNTRY_ADOPTION_TECHNICAL_ASSISTANCE_PROGRAMMEnepal_rpt09.pdf.

42. *Id.*

43. Hague Conference on Private International Law, The Implementation and Operation of the 1993 Hague Intercountry Adoption Convention: Guide to Good Practice, Guide No. 1 (2008).

44. Hague, *supra* note 41.

As soon as the Technical Assistance Mission arrived in Nepal, events occurred that raised suspicions and concerns by the delegation. Among these were that a number of programme sessions between the delegation and government officials were suddenly canceled "without reasonable explanation."[45] Nepalese government officials who were to be involved in the training programmes were unaccountably absent, and the Undersecretary of the Ministry of Women, Children and Social Welfare, who was believed to have a sound knowledge and understanding of the *Convention*, had been suddenly transferred prior to the arrival of the Mission.[46] The team interpreted these absences and programme changes as "a lack of commitment to adoption reform on the part of the Government."[47] Others might call this conduct public corruption.

Nevertheless, the Technical Assistance team set to work to review the *Terms and Conditions 2008* and found them to be inadequate and having serious omissions. Among these omissions was inclusion or adaptation of provisions found in the critical art. 21 of the *Convention on the Rights of the Child*.[48] The principles of the best interest of the child were entirely absent, raising questions as to the basis of decision-making for the child.[49] Also, there were no criteria in place for determining a child's adoptability, no procedures appeared to be in place to find a permanent family in Nepal for a child in need (for those concerned about international human trafficking, this particular point raises a significant red flag), and there was no procedure for providing counseling or support to biological parents about the legal ramifications of relinquishing a child.

The team also found that the principles and safeguards articulated in *The Hague Intercountry Adoption Convention of 1993*[50] were absent in the *Terms and Conditions 2008*; that the procedures were primarily concerned with administrative matters and the functions of a number of committees. The team was particularly concerned about a conflict of interest arising from "the inclusion of the orphanages' representatives on the Investigation, Recommendation and Monitoring Committee." The team also emphasized that since the role of that Committee is to investigate and verify the accuracy and au-

---

45. *Id.*

46. *Id.*

47. *Id.*

48. Convention on the Rights of the Child, G.A. Res. 44/25, 44 U.N. GAOR, Supp. No. 49, U.N. Doc. A/44/736 (1989).

49. Hague, *supra* note 41.

50. The Hague Convention on Protection of Children and Co-operation in Respect of Intercountry Adoption, May 29, 1993, 32 I.L.M. 1134.

thenticity of adoption documents, the representatives of orphanages "should not be permitted to investigate themselves as this creates a clear conflict of interest."[51]

Among the team's findings were the following conclusions:

1. Falsification of documents: there is evidence that this abuse is occurring regularly in order to declare a child adoptable and that this abuse has continued under the Terms and Conditions 2008;
2. False statements about the child's abandonment, origins, age and status: there is evidence that this abuse is occurring regularly in order to declare a child adoptable;
3. Lack of transparency and accountability for the money coming into Nepal (to the Government and institutions) from intercountry adoptions;
4. The absence of a policy on intercountry adoption as a child protection measure within an integrated policy of alternative care options for a child without a family;
5. A lack of alternative care solutions for children without parental care.

These are the kinds of gaps in policies and procedures, intentional or otherwise, that create the optics of misconduct, and may allow the presence of corruption to flourish and *become* the system rather than *influence* the system. The lack of oversight, transparency, and accountability not only invites abuse and fraud, but also allows dishonest actors to take advantage of weak oversight and lack of will to protect vulnerable populations.

What occurred in Nepal is endemic of conditions that allow some individuals to seize opportunities and to become figureheads and crusaders in humanitarian relief movements despite the possibility that they may be charlatans. One need look no further than the tale of Somaly Mam, whose rise to fame and celebrity as a jet-setting anti-human trafficking crusader was as meteoric as her spectacular flameout.

4. Celebrity and Sensationalism

A. The Downfall and Reinvention of Somaly Mam

The search for truth came calling several years ago for what was considered the most high-profile and successful HT NGO in the world, the Somaly Mam

---

51. Hague, *supra* note 41.

Foundation (SMF). The origins of SMF and the way it acquired massive sums of money to support the organization can be traced back directly to the seeming mythical rise of Somaly Mam, a Cambodian woman who wove together a fantastical story about being a trafficked child sex slave, survivor, and crusader against sex trafficking. Mam first began working in relief work with Doctors Without Borders (Médecins Sans Frontières) and in 1996 founded her first non-government organization, Acting for Women in Distressing Situations (AFESIP) (Agir pour les Femmes en Situation Precaire) with rescue operations in Cambodia, Laos, and Vietnam.

Her autobiographical story about the horrific abuse she suffered, her exotic looks, and her personal charm resonated with the Hollywood elite and socially conscious corporate executives, and by the mid-2000s, she was a global brand and cause célébre traveling among the rich and famous to promote herself and her organization, which she claimed had rescued more than 4,000 girls and women from sex trafficking.[52] In 2006, Mam founded the Somaly Mam Foundation to raise funds for AFESIP with the high-profile support of stars like Angelina Jolie, Susan Sarandon, and Sheryl Sandberg, the Chief Operating Officer of Facebook.[53] SMF soon had operating revenues in the many millions of dollars, and Mam was a sought after speaker, commanding hundreds of thousands of dollars in speaking and appearance fees worldwide. By 2009, Mam's international notoriety placed her on *Time* magazine's list of the 100 Most Influential People in the World.

But by 2012, concerns began to surface over discrepancies in Mam's autobiography and the personal stories of many of the trafficking victims she had rescued. The *Cambodia Daily* newspaper began a series of investigative reports that led to further additional scrutiny at the international level. Details of her life could not be verified, events she alleged took place seemed never to have happened,[54] and timelines in her narrative did not check out. Mam's situation quickly unraveled after some of her "girls" admitted to being told by Mam to falsify their stories in order to make them more sensational, and evidence sur-

---

52. Essemee, *Somaly Mam and the Dark Side of Charity*, SWALLOWING THE CAMEL, July 7, 2014, http://swallowingthecamel.me/2014/07/07/somaly-mam-and-the-dark-side-of-charity/comment-page-1/.

53. *Charity Watch Hall of Shame*, CHARITYWATCH.ORG (2015), https://www.charity watch.org/charitywatch-articles/charitywatch-hall-of-shame/63.

54. In a speech before the United Nations General Assembly in April 2012, Mam falsely asserted that the Cambodian army had killed eight rescued girls following a raid on her organization's Phnom Penh center in 2004. *See* Simon Marks, *Somaly Mam Admits to Inaccuracies in Speech to UN*, CAMBODIA DAILY, Apr. 26, 2012, https://www.cambodiadaily.com/archives/somaly-mam-admits-to-inaccuracies-in-speech-to-un-1590/.

faced that Mam violated the privacy of some of her survivors by allowing a journalist to "live tweet" a brothel raid in Cambodia in 2011,[55] parading them in front of the media and donors—a clear violation of the intent of art. 6(1) and art. 6(3) of the *Palermo Protocol*.

By 2014, her persona and many of her claims were challenged as fabrications by an investigative journalist's article published as the cover story in *Newsweek* magazine.[56] As was to be expected, the article received a considerable amount of blowback and criticism from Mam's legion of defenders. Mam later pushed back to clear her name and regain her reputation through an interview appearing in *Marie Claire* magazine in September 2014. In the article, Mam provided reasonable explanations for discrepancies in her background, and the journalist writing the story detailed her own investigation of documents and sources that refuted the *Newsweek* story's findings.[57] By then, however, Mam's credibility, along with her *de facto* "empire," was in shambles, and celebrities began distancing themselves from her. While the Cambodian government declined to pursue prosecuting her, in October 2014, it banned her from running any more NGOs in Cambodia.[58] That ban was soon lifted, but on October 18, 2014, Somaly Mam Foundation shut down its operations. By the end of October, a sophisticated public relations machine was already at work rebranding Mam's image in run-up to a December announcement of the creation of the New Somaly Mam Fund: Voices of Change, that commenced operations in January 2015 as a 501(c)(3) organization responsible primarily for being the new fundraising arm for AFESIP.[59]

---

55. Essemee, *supra* note 52.

56. Marks, *supra* note 54.

57. Abigail Pesta, *Somaly Mam's Story: "I Didn't Lie."*, Marie Claire, Sep. 16, 2014, http://www.marieclaire.com/culture/news/a6620/somalys-story/. Mam asserts in the article that her statements were misunderstood by many because English is her second language and that what she was trying to convey was unclear. In fairness to Mam, this is not, on its face, an unreasonable explanation.

58. Holly Robertson & Kuch Naren, *Gov't Says Somaly Mam Banned from Running NGO*, Cambodia Daily, Oct. 3, 2014, https://www.cambodiadaily.com/news/govt-says-somaly-mam-banned-from-running-ngo-68998/.

59. Lisa Anderson, *Disgraced Anti-Sex Slavery Crusader Mam Unveils Plans for New Group*, Reuters, Dec. 24, 2014, http://www.reuters.com/article/2014/12/24/us-advocacy-somaly-mam-new-foundation-idUSKBN0K215T20141224. Cambodian officials later changed their position about banning Mam from running any more NGOs. *See* Moore, *supra* note 9.

B. Chong Kim and *Eden*

Somaly Mam is not the only anti-human trafficking celebrity to have her story subjected to intense scrutiny. In 2012, filmmaker Megan Griffiths released a feature film entitled *Eden*, a fictionalized story based on supposedly true events in the life of American anti-human trafficking crusader and self-proclaimed sex trafficking survivor Chong Kim.[60] The film met with some critical acclaim and made Kim a minor celebrity in a similar vein as Somaly Mam. A portion of the film's proceeds were supposed to go to benefit anti-slavery organizations. But not long after the film was in circulation, skeptics about Kim's life and narrative began digging into her past and found that her life story simply did not make sense. In fact, it was another human trafficking organization that had initially attempted to work with her that raised concerns about her alleged deceit.

Kim's rise to notoriety began sometime around 2004 when her autobiographical essay titled, *No One's Concubine*, appeared in a collection of writings called *Not For Sale: Feminists Resisting Prostitution and Pornography*.[61] The narrative she embraced, in retrospect, contains nearly all the cliché elements one may associate with a tragic life that falls into sexual servitude—family violence at an early age, rape, low self-esteem, drug use, working as a stripper and being abused by clients, before finally emerging from the darkness to become a survivor.[62]

Kim skillfully parlayed the attention she gained from her story to become a motivational public speaker, writer, consultant, advocate against sex trafficking, and co-founder of a business entity called Velvet Brick Entertainment.[63] As her notoriety grew, her stories told in interviews became more fanciful. They also started not to make sense. In one account, she described how she escaped her traffickers in a major Las Vegas hotel by seducing a maintenance worker into giving her the plans of the air-conditioning system so that she could make her way out of the building through ductwork, reaching the end of the AC system and falling down the side of the building and injuring herself in an

---

60. *Eden*, Phase 4 Films, 2012.

61. Christine Stark & Rebecca Whisnant, eds., Not for Sale: Feminists Resisting Prostitution and Pornography 102 (Spinifex, 2005).

62. Mike Ludwig, *From Somaly Mam to "Eden": How Sex Trafficking Sensationalism Hurts Sex Workers*, Truthout, July 9, 2014, http://www.truth-out.org/news/item/24827-from-somaly-mam-to-eden-how-sex-trafficking-sensationalism-hurts-sex-workers.

63. Chong Kim is an LLC Incorporation, according to her webpage at http://www.chongnkim.net/resources/endorsement/.

awkward landing.[64] That tale was later challenged by James Barnes, the founder of the Florida-based HT NGO, Breaking Out, who spoke to the building engineer at the hotel about the air-conditioning ducting and learned that a human being could not possibly fit in the ducting or make it to an outside exit.

In Barnes, it appears that Kim came up against someone willing to confront her victim-as-crusader narrative. Prior to dedicating himself to fighting human trafficking, Barnes had a prominent career as a private investigator. Sensing that Kim might be someone other than she claimed to be, Barnes began digging into her background, and beginning in June 2014, posted a summary on his NGO's Facebook page detailing the results of his investigation into Kim's various claims and conducts.[65] Barnes wrote in his Facebook post that he took details from transcripts and interviews, in Kim's own words, "that showed a pattern of contradiction and deceit."[66]

Barnes began by looking at her claims about how long she had lived in the United States. In a statement made in 2006, Kim claimed to have been residing in the United States for 22 years, which would establish her date of residence at about 1984. But in her autobiographical book, *Broken Silence*, Barnes noted that Kim had stated that she had come to the United States from South Korea in 1977. Kim is also on record stating that she has never been arrested.[67] However, Barnes discovered that in 2007, Kim had indeed been arrested in her home state of Minnesota and charged with theft-by-swindle in a 2006 incident in which she was accused of cheating an actual human trafficking victim out of her life savings.[68] The court record shows that Kim was ordered to pay restitution in the amount of $15,246.92, complete her probation, perform 300 hours of community service, submit to a psychological evaluation and stay out of further legal trouble.

About her disability and walking with the use of a cane, she stated that her disability was due to beatings and abuse as a sex slave. Yet in her book, Kim states that she had become disabled as a child, and Barnes asserted that a former grade school teacher of Kim's told him that Kim had the disability since

---

64. Ludwig, *supra* note 62.

65. *See* the Breaking Out Facebook page at https://www.facebook.com/BreakingOut/?fref=nf. *See also* the posting on the Results of Chong Kim Investigation, posted Oct. 2, 2014, https://www.facebook.com/BreakingOut/posts/708922209196425.

66. Barnes has granted permission for the author to quote his statements from his Breaking Out Facebook page.

67. According to Barnes, Kim stated in her book that she was never arrested because one of the traffickers she worked with as a "madame" was a US Marshal who had inner connections with vice squads in Nevada, California, New York, and Florida.

68. Ramsey District court case number: 06166722. The terms of the outcome are public record and available as well from James Barnes.

she was seven years old and had been collecting Social Security checks for that disability up until at least 2005.[69]

To make matters more unclear, Kim claimed in her book that she was sold into sex slavery in 1994 while living in Texas. Yet, Barnes tracked down the 1994 yearbook of Bridge Creek High School in Blanchard, Oklahoma, containing a photo of Kim as a member of the junior class.[70]

When Barnes released his findings to the public, Kim promised swift and certain legal action against him (which has not occurred to date). Then on October 2, 2014, Barnes posted a detailed follow-up report of his investigations into Kim and her misrepresentations and conducts, reconfirming the veracity of his findings. Why did Barnes go to such trouble to expose Kim? He did so, he says, because he sees the work he is doing to help combat human trafficking as a calling, and he is not willing to allow individuals who may be charlatans to gain personal enrichment from the misery of true trafficking victims. Barnes also subscribes to the position that "anti-trafficking activism should be humble and honest, not a sensational, moneymaking machine."[71] At all times, the optics of misconduct and the potential for corruption must be avoided.

As for the film *Eden*, critics eventually panned the movie as Hollywood sensationalism replete with predictable plot lines, and it has been a revelation of sorts to some that Kim's assertions of having been involved in extreme violence, including murder, did not raise red flags sooner. Writing in *Salon*, Noah Berlatsky put the context of *Eden* and Kim's narratives into a sober perspective:

> To just point out the most obvious issue, the movie details a copious number of murders, several of them committed by the main character herself. This is standard issue for a Hollywood film, but in real life, this amounts to mass murder, including the killing of multiple law-enforcement personnel. That's a major story — if this happened in anything like the way Kim said, where's the massive investigation? Why is this being covered in an entertainment review, rather than on the front page?[72]

---

69. Results of Chong Kim Investigation, posted Oct. 2, 2014, https://www.facebook.com/BreakingOut/posts/708922209196425.

70. *Id.*

71. Ludwig, *supra* note 62.

72. Noah Berlatsky, *Hollywood's Dangerous Obsession with Sex Trafficking*, Salon.com, June 10, 2014, http://www.salon.com/2014/06/10/hollywoods_dangerous_obsession_with_sex_trafficking/.

In answering his own question, Burlatsky points out, as have other skeptics of narratives put forth by some HT NGOs and some survivor/activists, the public is hungry for salacious storylines and does not care to look too far below the surface of what is depicted on screen. Burlatsky concludes with a poignant insight that should become a central theme to how HT NGOs should conduct themselves, as well as how prospective donors should approach the organizations that are approaching them:

> Consuming exploitation films can be fairly harmless in itself—as long as you recognize that they're fiction…. The impulse to sensationalize doesn't help sex trafficking victims either. Hyperbolic narratives can make it hard to see more mundane abuses; … Donors end up sending money to the wrong people in the wrong places to solve the wrong problems. And, last but not least, portraying marginalized individuals as deviant and broken just ends up contributing to their further marginalization.[73]

Kim has never admitted to falsifying her life story and experiences. At the end of the day, some anti-human trafficking activists will be mortified and seek accountability of charlatans when they are exposed, and others will argue that the end justifies the means if the money generated by exaggeration and deceit comes into HT NGOs and funds the rescue of trafficking victims. There are still others who will urge charity and the benefit of the doubt by pointing out the gray areas between narratives that are perceived by others as false or inaccurate, and the effects of serious emotional and physical trauma that leave some trafficking victims convinced of a reality that may not exist, but in fact becomes a coping mechanism. This gray area, in fact, falls between the optics of misconduct and de facto corruption.

C. The Countess

In Southern California, a woman known as The Countess, aka Lady Katerine Nastopka, aka Lady Catarina Pietra Toumei, was investigated in 2014 by San Diego ABC news affiliate KGTV Channel 10 when calls came into the station that she might be scamming benefactors through her Rescue Children from Human Trafficking Foundation and using the money to fund a lavish lifestyle.[74] She was tracked down by an investigative reporter in an upscale

---

73. *Id.*

74. To view the investigative report, aired on July 17, 2014, *see Team 10 Questions Woman Formerly Known as 'Countess' about Fundraising Money*, https://www.youtube.com/watch?v=rYmLs1ekKXU.

neighborhood and asked to discuss her activities. She refused to answer any questions on video camera, but agreed to be interviewed with a regular television news camera. But when the news crew agreed to switch cameras, she began walking down the street away from the reporter and ducked into a fashion boutique and slipped out through a back door.

Nastopka apparently has a history of dubious conduct. In 2011 she portrayed herself as being a Countess with direct connections to the New York Guggenheim family. Her claims led to her arrest, along with two accomplices, to answer charges of fraud. She subsequently agreed to a plea deal promising never to use the Guggenheim name in the future.[75] The reporter later discovered that Nastopka, using the alias Kaitja Nastopka, sent out a mailing of fundraising letters and falsely represented that her organization's board of directors included the San Diego District Attorney Bonnie Dumanis, Police Chief Shelley Zimmerman, and the FBI San Diego station chief, Daphne Hearn.[76] The problem is that, according to the Channel 10 report, none of these luminaries actually served on or had any knowledge of her board of directors, and although her Foundation was listed as a 501(c)(3) organization on the

---

75. In 2011, Nastopka, then known as Lady Catarina Pietra Toumei claimed to be an investment relations manager, humanitarian and philanthropist and was a fixture among the rich and famous of San Diego high society. She was charged in criminal and civil suits in New York city for claiming to be a Guggenheim and trying to defraud investors in multimillion and billion dollar deals "for diamonds, gold, oil, works of art," among other commodities. According to Don Bauder, writing in 2013 in the *San Diego Reader*:

> In 2010, when Guggenheim Capital LLC and Guggenheim Partners LLC learned of the alleged misuse of the family name, they sued Toumei and her partners in New York, charging them with a nationwide scheme to defraud investors through false use of the Guggenheim trademarks and name, while claiming to be owners of the nonexistent Guggenheim Fund and Guggenheim Bank. The court banned them from further use of Guggenheim trademarks.

The civil suit filed by Guggenheim Capital LLC in federal court in San Diego accused Nastopka, then known as Lady Catarina Pietra Toumei, and two accomplices of trade infringement and fraud for using the family's name and logo on letters, financial documents and a bogus website. *See* Kristina Davis, *'Countess' Accused of Fraud Scheme Free on Bond*, SAN DIEGO UNION-TRIBUNE, Feb. 2, 2011, http://www.sandiegouniontribune.com/news/2011/feb/03/countess-accused-fraud-scheme-remain-free-bond/. Following her plea deal, she changed her name to Lady Katerine Nastopka in San Diego's North County Superior Court. She also disclosed in a notice published in the *New York Observer*, that she had been married three times and used eight different aliases over the years. *See* Don Bauder, *Lady Caterina Has a New Name*, SAN DIEGO READER, Nov. 20, 2013, http://www.sandiegoreader.com/news/2013/nov/20/citylights1-lady-catarina-pietra-toumei/#.

76. *See Team 10, supra* note 74.

Guidestar non-profit reporting website, it appears that Nastopka, as of this writing, has declined to file 990 tax forms as required by the IRS since her NGO's founding in 2012. Also, as of this writing, Nastopka's organization maintains a Facebook page for Rescue Children from Human Trafficking Foundation, but the link to the organization's webpage from the Facebook page leads to a "Server not found" result. Moreover, the phone number listed is for AT&T Directory Assistance.[77]

Law enforcement organizations were aware of Nastopka's activities and sent emails to anti-human trafficking agencies to avoid working with her. Apparently, Nastopka's website for her Foundation replaced a prior website of hers called *sextradebooks.web.com*, which among other things, promoted a novel called *Sex Trade, Part Memoir, Part Fantasy*, described as a "fictional thriller featuring a young prostitute, a showgirl, and a Harvard grad transvestite."[78] The proceeds of the book were said to cover the costs and pay fees for the establishment of a tax-exempt nonprofit, and that her nonprofit would in turn direct future funds to "about 14 charitable organizations throughout the world, that physically rescue children from brothels, street corners, and bars."[79]

Marisa Ugarte, one of the bona fide leading national experts on human trafficking and a highly regarded director of an HT NGO based in San Diego, stressed that Nastopka and her activities give anti-human trafficking organizations a black eye among the public and diminish the capacity of legitimate organizations to attract benefactors to fund sorely needed programs for trafficking survivors. Such fraudulent charities that claim to be helping trafficking victims, according to Ugarte, "Hurts the movement of the people who are real, here in San Diego and across the nation that really are doing the work."[80]

D. Human Trafficking and Reality Television

There is an insatiable, global thirst by the public for reality TV shows.[81] The competition in reality programming is so fierce that producers are constantly

---

77. As of October 17, 2016.

78. Bauder, *supra* note 75. For an interesting summary of Caterina's highly fabricated life, *see* Mike Taylor, *The Ersatz Aristocrats! The Undoing of Lady Caterina Toumei*, Observer, News & Politics, Mar. 3, 2011, http://observer.com/2011/03/the-ersatz-aristocrats-the-undoing-of-lady-catarina-toumei/.

79. Taylor, *supra* note 78.

80. See *Team 10*, *supra* note 74.

81. The value of reality programming in 2013 was believed to be in excess of $120 billion. *See* Michael Rose, *The Unreal Rise of Reality Television*, Huffington Post, Sept. 23,

looking for new and more outrageous ways to gain market share and viewer ratings, which translates to advertising revenue, profits, and professional success. The constant need to "one up" the competition and feed the voyeurism of the viewing public induces some producers to enter a gray area between informing the public about difficult reality topics and profiting from real life misery and human tragedy. It also occasionally places real people in potentially dangerous situations and raises the question of whether what reality program creators and producers are doing is a matter of public education or moral corruption at its most cynical and nihilistic base.

A case in point was a reality program called *8 Minutes*, which premiered to much pre-publicity and controversy on the A&E network on April 2, 2015. The premise of the program was to chronicle in real time the efforts of Kevin Brown, a retired police officer-turned pastor-turned anti-human trafficking crusader and founder of Safe Passage OC,[82] whose "ministry" was to rescue young women from sex servitude within 8 minutes of making contact with them.

The producer's press release said it all:

> With the help of strategically placed hidden cameras, the team undertakes harrowing undercover missions to offer help to women they believe may be in danger. In a non-descript hotel room, [Pastor Kevin] Brown poses as a client and once he established his credentials, he then brings in a victim's advocate—a woman who has successfully escaped being trafficked herself. Throughout the season, we meet over forty women; ranging from one who saw her twin sister killed in front of her to another woman sold at the age of 10 by a family friend. The stakes are high and there isn't much time to decide if they want to take the offer of help or return to their life on the streets.[83]

The idea of the eight minute time limit was explained as the outside amount of time Brown and his staff needed to effect an intervention and res-

---

2013, http://www.huffingtonpost.com/michael-rose/the-unreal-rise-of-realit_b_3976751. html.

82. A faith-based non-profit based anti-human trafficking organization based in Orange County, California. See the organization's webpage at https://www.facebook.com/ SafePassageOc. Brown is also a senior pastor at Side-By-Side Church International in Orange County, California. The Church's webpage is http://www.sidebysidechurch.com/. A prominent feature on the homepage is the link to Donate.

83. Sarah Seltzer, *Appalling New A&E Sex Worker Intervention Show '8 Minutes' Met with Protests*, FLAVORWIRE.COM (May 26, 2015), http://flavorwire.com/511253/appalling-new-ae-sex-worker-intervention-show-8-minutes-met-with-protests.

cue before the "victim's" pimp would become suspicious.[84] The show's producer, Tom Forman, described the time "concept" in far different terms that come off sounding a lot like someone exploiting the exploited for one's own agenda and professional aggrandizement: "The eight-minute rule that Kevin had made up for himself was a terrific framing device for a television show.... It is rare that I get to say the thing that is actually happening out there is happening exactly the way we would produce for TV."[85] Forman was also the producer of a We TV reality program called *Sex Box*,[86] described as an extreme therapy reality concept in which "couples discuss their relationship issues with a panel of experts and then retire to a camera-free, soundproof box on the show's set to have sex. They emerge to immediately discuss their experiences in the box and most intimate personal issues with the experts, as the cameras roll before a studio audience."[87] Several critics of *8 Minutes* described the show as an attempt by Forman to gain "respectability" in light of his producing *Sex Box*.[88]

Not surprisingly, *8 Minutes* was met with immediate, searing ridicule and criticism from many sectors, and even touched off a letter signing campaign initiated by the Chicago Alliance against Sexual Exploitation.[89] Scores of reputable anti-trafficking organizations and law enforcement agencies condemned the show and excoriated its premise that sex workers could be rescued from their situation in a matter of minutes.[90] The process of identifying trafficking victims, it has been stressed, requires highly specialized training, and even then, some victims are unable to self-identify as being trafficked.[91]

---

84. Kevin Ritchie, *A&E Explores Human Trafficking in "8 Minutes"*, REALSCREEN.COM, Apr. 2, 2015, http://realscreen.com/2015/04/02/ae-explores-human-trafficking-in-8-minutes/.

85. *Id.*

86. Taken from a similar concept program in the United Kingdom.

87. *We TV is Getting in the Box—The Sex Box!*, WETV.COM, Aug. 22, 2014, http://www.wetv.com/we-tell-all/blogs/introducing-our-newest-show-sex-box-yep-you-read-that-right.

88. Seltzer, *supra* note 83.

89. *See Sign on to Our Open Letter to A&E—Get '8 Minutes' Off the Air!*, CAASE.org, http://caase.org/action-alert-sign-on-to-our-open-letter-.

90. Samantha Allen, *To Catch a Sex Worker: A&E's Awful, Exploitative Ambush Show*, THE DAILY BEAST, Dec. 19, 2014, http://www.thedailybeast.com/articles/2014/12/19/to-catch-a-sex-worker-a-e-s-awful-exploitative-ambush-show.html.

91. Alana Massey, *A&E Completely Misunderstands the Reality of Sex Workers*, NEWRE-PUBLIC.COM, Apr. 2, 2015, http://www.newrepublic.com/article/121445/aes-show-8-minutes-damaging-sex-workers.

Some critics also challenged Brown's professional credentials and motivations. Brown first came into the public limelight after a *Los Angeles Times* feature article about him and his organization. The modus operandi of Safe Passage OC was to recruit volunteers from the faith-based community to engage in rescuing victims who are assumed to have been forced into prostitution. One reporter did not think much of the organization's methods:

> Volunteers only need to "attend a 16-hour course" in order to participate. That's only about half as long as it takes to get a learner's permit in the state of California—apparently learning when to use a turn signal is twice as complicated as conducting an undercover operation that jeopardizes women's lives.[92]

Other critics decried Brown and his organization as being part of the moralistic intervention side of the rescue industry.[93]

The *8 Minutes* program was cancelled after only 5 episodes, but the controversy did not end with the program's demise. In September 2015, the producers of the show, A&E Television Networks LLC, Long Pond Media LLC and Relativity Media, LLC were sued in state court in Houston, Texas, by three female plaintiffs on various allegations including fraud, breach of contract, fraudulent inducement, intentional infliction of emotional distress, and invasion of privacy.[94] The plaintiffs alleged that in exchange for participating in the program, Relativity Media "would provide them the ability to abandon sex work and would provide housing, medical and mental health care, educational, employment, legal and rehabilitation assistance."[95] They were also promised that their faces would be blurred to protect their identity, which did not occur when the episodes were edited. The production company subsequently filed for bank-

---

92. Allen, *supra* note 90.

93. Term coined by Dr. Laura Agustín, a noted anthropologist who studies and writes on undocumented immigration, human trafficking, and the sex industry. Agustín has a lot to say about the rescue industry, which springs from the idea that not being able to see social ills creates the need for self-identified experts to inform us about them. Her term "rescue industry" was created "after years of study to describe non-self-critical helpers who assume they Know Better than the rest of us how we all ought to live." *See* Laura Agustín, *Becoming Aware of Awareness-Raising as Anti-Trafficking Tactic*, The Naked Anthropologist, Jan. 7, 2015, http://www.lauraagustin.com/becoming-aware-of-awareness-raising-as-anti-trafficking-tactic. *See also* Allen, *supra* note 90.

94. *Jane Doe I v. A&E Television Networks et al.*, 2015-57344 (Harris County, Tex.).

95. James Rainey, *Sex Workers Who Sued Relativity Media Press for Case to Be Heard*, Variety, Mar. 20, 2016, http://variety.com/2016/biz/news/relativity-media-sex-workers-8-minutes-1201721226/.

ruptcy in federal court in New York, allegedly to protect itself from investors who had bankrolled a reality show that turned out to have been staged.[96] Almost immediately, sex worker rights advocates charged that the lawsuit was also a complete hoax because the women appearing in the episodes had been hired by the production company to be victims and were sought out and paid between $200 and $400.[97] One of the women, using the alias Kamylla, later related on the Sex Workers Solidarity webpage how she was recruited by the producers:

> One afternoon she receives a call from a woman, an assistant producer talking about a TV production. The producer explains that they are looking for women who have ads online to participate with the filming of a show called 8 minutes. The producer goes on to describe that the women who participate will be offered assistance to help them, and if they choose to they can "leave the life."
>
> Kamylla explained to them her situation, how she was facing an eviction at that moment; and she explained that she had tried very hard to find work. According to Kamylla, the producer excitedly stated, "[D]on't worry, they will help you! There will be assistance for you if you film for the show and compensation."[98]

Although the proceedings in the Texas court lawsuit were stayed pending the outcome of the bankruptcy case in New York,[99] one sobering point that emerged was that, "Simply handing these vulnerable women a list of numbers to overburdened organizations, many of whom had already denied help for these women, is not help at all but merely exploitation."[100] Moreover, as Kate D'Adamo, National Policy Advocate at the Sex Worker's Project, stated in the lawsuit:

> [U]nless this organization is offering jobs and not simply a referral to an organization who has already denied them services, they're just exploiting people's hope. This preys on marginalized people who aren't seeking public exposure and outing and publicly shames them for entertainment purposes. Forcibly outing a person can make them more vulnerable and isolated from their support systems. This is compli-

---

96. *Id.* Comment by a reader.

97. Emily Yahr, *A&E Pulls Heavily Criticized Show '8 Minutes', — Which Claimed to Help Sex Workers Leave the Trade,* Wash. Post, May 5, 2015, https://www.washingtonpost.com/news/arts-and-entertainment/wp/2015/05/05/ae-pulls-heavily-criticized-show-8-minutes-which-claimed-to-help-sex-workers-leave-the-trade/.

98. Domina Elle, *Brave Kamylla,* at http://sexworkersolidarity.com/kamylla/.

99. At this writing, the proceedings in Houston state court were still stayed.

100. *Jane Doe I, supra* note 94, at ¶ 13.

cated and delicate work to support someone exiting a difficult situation, and it can be very personal and take a great deal of trust. Treating it as carelessly as this show does, and then promoting it for entertainment value is not just disrespectful, it's despicable.[101]

Regardless of the outcome of lawsuits and accusations, one sex worker rights advocate raised the point as to what we must take into consideration with regard to using misery in real time (staged or otherwise) to attract donors to a cause:

> 8 Minutes now serves as a propaganda front for the faith based rescue industry. Observing the 8 Minutes twitter feed you find tweet after tweet praising what Pastor Kevin Brown and his advocates are doing, as if they are actually helping the women shown. Many people have fallen for the ruse of 8 Minutes. Subsequently, faith based rescue organizations are now tripping over themselves to grab their media bites in order to ride on the show's algorithm and popularity no doubt with the hopes of pulling in more funding and donations.[102]

Several HT NGOs also took issue with another television series aired on MSNBC in December 2013 called *Slave Hunter: Freeing Victims of Human Traf-*

---

101. *Id.*

102. Elle, *supra* note 98. Elle further wrote:

8 Minutes is a perfect allegory for the rescue industry. There is a great deal of rhetoric around "rescue" "restoration" and "help" but we aren't finding much in the way of actual services for people, despite the millions some of these organizations receive. We do find an increase in adult consensual sex workers being arrested and their already difficult lives made even more impossible. The 8 Minutes narrative is a treacherous lie which echoes the rescue industry it represents.

Many people working in the rescue industry know that most sex workers don't want their "rescue". This doesn't stop them from applying for federal grants or accepting donations. The money is predominantly used for hotlines and raising awareness. Watching a person like Kamylla fall through the cracks—being a person you'd assume the rescue industry would love to assist, is very telling. Kamylla's circumstances exposes the narrative for what it is, a ruse to be able to generate more funding for the rescue industry that never seems to manifest into tangible services.

It should be noted that the advocates serving the sex worker community are by no means in lock step. A careful review of the Internet reveals a slug-fest of charges back and forth among sex worker rights advocates. Domina Elle has been accused of having assumed the name of a dead woman and living and verbally attacking the work of another advocacy group in relation somehow to the *8 Minutes* debacle. *See Warning, Warning, Warning— Ratethatrescue.org and Sexworkersanonymous.org*, Trafficking and Prostitution Services Blog, Nov. 4, 2015, http://traffickingandprostitutionservices.blogspot.com/2015/11/warning-warning-warning.html#uds-search-results.

ficking, which chronicles the efforts of Aaron Cohen, a controversial anti-human trafficking activist who is well known for his unconventional tactics and self-promotion of his work. In a letter to Deb Finan, Vice-President for Production and Programming at MSNBC, more than twenty organizations involved in anti-trafficking and sex worker advocacy expressed concerns that Cohen's television show (and MSNBC producing it) misled the public about human trafficking and sex exploitation and "threatens the rights and safety of sex workers and survivors of human trafficking."[103] The signatories of the letter took particular issue with Cohen's portrayal of his work:

> [Cohen] reinforces an image of sex workers and human trafficking victims as powerless and requiring the help of a vigilante male rescuer whose motives are not questioned. Mr. Cohen is unassociated with any local trusted service provider or law enforcement official, unaccountable to any code of ethics. This series could encourage copycat initiatives, undertaken by individuals with no background or training, who are possibly well-meaning, or possibly have unexamined desires to interact with vulnerable women.[104]

The signatories further condemned "the dubious tactics of Mr. Cohen, the lack of distinction between sex and trafficking, the inappropriate contact that Mr. Cohen engages in with sex workers, and the danger in which Mr. Cohen potentially put sex workers and survivors."[105]

Critics also alluded to a loss of values and the element of moral degradation from this kind of reality entertainment. While "hunting" for slaves and trying to "free" women caught up in the sex trade "makes for good press and good story arcs," the actual conditions faced by sex workers before, during, and after their time in "the trade" get completely erased.[106] "The overlap between this kind of vigilante justice and entertainment media is becoming thinner and thinner.... If our primary motivation is supporting and serving people, using them for entertainment purposes is the opposite of that."[107] Ultimately, it is left to each of us to decide if reality programs like *8 Minutes* are the result of corrupt behavior, or just the product of avarice, very poor judgment, and bad taste.

---

103. Letter to Deb Finan, Dec. 9, 2013, http://sexworkersproject.org/downloads/2013/20131206-slave-hunter-msnbc-swp-letter.pdf.
104. *Id.*
105. *Id.*
106. Seltzer, *supra* note 83.
107. *Id.*

5. The Rescue Industry

Some trafficking survivors have a cynical view of the rescue industry, and feel that some HT NGOs place their agendas ahead of the trafficking victims they are supposed to serve. A few have become vocal activists in attempting to expose hypocrisy and corruption among the organizations. One trafficking survivor, Jacqueline Homan, now in middle age, has been trying to develop an online database that would serve as a watchdog tool to monitor the rescue industry. She holds no punches in stating her motivation:

> What started as a justice-seeking movement by the poorest, most marginalized older women (some like myself who have never [been] helped with unmet medical needs by any organization or agency)— women who've been human trafficking survivors decades before that word was even coined—ended up being usurped by unscrupulous people with significant socio-economic privilege who have turned this human rights catastrophe into something to use for their own personal cash cow—as a slush fund for privileged grafters with an agenda that isn't really about helping poor marginalized human trafficking survivors to get on their feet economically, reintegrate into society and rebuild their lives. And they stood on their upper-middle class, NON-survivor privileges in order to do it.[108]

The assertions by many trafficking survivors-turned-activists of widespread misconduct among many HT NGOs are notable, if not provable. Homan points to the experience of a fellow survivor and activist who was invited to speak at a fundraising event for an HT NGO. According to the individual, not only did the organization not pay her a speaking fee, but the group "hassled her for trying to sell a few copies of her book just so she could get some money to feed her kids and cover the cost of travel and child care that she had to incur in order to go speak. Ann [not her real name] said, 'They want to eat steak while forcing us to beg for oatmeal.'"[109]

Inquiries this author made among other sources suggest that older trafficking survivors have distanced themselves from the HT NGOs because they became disillusioned and appalled by troubling instances of misconduct and lack of assistance. One older trafficking survivor and founder of her own rescue organization asserted that she was "used" by a high-profile Washington,

---

108. Statement to the author on June 19, 2016.
109. Statement Jacqueline Homan to the author on June 19, 2016.

DC-based HT NGO when that organization was first becoming established, and that she and other older survivors were later discarded by the NGO when they were no longer of use. She ended up taking other survivors into her modest house because they had nowhere else to go. Another trafficking survivor, Alice Jay, the author of *Out of the Darkness: A Survivor's Story*,[110] struggled for several years while waiting to get social security benefits and was unable to get any help from "well-heeled" HT NGOs.

Older survivors also note that they face significant hardships for years after escaping being trafficked, and that some HT NGOs are indifferent to their long-term needs. Many have serious ongoing physical and mental health issues; those who have criminal records, particularly for prostitution, cannot afford legal counsel to expunge their records; and even when they are able to get college educations and acquire professional qualifications, their past criminal histories often prevent them from becoming gainfully employed and able to emerge from economic hardship. Older trafficking survivors also feel like outcasts because they do not fit the profile of young, vulnerable victims that many HT NGOs rely on to attract benefactors. Worse still, their stories of victimization and re-victimization are not deemed by marketing consultants working with some HT NGOs to resonate effectively—or more to the point, lucratively—with potential donors.

A. It's about the Brand

Early on in the evolution of HT NGOs, founders of both rescue and public awareness organizations realized they needed a brand to bring attention to their work. As we discussed earlier, they needed to create names as metaphors for the process of bringing trafficking victims out of darkness into the light of rescue, reintegration, and in the case of faith-based organizations, redemption. The imagery used by many HT NGOs evokes peace, security and sanctuary. Other organizations use imagery of young women in obvious states of distress and aloneness to evoke a sense of urgency in effecting rescues. According to the author of a provocative article addressing corruption in the rescue industry, some organizations choose names that suggest "recovery, light and sanctuary" to project a public image that is safe, redemptive, and nurturing.[111]

---

110. Published by Manifold Grace Publishing House, 2015. Amazon.com lists the book as One of the Best Books of 2016 So Far.

111. Moore, *supra* note 9.

At the opposite end of the branding spectrum, some HT NGOs embrace an aggressive "in your face" persona to attract attention to the work they do, and certainly there is nothing wrong with this approach. One organization, Operation Underground Railroad, chronicles their rescue operations of trafficking victims carried out around the world by the organization's founder, Timothy Ballard, whose chiseled looks, background as a former CIA agent and Homeland security agent, and his connection to the Church of Latter Day Saints make for an attractive media personality.[112]

A more "intense" organization is Bishop Outreach, a self-identified faith-based Christian organization, which portrays itself through social media as a pseudo-paramilitary-like operation that stages rescue operations of human trafficking victims while promoting a collective group persona in the vein of reality television star Duane Chapman and his Dog the Bounty Hunter exploits.[113] The colorful bio of the organization's "Shield Team Commander," who goes by the name Bishop, is replete with a photo of the man wearing a full face mask, ostensibly to protect himself from retribution related to his prior work as an undercover agent with the U.S. Department of Justice. Bishop's bio concludes:

> Bishop is available for speaking engagements. If you would like to book Bishop, please fill out the form here and select "Speaking Request" from the pulldown menu.

Bishop Outreach's Mobile Shield Team members likewise present a broad set of skills and experience in law enforcement, military training, and undercover investigations. Their mission to carry out victim rescues is singularly unique among HT NGOs, and their motto, "Awareness with Action," is supported by a claim that as a "highly trained and structured organization" they have the capacity to make rescues under any circumstance.[114]

In addition to fielding a rescue team, Bishop Outreach at one point supported a Legal Team under the acronym, B.E.S.T. (Building Empowerment by Stopping Trafficking). The Team's stated mission was to improve cooperatively the investigation and prosecution of human traffickers world-wide. As part of

---

112. Jamie Armstrong, *Rescuing Children from Sex Slavery: One Mormon's Inspired Mission*, LDSLIVING.COM, Feb. 27, 2015, http://ldsliving.com/story/78169-rescuing-children-from-sex-slavery-one-mormons-inspired-mission.

113. The Bishop Outreach webpage at https://bishopoutreachteam.wordpress.com/ posts video interviews and presentations of its work and also solicits partnership opportunities and donations online.

114. *Id.*

the B.E.S.T. programs, Bishop Outreach established the B.E.S.T. Academy, which it claimed was the only global Accredited Program for individuals to become certified in rescuing trafficking victims.[115] However, the accrediting entity was not identified on the website, and the link has since been removed.

Neither of these two examples suggest any kind of misconduct, whatsoever. But it is important to include in our discussion about establishing a presence among HT NGOs that some organizations may promote an identity for their own work and approach to the problem that, while well-meaning, could detract from the focus on helping victims of trafficking. This is something that should perhaps be avoided. Again, it is about how the optics and perception reflect on the anti-human trafficking movement as a whole.

B. It's about the Victims

While it is understood that there are unscrupulous people seeking to profit off the misery of fellow human beings, it is sometimes difficult to ascertain whether the actions and conduct of HT NGOs and those who run them are improper (or illicit), or the unintentional result of mismanagement and poor judgment by individuals who may not have the benefit of business degrees and management training to steer clear of making decisions that create the optics of misconduct. For this reason, it becomes even more critical that HT NGOs should be subject to some sort of regime, process, or sets of standards and guidelines for monitoring and vetting their activities so that the focus of the work they do, whether it be public awareness campaigns, law enforcement training, or rescue and restore work, is *always* on victims of trafficking.

The purpose of this discussion has not been to take any position for or against the HT NGOs that have been addressed in this chapter. But it is important to know that criticisms and allegations of misconduct and corruption within the rescue industry come from many voices, and that those voices speak from very different places and experiences. Addressing these concerns suggests strongly that the rescue industry needs to be monitored and vetted in a manner that is universally acceptable, meritorious, and collaborative, so that the focus of the movement remains on the victim. But, how can this be accomplished?

---

115. Bishop Outreach Legal Team, https://www.indiegogo.com/projects/bishop-outreach-human-traffickingrescue#/.

6. Monitoring and Vetting

Anna Rodriguez, the founder of the Florida Coalition Against Human Trafficking[116] and a pioneering anti-human trafficking crusader, has stated, "We do need more accountability regarding NGO's victim services and programs. But I believe it has to come from an independent organization or the federal government." This sentiment is also noted by Robert Bourgoing, the founder of an aid transparency website, who wrote, "There needs to be more pressure on NGOs to ensure they provide clear figures which are timely, reliable, useful and comparable."[117]

These suggestions mirror efforts that have been underway for some time to monitor domestic and international charities that focus on relief and humanitarian work, to make their operations transparent, and to inform their benefactors and the constituents they serve. The international relief organizations World Vision International, Care International, and Mercy Corps, to name a few, were the subject of a 2015 investigation conducted by the Thomson Reuters Foundation that examined financial losses in the global relief programs of 25 nongovernment organizations with the largest expenditures. The Foundation investigators found that 12 of the 25 NGOs reviewed reported annual losses of US$2.7 million during the reporting period of 2009–2014.[118] The findings suggest that the real figure for losses would have been far higher, but for the absence of reviewable data from the organizations, which collectively spend an estimated US$18 billion on their global programs annually. Some of the losses reported were due to fraudulent conduct by staff members in the organizations, or losses incurred during relief operations in places where conditions are often chaotic and uncertain. Such losses, regardless, need to be accountable, according to Craig Fagan, Head of Policy at Transparency International, who stated, "I would say in the last five years there has been a turning of the tide.... [There has been] a realization, at least at a global level, that this is part of their license to operate, that charities need to be accountable in a 360-degree way with people they are working with and those funding them."[119]

---

116. The FCAHT webpage and information on Anna Rodriguez is available at www.stophumantrafficking.org.

117. Tom Esslemont, *Exclusive: Aid Charities Reluctant to Reveal Full Scale of Fraud*, REUTERS.COM, July 15, 2015, http://www.reuters.com/article/us-aid-business-fraud-idUSK CN0PP00V20150715.

118. *Id.*

119. *Id.*

Many feel it is high time that similar efforts should begin to focus specifically on the human trafficking rescue industry, which operates in a climate of fundraising and revenue building that seems something of a free-for-all. Several ways to monitor and vet HT NGOs currently exist, and new capacities to uncover corrupt practices and/or address the optics of misconduct among HT NGOs are emerging.[120] One way to assess the credibility and the delivery of programs and services of anti-human trafficking organizations is to examine financial reports that HT NGOs are obligated to file in order to maintain nonprofit status.

Not-for-profit entities in the United States acquire tax exemption status under section 501(c)(3) of the United States Tax Code. Financial statements are required to be filed annually, and specific conditions set forth in the law must be met to retain tax-exempt status. Most 501(c)(3) organizations make their annual statements publicly available. However, some do not.

Two accessible and well regarded companies that track nonprofit organizations are GuideStar,[121] which tracks United States-based non-profits, and UK-based GuideStar International,[122] which focuses on making civil society

---

120. The following sample publications address issues of monitoring the work and work product of HT NGOs:

- United Nations Global Initiative to Fight Human Trafficking (UN.GIFT), *Research on Trafficking in Persons: Gaps and Limitations in Crime and Criminal Justice Data*, UN.GIFT B.P.: 024, 2008, https://www.unodc.org/documents/human-trafficking/2008/BP024QuantifyingHumanTrafficking.pdf.
- Ernesto U. Savona & Sonia Stefanizzi, Eds., MEASURING HUMAN TRAFFICKING: COMPLEXITIES AND PITFALLS (2007).
- U.S. GOV'T ACCOUNTABILITY OFF., GAO-06-825, Human Trafficking: Better Data, Strategy, and Reporting Needed to Enhance U.S. Antitrafficking Efforts Abroad (2006), http://www.gao.gov/assets/260/250812.pdf.
- U.S. GOV'T ACCOUNTABILITY OFF., GAO-07-1034, Human trafficking: Monitoring and Evaluation of International Projects Are Limited, But Experts Suggest Improvements (2007), http://www.gao.gov/new.items/d071034.pdf.
- Erin O'Brien, *Dark Numbers: Challenges in Measuring Human Trafficking*, DIALOGUE E-JOURNAL (undated), https://eprints.qut.edu.au/48257/.
- Lisa Fedina, *Improving the Statistics and Prevalence Data on Human Trafficking in the United States*, THE TRAFFICKING RESEARCH PROJECT (2014), https://thetraffickingresearchproject.wordpress.com/2014/06/06/improving-the-statistics-and-prevalence-data-on-human-trafficking-in-the-united-states/.
- Heather J. Clawson et al., *Improving Data to Combat Human Trafficking*, ICF INT'L (2008), http://thehill.com/sites/default/files/ICFI_ImprovingDataToCombat_0.pdf.

121. Guidestar was founded in Williamsburg, Virginia in 1994. *See* GuideStar webpage at http://www.guidestar.org/.

122. GuideStar International webpage at http://www.guidestarinternational.org/.

organizations (CSO) worldwide "more visible, accountable and effective" in order to enable "more confident and effective philanthropy."

Taking as an example the small HT NGO Born to Fly International (aka Born2Fly International) based in Lake Mary, Florida, the organization and its founder, Diana Scimone, are by many accounts doing good work world-wide in developing and implementing programs to raise awareness about human trafficking. The NGO's goal and indeed its motto appears to be "to reach kids before the traffickers do." Born2Fly's primary means of fulfilling this ambition involves spreading the word about human trafficking and empowering communities to become fortified against human trafficking crime. This is a great and noble aspiration.

While the organization's webpage provides many links to its programs, materials, and outreach formats, some elements of its webpage could perhaps be better clarified through a cooperative vetting and monitoring process that ultimately would help the organization become more transparent and less inscrutable. For example, the Donate page, which serves as the primary means for the organization to reach out to visitors for financial support online, raises some interesting questions. The first statement on the page reads:

> Your generosity allows us to give away the B2F anti-trafficking curriculums and wordless book without charge to groups all over the world. Most of them would have no way to pay. We don't want lack of funding to keep them from getting these life-saving materials, so as long as organizations register and we approve them, we'll share these materials without charge.

Let us look a bit more carefully at this statement. What is meant by giving away the materials to organizations for free, "so long as ... we approve them"? Would it be reasonable to explain the approval criteria? After all, how one's donation is utilized seems to be on a rather vague subjective basis. Born to Fly International states that it is a 501(c)(3) non-profit organization, that all U.S. donations are tax deductible, and that the NGO values the donor's "financial partnership" and works diligently to ensure that one's donations are invested wisely. In what manner? Where is the evidence?

Next, the Donor page poses a question, "How much is a little girl worth?" The question is followed by a statement by Ms. Scimone containing content that may not stand up to verification and bears the hallmarks of hyperbole that is the grist of many HT NGOs competing for the hearts and minds of potential donors. Ms. Scimone states that the value of a trafficked child is about US$300 and that the trafficker will make his money back "if she doesn't die of AIDS first." She continues by stating that the victim will be sold to a brothel and forced to service some 20 customers a night, and that many of the girls are just 5 years old.

This set of statements should raise enough red flags to give a donor pause before opening the checkbook. From what source does Ms. Scimone arrive at a value of US$300 for a trafficked child? Does she possess documentation to support her contention that the young girl will actually die of AIDS before the trafficker turns a profit? She also promotes the well-worn narrative that the child is a female and that the trafficker is a man, which while perhaps cinematic, is also problematic. Saying that the girl will have 20 customers a night is almost too random a number to be valid, and suggesting that many girls are just five years of age could be construed as highly irresponsible and misleading. Why not seven, or eight, or four years of age? Why five years of age? What is the factual basis underlying these statements?

At the bottom of the page, one has the opportunity to purchase two of Ms. Scimone's children's books, for which a "portion of the proceeds" goes to help support Born2Fly. Would not a discerning donor like to know exactly how much is a portion? The optics of this webpage leave one to wonder what is really going on here.

So, let us say that the interested donor decides to look up Born2Fly International on GuideStar to see what kind of information is available on the organization. What one finds raises more questions than it resolves. GuideStar relies on nonprofit organizations to self-report in response to questions presented by BoardSource, described on the GuideStar webpage as "the national leader in nonprofit board leadership and governance." Self-reporting should be a key element in the process of monitoring and vetting HT NGOs, and whether the NGOs listed in GuideStar respond to questions should help inform potential donors about whether to support an NGO (keeping in mind that the questions used by BoardSource may not be applicable to all HT NGOs).

The Summary page on GuideStar gives us a chart of Born2Fly's revenues from 2005 to 2014, with the most recent revenues of more than US$100,000. The Programs + Results portion of the GuideStar report is intended to answer the question, "How does this organization make a difference?" Despite Born2Fly International having been in operation since its founding in 2003, this section is absent any content. Might a potential donor like to know why a nonprofit organization in business for nearly a decade and a half has no content on the world's foremost nonprofit monitoring organization's website? Setting this question aside, a link to some of the NGO's tax filings is available, and it yields some interesting results. For instance, the Internal Revenue Service IRS 990 EZ form filed for tax year 2012 lists Born To Fly International Inc. as having received contributions, gifts, grants, and similar amounts of US$88,535. Total expenses were US$77,684. Of those expenses, US$62,130 went to salaries, compensation and employee benefits. Looking down the form, we see that 100 percent of that US$62,130 in salaries went to Ms. Diana Scimone. In other words, some 70 percent of all money taken in by Born To Fly International in 2012 went directly into Ms. Scimone's compensation. Of the remaining revenues, the Schedule O form of the 2012 filing, listing other expenses, shows US$4,918 in travel, as well as a US$1,000 donation to the Russian Orphan Project and US$1,038 for web site maintenance. Subsequent IRS 990 filings present an improved picture of income-to-expenditures for Born2Fly International, however, and when compared to other similar organizations, we see that the organization falls in step with other similar HT NGOs expenditures ratios.

GuideStar also reports on Governance of non-profit organizations. This is a key element for establishing a vetting process, and it is useful for a donor to have access to gain some insight into the leadership and core values of the leaders of a given organization. The questions GuideStar and BoardSource present with regard to Board Leadership practices are:

> 1. Board Orientation and Education: Does the board conduct a formal orientation for new board members and require all board members to sign a written agreement regarding their roles, responsibilities, and expectations?
> 2. CEO Oversight: Has the board conducted a formal, written assessment of the chief executive within the past year?
> 3. Ethics & Transparency: Have the board and senior staff reviewed the conflict-of-interest policy and completed and signed disclosure statements in the past year?
> 4. Board Composition: Does the board ensure an inclusive board member recruitment process that results in diversity of thought and leadership?
> 5. Board Performance: Has the board conducted a formal, written self-assessment of its performance within the past three years?

Returning to the GuideStar report on Born2Fly International, we see that these questions remain unanswered, although a review of other HT NGOs shows that the absence of responses to the questions is not uncommon. Nevertheless, between Born3Fly's webpage details and GuideStar's report, the optics of what we see raise reasonable questions.

In contrast, let us look at the GuideStar report on a large HT NGO. The Polaris Project is considered among the most prominent HT NGOs in the world. It is very well funded (the organization reported more than US$7 million in total assets in 2014), it has significant global name recognition, it is based in Washington, DC, and therefore has close connections with the Washington establishment, and it has a very successful fundraising operation. The data and detail available on GuideStar present a profile to any donor that Polaris Project has its "act" together and is unapologetic of its status, success, and its confidence in the delivery of its programs and services globally. We first see that Polaris Project presents a clear mission statement:

> Polaris's mission is to combat human trafficking and modern-day slavery and to strengthen the anti-trafficking movement through a comprehensive approach.

It then lists its programs, its top funding sources, and a narrative on each of its programs. Its financials are reported going back several years, and short bios of each of its primary officers are given under the Operations portion of the GuideStar report. Like Born2Fly International, Polaris Project also does not respond to the Board Leadership Practices questions. However, Polaris Project clearly seems to understand the ramifications of transparency and takes full advantage of a primary monitoring tool to reach potential donors and to sustain their support from year-to-year.

Within the rescue industry, monitoring entities are slowly beginning to emerge. But the self-policing efforts are not without controversy, and in some cases are little more than forums to express raw emotions and exchange recriminations.

End Slavery Now (ESN)[123] is an HT NGO that has taken on the responsibility of vetting other HT NGOs. ESN has established a set of standards that organizations must meet in order to be placed on both its Anti-Slavery Partners list and its Directory of Organizations, which contains entries for several hundred HT NGOs.[124] Inclusion in the Directory of Organizations database "is not an endorsement of effectiveness, stewardship or mission," and ESN states that it is not responsible for the accuracy or content of the information provided by the organizations listed. The organization also urges inquirers of both the Anti-Slavery Partners List and the Directory of Organization "to responsibly research them to determine if their policies and programs are suitable to your personal needs."[125] In other words, make sure they pass the smell test.

---

123. End Slavery Now, http://endslaverynow.org/.

124. The Directory is available at http://www.endslaverynow.org/connect.

125. End Slavery Now Anti-Slavery Directory, http://www.endslaverynow.org/connect?country=3417. The vetting policy is available upon request.

Lutheran Immigration and Refugee Service (LIRS) takes a slightly different approach to monitoring and vetting HT NGOs by tracking and debunking "the most common misinformation about human trafficking" that is used and reused by nongovernment anti-human trafficking organizations.[126] In early 2013, LIRS initiated its Human Trafficking Myth Buster website as "a unique resource in infographic form that empowers congregations and community leaders to debunk the most common misinformation about human trafficking."[127] The goal of the Mythbuster database is to meet "an urgent need for hard facts about this burning humanitarian issue, because the simple truth about trafficking is so much more powerful than all the misleading rhetoric that gets picked up and repeated."[128] This effort has exceptional potential to address increasing criticisms that some HT NGOs are careless in using vague and unsubstantiated figures and statistics, and intentionally mislead the public with bogus claims about the extent of human trafficking and related crimes in order to keep the revenue stream flowing.

While it is possible to monitor financial statements and records of anti-trafficking HT NGOs, it can be quite complicated to monitor and assess the actual work, programs, and services that HT NGOs perform. It is often a matter of taking the organizations at their word, and this can become quite problematic for donors and benefactors who want to engage in combating human trafficking by providing what can be robust financial resources.

One unique—and controversial—website that emerged in recent years was Ratethatrescue.org, described as "a community resource for sex work, where anyone can review organizations. Like Yelp for sex work."[129] Ratethatrescue.org self-described as "a sex worker-led, public, free, community effort to help everyone share information about both the organizations they can rely on, and those they should avoid."[130]

The prominent feature of Ratethatrescue.org was its Organizations link, where more than 550 rescue industry organizations from around the world were listed (as of mid-2016). Each listing followed a set taxonomy, and commenters posted statements, reviews, criticisms, and compliments about the organizations. The organizations were searchable by name, city, country, or

---

126. Lutheran Immigration and Refugee Service Mythbuster webpage, http://blog.lirs.org/human-trafficking-mythbuster-available-now/.

127. *Id.*

128. *Id.*

129. The Ratethatrescue webpage appears to have gone dormant as of June 2017, although there is still a presence on Twitter, #ratethatrescue.

130. Formerly at https://www.ratethatrescue.org/wp/about/.

rating rank (from unrated to 5, with 5 being the most favorable rating). The comments of the Organizations were uncensored and sometimes brutally frank, but this was important content for understanding how to devise a future monitoring and vetting protocol that would result in some kind of standards or code of conduct, ethics, and best practices for HT NGOs.

The Ratethatrescue.org Organizations taxonomy was based on responses to a basic set of questions followed by responses, using a five-star rating system (Not Answered to 5 for highest), to a set of factors that together yield a composite score. This scoring would allow the capacity to paint an in-depth and potentially useful assessment of an HT NGO. These unusually comprehensive factors were:

> Overall Rating
> How came in contact (some of the choices include)
>> Law enforcement
>> Another organization
>> Court
>> Jail
>> I called them
>> They called me
> Asked to sign documents
>> I understood them
>> I did not understand them
> Copies of documents signed
>> Yes
>> Promised but not received
>> No
> The following rated with 5 stars to 1 star and Not answered:
>> Food
>> Clothing
>> Housing: temporary
>> Housing: permanent
>> Money
>> Childcare
>> Healthcare: emergency
>> Healthcare: preventative
>> Healthcare: dental
>> Healthcare: information
>> Legal: criminal case
>> Legal: immigration

Legal: domestic violence
Legal: child custody
Identification
Counseling: group
Counseling: private
Education
Referrals
Community
Outreach
Advocacy
Research
Advertising
Photography
Website
Communications
Financial
Safety
Reviews
Business
Assistant
Agency
Workplace

The comments about the organizations listed on Ratethatrescue.org were frank and entirely unedited. While in some ways this is a good thing because it allows a visitor to get a visceral sense of the passion and raw emotions present in the opinions of some reviewers, the level of unregulated vitriol could be counterproductive and potentially libelous. While it is unnecessary for this discussion to reproduce strongly worded exchanges and invective between commenters, the ratings and postings regarding the HT NGO organization The Cupcake Girls in Portland, Oregon, and Polaris Project, were illuminating examples of the open character of the Ratethatrescue.org forum. Within the comments, one found details and information, that while anecdotal, shed light on issues of concern that have been raised about alleged conduct and practices of the two organizations by individuals who appear to have more than a passing familiarity with the entities.

Also noteworthy about Ratethatrescue.org's Organizations rating page was that of the 553 organizations listed at the time of this writing, 60 were organizations outside the United States, 50 of them had review comments, and of those 50, only 20 were rated higher than 3 stars. This would suggest that HT

NGOs worldwide share some common traits that invite criticism for alleged conduct or practices that might raise some red flags.[131]

Another promising HT NGO monitoring website recently attempted to secure financial support. In early 2015, an intriguing proposal was posted on the crowdfunding website GoFundMe, asking for financial backing for an online application called Anti-Trafficking NGO Fraud-Buster.[132] The App was inspired by the controversial report published by investigative journalist Anne Elizabeth Moore, whose article, *Money and Lies in Anti-Human Trafficking NGOs*,[133] asks probing questions about the continual use of facts and figures that fall apart under close scrutiny, and raises serious questions about corruption and the optics of misconduct among HT NGOs.

The Fraud-Buster App was intended to do three functions, that if put into use could be extremely beneficial for policing and vetting thousands of HT NGOs because it went beyond tracking information provided from self-reporting and included assessments of survivors who were served by the NGOs. This was accomplished in three ways:

1. It was to be a data-rich cross-platform app that would enable sex trafficking survivors to report anonymously (and free of charge) the outcomes of their requests for help from anti-trafficking NGO's claiming to provide victims' services, material aid, and long-term support to poor sex trafficking survivors. It would serve as a "report card" of sorts for the public, and thus, the organizations that really are doing the work in providing the help that survivors need could be whitelisted.

2. The app would catalog the outcomes of survivors' help requests, which were represented in hundreds of data points, and index them by the name of each NGO the survivors contacted in the referral pipeline, and the type of help or services for survivors the NGO's claimed to provide.

3. It would provide reports on each reported NGO by sector, name, funding sources, services provided, whether there was any advocate follow-up with the survivors requesting help, and whether or not the NGO is "faith-based."[134]

---

131. Formerly at https://www.ratethatrescue.org/.

132. GoFundMe, http://www.gofundme.com/ngofraudbuster. At last check before the link was taken down as of sometime in November 2016, there were 638 total shares with visitors to the page and 45 people had contributed a combined US$3,281 during four months of the request being posted on the site.

133. Moore, *supra* note 9.

134. GoFundMe, http://www.gofundme.com/ngofraudbuster (no longer available).

The app developer stressed that one of its strongest features was the anonymous reporting structure because it could build trust with survivors of extreme abuse and show that their lives really do matter. More significantly, the app would make survivors interactive in their own healing process while simultaneously helping to improve the entire anti-human trafficking community, "by empowering survivors to report an offense or evidence of fraud that will be investigated by trained professionals committed to this cause."[135] Moreover, the app provided a venue to recognize the honest organizations that do great work and "should not be forced to compete with frauds for very limited anti-trafficking funding."[136]

Monitoring and vetting should also target the funding side of an NGO's operations, and not just track programs and the delivery of services. Suzanne Hoff, the International Coordinator of La Strada Association (La Strada International) published an outstanding and comprehensive article in 2014 on the subject as it pertains to HT NGOs in Europe.[137] The premise of her article is that "little is known about the amount of money spent on anti-human-trafficking programmes today, much less what the impact of this funding is."[138] Her goal was to examine "(inter)governmental, public and private funding, looking at problematic policies to do with geographical restrictions or restrictions on what funds can be spent on" and to comment on "inefficiencies in funding and a great need for impact evaluations to ensure future funds are well spent." Established in 1995, La Strada International[139] is one of the preeminent anti-human trafficking network organizations in Europe, with a long and distinguished record. Anyone wishing to gain a better idea of how to monitor the work of HT NGOs should refer to Hoff's work in order to gain a clearer picture of how NGOs receive funding, are accountable to established standards, and demonstrate that available funding sources are adequate to meet ever-increasing victim needs.

Monitoring and vetting HT NGOs in more remote parts of the world present unique challenges. In many cases, the benefactors/sponsors and the programs they support live on separate continents. Because it is unlikely that most sponsors will ever have in-person contact with an NGO and its staff, it becomes a matter of faith that the programs and services donors support are

---

135. *Id.*

136. *Id.*

137. Suzanne Hoff, *Where is the Funding for Anti-Trafficking Work? A Look at Donor Funds, Policies and Practices in Europe*, Anti-Trafficking Review 109 (2014), http://www.antitraffickingreview.org/index.php/atrjournal/article/view/67/65.

138. *Id.*

139. La Strada International webpage, http://lastradainternational.org/.

being carried out in an ethical and responsible manner. This dynamic creates the temptation for some NGOs to inflate statistics or misrepresent the work being done because they assume that no one is going to bother to look too closely at what they are actually doing or not doing.

Recall that Professor Michele Kaufman of Johns Hopkins University observed that relief and anti-human trafficking NGOs in Nepal are "just doing their own thing."[140] Many of the HT NGOs in developing nations are trying to do good work, but reliable statistics about programs and services and success rates are hard to come by. Those HT NGOs that provide program reports on activities "may outline their projects in the number of participants, but provide little data that the activities actually helped stem trafficking."[141] University of Connecticut Professor Mary Crawford, who also researches anti-trafficking NGOs in Nepal, described the situation more succinctly. "There are a couple of hundred [NGOs] in Nepal that say that they're working on trafficking, but only a small handful actually run shelters and care for trafficked women.... It's a cut-throat world out there, trying to get donors to support your foundation and your anti-trafficking initiatives."[142]

In such a competitive environment with very little oversight, it is not difficult to imagine that corruption, or at least acts of intentional misconduct, are present, as seen in Nepal with regard to child trafficking and the abundance of shady orphanages. Some NGOs also are operating in a vacuum of sound advice and guidance on best practices and end up causing more harm than good. In one instance, an HT NGO in Nepal staged an awareness campaign using a street performance in which young girls were portrayed as being dragged off to brothels and then dying of HIV-AIDS. Parents in the village where the performance occurred later kept their daughters home from school for fear that they would be kidnapped if they went outdoors.[143]

The collapse of the Somaly Mam Foundation makes a compelling case for the need to have strong monitoring and vetting mechanisms in place to help maintain the integrity of HT NGOs worldwide. Thousands of Somaly Mam Foundation donors took it solely on faith and on face value that Mam was everything that she said she was, and that her organizations were everything that she claimed they were. Her years of success encouraged many HT NGOs, and her methods of self-promotion and public relations campaigns became a model for other NGOs to follow. Yet, Mam's actions constituted behavior

---

140. Browne & Dharssi, *supra* note 35.
141. *Id.*
142. *Id.*
143. *Id.*

that is very complex and difficult to monitor, and it should be concerning that it took investigative journalism, rather than the actions of a government agency or non-government watchdog, to uncover irregularities. Once exposed, Mam's activities were of such a perceived magnitude that not only did her acts hurt her own organization, but the fallout may have tainted the work and image of HT NGOs that have no record of questionable activities. For this and other reasons, the rescue industry needs to be monitored and vetted, if for no other purpose than to protect the good name and work of honest organizations from those individuals (and entities) who use human trafficking to advance personal agendas and/or to gain personal financial benefit.

Moore's article on corruption in the HT NGO sector points to the need for much better monitoring. When looking at the financial reports of several prominent anti-human trafficking NGOs, one begins to see a possible baseline to divide responsibly managed organizations from those that may fall short. For instance, on paper, the Polaris Project appears to set a high standard for HT NGOs—more than 86.5 percent of more than US$5.6 million in revenues went to programs and services in 2013.[144] Likewise, another well-known organization, Free the Slaves, spent 82 percent of more than US$2.6 million in revenue on programs and services in 2013. Many of the HT NGOs that report on Charity Navigator, an exceptional web-based tool for assessing the financials of a variety of charitable organizations, devote between 80 and 90 percent of total revenues on programs and services. While these percentages are admirable, other figures should be reviewed that may give some indication of how responsibly an organization's funding from private donations, government grants, and corporate partnerships are being managed.

For example, 87.3 percent of total expenses at Children of the Night are spent on programs and services, but the organization's founder/president draws more than US$220,000 in annual compensation, or nearly 11 percent of expenses for the organization. In contrast, the Coalition against Trafficking in Women spends less than 80 percent of revenues on programs and services, while the compensation of its director is also nearly 11 percent of total expenses.

In addition to executive compensation, fundraising costs appear to take a significant portion of total revenues for many organizations. Upon examining several other financial reports of HT NGOs on Charity Navigator, a few assessments emerge that might be considered benchmarks for vetting purposes:

---

144. *Charity Navigator*, Polaris webpage, http://www.charitynavigator.org/index.cfm?bay=search.summary&orgid=12434#.VXICx0YR8Xh.

- Executive compensation for any one individual should not exceed more than 10 percent of total expenses. In fact, some HT NGOs report executive compensation as being around 5 percent or less of total expenses.
- Fundraising expenses should not be more than 12 percent.
- Administrative expenses should be somewhere in the area of 6 to 8 percent.
- Target expenditures for programs and services should ideally be in the 80 to 90 percent range.

The ongoing challenge that should be of concern for those who wish to monitor and vet HT NGOs is well expressed by the director of a nonprofit organization based in Florida who stated, "How can the grant providers [and private donors] be substantively advised about their specifications as well as the resources and objectives of the grant seeker? Standards, validations and quality review of results, perhaps might start to reshape what is considered to be a public need but is more of private gain.... Valid and verifiable truth is a key hallmark for all programs serving in this difficult social, political, human arena."[145]

Professor Ronald Weitzer of Georgetown University stresses that, "Today, trafficking has been socially constructed in a particular way—both in terms of its magnitude and in the often-melodramatic depictions of victims, who are usually presented as victims of sexual (rather than labor) exploitation and in an extreme manner that is often formulaic and decontextualized."[146] This makes the process of monitoring HT NGOs all the more vital to continuing the fight against this pernicious human rights calamity, and it therefore becomes critically important to attach accountability for the corrupt or morally corrupt acts, or the misconduct of individuals in the rescue industry who by their actions threaten the legitimacy of the good work and best practices of the many organizations so dedicated to combating human trafficking.

This leads to the question, then, of who should be monitoring and vetting the rescue industry in a method that is effective at reducing corrupt and irresponsible activities? One of the fundamental problems with self-policing is that

---

145. Statement of Mary Elizabeth McIlvane, founder/director of the Center for Truth and Trust, www.truthandtrust.org.

146. Ronald Weitzer, *New Directions in Research on Human Trafficking*, 635 ANNALS OF THE AMERICAN ACADEMY OF POLITICAL AND SOCIAL SCIENCE 9 (2014), http://www.research gate.net/profile/Ronald_Weitzer/publication/273133970_New_Directions_in_Human_Trafficking_Research/links/54f8c97a0cf210398e96caa4.pdf.

it can become highly contentious and litigious. When it involves a smaller organization calling out a larger organization that has friends in government or in other positions of influence, attempts to hold the more influential organization accountable can end up damaging the smaller organization that is just trying to uncover misconduct in order to compel all HT NGOs to do the right thing. In the face of government reticence to go after HT NGOs and to clean up fraud, corruption, misconduct, and practices that create the optics of misconduct, some victim advocates feel that it has been left up to them to create public forum websites through which trafficking victims and others can voice their concerns. While there is a place for self-regulated forums like those we have discussed, there must be other alternatives.

7. Accountability

A. Raising Public Opinion and Awareness

Consider the following statement for a moment:

> There is no legal right of redress or adequate remedy at law readily available to destitute sex trafficking survivors in the event of abuse, denial of access to proper victims' services, or slave labor within the NGO system. NGOs are not accountable to the public in the way that government-run agencies are with regards to discrimination. There is no oversight and no recourse for either the survivors or the public at large who must make up the tax shortfall that these tax-exempt charities are not paying, except reporting a fraudulent, [abusive] or otherwise criminally acting NGO to the IRS.[147]

The forum of public opinion currently seems to be the most expedient method of holding HT NGOs accountable for their conduct. But even public vilification has not deterred Somaly Mam from continuing her fundraising campaigns after rebranding herself in the form of a new foundation. Mr. Morrish of SISHA International stepped down briefly while an independent auditor went through the organization's records and cleared it of wrongdoing, at which point he reemerged in the SISHA leadership. There must be some better way to hold HT NGOs accountable, and it should not be incumbent upon only government authorities to do so.

---

147. Homan's Anti-trafficking NGO Fraud Buster presentation on the gofundme.com webpage posted at https://www.gofundme.com/ngofraudbuster (no longer available).

We know that the proliferation of HT NGOs in recent years creates an unrelenting competition for funding resources. We also know that intense competition has created a tendency for organizations to make some outrageous claims about the extent of human trafficking, the number of trafficking victims rescued, the kinds of assistance and advocacy being offered, and program success rates. Moreover, we have found that among this proliferation of HT NGOs there are some founders, directors, and managers who have rather suspicious backgrounds and/or engage in unorthodox and sometimes illegal practices.[148] Some directors of HT NGOs have no professional credentials or work experience relative to the rescue work they are doing; their primary skill seems to be self-promotion and being engaging public speakers. Unethical individuals working in the rescue industry know the difficulty of proving that someone is perpetrating a scam or a fraud and know that the chances of being held accountable are remote. Absent a monitoring and vetting regime, anecdotal stories about misconduct within HT NGOs abound, including reports such as siphoning off funds to support lavish lifestyles, purchasing expensive automobiles and real property, engaging in executive perks such as first-class travel, dining in expensive restaurants, having memberships in clubs and spas, and in one instance, actually using trafficking rescues to do gardening and menial labor and calling it part of the rehabilitation process.

While some of this conduct may not constitute actual corruption, awareness of the practices of HT NGOs is important so that donors and sponsors can make informed decisions about which organizations to support and which organizations to avoid. There are some donors who would possibly support unconventional methods of helping trafficking victims, while others would be abhorred by it. Some donors may choose to support only faith-based organizations, while others will prefer not to do so. The best way to know what an organization is up to before deciding to support it would be to have some sort of umbrella association that sets standards for its members and does regular monitoring and vetting of its organizations as a condition for continuing membership and/or program certification. The glue that would hold the organizations together within a larger association would be commitment to a code of conduct and guidelines for best practices. This is already done in business sectors, and elsewhere in the non-government and non-profit sectors, and is a readily attainable aspiration for HT NGOs.

---

148. The director of one HT NGO in the southeastern United States is said to subject its trafficking rescues to exorcisms, while another organization uses trafficking victims in its care in the production of marketing videos without taking any steps to protect the victims' privacy, even as criminal proceedings are ongoing against an individual's trafficker.

B. Toward a Code of Conduct for HT NGOs

The World Association of Non-Governmental Organizations (WANGO) has a membership spanning 120 nations with international headquarters in Tarrytown, New York. According to its webpage, WANGO aspires "to provide the mechanism and support needed for NGOs to connect, partner, share, inspire, and multiply their contributions to solve humanity's basic problems."[149] Founded in 2000, this global organization provides services and support for its member organizations to fulfill their goals and accomplish their tasks of "better society and world: economically, socially, environmentally, politically, and morally."[150] In 2002, WANGO recognized the need for establishing a code of conduct and ethics that would be a suitable, applicable code for guiding NGOs worldwide.

Just as there are trafficking in persons country reports issued annually by the United States Department of State that ranks nations in a tier system from full compliance to noncompliance, perhaps a tiered system could be developed for measuring and long-term monitoring of HT NGOs. Those organizations found to be lacking in their conduct and management could be placed on a watch list, and sanctions or restrictions such as probation of some form could be levied on organizations that fail to adhere to the standards and expectations articulated in the code of conduct. This raises the question, however, over what kind of sanctions would be available, who would be sanctioned (the organization itself or the directors individually), who would oversee the sanctions, and what would be the long-term pitfalls from applying a sanctions regimen?

The question also arises as to who monitors the monitoring entities? Human nature being what it is, jealousy among individuals and HT NGOs is present and would need to be addressed. This means that if there were some official sanctioning authority, then there must also be mechanisms for appealing sanctions. Could this method include the use of an ombudsman or some form of alternative dispute resolution? These are just a few of the questions that must be considered in a discussion about how to hold HT NGOs accountable to the private sponsors who fund them, to the government institutions that provide grants and intelligence in exchange for programs and services, to the corporate partners that to a significant extent place their trust, good name, resources, and public image in the hands of the individuals running HT NGOs, and most critically, to the victims and survivors of human trafficking whose needs should always come first.

---

149. WANGO About section, http://www.wango.org/about.aspx.
150. WANGO Mission statement, http://www.wango.org/about.aspx?section=mission.

Anti-human trafficking NGOs (and the work they do) need to become subject to transparency indicators and proper analytical methodologies to achieve two goals: (1) to have more NGOs offering much needed services to victims, and (2) to have reliable and trustworthy information publically available. The current WANGO Code of Ethics and Conduct for NGOs is divided into the following sections that would also be uniquely applicable for nonprofit organizations working to combat human trafficking. These sections are: I. Guiding Principles; II. NGO Integrity; III. Mission and Activities; IV. Governance; V. Human Resources; VI. Public Trust; VII. Financial and Legal; VIII. Fundraising; and IX. Partnership, Collaboration and Networking. The sections covering public trust, financial, legal, and fundraising activities are of particular importance for HT NGOs, particularly given that to date, the hundreds of organizations are largely unregulated beyond requirements to file tax paperwork annually in order to maintain nonprofit status.

Among HT NGO executives, James Barnes has called for setting up an organization that would vet and monitor members and hold them accountable to public scrutiny.[151] His goal is to form a coalition that would "bring integrity back into the cause." Barnes writes:

> This coalition will create a symbol that will be given to organizations or individuals that have been thoroughly vetted. If your organization checks out and your funds are being used correctly, you get to use this symbol on all your advertising and marketing materials. It will let the public know if they want to donate to an anti-human trafficking organization, their money is going to a legitimate cause and that organization is doing the job they claim to be doing.[152]

Unfortunately, some working in the rescue industry may feel that imposing some form of model code of conduct on HT NGOs goes against the DNA of nongovernment organizations. "NGOs are notorious for their wish for independence. Coordinating NGOs is, just like coordinating states, 'like herding cats,'" according to Dr. Peter Baehr, a prominent human rights researcher.[153]

---

151. Results of Cheong Kim Investigation, posted Oct. 2, 2014, at https://www.facebook.com/BreakingOut/posts/708922209196425.

152. Id.

153. Peter R. Baehr, *Mobilization of the Conscience of Mankind: Conditions of Effectiveness of Human Rights NGOs*, Presentations Made at a UNU Public Forum on Human Rights and NGOs on 18 September 1996, http://archive.unu.edu/unupress/lecture14-15.html (noting as well that among NGOs, "Amnesty International has traditionally stood out for its aloofness and unwillingness to associate itself with other human rights NGOs for fear of

On the other hand, nongovernment organizations recognize that accomplishing individual goals may require working together to achieve "common aims."[154] If the common aim is accountability in order to maintain the integrity of the anti-human trafficking movement, then it may not be so difficult to achieve some form of consensus for establishing both measurements and vetting regimens, as well as levels of sanctions for noncompliance or misconduct.

In concluding the discussion of accountability of anti-human trafficking NGOs, Dr. Baehr's views are well worth reflection with regard to getting organizations to agree to a set of standards of conduct and to submit to an accountability regimen:

> Coordination [of NGOs] at least, and mutual cooperation if possible, are helpful for human rights NGOs. They may decide to channel their efforts and thus be more effective. Yet, such coordination and cooperation must not be the result only of government prodding. Governments may find NGOs troublesome and try to limit their activities by calling for "restraint" and "self-discipline", however reluctant they may be to display such restraint and self-discipline themselves. NGOs should opt for coordination and cooperation only if they find that helpful to carry out their activities. Such cooperation may be found in the realm of exchange of information and pooling of efforts. On the other hand, the existence of some form of healthy competition among NGOs is not necessarily a bad thing. It may actually be helpful to the cause of human rights and to the plight of victims of human rights violations.

---

endangering its cherished limited mandate."). Peter R. Baehr is Professor Emeritus of human rights at Utrecht University, Netherlands.

154. *Id.*

Chapter 10

Conclusions and Recommendations

Summary: We conclude this book with a chapter offering several sets of recommendations to consider in confronting the elements of corruption, misconduct, and the optics of misconduct as it relates to human trafficking, and strengthening the capacity of organizations and entities to combat human trafficking.

We have seen throughout this book the many forms of corruption, misconduct and the appearance of misconduct that are both a component and a result of human trafficking crimes. Addressing the elements of corruption and human trafficking requires looking at the problem in new ways and constructing a new set of recommendations, and categorizing them in a clear and usable manner.[1]

Trafficking survivors, particularly women, face many daunting obstacles, such as lifelong marginalization, mental distress, and other psychological consequences.[2] Being re-victimized by public, private, and non-government actors that are supposed to be helping them should not be among those obstacles.

---

1. The United States State Department and the Organization for Economic Cooperation and Development have proposed several ideas for providing the basic foundation upon which to build better domestic legislation and better enforcement regimes to curb corruption in the context of human trafficking. For a comprehensive discussion of these ideas *see* Virginia M. Kendall, *Greasing the Palm: An Argument for an Increased Focus on Public Corruption in the Fight Against International Human Trafficking*, 44 CORNELL INT'L L.J. 33, 40–47 (2011).

2. Chandra Kant Jha & Jeanne Madison, *Antecedent and Sequalae Issues of Nepalese Women Trafficked into Prostitution*, 12 J. INT'L WOMEN'S STUDIES 79, 81 (2011).

A corrupt public servant is going to be reticent to encourage public awareness or to influence changing public perceptions about trafficking victims if that corrupt official is himself or herself involved in human trafficking. Such corrupt officials by reason of what they do in conspiring to trafficking human beings are not going to "cut off their nose to spite their face." They have no incentive to participate in awareness campaigns or reform efforts or the implementation of any type of legislation that would hurt their ability to make profits through their corrupt conduct. One would think that the only viable response to confronting such corruption in the public sector would be to make the punishment severe enough to dissuade individuals from taking the risks. Public humiliation, loss of position and status, loss of income, and loss of freedom can be powerful disincentives.

Business people too often place the "bottom line" ahead of all other considerations. Whether it be due to strong competition in a particular market, a demand for labor that exceeds available manpower, taxation regimes that place pressure on businesses to survive, unrealistic deadlines for fulfilling supply contracts, or simply corporate greed and avarice, some executives approach corruption using a cost benefit analysis, weighing the benefits to be gained through a corrupt act against the odds of getting caught, and factoring in the impact of punishment. One may expect a corporation to be a good corporate citizen, but sometimes a carrot and stick approach may be necessary to keep businesspeople focused on compliance and respect for the law.

Then there is the Wild West character of the rescue industry, where the prospect of making money is to a charlatan like chumming the waters to attract a shark. Among the recommendations the United States State Department makes in its TIP reports to countries struggling to achieve greater success in combating human trafficking is to fund HT NGOs by sustainable means. However, such a policy sets a dubious and troubling precedent, and could have the unintended effect of a flawed government system continuing to be engaged in a flawed relationship with a flawed non-government actor, as we saw in the United Conference of Catholic Bishops matter. Governments cannot continue to fund HT NGOs without there being some methodical and institutionalized process for monitoring organizations receiving government support. Such a process should also have some third party oversight by an independent entity that has no horse in the race and is above reproach. This is an open-ended question, but one that merits future debate and dialog. So, let us conclude with the following suggested recommendations.

The first set of recommendations must focus on improving domestic anti-trafficking laws to include specific anti-corruption provisions involving both private and public corruption as related to trafficking activities.[3] There must be unambiguous certainty in the law that both public officials and private individuals who engage in corrupt acts involving human trafficking will be brought to justice, and that an adequate selection of laws are available to prosecutors to bring indictments. Domestic legislation must also provide for monitoring, reporting, and analyzing corrupt acts along the human trafficking chain. Moreover, there must be a means embedded in domestic legislation for constantly evaluating and improving the laws and closing loopholes. One jurist has proposed a two-part process in this regard:

- Develop a comprehensive Anti-Corruption Strategy built around the existing public corruption laws, and focused on identifying where the laws could be improved. The Strategy should build on an analysis of the patterns of corruption in the country and be developed in a participatory process.
- Establish a national multi-stakeholder Anti-Corruption Council to facilitate the development and implementation of the Anti-Corruption Strategy. Stakeholders of the body should include representatives of all branches of government, as well as civil society, as equal partners.[4]

The second set of recommendations should address improving enforcement capacity to combat corruption in human trafficking. Some of the ideas[5] proposed include:

- Ensuring effective training for police officers, prosecutors, and judges on current anti-human trafficking principles, procedures, and best practices.
- Subject police officers, prosecutors, and judges to continuing education programs and where warranted, unannounced inspections and review of records and procedures.
- Integrate an anti-trafficking module into the basic training of the police officers and make advancement in the police force predicated upon successful completion of those training modules.
- Monitoring prosecutions for trafficking-related corruption in order to educate law enforcement regarding the unique methods used by

---

3. Kendall, *supra* note 1, at 41.
4. Some of these proposals and those that follow are promoted and articulated by United States District Court Judge, the Hon. Virginia M. Kendall. *See* Kendall, *supra* note 1, at 41.
5. *Id.* at 41–47.

a particular trafficker in a particular country, which in turn provides guidance on how to effectively close corrupt loopholes along the trafficker's route.

- Establishing a special anti-corruption agency tasked to detect, investigate, and prosecute corruption offenses related to human trafficking. Such an agency would have a degree of autonomy and possibly be integrated in the Prosecutor's Office with officers seconded from the main law enforcement agencies, and should have investigative, administrative, and analytical specialists, as well as specialized/dedicated prosecutors. The agency would work on actual corruption cases, raise public awareness of the problem, facilitate interagency cooperation (including security, law enforcement, and financial/bank bodies), and maintain and disseminate statistical and comparative findings through a centralized database.
- Adopting a protocol for enhanced cooperation, information exchange, and resource sharing between agencies responsible for combating organized crime, private and public corruption, and human trafficking.
- Organizing corruption-specific joint training for police, prosecutors, judges, and other law enforcement officials.

The third set of recommendations should focus on monitoring the many organizations and agencies involved in combating human trafficking to ensure that: (1) victim privacy is protected; (2) best practices in financial and programs management are observed and reported; (3) individuals involved in anti-human trafficking work adhere to some uniform model of standards for transparency and accountability; and (4) trafficking victims do not become a vehicle for private gain by unscrupulous individuals, such as we have noted in the burgeoning reality show sector of the entertainment and broadcasting industry. This could be accomplished by criminalizing specific related acts such as endangering victims' privacy, interfering with ongoing law enforcement investigations, and even conspiracy and racketeering.[6] The current most effective means of monitoring the conduct of HT NGOs is: (1) through reporting

---

6. There is precedent for this concern, as noted by a UNODC report from 2011 in which several cases from Eastern Europe and West Africa indicated that "individuals working with non-governmental organizations that assisted women were implicated in disclosing the addresses of shelters to traffickers." In at least one case, the report stated, a woman was re-trafficked directly out of the victim shelter. UNODC, *Issue Papers: The Role of Corruption in Trafficking in Persons* 14 (2011).

entities such as GuideStar and GuideStar International; (2) NGO watchdog organizations that are already at work compiling data, and; (3) emerging mechanisms for reporting and tracking questionable activities and practices of HT NGOs.

The fourth set of recommendations should concern the preparation, training, and continuing education of consular officials who are often the first point of contact with transborder human trafficking activities. In many cases, consulate and embassy officials are relatively new to their positions and may have only recently graduated from diplomatic training programs. Many lack the experience and the time in country to understand the challenges they face. They may not yet recognize the indicators consistent with human trafficking activities occurring in their duty stations. Consular officials should also be constantly monitored and vetted in an effort to reduce and curtail corruption. This would also include keeping an eye on their activities and conduct when they are off the clock. They are, after all, accountable to the governments they serve, to the people back home whose taxes pay their salaries, and to the citizens of the host countries in which they are posted. Training should include "ensuring sensitivity of consular officers to trafficking victims,"[7] and there should be a committed effort to ensure that trafficking victims when identified abroad are referred to care in the host country.[8]

The fifth set of recommendations involves determining what entities, government or non-government, should be responsible for implementing guidelines, issuing recommendations, and promoting modifications to current domestic and international antitrafficking instruments on human trafficking. Because some relevant international instruments that are not human rights-based may violate the rights of trafficking victims, framing a better definition of corruption with regard to human trafficking crimes should be a high priority.

The sixth set of recommendations entails how understanding the nexus of human trafficking and corruption can result in: (1) obtaining better data and reporting; (2) developing tools that can be more effective in prevention and detection of corruption in the human trafficking chain; and (3) disrupting the elements that corruption requires to flourish. One of the ways to accomplish these goals would be, again, to create a database of public, private, and non-government sector corruption and misdeeds involving human trafficking crimes. This is particularly vital in areas of human trafficking in which we are still lacking reliable data such as labor trafficking, trafficking in infants, traf-

---

7. U.S. Dep't of State, The Trafficking in Persons Report 226 (2012).
8. *Id.*

ficking for purposes of organ removal, pan handling, and committing petty larceny.

The seventh set of recommendations addresses the need to have a holistic approach to human trafficking and the elements of human trafficking that encourage corruption to flourish alongside trafficking crimes. The comments of HT NGO monitor, trafficking survivor and victim advocate Jacqueline S. Homan are particularly salient:

> The current system we have does not work. I personally feel that the systemic problems of poverty due to discrimination, of which human sex trafficking is a direct result, cannot be solved by the NGO/ charity model alone. Systemic solutions for helping poor trafficking survivors—and—the unemployable jobless poor in general—have to be implemented, such as implementing either a guaranteed basic income provision and universal healthcare, or a robust and adequate welfare safety net, for starters.
>
> That is what we should be talking about … if we're truly committed to taking a bite out of human trafficking. Because let's face it, we all know that it's not rich white men or upper-middle class and rich women, that are being trafficked and then left for dead.[9]

Human trafficking is a global societal problem involving a multitude of crimes, including economic crimes, transborder crimes, crimes of violence, and deprivation of a person's most basic human rights. Corruption is a result of opportunities to engage in unethical and illicit conduct by individuals from many stations in life who lack the rectitude and moral judgment to resist temptations. The nexus of human trafficking and corruption presents us with serious, daunting challenges requiring robust, long-term responses. Governments are only effective if public officials are honest and faithfully carry out their duties. Businesses must practice good corporate governance and resist placing profit ahead of human rights. Non-government organizations must be accountable to higher authorities and transparent to scrutiny and ongoing monitoring. Finally, the justice system must pursue far stronger punishments for both human traffickers and for corrupt actors. These are attainable aspirations.

We all have a choice to make as our societies continue to rush through the twenty-first century. Either we carry on with a firm devotion to time-honored universal principles of human rights and rededicate ourselves continually to upholding those principles, or we succumb to illegality, temptation, and crim-

---

9. Statement of Jacqueline S. Homan on file with the author.

inal acts that debase human dignity and turn vulnerable people into human chattel. Either we become careful stewards of fair commerce and the rule of law, or we allow corruption and greed to erode and undermine the basic element of civil society to the point that no law is enforceable, and no conduct is too profane. The core value of who we are as human beings is that we are our brother's keeper. This is a constant that transcends all societies, cultures and points on the globe.

Appendix

Palermo Protocol[1]
I. Protocol to Prevent, Suppress and Punish Trafficking in Persons
Especially Women and Children, supplementing the
United Nations Convention against Transnational Organized Crime
II. Adopted and opened for signature, ratification and accession by
General Assembly resolution 55/25 of 15 November 2000

Preamble

The States Parties to this Protocol,

Declaring that effective action to prevent and combat trafficking in persons, especially women and children, requires a comprehensive international approach in the countries of origin, transit and destination that includes measures to prevent such trafficking, to punish the traffickers and to protect the victims of such trafficking, including by protecting their internationally recognized human rights,

Taking into account the fact that, despite the existence of a variety of international instruments containing rules and practical measures to combat the exploitation of persons, especially women and children, there is no universal instrument that addresses all aspects of trafficking in persons,

Concerned that, in the absence of such an instrument, persons who are vulnerable to trafficking will not be sufficiently protected,

Recalling General Assembly resolution 53/111 of 9 December 1998, in which the Assembly decided to establish an open-ended intergovernmental ad hoc committee for the purpose of elaborating a comprehensive international con-

---

1. Source: http://www.ohchr.org/EN/ProfessionalInterest/Pages/ProtocolTraffickingIn Persons.aspx.

vention against transnational organized crime and of discussing the elaboration of, inter alia, an international instrument addressing trafficking in women and children,

Convinced that supplementing the United Nations Convention against Transnational Organized Crime with an international instrument for the prevention, suppression and punishment of trafficking in

Have agreed as follows:

I. General provisions
Article 1
Relation with the United Nations Convention against Transnational Organized Crime

1. This Protocol supplements the United Nations Convention against Transnational Organized Crime. It shall be interpreted together with the Convention.

2. The provisions of the Convention shall apply, mutatis mutandis, to this Protocol unless otherwise provided herein.

3. The offences established in accordance with article 5 of this Protocol shall be regarded as offences established in accordance with the Convention.

Article 2
Statement of purpose

The purposes of this Protocol are:

(a) To prevent and combat trafficking in persons, paying particular attention to women and children;

(b) To protect and assist the victims of such trafficking, with full respect for their human rights; and

(c) To promote cooperation among States Parties in order to meet those objectives.

Article 3
Use of terms

For the purposes of this Protocol:

(a) "Trafficking in persons" shall mean the recruitment, transportation, transfer, harbouring or receipt of persons, by means of the threat or use of force or other forms of coercion, of abduction, of fraud, of deception, of the abuse of power or of a position of vulnerability or of the giving or receiving of payments or benefits to achieve the consent of a person having control over another person, for the purpose of exploitation. Exploitation shall include, at a minimum, the exploitation of the prostitution of others or other forms of sexual exploitation, forced labour or services, slavery or practices similar to slavery, servitude or the removal of organs;

(b) The consent of a victim of trafficking in persons to the intended exploitation set forth in subparagraph (a) of this article shall be irrelevant where any of the means set forth in subparagraph (a) have been used;

(c) The recruitment, transportation, transfer, harbouring or receipt of a child for the purpose of exploitation shall be considered "trafficking in persons" even if this does not involve any of the means set forth in subparagraph (a) of this article;

(d) "Child" shall mean any person under eighteen years of age.

Article 4
Scope of application

This Protocol shall apply, except as otherwise stated herein, to the prevention, investigation and prosecution of the offences established in accordance with article 5 of this Protocol, where those offences are transnational in nature and involve an organized criminal group, as well as to the protection of victims of such offences.

Article 5
Criminalization

1. Each State Party shall adopt such legislative and other measures as may be necessary to establish as criminal offences the conduct set forth in article 3 of this Protocol, when committed intentionally.

2. Each State Party shall also adopt such legislative and other measures as may be necessary to establish as criminal offences:

(a) Subject to the basic concepts of its legal system, attempting to commit an offence established in accordance with paragraph 1 of this article;

(b) Participating as an accomplice in an offence established in accordance with paragraph 1 of this article; and

(c) Organizing or directing other persons to commit an offence established in accordance with paragraph 1 of this article.

II. Protection of victims of trafficking in persons
Article 6
Assistance to and protection of victims of trafficking in persons

1. In appropriate cases and to the extent possible under its domestic law, each State Party shall protect the privacy and identity of victims of trafficking in persons, including, inter alia, by making legal proceedings relating to such trafficking confidential.

2. Each State Party shall ensure that its domestic legal or administrative system contains measures that provide to victims of trafficking in persons, in appropriate cases:

(a) Information on relevant court and administrative proceedings;

(b) Assistance to enable their views and concerns to be presented and considered at appropriate stages of criminal proceedings against offenders, in a manner not prejudicial to the rights of the defence.

3. Each State Party shall consider implementing measures to provide for the physical, psychological and social recovery of victims of trafficking in persons, including, in appropriate cases, in cooperation with non-governmental organizations, other relevant organizations and other elements of civil society, and, in particular, the provision of:

(a) Appropriate housing;

(b) Counselling and information, in particular as regards their legal rights, in a language that the victims of trafficking in persons can understand;

(c) Medical, psychological and material assistance; and

(d) Employment, educational and training opportunities.

4. Each State Party shall take into account, in applying the provisions of this article, the age, gender and special needs of victims of trafficking in persons, in particular the special needs of children, including appropriate housing, education and care.

5. Each State Party shall endeavour to provide for the physical safety of victims of trafficking in persons while they are within its territory.

6. Each State Party shall ensure that its domestic legal system contains measures that offer victims of trafficking in persons the possibility of obtaining compensation for damage suffered.

Article 7
Status of victims of trafficking in persons in receiving States

1. In addition to taking measures pursuant to article 6 of this Protocol, each State Party shall consider adopting legislative or other appropriate measures that permit victims of trafficking in persons to remain in its territory, temporarily or permanently, in appropriate cases.

2. In implementing the provision contained in paragraph 1 of this article, each State Party shall give appropriate consideration to humanitarian and compassionate factors.

Article 8
Repatriation of victims of trafficking in persons

1. The State Party of which a victim of trafficking in persons is a national or in which the person had the right of permanent residence at the time of entry into the territory of the receiving State Party shall facilitate and accept, with due regard for the safety of that person, the return of that person without undue or unreasonable delay.

2. When a State Party returns a victim of trafficking in persons to a State Party of which that person is a national or in which he or she had, at the time of entry into the territory of the receiving State Party, the right of permanent residence, such return shall be with due regard for the safety of that person and for the status of any legal proceedings related to the fact that the person is a victim of trafficking and shall preferably be voluntary.

3. At the request of a receiving State Party, a requested State Party shall, without undue or unreasonable delay, verify whether a person who is a victim of trafficking in persons is its national or had the right of permanent residence in its territory at the time of entry into the territory of the receiving State Party.

4. In order to facilitate the return of a victim of trafficking in persons who is without proper documentation, the State Party of which that person is a national or in which he or she had the right of permanent residence at the time of entry into the territory of the receiving State Party shall agree to issue, at the request of the receiving State Party, such travel documents or other authorization as may be necessary to enable the person to travel to and re-enter its territory.

5. This article shall be without prejudice to any right afforded to victims of trafficking in persons by any domestic law of the receiving State Party.

6. This article shall be without prejudice to any applicable bilateral or multilateral agreement or arrangement that governs, in whole or in part, the return of victims of trafficking in persons.

III. Prevention, cooperation and other measures
Article 9
Prevention of trafficking in persons

1. States Parties shall establish comprehensive policies, programmes and other measures:

(a) To prevent and combat trafficking in persons; and

(b) To protect victims of trafficking in persons, especially women and children, from revictimization.

2. States Parties shall endeavour to undertake measures such as research, information and mass media campaigns and social and economic initiatives to prevent and combat trafficking in persons.

3. Policies, programmes and other measures established in accordance with this article shall, as appropriate, include cooperation with non-governmental organizations, other relevant organizations and other elements of civil society.

4. States Parties shall take or strengthen measures, including through bilateral or multilateral cooperation, to alleviate the factors that make persons, especially women and children, vulnerable to trafficking, such as poverty, underdevelopment and lack of equal opportunity.

5. States Parties shall adopt or strengthen legislative or other measures, such as educational, social or cultural measures, including through bilateral and multilateral cooperation, to discourage the demand that fosters all forms of exploitation of persons, especially women and children, that leads to trafficking.

Article 10
Information exchange and training

1. Law enforcement, immigration or other relevant authorities of States Parties shall, as appropriate, cooperate with one another by exchanging information, in accordance with their domestic law, to enable them to determine:

(a) Whether individuals crossing or attempting to cross an international border with travel documents belonging to other persons or without travel documents are perpetrators or victims of trafficking in persons;

(b) The types of travel document that individuals have used or attempted to use to cross an international border for the purpose of trafficking in persons; and

(c) The means and methods used by organized criminal groups for the purpose of trafficking in persons, including the recruitment and transportation of victims, routes and links between and among individuals and groups engaged in such trafficking, and possible measures for detecting them.

2. States Parties shall provide or strengthen training for law enforcement, immigration and other relevant officials in the prevention of trafficking in persons. The training should focus on methods used in preventing such trafficking, prosecuting the traffickers and protecting the rights of the victims, including protecting the victims from the traffickers. The training should also take into account the need to consider human rights and child- and gender-sensitive issues and it should encourage cooperation with non-governmental organizations, other relevant organizations and other elements of civil society.

3. A State Party that receives information shall comply with any request by the State Party that transmitted the information that places restrictions on its use.

Article 11
Border measures

1. Without prejudice to international commitments in relation to the free movement of people, States Parties shall strengthen, to the extent possible, such border controls as may be necessary to prevent and detect trafficking in persons.

2. Each State Party shall adopt legislative or other appropriate measures to prevent, to the extent possible, means of transport operated by commercial carriers from being used in the commission of offences established in accordance with article 5 of this Protocol.

3. Where appropriate, and without prejudice to applicable international conventions, such measures shall include establishing the obligation of commercial carriers, including any transportation company or the owner or operator of any means of transport, to ascertain that all passengers are in possession of the travel documents required for entry into the receiving State.

4. Each State Party shall take the necessary measures, in accordance with its domestic law, to provide for sanctions in cases of violation of the obligation set forth in paragraph 3 of this article.

5. Each State Party shall consider taking measures that permit, in accordance with its domestic law, the denial of entry or revocation of visas of persons implicated in the commission of offences established in accordance with this Protocol.

6. Without prejudice to article 27 of the Convention, States Parties shall consider strengthening cooperation among border control agencies by, inter alia, establishing and maintaining direct channels of communication.

Article 12
Security and control of documents

Each State Party shall take such measures as may be necessary, within available means:

(a) To ensure that travel or identity documents issued by it are of such quality that they cannot easily be misused and cannot readily be falsified or unlawfully altered, replicated or issued; and

(b) To ensure the integrity and security of travel or identity documents issued by or on behalf of the State Party and to prevent their unlawful creation, issuance and use.

Article 13
Legitimacy and validity of documents

At the request of another State Party, a State Party shall, in accordance with its domestic law, verify within a reasonable time the legitimacy and validity of travel or identity documents issued or purported to have been issued in its name and suspected of being used for trafficking in persons.

IV. Final provisions
Article 14
Saving clause

1. Nothing in this Protocol shall affect the rights, obligations and responsibilities of States and individuals under international law, including international humanitarian law and international human rights law and, in particular, where applicable, the 1951 Convention and the 1967 Protocol relating to the Status of Refugees and the principle of non-refoulement as contained therein.

2. The measures set forth in this Protocol shall be interpreted and applied in a way that is not discriminatory to persons on the ground that they are victims of trafficking in persons. The interpretation and application of those measures shall be consistent with internationally recognized principles of non-discrimination.

Article 15
Settlement of disputes

1. States Parties shall endeavour to settle disputes concerning the interpretation or application of this Protocol through negotiation.

2. Any dispute between two or more States Parties concerning the interpretation or application of this Protocol that cannot be settled through negotiation within a reasonable time shall, at the request of one of those States Parties, be submitted to arbitration. If, six months after the date of the request for arbitration, those States Parties are unable to agree on the organization of the arbitration, any one of those States Parties may refer the dispute to the International Court of Justice by request in accordance with the Statute of the Court.

3. Each State Party may, at the time of signature, ratification, acceptance or approval of or accession to this Protocol, declare that it does not consider itself bound by paragraph 2 of this article. The other States Parties shall not be bound by paragraph 2 of this article with respect to any State Party that has made such a reservation.

4. Any State Party that has made a reservation in accordance with paragraph 3 of this article may at any time withdraw that reservation by notification to the Secretary-General of the United Nations.

Article 16
Signature, ratification, acceptance, approval and accession

1. This Protocol shall be open to all States for signature from 12 to 15 December 2000 in Palermo, Italy, and thereafter at United Nations Headquarters in New York until 12 December 2002.

2. This Protocol shall also be open for signature by regional economic integration organizations provided that at least one member State of such organization has signed this Protocol in accordance with paragraph 1 of this article.

3. This Protocol is subject to ratification, acceptance or approval. Instruments of ratification, acceptance or approval shall be deposited with the Secretary-General of the United Nations. A regional economic integration organization may deposit its instrument of ratification, acceptance or approval if at least one of its member States has done likewise. In that instrument of ratification, acceptance or approval, such organization shall declare the extent of its competence with respect to the matters governed by this Protocol. Such organization shall also inform the depositary of any relevant modification in the extent of its competence.

4. This Protocol is open for accession by any State or any regional economic integration organization of which at least one member State is a Party to this Protocol. Instruments of accession shall be deposited with the Secretary-General of the United Nations. At the time of its accession, a regional economic integration organization shall declare the extent of its competence with respect to matters governed by this Protocol. Such organization shall also inform the depositary of any relevant modification in the extent of its competence.

Article 17
Entry into force

1. This Protocol shall enter into force on the ninetieth day after the date of deposit of the fortieth instrument of ratification, acceptance, approval or accession, except that it shall not enter into force before the entry into force of the Convention. For the purpose of this paragraph, any instrument deposited by a regional economic integration organization shall not be counted as additional to those deposited by member States of such organization.

2. For each State or regional economic integration organization ratifying, accepting, approving or acceding to this Protocol after the deposit of the for-

tieth instrument of such action, this Protocol shall enter into force on the thir-
tieth day after the date of deposit by such State or organization of the relevant
instrument or on the date this Protocol enters into force pursuant to paragraph
1 of this article, whichever is the later.

Article 18
Amendment

1. After the expiry of five years from the entry into force of this Protocol, a
State Party to the Protocol may propose an amendment and file it with the Secretary-General of the United Nations, who shall thereupon communicate the
proposed amendment to the States Parties and to the Conference of the Parties to the Convention for the purpose of considering and deciding on the proposal. The States Parties to this Protocol meeting at the Conference of the
Parties shall make every effort to achieve consensus on each amendment. If all
efforts at consensus have been exhausted and no agreement has been reached,
the amendment shall, as a last resort, require for its adoption a two-thirds majority vote of the States Parties to this Protocol present and voting at the meeting of the Conference of the Parties.

2. Regional economic integration organizations, in matters within their
competence, shall exercise their right to vote under this article with a number
of votes equal to the number of their member States that are Parties to this
Protocol. Such organizations shall not exercise their right to vote if their member States exercise theirs and vice versa.

3. An amendment adopted in accordance with paragraph 1 of this article is
subject to ratification, acceptance or approval by States Parties.

4. An amendment adopted in accordance with paragraph 1 of this article
shall enter into force in respect of a State Party ninety days after the date of the
deposit with the Secretary-General of the United Nations of an instrument of
ratification, acceptance or approval of such amendment.

5. When an amendment enters into force, it shall be binding on those States
Parties which have expressed their consent to be bound by it. Other States Parties shall still be bound by the provisions of this Protocol and any earlier
amendments that they have ratified, accepted or approved.

Article 19
Denunciation

1. A State Party may denounce this Protocol by written notification to the
Secretary-General of the United Nations. Such denunciation shall become ef-
fective one year after the date of receipt of the notification by the Secretary-
General.

2. A regional economic integration organization shall cease to be a Party to this Protocol when all of its member States have denounced it.

Article 20
Depositary and languages

1. The Secretary-General of the United Nations is designated depositary of this Protocol.

2. The original of this Protocol, of which the Arabic, Chinese, English, French, Russian and Spanish texts are equally authentic, shall be deposited with the Secretary-General of the United Nations.

In witness whereof, the undersigned plenipotentiaries, being duly authorized thereto by their respective Governments, have signed this Protocol.

Index